PART TWO

THE AMERICANS: A Brief History Since 1865

PART TWO

THE AMERICANS

A BRIEF HISTORY SINCE 1865

HENRY F. BEDFORD

Phillips Exeter Academy

TREVOR COLBOURN

University of New Hampshire

Under the General Editorship of John Morton Blum
Yale University

Harcourt Brace Jovanovich, Inc.

New York   Chicago   San Francisco   Atlanta

COVER *Totems in Steel 1935*, by Charles Sheeler.
Fogg Art Museum, Harvard University. Bequest of Meta and Paul J. Sachs.

ISBN: 0-15-502601-1

Library of Congress Catalog Card Number: 71-182337

Printed in the United States of America

SOURCES OF ILLUSTRATIONS

Ollie Atkins: pp. 472, 474
Bettmann Archive: pp. 191, 238, 250, 373
Brown Brothers: pp. 45, 346, 384
John Carter Brown Library, Brown University: p. 22
Culver Pictures: pp. 160, 167, 294, 326, 388, 401
Courtesy of Essex Institute, Salem, Mass.: p. 42
Michael Gregory/Pix: p. 481
The Historical Society of Pennsylvania: p. 30
Bern Keating/Black Star: p. 454
Library of Congress: pp. 17, 25, 36 (*top*), 52, 56, 69, 72, 100, 123, 149, 155, 168, 195, 196,
   197, 205, 217, 218, 222, 227, 231, 235, 268, 276, 279, 287, 299, 315, 322, 325, 331, 337, 349,
   355, 426
Mariner's Museum, Newport News, Va.: p. 126
The Metropolitan Museum of Art: pp. 63 (Gift of Mrs. Russell Sage, 1910), 77
   (Bequest of Charles Munn, 1924), 102 (Gift of Henry Marquand), 131 (Bequest of
   Seth Low), 142, 185, 211
Museum of the City of New York: pp. 140, 246 (*bottom*) (The Jacob A. Riis Collec-
   tion)
National Archives/Signal Corps: p. 342
National Maritime Museum: p. 36 (*bottom*)
National Portrait Gallery: p. 43
New York Historical Society: pp. 98, 111, 125, 127, 162, 258, 267, 364
New York Public Library: p. 310
Lloyd Ostendorf Collection: p. 209
Preservation Society of Newport County: p. 246 (*top*)
Public Library of Cincinnati and Hamilton County: p. 171
Ben Shahn, *The Passion of Sacco and Vanzetti*. Whitney Museum of American Art,
   New York: p. 366
Edward Sorel: p. 492
TVA: p. 397
United Press International: pp. 438, 445
Virginia Museum: p. 91
White House Collection: pp. 116, 312
Wide World: pp. 416, 420, 427, 434, 448, 455, 461, 488

A NOTE

ON THE TWO-VOLUME EDITION

This volume is part of a variant printing, not a new or revised edition, of *The Americans: A Brief History*. Many instructors have requested a two-volume version that would enable them to fit the text into the particular patterns of their teaching and scheduling. To meet that request, the publishers have prepared this printing, consisting of two separate volumes that exactly reproduce the text of the one-volume version of *The Americans: A Brief History*. The first of these volumes continues through Reconstruction. The second volume repeats the chapter on Reconstruction (Chapter 12), and carries the account forward to the present day. The variant printing, then, is intended as a convenience to those instructors and students who have occasion to use either one part or the other of *The Americans: A Brief History*. Consequently, the pagination and index of the one-volume version, as well as its illustrations, maps, and other related materials, are retained in the new printing. The difference between the one-volume and the two-volume versions of the book is a difference only in form.

PREFACE

Some four centuries ago an Elizabethan scholar pondered the importance of history: "Man without learning and remembrance of things past," concluded Sir William Dugdale, "falls into a beastlye sottishnesse and his life is noe better to be accounted of than to be buried alive." Two centuries later, David Hume thought history "the greatest mistress of wisdom," and Benjamin Franklin praised "Good History" because it could "fix in the Minds of Youth deep Impressions of the Beauty and Usefulness of Virtue of all kinds." More recently American Presidents have erected great stone shrines in which their papers might be cataloged for study by future generations of historians.

The importance of the American historical experience seems generally accepted, even if its relevance is not always appreciated. The most casual observer of the American scene cannot fail to notice the seemingly unceasing flow of historical books, periodicals, and monographs from the nation's presses. No other nation boasts such a profusion of textbooks that attempt to analyze, describe, and synthesize its history. In spite of this abundance there is a case to be made for a textbook that seeks brevity without lamentable omissions, succinctness without tantalizing allusions, interpretation without prejudice. We have written *The Americans: A Brief History* in the hope of providing such a book.

As we were writing this book, young Americans in particular were questioning their national heritage: Have Americans constructed a racist society? Must Americans change the balance of nature and foul the environment? Can the American political system respond to human needs? Are Americans inherently greedy, imperialistic, conforming, prudish, and apprehensive? In raising such questions, many students implied a criticism of their earlier courses in American history, where they studied the details but gained little sense of historical perspective. This book reminds students of the facts and also tries to suggest, rather briefly, the dimensions of the relevant past.

The opening chapter discusses those values that have characterized the American people—the Puritan work ethic, thrift, the profit motive, emphasis on education, the belief in political solutions to problems—and these themes are addressed (often obliquely) throughout the book. We hope, for instance, that readers will better understand the nation's faith in its political process as they consider its political history; we hope to have made the aspirations of American industrial workers as clear as the chicanery of some of their employers; we hope the black American emerges as more than an unstated exception to generalizations about American ideals.

Any text must derive substantially from the learning and judgment of others. The authors are particularly indebted to John M. Blum, Yale University, and Donald B. Cole, Phillips Exeter Academy, for their helpful suggestions, and to Thomas A. Williamson and Virginia Joyner for their encouragement and patience. We owe thanks also to G. Wallace Chessman, Denison University, William W. Freehling, University of Michigan, and Robert Middlekauff, University of California, Berkeley, who read and commented on portions of the manuscript. Every historian cited at the end of each chapter is our unacknowledged collaborator, as are scores of others in the historical fraternity.

Henry F. Bedford
Trevor Colbourn

CONTENTS

THE AMERICANS: A Brief History Since 1865

CHRONOLOGY

1864 Wade-Davis Bill, vetoed by Lincoln

1865 Lincoln assassinated; Andrew Johnson succeeds
Thirteenth Amendment abolishes slavery
Presidential Reconstruction: Amnesties for whites and
enactment of Black Codes

1866 Civil Rights Act
Freedmen's Bureau

1867 Congressional reconstruction: Reconstruction Act imposes military districts on South; Tenure of Office Act

1868 Fourteenth Amendment ratified
Johnson impeached but conviction not secured
Presidential election: Ulysses S. Grant (Republican) defeats Horatio Seymour (Democrat)

1870 Fifteenth Amendment ratified

1870–71 Force Acts to combat Ku Klux Klan

1872 Presidential election: Ulysses S. Grant (Republican) defeats Horace Greeley (Liberal Republican, Democrat)

1876 Presidential election: Rutherford B. Hayes (Republican) defeats Samuel J. Tilden (Democrat) when a special electoral commission awards Hayes all 20 disputed votes in January, 1877

1883 Civil Rights cases

1895 Booker T. Washington addresses Atlanta Exposition

1896 *Plessy* v. *Ferguson* establishes doctrine of "separate but equal"

XII

RECONSTRUCTION

Reconstruction, Abraham Lincoln remarked as he received the news of Appomattox, "is fraught with great difficulty." The President's victory speech soberly emphasized the uncertain future, not the triumphant past, for Lincoln lacked specific programs for rebuilding his shattered nation. In the dozen years after Lincoln's death this national effort to reconstruct subtly changed to a search for peaceful accommodation. And the dilemmas Lincoln had foreseen endured, like the monuments both sections erected to the dead.

There are no monuments to Reconstruction, for nations do not celebrate their failures. Reconstruction just ended; it was never completed. Although the South rejoined the Democratic party and once more participated in the national political process, regional peculiarities have ever since set the section off from national politics. Although diligent southerners of both races slowly rebuilt their agrarian economy, industry rapidly transformed the rest of the country, creating problems and opportunities that much of the South did not share. Finally, although emancipation made racial equality possible, postwar generations never completed the task.

LINCOLN PLANS FOR RECONSTRUCTION

Lincoln foresaw the difficulty of reconstruction partly because he had to improvise a southern policy as Union armies began to occupy sections of the Confederacy. In 1863 the President promised amnesty to all southerners (except a few Confederate officials) who would swear allegiance to the Constitution and the Union. When the number of oath-taking voters reached 10 percent of a state's vote in the presidential election of 1860, military authorities were to permit the formation of a state government. Lincoln promised the executive recognition that signified the completion of reconstruction as soon as that state government abolished slavery.

But executive recognition, as the South was to discover repeatedly, was only one hurdle. Congress alone could permit southern states to rejoin the national legislature. Many Republicans in Congress thought the President too lenient and his conception of reconstruction too narrow. Charles Sumner, Thaddeus Stevens, Ben Wade, and other Republican critics who had earlier objected to Lincoln's cautious approach to emancipation were called Radicals. They believed that a victorious Union should punish rebellion and create a new pattern of southern life.

Radicals countered Lincoln's "ten-percent plan" with the Wade-Davis Bill, which Congress passed in July, 1864. Whereas Lincoln had been willing to accept a promise of future loyalty from a minority, the Radicals demanded proof of past loyalty from a majority. Before military occupation could give way to civil government, Radicals insisted, a majority of white male citizens must take an oath of past and future allegiance to the federal Constitution. No one who had supported the Confederacy could vote or participate in the formation of reconstructed state governments, which must abolish slavery, repudiate any debt incurred during the war, and deprive former Confederates of political rights.

Although Lincoln killed the Wade-Davis Bill with a pocket veto, he indicated a willingness to modify his own policy. The President did not insist on one method of reunion; if a southern state wished to reconstruct itself as the Wade-Davis Bill prescribed, Lincoln would not object. Lincoln's pose of flexibility conceded nothing, since no southern state would choose harsh congressional terms while the President's less demanding option was available. Radical sponsors of the bill responded to the veto with an indignant manifesto. The dispute over reconstruction, which divided Congress and the President more deeply than any other issue in American political history, had begun in earnest.

On the surface, the protracted debate centered on legal and constitutional questions. Were southern states still states with full constitutional rights? Or were they, as Thaddeus Stevens claimed, "conquered provinces," subject to the unlimited power of Congress to regulate federal territories? Was reconstruction a presidential function—for the executive power to pardon was clearly relevant—or could Congress assume full responsibility, since it must consent before a southern state could rejoin the national legislature?

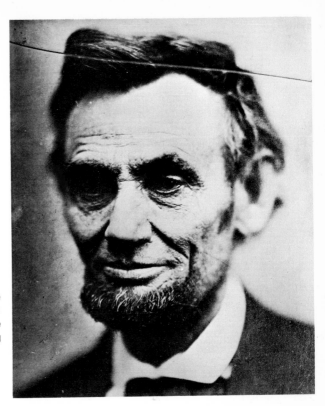

Lincoln's last portrait. Compare with the 1860 portrait (p. 209) for a visual indication of the strain of the presidency during the Civil War.

These questions, and dozens of others like them, disclose American political ritual. For at bottom, the questions of reconstruction were racial and economic, and at stake was the power to remake a great nation. But post–Civil War Americans, as their descendants have since, masked such visceral issues as racial equality and agrarian peonage with a constitutional façade that usually permitted civilized political discourse.

Abraham Lincoln knew that reconstruction was more than a constitutional nicety and dismissed the whole controversy over the legality of secession as "a merely pernicious abstraction." He thought reconstruction might be accomplished "without deciding or even considering" whether the Confederacy had ever been outside the Union. Lincoln hoped to subordinate dispute to agreement: "We all agree that the seceded states, so called, are out of their proper practical relation with the Union; and that the sole object of the government . . . is to again get them into that proper practical relation." Perhaps Lincoln, with his political genius, could have continued his uneasy coalition with the Radicals and still reconstructed the Union without bitterness. The assassin did not give him the chance.

THE RADICAL VIEW OF RECONSTRUCTION

Not all Republicans were Radicals in 1865, and not even all Radicals agreed on the entire program for remolding the South. At the very least, Radicals hoped to replace illiteracy and discrimination with education and tolerance. They proposed to educate, or coerce, the South toward com-

227

plete acceptance of emancipation and to finish that "more perfect Union" that the Constitutional Convention had begun.

The vision of some Radicals, of whom Thaddeus Stevens was most prominent, extended beyond social and political rights to economic equality for the freedmen. In place of ruined or neglected plantations, these Radicals saw economically independent farmers of both races tilling their own small farms. Stevens proposed to confiscate all southern land except individual holdings of less than two hundred acres. He suggested that some of the land thus obtained be granted to the former slaves who had worked it in order to assure their economic independence. The rest of the confiscated lands, Stevens said, should be sold at auction and the proceeds put toward reducing the national debt, establishing a fund for Union soldiers or their widows and children, and replacing northern property destroyed during the war. The South must pay for the hardship its war had brought. If the losers paid no reparation, northern taxpayers would in effect subsidize the defeated enemy by bearing the war's indirect costs. That situation, Stevens charged, was absurd.

Stern, unforgiving Thaddeus Stevens may have been right. Without economic security the freedom of the black man was not firmly based; peonage and slavery have much in common. Yet the radicalism of most of Stevens' Republican colleagues did not extend to the confiscation of slaveholders' plantations. Congress did not give farms to the freedmen, but it did temporarily support and protect them in their transition to freedom.

The Freedmen's Bureau, established about a month before the end of the war, was to provide this support. In the confusion immediately after Appomattox the bureau fed refugees of both races and helped them to relocate. It helped freedmen secure jobs and then supervised employers to prevent the concealed reestablishment of slavery. The agency also established and maintained schools and hospitals, in both of which the South had previously been deficient. And it attempted to protect the legal equality of blacks and to prevent social discrimination. But the Freedmen's Bureau did not function equally well in all places. Some agents were corrupt; some abused black trust; some used the political possibilities inherent in the bureau to promote their own careers.

Indeed, no part of Radical Reconstruction was free of political overtones. Thaddeus Stevens, forthright as usual, declared that any program must "secure perpetual ascendancy to the party of the union. . . ." The Thirteenth Amendment, Stevens pointed out, abolished the former practice of counting a slave as three-fifths of a person; consequently, the South, once readmitted, would be entitled to more congressmen than had represented the section before the war. More congressmen meant more electoral votes, thus endangering Republican control of the White House, for Democrats could fuse their northern minority with white voters of the South to create a national majority. Stevens' uncompromising demand for black suffrage was a function of his desire to perpetuate Republicanism through southern support, as well as a result of egalitarian convictions.

Stevens was probably honest in his conviction that the republic could not be entrusted to "whitewashed rebels" and those whom he regarded as apologists for treason. But his motive may have been less disinterested than he acknowledged, and some Republicans certainly hoped to use Reconstruction to serve themselves. Stevens, for instance, owned an iron mine in southern Pennsylvania that Confederates had damaged extensively during the war; his interest in compensating northern property-holders for wartime destruction may have been related to his own losses. Like other owners of iron mines, Stevens was also a confirmed advocate of the protective tariff; protection seemed to depend upon continued Republican supremacy, for Democrats had traditionally opposed the policy.

As Stevens' motives were mixed, so too were those of other Republicans. They believed in the comprehensive legislative program that the fortuitous secession of the South had allowed them to bring about—protective tariff, the national banking system, the Homestead Act, and federal grants to transcontinental railroads. Before the war southern Democrats had blocked this legislation. Postwar Democrats were still hostile to some of it, and were also flirting with various forms of economic heresy, such as the notion that national bonds should be redeemed in the inflated greenbacks with which they had often been purchased, instead of in gold as the bond promised. Northern businessmen, whose opinions weighed heavily with Republican politicians, preferred fiscal orthodoxy. Moreover, the North glimpsed industrial affluence in the future; it seemed no time for economic experimentation.

The white South was equally unready for social experimentation, and Abraham Lincoln may have agreed. Once a staunch Whig, Lincoln perhaps hoped to gain support for gradual change from the same coalition of moderates in both sections that had sustained his old party. Some Radicals so mistrusted the President that they welcomed Vice-President Andrew Johnson's succession. For Johnson, a self-made man from Tennessee and a thoroughly Jacksonian Democrat, seemed to have nothing in common with those substantial southerners whom Lincoln hoped might become the pillars of a southern Republican party. But to the surprised dismay of the Radicals, Andrew Johnson, who had never acted like a southerner during the war, seemed to join the Confederacy after Appomattox.

PRESIDENTIAL RECONSTRUCTION

The new President began immediately to exercise his power to pardon almost without limit. While Radicals fumed because the recessed Congress could not respond, Johnson encouraged amnestied southerners to establish new constitutions, hold elections, and complete reconstruction before Congress resumed in December, 1865. He insisted only that the South ratify the Thirteenth Amendment, repudiate the Confederate debt, and repeal the ordinances of secession. White southerners hastened to adopt Johnson's terms, which were surely among the most generous ever imposed upon a defeated foe. Although the President withheld political rights from a few prominent former Confederates, voters all over the South chose many of the same men who had led them out of the Union to lead them back in. Mississippi and South Carolina elected governors who had been Confederate generals; Georgia chose Alexander Stephens, the Confederacy's Vice-President, for the Senate of the United States. Neither the southern voter nor Andrew Johnson made any tactful gesture to quiet mounting northern suspicion that a costly victory was being cheaply given away.

Blacks, Radicals, and others who had added equality to the war aims of emancipation and union thought Johnson's terms too generous. A group of blacks in Virginia, for example, pointed out that Johnson's plan would subordinate both black and white supporters of the Union to those former Confederates who were organizing and dominating the state government. The President had left them, these freedmen complained, "entirely at the mercy of . . . unconverted rebels." Maintaining that they were " 'sheep in the midst of wolves,' " the blacks asked for "an *equal chance* with the white *traitors*" whom the President had pardoned. Without the protection of the ballot and federal arms to enforce equal rights, the freedmen feared their former masters would make freedom "more intolerable" than slavery.

Those whom Johnson pardoned did indeed try to preserve as much as possible of the prewar social order. Most white southerners were not ready to believe that legal freedom made their former slaves the equals of other men. So the Black Codes that southern legislatures adopted to replace slave codes made only grudging concessions to the new free status of the blacks.

These Black Codes permitted blacks to form families. One black might marry another, and black parents were responsible for their children. Most statutes also defined the legal rights of freedmen and sometimes made the black man almost the equal of the white man in court, although in some states blacks could not testify against whites.

But equality did not go beyond these provisions. Apprenticeship regulations bounded the economic and social freedom of young blacks; courts had to order the apprenticeship of unemployed young freedmen and give preference to their former masters. The resulting arrangement often differed little from slavery. Vagrancy regulations and laws forbidding disorderly conduct gave enforcement officers wide discretion and restricted the social and economic life of black adults. Any Mississippi black who lacked regular employment or could not pay the poll tax was guilty of vagrancy. Those convicted could be leased to employers who paid fines and costs; former masters again had preference and the result again might be only technically distinguishable from bondage. Even if a black obeyed all these statutes, other laws kept him out of the white community. The only black passengers permitted in first-class railroad cars in Mississippi, for instance, were maids, who were allowed to wait on their white mistresses.

The freedman's lack of land and money reinforced those provisions of the Black Codes that limited his mobility. Any black who lacked a contract certifying steady employment had to have a license. Contracts often specified annual wage payments, a practice that forced the employee into debt for expenses incurred while earning the first year's wage. And if he left his employer before the expiration of the year, he forfeited any wages earned up to that time.

RUIN IN DIXIE

Postwar economic distress impartially afflicted both black and white southerners and sharply limited the chance for anyone to get ahead. Losses, either through battle or through years of negligent cultivation, required capital to replace. Southern wealth had traditionally taken the form of land and slaves. Since slaves were gone, land had to serve as the basis for rebuilding southern prosperity. Yankee investors who might have advanced credit found their economic opportunity at home, where railroads and industry brought a larger and faster return at less risk than investment in southern agriculture.

Although some parts of the South escaped desolation, others had become wastelands. General Philip Sheridan's troops destroyed so much in the Shenandoah Valley that he boasted that even a crow would have to carry rations to survive a flight over the area. General William T. Sherman's army had left its mark along its route through Georgia and South Carolina. Where war had reached town, waste was sickeningly evident. One northern reporter described Charleston, South Carolina, as a city "of ruins, . . . of vacant houses, of widowed women, of rotting wharves, of deserted ware-houses, of weed-wild gardens, of miles of grass-grown streets, of acres of pitiful and voiceful barrenness. . . ." But at least the houses and warehouses still stood in Charleston. Columbia, the same reporter noted, was a "wilder-ness of ruins, . . . blackened chimneys and crumbling walls." In the business district "not a store, office, or shop escaped; and for a distance of three-fourths of a mile on each of twelve streets, there was not a building left."

Damage in the countryside was less immediately visible, but not less economically severe. Even where plantation houses still stood, weeds ruined

Columbia, South Carolina, after the war

cotton fields as surely as they had Charleston's gardens. Throughout the rural South, men had to restore fertility to the soil, fences to the fields, and stock to the barns and to produce an initial crop for food and seed. When buildings had to be rebuilt, the hardship was compounded.

Some rural southerners at first avoided the task. To many newly emancipated blacks, freedom meant the right to leave the plantation, and this action upset the traditional pattern of southern agriculture. Gradually, sharecropping evolved to replace slavery as a method of harnessing labor. In this system, which spread throughout the South before 1880, impoverished landowners allowed impoverished tenant farmers of both races to work the land. Owner and laborer then shared the crop according to a formula that depended partly on prevailing rates in the community and partly on whether the tenant furnished his own seed and mule. Both parties often had to survive between harvests on credit advanced by the local store, so interest charges added to costs. Profits were frequently inadequate to carry either owner or tenant through the following season, when the cycle began again. In spite of important differences, sharecropping was in many respects more similar to prewar plantation agriculture than to farming in the rest of the nation.

Tenant farming enabled the South to use the land, but it produced a meager living for most southerners. The sharecropping system, like slavery,

A Georgia Plantation in 1860 and 1881

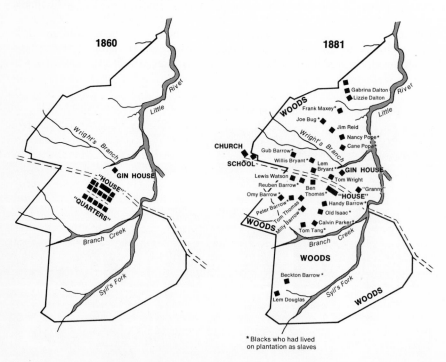

* Blacks who had lived
on plantation as slaves

discouraged agricultural innovation that might have helped the region develop more diversified farming. Sharecropping required the sale of a cash crop to pay bills already incurred. Creditors preferred the continued production of familiar crops to experimentation with new ones. Methods of cultivation were perhaps less efficient than those employed on large plantations before the Civil War. Plots were smaller; management was sometimes less competent and nearly always unable to purchase machinery, which was increasingly employed on northern farms.

CONGRESSIONAL RECONSTRUCTION

The economic transition from slavery to sharecropping was less dramatic and less frenzied than the political transition from Confederacy to reunited states. Once southern legislatures had been reestablished and federal elections held in 1865, Andrew Johnson was anxious to welcome the states back into the Union. Johnson's readiness to readmit the South was not shared by Congress, whose reaction to the Black Codes was prompt and hostile. Even Republican moderates were unconvinced that the governments Johnson had approved represented loyal, reformed, and contrite southerners.

Radicals renounced Johnson's work as a sham and urged Congress to undertake genuine reconstruction. The rebels had proudly reestablished "'the white man's Government,'" Thaddeus Stevens reported, and Congress should resolutely prove that such governments were entirely unacceptable components of the federal republic. Demagogues, including "some high in authority," he continued, with a barbed reference to the President, had appealed to the "lowest prejudices of the ignorant" to maintain the dominance of southern whites. Stevens held that the white race had "no exclusive right forever to rule this nation," nor could it convert "other races and nations and colors" to mere subjects. He did not shrink from the conclusion: this nation, he said, must be "the Government of all men alike. . . ."

Most Republicans stopped short of Stevens' stand. Yet if they were not ready to admit the black man to full political equality, as Stevens demanded, they did insist on more change than Johnson had required. So, in December, 1865, Congress refused to let southern legislators take the oath and sent them home. Congress then began work on two bills and a proposed constitutional amendment that became the congressional terms for reunion. The President vetoed both bills and encouraged those who opposed the amendment. His intransigence blighted any hope for a compromise program, for when moderate Republicans were forced to choose between Stevens' radicalism and the unreconstructed white governments Johnson had permitted, they chose radicalism. Andrew Johnson's political ineptitude and the adamant refusal of white southerners to concede to the blacks more than technical emancipation eventually drove the Republican party to Thaddeus Stevens and military reconstruction.

Moderates began with a bill to prolong the life of the Freedmen's Bureau and to give it a quasi-judicial authority over disputes arising from discrimination or denial of civil rights. The bill deprived state courts of jurisdiction in such cases, and specifically contradicted southern black codes by making punishable the sort of discrimination they permitted. Although the bill's sponsors thought they had secured the President's approval, Johnson vetoed the measure in February, 1866. The bureau, the President held, had grown out of the war's emergency and was based on the constitutional grant of power for war, which Congress could not legitimately invoke in peace. Once ordinary institutions, including civil courts, were reestablished, the bureau should disband.

Congress could not immediately assemble the majority necessary to override Johnson's veto, and moderates tried again to resolve the impasse with the Civil Rights Bill of 1866. The bill declared blacks to be citizens of the United States, thus burying the Dred Scott decision, and guaranteed "the full and equal benefit of all laws . . . for the security of person or property" to black citizens. Federal courts were to have jurisdiction over cases in which citizens had been deprived of equal rights. The bill received the support of every Republican in the House and all but three in the Senate. And Andrew Johnson vetoed it because it infringed the reserved powers of the states.

This time Congress overrode the veto and, for good measure, salvaged the Freedmen's Bureau bill too. To preserve its handiwork, Congress framed the constitutional amendment that eventually became the Fourteenth, which confirmed the status of the blacks as citizens and prohibited state legislation that denied equal legal protection to all citizens. Johnson could not prevent the submission of the amendment to the states, but his hostility encouraged southern states to reject it and temporarily blocked ratification. Tennessee, the President's own state, ratified the amendment and was rewarded by full restoration to the Union. Other southerners rejected the amendment and waited.

They waited too long, for the Congress that assembled in 1867 raised the price of readmission. In the crucial congressional election of 1866 Andrew Johnson had taken his cause to the country. His performance on the stump struck people as undignified and seemed as inept as his performance in the White House. Voters sent a new Congress to Washington with enough Radical votes to overwhelm the President.

The Radicals lost no time. In 1867 Congress passed a Reconstruction Act that combined ten southern states into five military districts and subordinated state governments to military commanders. The governments and constitutions Johnson had approved in 1865 were to be discarded and new constitutions granting suffrage to blacks and guaranteeing their equality were to be established. This legislation unquestionably mocked the traditional rights of the states, as both Johnson and the South claimed. The Radicals, however, were trying to crush traditions and had minimal interest in the constitutional pretenses of the defeated section. Radicals counted the doctrine of state rights an unmourned casualty of the Civil War.

Congress abridged the President's powers, as it had the rights of the states. Johnson's power to direct the army was limited by a requirement that all orders be issued through the General of the Army, who could not be removed or reassigned without the Senate's consent. The Tenure of Office Act required the Senate's approval for removal of any official for whom senatorial confirmation was necessary. Radicals hoped thereby to protect Secretary of War Edwin Stanton, who opposed the President's program, and whose support for military reconstruction was crucial.

The Radicals then turned to impeachment, both to remove the stubborn President and to warn future presidents. The charge against Johnson specified eleven offenses, most of which arose from his attempt to remove Stanton from the Cabinet. But, Thaddeus Stevens confessed, he did not mean to impeach the President for any particular offense or even for all of them together. Stevens meant to banish Johnson for his political mistakes, not for moral or legal lapses. Stevens wanted nothing less than to subordinate the President to Congress—to make future Presidents responsible to future Congresses—and impeachment was the means to his end.

The House debated all of Andrew Johnson's alleged crimes: his partiality toward the South, his public disrespect of Congress and its leadership, his drunken inauguration as Vice-President, his alleged complicity in Lincoln's assassination, and his deliberate violations of the Tenure of Office Act. The President was acquitted partly because the Senate found the bill of particulars too flimsy a basis for so unprecedented a step and partly because a few senators decided to support the independence of the executive branch rather than establish a precedent that might lead to a ministry responsible to the legislature, as is a parliamentary cabinet. The margin in the Senate was slim; Johnson survived by one vote. Thirty-five Republicans voted to convict; twelve Democrats and seven Republicans found for the President. After the roll calls in the Senate, Washington ceased to be the main forum for debate over reconstruction.

Thaddeus Stevens summarizes the case for Andrew Johnson's impeachment.

RECONSTRUCTION—A SOUTHERN VIEW

Radical Reconstruction, so the legend runs, was an undignified, corrupt, expensive, regrettable social experiment from which enlightened white conservatives freed the South in 1877. Blacks, their venal northern allies the carpetbaggers, and a few unprincipled southern opportunists called scalawags looted southern treasuries, discredited themselves, and demonstrated that the freedmen had no political capacity. The return to white control, many Americans have complacently believed, preserved the South from bankruptcy and barbarism.

Until recently, Americans have used Radical Reconstruction to confirm racial stereotypes that developed in the seventeenth century and persist in the twentieth. A simple illustration of the nation's stern judgment of that reconstruction has been the connotation and currency of the term "Black Reconstruction" applied to the period. D. W. Griffith's classic film *Birth of a Nation*, released in 1915, portrays the Southern white as the victim of Reconstruction. The narratives of professional historians, less emotionally charged and incomparably more dull than Griffith's movie, have too often made the same point.

This belief, like most myths, has a factual basis. Reconstruction did bring unprecedented taxes to the southern states, and not all the money was honestly spent. Blacks did not universally resist financial temptation, nor were they always dignified and wise in their legislative deliberation. Illustrative statistics abound. Florida spent more for printing in 1869 than the entire state government had cost in 1860. Sometimes bookkeeping was so casual that even a legislature could not calculate the state's debt; according to one estimate, South Carolina's debt tripled in three years, while another figure indicated that it had increased nearly six times. South Carolina also maintained at public expense a luxurious restaurant and bar that impartially dispensed imported delicacies to both black and white legislators.

But the term "Black Reconstruction" is misleading. Only in South Carolina did blacks ever become a majority of the legislature. They held high office elsewhere in the South—Mississippi sent two black senators to Washington—but they were by no means so dominant as the term "Black Reconstruction" implies. Many white officeholders, to be sure, did not belong to the social class that had ruled the prewar South; some were recently transplanted northerners, known as carpetbaggers. These white politicians had to have black support to succeed, but the simplistic picture of black rule is incorrect.

Nor is the myth of corrupt extravagance entirely justified. Rebuilding after a war is always expensive, and taxpayers always resent the bill. Further, Reconstruction governments not only had to restore public buildings and services; they also had to furnish new facilities and services that had been inadequate in most of the South. In many southern states, for example, public education for both races dates from these legislatures. For the first time, in some cases, states also accepted limited responsibility for the welfare of the indigent and sick. These were among the constructive accomplishments of the Reconstruction legislatures.

The notorious corruption of Reconstruction often came from the attempt by ambitious southerners to bring to the area the blessings of railroads and factories. Only the state commanded enough credit to entice the railroads that seemed to be the indispensable beginning of prosperity. Southern states issued bonds to finance railroad construction, but the proceeds sometimes vanished before the rails were laid. Fraud in the development of the American rail net was not peculiar to the South; in other states as well, public funds were converted to private use and politicians occasionally pocketed "fees" that might more candidly have been called bribes. Nor were corrupted legislatures confined to the South in the post–Civil War era. The peculation of southern legislators was trifling by comparison with scandals in the Grant administration.

Finally, not all corrupt southerners were black. Although some black politicians accepted bribes and some misused public funds, none stole as much as the white treasurer of Mississippi embezzled immediately after the state was supposedly saved from the irresponsible blacks. And for every purchased politician, there must have been a buyer. The fast-buck promoters of railroads and industries were whites, not blacks, few of whom were enriched by the plunder they had supposedly secured from public treasuries.

RECONSTRUCTION ENDS

Most southern whites resented any sign of racial equality and found black political participation particularly threatening. Although the Fourteenth Amendment extended most rights of citizenship to blacks and the Fifteenth Amendment gave them the franchise, white southerners did not always abide by these provisions. As Congress readmitted southern states to full membership in the union, the Ku Klux Klan and other terrorist bands perfected new ways to return the black man as nearly as possible to his old bondage.

These groups adopted mystifying hierarchies, rituals, and regalia, but no mystery shrouded their central purpose: they proposed to reestablish white supremacy by terrifying the blacks into giving up their quest for equality. The Klan and its imitators used direct, brutal, and highly visible methods: torch, lash, and rope were standard equipment. A frightened Louisiana tax-collector wrote a northern senator that thirty-eight blacks in his district had recently met violent death. The lives of the "few white Republicans now left," he continued, were jeopardized. The official asked urgently for federal intervention, a plea that Congress met with the Ku Klux Klan Acts, or the "Force Acts," of 1870 and 1871. These measures set stiff penalties for those convicted of interfering with the right of any citizen to vote and permitted the use of troops against terrorists, as if they constituted a renewed Confederate rebellion.

The Klan was no match for the army; while troops remained in the

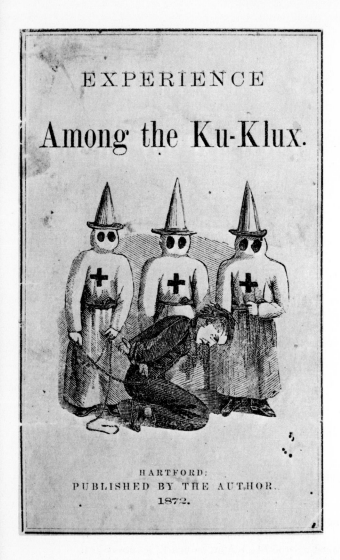

EXPERIENCE

Among the Ku-Klux.

HARTFORD:
PUBLISHED BY THE AUTHOR.
1872.

South, federal law was outwardly obeyed. Had vigilant national administrations kept garrisons in the South for a generation, perhaps an equitably biracial society might have developed, even if racism remained. But within a decade after Appomattox, northern voters' interest in Reconstruction dwindled. Rutherford B. Hayes, the Republican presidential nominee in 1876, favored removing the occupying forces from the three unreconstructed states. His party ran its standard campaign, which blended emotional appeals to Union veterans with denunciation of Democratic "treason,"—a tactic known as "waving the 'bloody shirt' "—but this emotional Radicalism no longer produced a political mandate.

The voters in 1876 did not even produce a clear decision. The majority of the popular vote went to the Democratic candidate, Samuel J. Tilden, a financially conservative governor of New York who had successfully battled the notoriously corrupt Tweed Ring. Republicans conceded Tilden 184 electoral votes; while Hayes had won only 165 for certain. But Republicans also claimed the nineteen contested electoral votes from Louisiana, Florida, and South Carolina, where fraud and federal troops raised the Republican total, and one disputed vote of Oregon that had been awarded to Tilden on a legal technicality. Since the contested electors could determine the winner, public dispute was bitter and private bargaining intense.

To decide the dispute, Congress established a presumably bipartisan commission consisting of five members each from the House, Senate, and Supreme Court. The appearance of impartiality disappeared when the commission's one uncommitted member withdrew and was replaced by a convinced Republican. There was chicanery and intimidation on both sides, but the commission's award of all twenty votes to Hayes was unquestionably partisan and probably unjust.

Republicans paid a political price for the White House. Southern Democrats won assurance that federal funds would become available for construction of southern railroads, for improvements to southern harbors, and for projects that would make southern rivers more navigable and less apt to flood the countryside. In addition to capital for internal improvements, white southerners were to be given the respectability (and the salaries) of federal jobs. Hayes appointed David M. Key, a former Whig from Tennessee, as Postmaster General, the traditional post for the adminis-

The Election of 1876

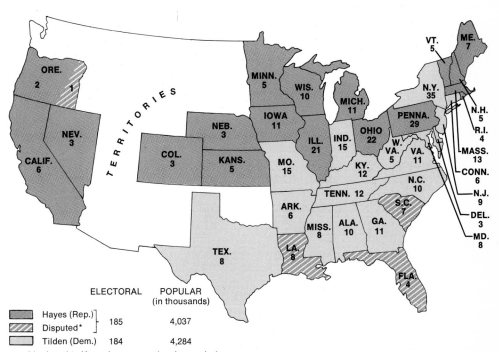

	ELECTORAL	POPULAR (in thousands)
Hayes (Rep.)		
Disputed*	185	4,037
Tilden (Dem.)	184	4,284

*Assigned to Hayes by congressional commission.

tration's patronage broker. Finally, civil government was restored throughout the South when Hayes recalled the last of the troops.

The experiment in Radical Reconstruction was over. Although the settlement in 1877 meant different things to different people, it clearly signalled a return to the politics of compromise. Republicans probably hoped that conciliation would persuade conservative southerners to make common cause with conservatives to the north. The promised flow of federal capital seemed to southerners to herald a "New South," where industry and transportation would complement agriculture and produce unparalleled prosperity. For blacks, however, the New South turned out to be quite like the old.

The tragedy of the Reconstruction is that so little was permanently accomplished. White southerners naturally wanted to preserve what they could of the sentimentalized past in which so many had taken refuge. Some were deceitful and harsh; most were unyielding on the central issue of white supremacy. Blacks understandably wanted to become wholly free Americans. In the attempt some were foolish and some corrupt, but most were humbly patient. Radicals wanted to reconstruct the South. Most expected the process to assure continued Republican supremacy; some intended to get rich; others meant to do full justice to the blacks. But Radicals retired or died, and their party soon found other causes more congenial than racial equality.

THE NEW SOUTH

Even while the politicians were preoccupied with Reconstruction, most of the rest of the nation had more important business to attend to. The North's business of the moment was industrialization. Prophets of the New South, like Henry Grady, editor of the Atlanta *Constitution*, urged their section also to pursue the profits of commercial enterprise and the promise of industrial plenty. Before 1900, the essential transportation was available; southern railroad mileage more than doubled in the 1880s alone, far exceeding growth in the rest of the nation. The pace of southern industrial development, though impressive, was less rapid.

Southern industry processed the region's agricultural staples and exploited such natural resources as bauxite, sulphur, and the oil of Texas and Oklahoma. Coal and iron deposits made Birmingham a major center for the production of pig iron. The American Tobacco Company, which James Buchanan Duke organized in North Carolina in 1890, brought new machines and new marketing techniques to one of the South's oldest crops. Textile mills sprang up in Georgia, Alabama, and the Carolinas, taking advantage of cheap labor and eliminating the need for transportation of raw cotton to northern mills. In 1900 investment in southern textile factories had increased seven times over the total for 1880.

While the South wooed industry, tenant farming continued to burden the agricultural base of the economy. In some parts of Georgia, perhaps 1 percent of black farmers owned land in 1880; the blacks' share of total

Tenancy on Southern Farms

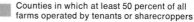

Counties in which at least 50 percent of all
farms operated by tenants or sharecroppers

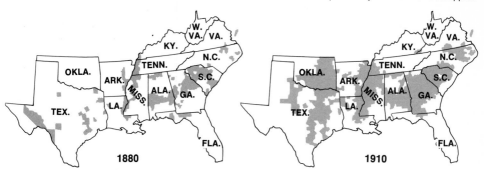

1880

1910

wealth in stock and soil was probably even smaller. Absentee land ownership and soil depletion through cash-crop farming increased along with
sharecropping after Reconstruction. The lack of capital to buy fertilizer or
to enable a shift to other crops doomed the South to soil-mining that could
only bring diminishing yields and rural penury.

And the racial dilemma persisted with the poverty. The distinction
between sharecropping and bondage was not apparent to many blacks.
Blows hurt both pride and body, whether delivered by masters to slaves or
by Klansmen to freedmen. Lacking troops to ensure equality, Hayes and
his successors exhorted the South to respect the amendments and the civil
rights laws, but presidential pleas were less effective than force. The
"Redeemers," conservatives who ran the South for a generation after
1877, did not immediately disfranchise and segregate the black man. Rather
they secured political support from freedmen, with promises, polite words,
and a few local offices. Black support, in turn, helped these conservatives
retain control when discontented whites in the 1880s and 1890s demanded
increased public services, such as new schools. As rivalry among whites
grew sharper, the votes of blacks in some areas were bought more or less
openly, while intimidation in other places kept blacks at home on election
day. When an honest count in a free election could no longer be assumed,
white southerners blamed blacks, whose support was being corruptly
sought, rather than white politicians who profited from public office. So the
black man lost his right to vote in the cause of reform and honest elections;
black men were disfranchised so that white men would no longer have to
count one another out.

The North acquiesced to disfranchisement with only occasional bursts
of self-righteous outrage. While in the House, James A. Garfield three times
introduced bills to reduce the number of congressmen from southern states
as the Fourteenth Amendment required. Garfield's bills failed to pass, and
he dropped the crusade before he became President in 1881. In 1890, Henry
Cabot Lodge, a young Republican congressman from Massachusetts, sponsored a bill to permit federal supervision of federal elections. Some Republicans hoped, as had their predecessors during Reconstruction, to break the
Democratic hold on the South with the black vote. But the Lodge bill failed
to pass, and northern interest in helping southern blacks vote died with it.

One important northern newspaper consoled its readers with the observation that disfranchisement by law was less wrong than disfranchisement through terror.

The threat of renewed federal supervision made the South hasten to find legal means for securing exclusive white control of the political process. Between 1890 and 1905, various methods of restricting black suffrage were proposed, refined, and adopted. Some states used property qualifications and poll taxes, but these devices also excluded a great many poor whites. Literacy tests or tests requiring an "understanding" of selected passages from the state or national constitution left more discretion to the local examiners who administered the test. Louisiana permitted an exemption from such tests for those entitled to vote on January 1, 1867, or for sons and grandsons of such voters. Because blacks did not vote before the Reconstruction Act of March, 1867, Louisiana's "grandfather clause" exempted only whites. The president of the convention that proposed the change admitted that it seemed a bit ridiculous. But, he asked, "Doesn't it let the white man vote and doesn't it stop the negro from voting, and isn't that what we came here for?" No one could quarrel with results: the number of registered black voters in Louisiana promptly fell from over 130,000 to 5,320.

Although the Supreme Court of the United States subsequently invalidated the crude "grandfather clause" technique, other methods of disfranchisement survived the Court's scrutiny. The Court was also tolerant of the growing southern demand for social separation of the races. In 1873, in the Slaughterhouse cases, which did not directly involve the rights of blacks, the Court held that the Fourteenth Amendment protected only those rights derived from federal citizenship. Most civil rights, the Court decided, derived from state citizenship, and a citizen must appeal to his state to protect them.

In the Civil Rights cases of 1883, the Court held that the Fourteenth Amendment only prevented the discriminatory political acts of states, and did not outlaw social discrimination by individuals. Congress had exceeded its authority, then, in passing the Civil Rights Act of 1875, which required individuals to furnish equal access to such public facilities as inns, theaters, and transportation. In spite of a prescient and persuasive dissent from Justice John Marshall Harlan, the Court told blacks to appeal to state legislatures to secure equal public accommodations.

The Court's decisions permitted discrimination on racial grounds; southern legislatures in the next two decades gradually required the practice. Separate sections of public buildings or vehicles, separate schools, churches, lodges, and jails kept the races from social contact. And in 1896 the Supreme Court, in *Plessy* v. *Ferguson*, again went along. So long as the facilities were substantially equal, even if separate, the Court said no rights were abridged. Separation did not imply inferiority, the Court held, nor could either the Constitution or legislation "eradicate racial instincts or . . . abolish distinctions based upon physical differences. . . ." Justice Harlan was still unconvinced. "Our Constitution," he wrote, "is color-blind. . . ." The pose of equal accommodations for black citizens he called a "thin disguise" that would neither "mislead any one, nor atone for the wrong this day done. . . ."

Even before the Court accepted segregation, Booker T. Washington, the respected head of Tuskeegee Institute, indicated the black man's acceptance. At the Atlanta Exposition, where the New South displayed its initiative and its produce, Washington gave a widely acclaimed speech in which he appealed to his fellow blacks to learn trades, to become producing members of society, to earn—not demand—equality. He asked whites for help, for employment, for a chance to hew the wood and draw the water of the New South. But discussion of social equality Washington branded "the extremest folly," and he seemed to accept the Jim Crow laws that were requiring racial separation. "In all things that are purely social," said Washington with a superb metaphor, "we can be as separate as the fingers, yet one as the hand in all things essential to mutual progress."

Washington specifically did not accept disfranchisement and opposed any measure that permitted "an ignorant and poverty-stricken white man to vote" while it kept a "black man in the same condition" from the polls. But whites heard only Washington's seeming renunciation of equality. This was one time when they took the black man at his word.

Suggested Reading

Walter L. Fleming's *A Documentary History of Reconstruction* (1960), compiled nearly seventy years ago, has been reprinted and contains extensive source material for a study of the period. Kenneth M. Stampp's *The Era of Reconstruction** (1965) is a distinguished interpretive work that surveys the period, as does John Hope Franklin's *Reconstruction** (1962), and an older account by Paul H. Buck, *The Road to Reunion** (1937).

More specialized than these books are Howard K. Beale, *The Critical Year* (1930), which focuses on the election of 1866, C. Vann Woodward, *Reunion and Reaction** (1951), which analyzes the Compromise of 1877, and Joel R. Williamson, *After Slavery** (1965), which deals with the progress of the freedmen. W. E. Burghardt DuBois, *Black Reconstruction** (1935), stresses the positive accomplishments of the Radicals of both races. Fawn Brodie, *Thaddeus Stevens** (1959), illuminates all of Radical Reconstruction. Eric L. McKitrick, *Andrew Johnson and Reconstruction** (1960), documents Johnson's political ineptitude. Thomas F. Gossett's *Race: The History of an Idea in America** (1963) is a social and intellectual history of racism. Booker T. Washington argues his views in *Up From Slavery** (1901). In *Origins of the New South** (1951) C. Vann Woodward carries the history of the South from Reconstruction into the twentieth century.

*Available in paperback edition

CHRONOLOGY

THE INDUSTRIAL

TRANSFORMATION

The last three decades of the nineteenth century were years of contrast and contradiction. The age was at once dynamic and unchanging, certain and confused, vulgar and genteel, imitative and original. The poor man believed the rich man's creed; rural attitudes persisted in teeming cities; economic principles of family and farm were applied to corporations and industries; and humanitarianism became a cause for an imperialistic war. Mark Twain called the period "the gilded age," and it was indeed a shoddy alloy of precious and base—cheap, shiny, tasteless. It was also the Victorian age—massive, ornate, cluttered, and prudish. And it was "the age of excess," when the economic system did not provide the population with the means to consume what could be produced and when there was too much façade on both the homes and the lives of too many Americans.

If some parlors were overly full, others were bare; it was an age of too little as well as too much. In the stables of the Vanderbilts' summer estate at Newport, Rhode Island, grooms carefully spread sand on the wooden floors and then with sand of another color traced a monogram as exquisite as an Italian mosaic. In many American homes a clean sand floor would itself have been a luxury. On the same estate was a playhouse with

The Breakers

its own setting of imported English china; elsewhere families of eight or ten people lived in quarters smaller than that playhouse, and they furnished them with less than the cost of a half-dozen of the Vanderbilts' salad plates. The main mansion, called The Breakers, was a triumph of Victorian architecture, complete with gargoyles, French furniture, Italian marble, and Norman tapestry. The house required a staff of about thirty servants and was used by the Vanderbilt family for but a few weeks during the summer season. To house his family of five or six in a four-room tenement a textile-worker not far from Newport paid two or three dollars of his eight- or ten-dollar weekly wage.

Tenement housing: "an age of too little as well as too much"

The gap between rich and poor was only one of the contrasts of the age. Laborers, for instance, worked from sixty to eighty-four hours each week, but they still found time to watch professional baseball, burlesque, P. T. Barnum's Greatest Show on Earth, and touring theatrical companies, all of which flourished in the late nineteenth century. Nearly every year brought farmers larger harvests and smaller income, a contrast that at first puzzled, and then outraged, rural America. Horatio Alger's banalities were widely read, but a generation that produced the prose of Mark Twain, William Dean Howells, and Henry James, the poetry of Emily Dickinson, and the philosophy of William James and Charles Peirce cannot have been entirely undiscriminating. Many American architects built imitations of Greek, Gothic, Romanesque, and Italian Renaissance buildings, but here and there a Louis Sullivan or a Henry H. Richardson followed his American imagination rather than a European model. "Victorian" since 1900 has come to mean gentility, propriety, and stern morality. Yet flamboyance often obscured gentility; propriety often ended in the parlor; and morality was a myth in an age of bosses, stock-watering, and scandals in the private lives of a President of the United States and the nation's best known preacher. Pretense contrasted with performance.

On every hand was confusion—a welter of ideas, political programs, and economic nostrums, paradoxically combined with a resignation to let events take their course, which they did at an accelerating pace. In 1870 Indians and buffalo still roamed the plains; Minneapolis had only about 13,000 inhabitants; few Americans knew where Samoa was; and Andrew Carnegie had not yet devoted himself to the steel business. By 1900 Indians were wards of the nation on reservations and buffalo were protected in zoos; Minneapolis was a thriving city of more than 200,000; Americans had governed part of Samoa for a dozen years; and Andrew Carnegie was about ready to sell his steel business for several hundred million dollars. Confusion grew out of rapid change, and rapid change, in large measure, grew out of the nation's industrialization.

PREREQUISITES FOR INDUSTRIALIZATION

Most of the elements essential to the nation's industrial growth had been present before the Civil War. The first American factories had processed the products of mine and soil—iron, coal, timber, wheat, and cotton. These factories furnished a prototype for subsequent industrial organization and tested the technology of mass production, in particular the idea of interchangeable parts. Sir Henry Bessemer's process of refining steel, developed in the 1850s, went into production in the United States during the Civil War. A pool of factory labor had also developed before 1860, for discontented farmers needed only a nudge to join the Irish immigrants that already crowded the seacoast towns of New England and the middle states. Other more fortunate farmers had mechanized farming and provided a firm base of agricultural productivity. Just as essential to industrialization as cotton or iron, and just as abundant, was the spirit of enterprise. Americans long before 1860 had had a highly developed acquisitive-ness. They figured that change meant improvement, and they measured improvement in cash.

Above all, industrialization required capital. Unless a society can secure unlimited foreign funds, it must produce more than it consumes and then invest its collective savings productively in railroads, factories, housing, and education. Europeans did invest heavily in American industrial development, but domestic investment was perhaps three or four times greater. Americans, as a society, postponed present consumption in the expectation of an improved standard of living in the future. The economic process was not substantially different from earlier industrial development in England or the later development in Japan and the Soviet Union.

Some of the capital came from farmers and industrial laborers. Farmers received a progressively smaller portion of national income in return for progressively larger output, which, when exported, secured the foreign exchange that was essential to economic growth. Workers received inadequate wages for long hours of tedious work. Even the capitalists, whose profits were the first return on society's investment in industry, were productive. In the ordinary course of business, bankers created capital. Railroads by their very existence increased land values and thereby added enormously to national wealth. The growth of railroads stimulated new economic activity in steel, mining, and in many new industries that sprang up to supply the railroads' needs. And the expansion of the rail net into the most remote parts of the nation created the possibility of national distribution and of profit on a comparable scale.

Natural resources, technology, labor, agricultural productivity, a receptive domestic market, transportation facilities, a spirit of enterprise, and capital—all these prerequisites for industrialization were interlocked. The immigrant who furnished his labor was also a source of capital because he brought a little money with him, and, more importantly, because his unproductive years had been spent in Europe. The railroad that created a national market created capital as well. One technological improvement in machine tools led to several more improvements in production equipment. In short, industrialization fed on itself, and once well begun, growth became the ordinary economic condition.

RAILROADS: THE "FIRST BIG BUSINESS"

According to laissez faire, the dominant economic theory of the age, a dormant government was an economic blessing. Since economic forces were assumed to be immutable, governmental interference was at best futile and might be mischievous. The argument was directed primarily at those who wished to curb business or mitigate some of the social inequi-ties that accompanied industrialization. But when business needed help—a tariff, a land grant, even a subsidy—politicians discovered that laissez faire permitted government aid to business.

Railroads were the chief beneficiaries of this political bounty. Before

Federal Grants to the Railroads

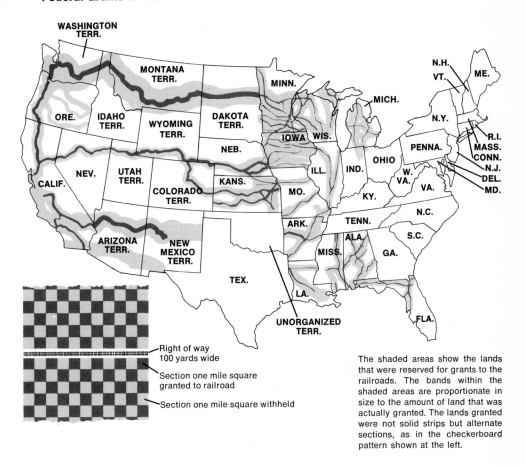

Right of way 100 yards wide

Section one mile square granted to railroad

Section one mile square withheld

The shaded areas show the lands that were reserved for grants to the railroads. The bands within the shaded areas are proportionate in size to the amount of land that was actually granted. The lands granted were not solid strips but alternate sections, as in the checkerboard pattern shown at the left.

the Civil War, Congress had granted public lands to aid construction of the Illinois Central. When construction of transcontinental lines began in earnest after the war, the practice of granting land was revived and refined. Ordinarily a railroad received alternate square miles of land to a depth of ten to twenty miles on either side of the right of way in states and to a depth of forty miles in territories. For each mile of track, then, the railroad received at least ten square miles of public domain. Nor was that the limit of the subsidy. States and local governments outbid one another to attract railways; communities used tax concessions, land grants, and governmental purchases of stock to get on the tracks that promised to be the route to prosperity.

Total public aid for railway construction can only be estimated. Apparently, total land grants approximately equaled the combined area of New York, New England, and Pennsylvania. And land was only the beginning. Both the Union Pacific and the Central Pacific, which met at Promontory Point, Utah, in 1869 to complete the first transcontinental, received federal loans for construction. The government advanced $16,000 per mile of track laid on the plains, and increased the amount to $32,000 and $48,000 per mile in more difficult terrain. The railroads eventually retired the second mortgage bonds that secured these federal loans, but less wary state and local governments occasionally lost subsidies to unscrupulous promoters who never laid a rail. Missouri, for instance, spent nearly $25 million in subsidies, of which about $19 million was wasted.

In spite of occasional corporate chicanery, land grants and subsidies made economic sense. The value of the alternate sections of land retained by the government more than doubled because of the railroad's presence. The public could give half the land away, sell the remainder at double the original price, break even on the transaction, and still have the railroad, which would not otherwise have been built. Postwar American railroads were built in the expectation of future traffic from future settlement. Unsettled public land offered no immediate market for the railroad's service, but the American people, as is their custom, were impatient. The public demanded railroads and opened public treasuries to help pay for them.

The public money poured into railroads was but a small fraction of their total cost; private investors paid far more. This total cost may well have been exorbitant, for private investment, like public funds, also tended to disappear into the pockets of railroad financiers, as gaudy a collection of entrepreneurs as the American economy ever produced. Some of these capitalists performed an economic service in return for their fortunes. The Vanderbilts improved rail service between New York and Chicago by merging small competitors into the New York Central. James J. Hill turned the rusting St. Paul and Pacific into the prosperous Great Northern, extended it from Minnesota across the northwest to the Pacific, and strengthened the economy of the region and of several Canadian prov-

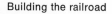

Building the railroad

inces as well. But other railroad tycoons provided less service and more scandal. Daniel Drew, Jay Gould, and Jim Fisk, in concert and as individual operators, amassed fortunes by manipulating railroad securities. At one time or another between 1870 and 1900, almost every American railroad fell prey to some financial freebooter whose interest was in stocks and bonds, not in tracks and locomotives. Reduced to essentials, the usual method of making money while bankrupting the railroad required four steps. First, control of the corporation was secured through quiet purchases in the stock market. Second, whatever the financial condition of the corporation, new management then declared a whopping dividend. This declaration doubly enriched those who had obtained control: they received the dividend itself, which also attracted new investors to the stock, thus driving the price up, sometimes severalfold. Third, to pay for the dividend, management voted to float new stock in the market. And finally, before too many investors suspected the scheme, those with inside information sold out and left the railroad floundering with a higher capitalization on which stockholders expected to receive a dividend bonanza.

As a result of such deception, and because railroads require an immense investment even when honestly managed, the capital costs—interest and dividends—of the nation's railroads were very high. In addition, neither capital costs nor such other expenses as taxes, insurance, and many salaries, vary with the amount of freight the railroad carries. These fixed costs, together with the proliferation and increasing competition of the railroads after the depression of 1873, produced unscrupulous competitive practices, or "abuses," which, in turn, led to demands that the government abandon laissez faire for public regulation.

REBATES AND REGULATION

Since many of a railroad's expenses were fixed, almost any freight carried at almost any fee was better than no freight at all. Securing large, regular shipments was worth extraordinary effort, and shippers fortunate enough to be served by competing lines soon discovered that published rates were negotiable. A railroad often charged its favored customers the published rates but regularly refunded a portion of the charge, thereby, in effect, giving a discount for heavy volume. Some shippers even coerced railroads into paying rebates on shipments made by other competing customers. This concession, usually called a "drawback," gave the privileged customer a double competitive advantage: not only were his freight costs lower than those of his rivals, but in effect the railroad paid him part of his competitor's freight charge.

Those who lacked competitive leverage because their shipments were small, or because they could ship on only one railroad, paid "what the traffic will bear." Fees from large-volume shippers helped meet a railroad's fixed costs; profit came from those who paid full fare. Sometimes the fare seemed exorbitant. A farmer in Elgin, Illinois, taking advantage of competing railroads, could send a tub of butter to New York City for thirty cents; less fortunate farmers within 165 miles of New York, who were served by only one line, paid seventy-five cents for the same service. The patent injustice of this long-haul/short-haul discrimination gave critics a weapon they lacked in attacking rates that were less obviously outrageous.

Critics of railroads had sought legislative redress even before the Civil War. Several states had established regulatory commissions before 1860, and other states followed. But regulation proved less effective than its sponsors had hoped. Often a complimentary pass from the railroad was enough to corrupt a public official. And when a commission or legislature was incorruptible, railroads retreated to the courts where endless litigation delayed effective regulation.

In the 1870s, angry citizens in Illinois, Iowa, and Wisconsin denounced the discriminatory freight rates which, they believed, siphoned rural prosperity to the city. Some of them were members of the Patrons of Husbandry, a fraternal lodge usually called the Grange. Founded in 1867 by Oliver H. Kelley, a functionary in the Department of Agriculture, the Grange was initially designed to break the isolation and tedium of life on the farm. Soon the organization began to devise ways to enhance rural purchasing power as well. Several Granges sponsored cooperatives and others attempted to induce governmental regulation of warehouses, grain elevators, and railroads.

"Granger laws" of the 1870s permitted inspection of storage facilities, established commissions with power to set rates for storage and transportation, and prohibited such practices as favoring a long haul over a shorter one. The impulse for railroad regulation was not exclusively rural; merchants in Iowa, for instance, also wanted to reduce costs by curbing the railroads. In fact, between 1870 and 1880 freight rates fell faster than the price of agricultural products. But farm prices did drop about 25 percent, and farmers continued to seek legislative help.

So the railroads sought protection in the courts. Initially, in *Munn* v. *Illinois* (1877), the Supreme Court upheld the right of the state to regulate private property when it was "used in a manner to make it of public consequence," and when it affected "the community at large." The particular case derived from an Illinois law regulating warehouses, but the court applied the rule to railroads as well, since they were of even greater "public consequence." Yet railroads continued to contest legislation, and in 1886, in the *Wabash, St. Louis, and Pacific Railway Co.* v. *Illinois*, the Supreme Court limited the effectiveness of state regulatory laws. The Illinois statute outlawed long-haul/short-haul discrimination on shipments from the state to New York City. The Court held that only Congress could regulate interstate commerce and effectively removed control of interstate rates from state legislatures.

A year later, in 1887, Congress stepped into the legislative gap that the Wabash case created. Although the Interstate Commerce Act did not specifically authorize governmental rate-setting, it did require railroads to publish rate schedules and insisted that the fees be "reasonable and just." Congress failed to provide a procedure for determining fair rates or an effective means of enforcing them, and the Interstate Commerce Commission, which was created to administer the act, had to enforce its orders through the courts. The ICC heard complaints, summoned witnesses, examined records, and issued decrees, but for almost two decades, discrimination, rebates, and arbitrary rate-setting continued. Between 1887 and 1905 sixteen cases contesting orders of the ICC reached the Supreme Court; the railroads won fifteen. Justice John Marshall Harlan noted in a dissent in one such case that the Court had reduced the Commission to the power "to issue reports and make protests." Richard Olney, an astute railroad attorney who became Attorney General in the second Cleveland administration, thought the Interstate Commerce Act entirely satisfactory. It satisfied, he wrote, "the popular clamor for governmental supervision" while keeping control "almost entirely nominal." Effective railroad regulation was not achieved until the twentieth century.

Governmental supervision remained nominal because the attitude of the voting population was ambivalent. As was to be the case with industry, Americans wanted all the advantages of railroads without any disadvantages. The public insisted that tracks follow the route of political expediency instead of that of economic need and then expressed surprise when promoters and politicians proved to be in cahoots. The public expected railroads to expand well before ordinary traffic could support the investment and then was furious when financial sleight of hand and exorbitant rates were required to make an unprofitable route profitable. The public demanded regulation, but not enough regulation to still the steam whistle that seemed to every hamlet the herald of prosperity.

By 1900 whistles echoed in all but the most remote sections of the country. Between 1865 and 1870 the nation's rail network increased from 35,000 to 53,000 miles. In the next decade it jumped to 93,000 miles, and in the 1880s more than 70,000 additional miles were built. By 1900 193,000 miles of track crisscrossed the United States; more than $10 billion were invested in the nation's railroads, over $2 billion more than the total investment in manufacturing. And the stimulus to a developing economy was immense. In 1880 railroad construction required three-quarters of the steel produced in the United States. The railroads also were a primary market for coal, timber, and petroleum products. They employed more than a half-million Americans, who received more than $500 million in wages in 1900.

American businessmen were ill prepared to cope with enterprise on so gigantic a scale. Techniques adequate for managing local concerns failed to control a corporation that made a business of spanning the continent. Making a decision in New York about routing cars from St. Louis to Chicago presented unprecedented difficulty. Similarly, the collection of capital to expand the railroads forced financial innovation. The railroads pioneered in developing the financial, managerial, and accounting procedures that other national corporations then adapted to their own needs. The development of railroad regulation also foreshadowed a new relationship for business and government. Railroads created a national market, made national businesses possible and profitable, consumed the products of the nation's heavy industry, and attracted billions of dollars in capital. They were indeed, as Alfred D. Chandler has written, "the nation's first big business."

INDUSTRIAL GROWTH

In retrospect, the late nineteenth century seems a time for making fortunes, for building factories, for consolidating companies or railroads or acreage. If economic change had simply been growth, the process might not have been so disruptive, and perhaps the 1890s could justifiably be called the "gay nineties." But while the economy grew rapidly, it grew irregularly. Each time prosperity paused or its index dipped, rich and poor, wise and unwary alike were ruined. The "gay nineties" were years of strident agricultural protest, of strikes that occasionally escalated to industrial warfare, and of a deep and persistent depression.

Still, the age had the stamp of those who succeeded, and everyone knew who they were. A generation's heroes reflect the values and concerns of the times: the heroes of the post–Civil War generation were those who mastered and directed economic change. Andrew Carnegie, John D. Rockefeller and J. P. Morgan are the most prominent of dozens of men whose fortunes made their names familiar in every American household. Critics abused the Carnegies and Rockefellers and Morgans, but such criticism merely confirmed the commanding importance of economic leaders. By contrast, business executives and bankers in the generation after the Second World War are relatively anonymous, their private lives less a matter of public interest than those of entertainers, athletes, and politicians.

Statistics indicate the dimension of the economic change that rocked the United States after the Civil War. Population nearly doubled between 1870 and 1900, increasing by slightly more than 1 million people every year. About one-third of the increase between 1870 and 1880 came from nearly 3 million immigrants; in the next decade, the number of immigrants climbed to more than 5 million, and the population rose by 13 million. A rapidly expanding population meant a rapidly expanding market, and productivity jumped in response.

America's gross national product more than doubled in the quarter-century after 1870. By 1885 the total market value of manufactured products exceeded that of any other nation, and between 1885 and 1900 the production of American manufactured goods more than doubled. In 1870 millers shipped 48 million barrels of flour; by 1896 the figure had doubled. In 1870 American steel production was less than 70,000 tons; two years later it exceeded 140,000 tons; by 1880 the figure was over 1 million, and before the end of the century more than 10 million tons of steel came from American foundries. In 1871 American railroads bought less than 2,000 freight cars. In the decade thereafter, the annual figure was never less than 4,500 and in 1880 railroads needed more than 46,000 new cars to supply the booming national market. In 1890 Americans spent about three times as much as they had in 1870 for household furnishings, tombstones, and newspapers, and more than twice as much for clothes. Technological innovation spurred the pace. In 1860 the Patent Office registered less than 4,000 inventions; in 1870 the number exceeded 12,000, and in 1890 it had increased to more than 25,000—a figure greater than the total for the entire decade before the Civil War.

While industrial activity rose dramatically after Appomattox, the war itself may well have retarded a process that began earlier. Secession did remove southern opposition to protective tariffs and central banking. And managing a national war effort perhaps gave some entrepreneurs experience in directing nation-wide enterprises. But immigration lagged between 1860 and 1866, and desolation and neglect spread poverty across the South. More than a half-million men died before they could become productive in the economy. Capital that might have been employed in manufacturing or transportation had been diverted to destruction.

The ascent to industrial affluence was neither quick nor smooth. A dynamic economy is also unstable. Fourteen of the twenty-five years after 1873 were years of recession or depression, which exacted a capital toll in ruined businesses and a human price in unemployed workers. Farmers, small tradesmen, and artisans found that their lives became more difficult as a result of economic forces they could neither understand nor combat. Manufacturers and merchants, as well as the laboring population, had anxieties, tensions, and failures.

Productivity went up, however, even during depression. And, perhaps partly as a result of depression, prices went down. In the thirty years after Appomattox, the cost of living dropped about 25 percent, and manufactured goods and transportation, farm products and wages, all declined sharply. The price of refined petroleum fell about 90 percent in these three decades; steel rails dropped nearly 75 percent. Agricultural prices, by contrast, declined roughly 50 percent, though the decline in wheat, a crucial commodity, was greater. Increasing productivity and decreasing prices meant more and cheaper goods were available to more people. To be sure, some Americans could afford few goods at any price; but in spite of the dislocation it caused, industrialization offered many Americans a better standard of living.

TRUSTS AND ANTITRUSTS

The economies of large-scale production enabled some manufacturers to maintain their profits even while reducing prices. Andrew Carnegie's steel empire included everything from iron and coal deposits to factories for making finished steel products. Carnegie owned a railroad, ore boats, coking ovens, blast furnaces, and steel mills. The Carnegie Steel Company—called a vertical combination because it controlled the product from raw material to consumer—achieved internal saving by eliminating the profits of middlemen. Carnegie recorded the miraculous result:

> Two pounds of ironstone mined upon Lake Superior and transported nine hundred miles to Pittsburgh; one pound and one-half of coal, mined and manufactured into coke, and transported to Pittsburgh; one-half pound of lime, mined and transported to Pittsburgh; a

small amount of manganese mined in Virginia and brought to Pittsburgh—and these four pounds of materials [are] manufactured into one pound of steel, for which the consumer pays one cent.

John D. Rockefeller achieved comparable savings and perhaps greater profits by a horizontal combination in the oil industry. His Standard Oil Company secured almost complete control of oil refining. Through its domination of one segment of the industry Standard Oil gradually extended its influence into production, transportation and marketing and eventually became, like Carnegie Steel, a vertically integrated combination.

Before Rockefeller's domination, the oil industry could have served as a model of free competition. The risks were great, for drillers selected sites by hunch, and the result was often an expensive dry hole. Yet the capital required to become a driller was so small that many marginal operators entered the business. With many producers, most of whom lacked the capital to provide storage facilities, both production and price fluctuated wildly. In 1859, crude oil sold for $18 a barrel; at times in 1862, the same amount of oil brought a dime. Uncontrolled production also wasted the resource, for unsold oil seeped through wooden storage tanks or spilled away at the wells. Few drillers could invest in research or technological improvements when the price of their product changed so quickly.

Oil refining was somewhat more stable than the production of crude, but it became even more stable as Rockefeller and his associates either bought or crushed most of their competition. Standard Oil used its competitive advantage to secure rebates from the railroads. Rockefeller's firm also cut costs, developed new marketing techniques, and sold a product that was in fact standard—a uniform product that compared favorably in quality with the output of competitors. There were, in short, legitimate economic reasons for Standard's domination of the industry.

But other reasons for Standard's success were less a result of economy than of power. Standard occasionally secured not only discounts on its own freight, but rebates on shipments of other firms as well. The sequel to price wars that ruined independent refiners was sometimes monopolistic control of a market, with resulting price increases and mounting profits that seemed illegitimate. Like other firms in the period, Standard engaged in industrial espionage and perhaps bought political influence and a favorable press as well.

Consolidated economic power brought demands for public control and changes in corporate structure. In 1882 major stockholders in the various component companies of Standard Oil gave managerial control to Rockefeller and eight other trustees in return for trust certificates. In 1892 Ohio, which had chartered Standard Oil, moved to dissolve this trust that now controlled the corporation. A decision of the state's Supreme Court required the trustees to disband, but centralized management was retained through an informal agreement among the major stockholders. In 1899 Standard Oil established a holding company under a New Jersey statute that permitted one corporation to own stock in another. Standard Oil of

New Jersey acquired the stock of the other firms in the combination, and until 1911, when the Supreme Court ordered the holding company split into separate operating firms, the directors of the New Jersey corporation managed the whole Standard empire.

While Standard Oil was unusual in size, profits, and power, the cycle of its development occurred repeatedly in the American economy in the later nineteenth century. Free competition—unstable, chaotic, inefficient— gave way to various forms of consolidation that were usually inaccurately labeled "trusts." If the combination succeeded in imposing on an industry what businessmen called order, customers and competitors objected to the corporation's dominance. Since only the whole society seemed capable of checking the power of the largest corporations, state governments, and eventually the national government too, required the restoration of competition; presumably the cycle would then begin once more. In fact, competition did not ordinarily follow governmental action, but the principle that the public might control private economic matters was forcefully asserted if not conclusively established.

Yet American industrialization is not a continuous story of "robber barons" and monopolies that fleeced the public, which in turn rose in righteous anger and demanded that governments check corporate greed. There were robber barons and monopolies and bloated profits and righteous anger, and there was a great deal of greed, not all of it corporate. But the American economy was so diverse that generalizations about "industry" or "business" have to be so qualified as to be nearly meaningless. Most businesses were small; most profits were small; most businessmen were harassed and uneasy about dizzying, unpredictable economic change. Some businessmen, indeed, far from fearing governmental regulation, welcomed it as a means of creating stability. Eventually the largest corporations came to prefer uniform federal action to state regulation with bewildering local variations. Finally, in spite of great concern about the potential danger of big business, few Americans wanted to return to preindustrial bliss. For whatever their economic status or profession, all Americans were consumers. And industry produced goods, ordinarily at a reasonable price. The nation hoped to keep the prices reasonable, but above all it hoped to keep goods pouring from the factories. Nobody wanted to smash the cornucopia.

So although critics of millionaires abounded and Standard Oil became a symbol of inordinate economic power, there was little criticism of industry itself. Industrialization unquestionably exacted social costs and upset every sector of the society. Farmer, merchant, laborer, clergyman, politician, and everybody's maiden aunt all found that industry had changed their world; but Americans did not find all those changes bad. They tended to agree with Andrew Carnegie when he said it would "be a great mistake for the community to shoot the millionaires. . . ." Most millionaires worked hard, and as Rockefeller once observed, they performed a public service by furnishing both goods and employment for a great many Americans.

THE GOVERNMENT STEPS IN

Before 1900 states had begun to regulate both utilities and factories. Municipal franchises for water, trolley lines, electricity, or gas provided an opportunity for public control; a few municipalities owned and operated their utilities. States established commissions with authority to regulate rates of natural monopolies like railroads. Gradually many states began to regulate manufacturing as well, requiring safety devices to protect workers and occasionally establishing maximum hours of employment or prohibiting child labor.

States also responded to the popular fear of consolidation, as had Ohio in the case of Standard Oil. But states seemed no match for giant corporations, whose annual budget and legal staff dwarfed those of any state. By 1888 both political parties promised national legislation to curb monopolies, and in 1890 the Sherman Antitrust Act declared "Every contract, combination in the form of trust or otherwise, or conspiracy, in restraint of trade or commerce . . . illegal." Not only were monopolists subject to prosecution, but those whom the monopoly had injured might institute civil suits to recover three times the damage incurred.

Lacking the guidance of precedent, Congress wrote an ineffective law. Though the intent seemed clear from the title, one senator remarked that the bill was not really intended to prohibit or punish trusts. Rather, charged Senator Orville Platt of Connecticut, politicians wanted to hush the popular outcry with a bill that included antitrust as a part of the title. For a dozen years after 1890 the Justice Department used the Sherman Act sparingly. Nor did the Supreme Court of the United States apply the statute invariably to punish trusts.

Antitrust rhetoric

The rhetoric of the trust-busters once more disclosed the nation's ambivalence about industrialization. To be sure large enterprise had undeniable economic advantages for the entire society. On the other hand, most Americans believed competition an absolute moral virtue as well as a theoretical economic one; they responded, as they had since the days of Jefferson and Jackson, to political leaders who warned of the potential danger of concentrated economic power. Yet, most Americans also meant to emulate the rich, not to confiscate their fortunes. Industry was the current path to quick wealth, a tempting and thoroughly traditional American goal. Americans listened attentively to the trust-busters, approved the appropriate legislation, and then permitted consolidation to continue apace. In 1901 J. P. Morgan merged the Carnegie Steel Company with other firms in United States Steel to make the nation's first billion-dollar corporation. Competition was actually more prevalent in the later nineteenth century than it would become in the twentieth.

THE GOSPEL OF WEALTH AND ITS CRITICS

Andrew Carnegie was industry's foremost philosophical advocate as well as a primary example of sudden industrial riches. In 1889 he sent to the *North American Review* an article entitled "Wealth," which the editor proclaimed the finest piece he had ever published. In it Carnegie caught the spirit of his age.

The Gospel of Wealth, as Carnegie and his contemporaries formulated it, rested on the Protestant ethic. The values and virtues were familiar: industry, sobriety, frugality, perseverance. The goal, by the nineteenth century, had become a secular salvation through wealth, and Biblical texts, such as the parable of the talents, seemed to lend authority to the doctrine. Civilization, Carnegie wrote, began "the day that the capable, industrious workman said to his incompetent and lazy fellow, 'if thou dost not sow, thou shalt not reap'. . . ." Those who gathered the largest harvest, therefore, were those of greatest diligence. Or, as William Lawrence, the Episcopal Bishop of Massachusetts, wrote in 1901, "in the long run, it is only to the man of morality that wealth comes." Only by following God's laws, the Bishop continued, can "we . . . work with efficiency"; only by "right thinking and right living can the secrets and wealth of Nature be revealed." Russell Conwell, the Baptist minister who founded Temple University, remarked that ninety-eight of every hundred rich Americans excelled their fellows in honesty. "That," Conwell asserted, "is why they are rich."

Since riches were the reward for Christian virtue—as Bishop Lawrence said simply, "Godliness is in league with riches"—poverty was a sin, and critics of the system that led to swollen personal fortunes were challenging God's law. Carnegie ruled "objections to the foundations upon which society is based . . . not in order." Civilization itself, he said, depended on "the sacredness of property. . . ." Individualism and competition were essential to human progress, and "inevitably" gave "wealth to the few."

But, Carnegie continued—and here some of his disciples refused to follow—responsibility accompanied wealth. The rich man acted as society's steward, accumulating what could be spared as a trust to be returned to society as his wisdom directed. "Wealth passing through the hands of the few, can be a much more potent force for the elevation of our race than if it had been distributed in small sums to the people themselves," who would waste it "in the indulgence of appetite." The rich man must invest in the improvement of humanity with the same care he used to build his fortune; if he did not return his riches quickly enough, the state would be entirely justified in reclaiming them with inheritance taxes.

Carnegie practiced what he preached. He built libraries, stocked them with books, supported colleges, and endowed a search for international peace. Although he was not exactly a pauper when he died, the gospel according to Carnegie sounded less self-serving than it did in other mouths. Neither Carnegie nor his less refined imitators who spoke of a divine right of property were saying anything very new anyway. The "Gospel of Wealth" had its roots in colonial Puritanism and a more immediate ancestor in the individualism of Jackson and Emerson. Industrialization had made fortunes larger; it had not changed society's values.

If an apologist for the rich wanted to be up-to-date, he used the discoveries of Charles Darwin to defend his economic and social ideas. Darwinism and religion seemed in some respects incompatible, and clergy and scientists argued into the twentieth century about the origin of man and the creation of the earth. But Darwinism and the Gospel of Wealth complemented one another in demanding work, competition, and wealth. Those who rejected divine law as man's code—and there were precious few— replaced it with the law of nature. After Darwin, natural law meant "the survival of the fittest." Carnegie himself wrote of the "law of competition" which was "beneficial to the race." Whether "the law be benign or not," Carnegie said, man must conform because it ensured "the survival of the fittest." In his autobiography, Carnegie remembered that evolution had provided him with the spiritually comforting idea that " 'All is well since all grows better.' "

No exponent of Social Darwinism had better credentials than the steel magnate, but some were more prolific and lent the doctrine academic respectability. Indeed Social Darwinism was much more an academic than a popular phenomenon. With rare exceptions, businessmen neither speculated about their wealth nor felt compelled to justify it; philosophy was a professional concern. William Graham Sumner, a Yale professor, applied Darwin's biological theories to social and economic questions and popularized Social Darwinism for the American market. Sumner's faith in the immutability of evolution was evident in the title of an essay published in 1894: "The Absurd Effort to Make the World Over." Sumner made economic competition the evolutionary test and concluded that the thrifty, hardworking enterpriser was America's fittest and that his survival advanced the nation and the race. Capital, Sumner held, was the product of self-denial. Those who had capital naturally had a competitive advantage over those without. But the advantage, procured through abstinence and prudence, was deserved, for millionaires were "naturally selected agents" who served society. Society's bargain, Sumner said, was "a good one."

Whether the law was natural or divine, it brooked no interference. The Darwinian response to injustice was to wait for change through evolution. "Perhaps," wrote a resigned Darwinian, "in four or five thousand years evolution may have carried man beyond this state of things." Sumner said man must bend to the tide of his age: ". . . it is the greatest folly of which a man can be capable to sit down with a slate and pencil to plan out a new social world." "Indiscriminate charity," Carnegie wrote, was a most serious obstacle "to the improvement of the race."

Above all, government must not rush in where philanthropists wisely refused to enter. Government, Sumner held, must be economically neutral; its only function was to protect "the property of men and the honor of women." From this truly laissez faire premise, Sumner deduced that a protective tariff was no more legitimate than an income tax. Although Sumner's conclusions about the tariff were controversial, his view of poverty was orthodox. The poor had simply lost the race, and according to an unofficial Gospel of poverty, they were profligate and idle. To encourage such qualities would shatter civilization and bring universal sorrow.

An occasional critic pointed out that sorrow was no stranger in Sumner's America. With the progress to which Darwinians constantly pointed went poverty, wrote Henry George, a California newspaperman who had made a habit of losing the competitive struggle. His *Progress and Poverty*, which began to sell widely in 1880, sternly indicted the "contrast between the House of Have and the House of Want." Society, George predicted, would collapse: "The tower leans from its foundations, and every new story but hastens the final catastrophe. To . . . base on a state of most glaring social inequality political institutions under which men are theoretically equal, is to stand a pyramid on its apex."

But Henry George hoped that the tower would not topple. He preferred to fix the foundation by making society more just. He offered no direct challenge to industrialization and he certainly approved of diligence and thrift. Property was the product of man's labor, and an individual had a natural right to what he produced. But he had no right to what society produced, and society, George claimed, was responsible for the value of land. "The wide-spreading social evils which everywhere oppress men . . . spring from a great primary wrong—the appropriation, as the exclusive property of some men, of the land on which and from which all must live." The government must levy a confiscatory tax on any increase in land value that was not a direct result of the owner's effort. By such a tax, the value society added would be returned to the society, and the government would need but the single tax to sustain itself.

Henry George was soon a celebrity and his single tax the program of a political movement that caused a momentary sensation. In 1886 George ran for mayor of New York and finished second to a conservative Democrat, but he finished well ahead of an aspiring young Republican named Theodore Roosevelt. Yet a single tax on land had no political appeal to farmers, who after the Civil War frantically sought an income tax to relieve the tax burden on land. And, since the single tax penalized speculation, it had a narrow appeal in a country where cities, countryside, and cemeteries alike were full of land-speculators.

Like Henry George, Edward Bellamy wrote a best seller that criticized the economic orthodoxy of his time. *Looking Backward,* which appeared in 1887, contrasted the idyllic society of 2000 A.D. with the tension of the late nineteenth century. In Bellamy's utopia, cooperation replaced competition, corruption disappeared, industry enriched everyone, and human kindness, social harmony, and international peace prevailed.

The change Bellamy envisioned was gradual, indeed evolutionary. During the twentieth century, as business consolidated and economic power concentrated in fewer hands, government simply assumed the right to manage the economy in the public interest. The state became the final big business. Bellamy called his system "nationalism" and defined it as state ownership of the means of production and distribution. He had read none of the standard texts of European socialism and did not like what he knew of the activity of the microscopic American socialist movement. But his economic collectivism was a rather gentle, humane version of socialism, and *Looking Backward* gained both an audience and a respectability that socialistic ideas had never before attained in America. Such as it was, the American socialist movement owed more to Edward Bellamy than to Karl Marx.

Before 1900 the American socialist movement had only a local impact. A few immigrants, who had brought Marxism with them from Europe, formed the nucleus of the Socialist Labor party. This organization convinced a few hundred workingmen that their salvation lay in socialism but soon gave up any serious attempt to participate in politics and concentrated on keeping its ideology unadulterated. Most English-speaking socialists came to the movement through Nationalist clubs formed to promote Bellamy's ideal. And the members of these groups, as often as not, were professional people, respectable middle-class or even upper-class members of their communities. The official journal of the Nationalists boasted that Bellamyites were "men of position, educated, conservative in speech, and of the oldest New England" families.

But socialists, single-taxers, and patrician reformers were less in touch with their contemporaries than was Horatio Alger, who outstripped even Carnegie in popular appeal. In novel after novel, with titles like *Jed the Poorhouse Boy* and *Struggling Upward,* Alger told Americans what they wanted to hear: he told them they could all be rich. Horatio Alger's heroes were invariably poor, but honest, industrious, humble chaps. They performed menial duties with good cheer and good manners. And they succeeded mightily, though not usually as a result of these virtues. Rather, Alger's heroes were lucky; they were adopted by some sentimental tycoon, or they overheard a conversation that could be converted into money. Americans in the nineteenth century still thought theirs was the land of the fortunate as well as the free. And they expected the reward for character and virtue to be nearly instant and always in cash.

Suggested Reading

Edward C. Kirkland's *Industry Comes of Age: Business, Labor and Public Policy, 1860–1897* (1961) is a good place to begin a study of industrialization. Kirkland's *Dream and Thought in the Business Community** (1956) discusses the ideas and hopes of industrialists, and Andrew Carnegie reveals his own in his *Autobiography* (1920).

Alfred D. Chandler has edited a useful collection of sources in *Railroads: The Nation's First Big Business** (1965). Gabriel Kolko, *Railroads and Regulation** (1965), suggests that the railroads sought governmental regulation.

Robert McCloskey discusses laissez faire in *American Conservatism in the Age of Enterprise** (1951), and Irvin G. Wyllie in *The Self-Made Man in America** (1954) considers the popularization of the myth of individual enterprise. Richard Hofstadter's *Social Darwinism in American Thought** (1959) is indispensable. Eric F. Goldman discusses both Social Darwinism and the reform reaction in *Rendezvous with Destiny** (1953).

In *John D. Rockefeller* (1940) Allan Nevins treats Rockefeller much more favorably than does Henry D. Lloyd in *Wealth Against Commonwealth** (1894). Other older works useful in understanding the reaction of contemporaries to the process of industrialization include Edward Bellamy, *Looking Backward** (1888), and Henry George, *Progress and Poverty* (1879).

NOTE: See also works cited in *Suggested Reading* for Chapters 14 and 15.

* Available in paperback edition

CHRONOLOGY

1866   National Labor Union organized

1869   Knights of Labor founded

1882   Chinese Exclusion Act

1886   Haymarket riot
American Federation of Labor (AFL) organized

1887   Dawes Act confirms end of Indian independence

1890   Census shows end of frontier

1892   Homestead strike

1894   Pullman strike

1917   Literacy test restricts European immigration

XIV

A PEOPLE ADJUSTS

People all over America had to make a private peace with the industrial economy that boomed after the Civil War. Statistics revealing the quantitative impact of industrialization are too impersonal to show a change that most Americans knew only as it forced them to modify habits and attitudes or shift homes and jobs. The impact of industrialization could be read in the despair of the shoemaker whose skill became irrelevant when machines manufactured shoes too efficiently. Or in the bewilderment of the wheat farmer whose mortgage remained constant while the price of his product plummeted. Or in the anguish of the Italian or Polish peasant, uprooted from a familiar village and half-settled in a strange city where more people lived in one overflowing tenement than in a half-dozen villages in the old country. Or in the endless meetings of endless city councils where politicians grappled with problems of slums and sewage and greed and garbage and parks and police and too many people in too little space.

For generations the unsettled West had provided one way out for Americans who resisted or resented change. But the new West that lay beyond the Mississippi Valley was a different West; it lacked trees, streams, rainfall, and the gently rolling contours of familiar eastern landscapes and midwestern prairies. Those settlers who left industrial America for the Great Plains found a new environment that tested their ability to adjust no less rigorously than did the industrial environment back east.

THE LAST FRONTIERS

In 1859, Horace Greeley made the arduous overland journey from New York to San Francisco. What he saw repelled him; Greeley advised young men to "Go West" only if they had no farm or shop to inherit and no family to set up a venture at home. Greeley had a glimpse of what his contemporaries called "The Great American Desert," an area without precise boundaries that encompassed roughly the western third of the nation, omitting California and parts of Oregon. Greeley thought the area might be settled in the course of a century; his description made his prediction sound optimistic.

The flat land Greeley found so desolate in fact supported a good deal of life. Most prominently, the plains grass supported the buffalo, which, in turn, was a walking shopping center for the Indians. At the beginning of the Civil War, perhaps twelve million buffalo roamed the grasslands; from these beasts Sioux, Blackfeet, Pawnees, and other tribes of the plains derived their meat, their dwellings, their clothing, and even some of their tribal ritual and religion.

Unlike Indians, white men did not regard buffalo as an infallible sign of good country. Conventional crops required an annual rainfall greater than the ten to twenty inches that could be expected on the Great Plains west of the ninety-eighth meridian. Climate varied from parching summer heat to numbing Arctic cold. Settlers before 1860 hurried across the region to get to Oregon and California; better yet, they took a boat to avoid the dreary overland trip.

Eventually, railroads made the trip less formidable and the "desert" more inviting. Temporary shelters could be made of sod, until lumber arrived for more permanent dwellings. Rainfall, said promoters, followed the plow, and would commence with cultivation. Wheat grew tall on the plains, it was said, and cattle fattened on the unfenced range. Gold, prospectors whispered, was in the hills. Americans seeking an elusive short-cut to riches in beef, mining, and land speculation poured into the Great Plains. In twenty years the open spaces of the western frontier became the stuff of folklore and history.

The first crop was buffalo. Those who ran the railroads thought the animals a dangerous nuisance and hired buffalo hunters; "Buffalo Bill" Cody made his reputation hunting for the Kansas and Pacific Railway. When the price of hides jumped in the 1870s, the slaughter became a business. By the end of the decade, the herd had become rugs and leather.

Dependent on the buffalo for food and shelter, Indians grew more desperate and more pathetic as whites systematically eliminated the animal. Deprived of the opportunity to be independent, Indians were gradually confind to reservations, robbed of both self-respect and property by unscrupu-

SIXTEENTH ANNUAL CIRCULAR.

BUFFALO ROBES!

HART, TAYLOR & CO.
BOSTON.

COLLECTION OF
BUFFALO ROBES 1876.

UNLINED ROBES.

No. 1 Seasonable, Sewed Robes,	$9.00
" 2 " " "	8.00
" 3 " " "	7.00
" 1 " XX whole " "	12.00
" 2 " " "	10.50
" 1 " " "	9.00
" 3 " " "	8.00
Calf, according to size,	4.00 to 8.00
Choice Whole and Split Robes,	12.00 to 15.00

LINED BUFFALO ROBES.

Medium and Small Lined Buffalo, $8, and $9.00
" Lined " " 11.00
" X " " 12.00
Large " " " 13.50
" X " " 15.00
" XX " " 16.50
Extra Lined Robes, 18.00 to 24.00

BUFFALO COATS.

Buffalo Overcoats, Buffalo Trimmings,	$13.50
" " Nutria,	15.00
" " Beaver Collar,	16.50
" " Beaver Collar and Facings,	18.50
Extra Length and Quality, $1.50 to 5.00 Extra.

WE HAVE REDUCED THE PRICE OF OUR COATS AS LOW EACH FROM LAST SEASON PRICES AND HAVE NOT REDUCED THE QUALITY.

Coon Coats,	33.00 to 45.00
Beaver "	75.00 " 100.00

WOLF AND OTHER FUR ROBES.

Black Bear Robes,	$35.00 to $100.00
Russia "	25.00
Wolverine,	40.00 to 75.00
Beaver,	60.00 " 80.00
Raccoon,	18.00 " 30.00
Genet,	12.00 " 20.00
"Japanese" Wolf Robes,	20.00 " 25.00
Hudson Bay " 8 skins,	35.00 " 45.00
" " "	25.00 " 35.00
" " Medium Grade,	21.00 " 25.00
Prairie Wolf,	15.00 " 21.00

THE ABOVE WE HAVE WITH JAPANESE WOLF ROBES LAST SEASON.

CARRIAGE ROBES, &c.

Imported Lamb's Wool,	$13.00 to $15.00
Chenille,	8.50 " 9.00
Alaska, very heavy and durable,	4.00 to 4.80
Alaska Tufted,	4.50
Oxford,	3.00
Double Oxford,	5.00
Balmoral,	2.50
Polar Grecian border,	3.00
Fancy Animal pattern,	2.75
Medium,	3.50
Super,	5.00

HORSE SQUARE BLANKETS.

XX Fine Kersey,	$7.00, 8.00 and 9.00
New Hampshire, full size and weight,	1.25
Huntington Mills, very extra, N. H.,	1.35
White Plaid, New Hampshire,	1.50 to 1.75
Square, Scarlet and Blue 76×80,	6.50
" 80×90,	6.50 to 4.00
Army, per pair,	2.00 " 4.50
Rubber, (U. S. Gov't),	1.00
Printed Felt Robe Lining,	.80, .90 and 1.00
Seal Cloth,	1.00
Single Pinked, Robe border,	8c. to 15c.
Double, (two colors,)	18c. " 25c.
Treble, (three colors,)	25c. " 35c.

Our Terms for the above Goods are in all cases strictly NET CASH.

OUR FINE FUR DEPARTMENT

Is now complete with goods manufactured under the supervision of a member of the firm, and is suitable for best retail trade as follows:—

SEAL SACKS, SEAL MUFFS AND BOAS, A.M. SABLE MUFFS AND BOAS, FRENCH SEAL MUFFS AND BOAS, CHILDREN'S SACKS, ALASKA MUFFS AND BOAS, ASTRAKAN MUFFS AND BOAS, CHINCHILLA MUFFS AND BOAS, SEAL CAPS, OTTER MUFFS AND BOAS, LADIES' AND GENTS' FUR GLOVES, IN GREAT VARIETY.

A full line of FUR TRIMMINGS.

We would recommend a personal examination in all instances, when practicable.

Our HAT and CAP department is SECOND TO NONE in variety, and all new styles constantly received, at lowest jobbing prices.

HART, TAYLOR & CO.,
34, 36, 38 & 40 CHAUNCY ST., opposite AVON and near SUMMER ST.

BOSTON, OCTOBER 1, 1876.   **SHIPPING FURS BOUGHT.**

---

lous government agents. In an era noted for its graft, the Bureau of Indian Affairs was conspicuously corrupt. Its agents debased the Indians with alcohol, cheated them with cheap goods at inflated prices, and when possible, stole the best of the Indian land. Reservations usually kept Indians in, but never effectively kept white men out. Post–Civil War prospectors and farmers had no more regard for the Indian's rights than had their ancestors.

Before they gave up, the plains tribes were formidable antagonists. As horsemen, they surpassed the regular cavalry; as tacticians, they were at least the equal of most of the Civil War veterans whom they opposed. Except for the repeating revolver, their weapons were as deadly as those of the regulars; a skilled brave could keep several arrows in the air simultaneously, and each arrow had enough force to stop a buffalo. The estimated cost of three Indian wars in the 1860s was $100 million.

Wars continued in the 1870s, even though reservations were supposed to prevent friction through separation. Trespassing prospectors may have provoked the Sioux to take to the warpath in 1876; the Indians wiped out General George Custer's force at the Little Bighorn, but victory only delayed eventual capitulation. Resentment of other miners drove Chief Joseph's Nez Percé to skirmishes with federal troops between 1877 and 1880. Geronimo led the Apaches in a futile rebellion that ended with his capture in 1886. In 1878, Chief Joseph talked with his braves about surrender; although a few years premature, his was an eloquent epitaph for the free American Indian:

Geronimo: from the open prairie to a fenced reservation

I am tired of fighting. . . . The old men are all dead. . . . It is cold and we have no blankets. The little children are freezing to death. . . . I want to have time to look for my children and see how many of them I can find. Maybe I shall find them among the dead. . . . My heart is sick and sad. From where the sun now stands I will fight no more forever.

In 1887, when Indian resistance was crushed, Congress passed the Dawes Act to provide for the docile remnant of a once proud people. The act dissolved tribal ties and gave a 160-acre homestead to the head of each family. After twenty-five years, the family would become full citizens of the United States and would receive clear title to the land. But land ownership and agriculture were not the Indian way, and the Dawes Act proved just one more opportunity for unscrupulous whites to cheat Indians. In the Wheeler-Howard Act of 1934 Congress attempted to revive tribal organization by making the tribe again the basic landowner.

THE WESTERN ECONOMY

Even before Indians and buffalo left the plains and mountains, the white man moved in with his prospecting kit, his saddle and lariat, or his plow. Western mining, ranching, and farming all went through the same economic cycle that had characterized industrial organization back east.

Individual prospectors, cowboys, and homesteaders gave way to corporations, ranches, and larger farms, each of which in turn consolidated. Mining required increasingly more capital for expensive equipment. Ranchers who could no longer rely on free government grazing had to invest in their own pastures. And farmers found that small plots produced small profits.

The mining frontier moved east from California, and with it came the techniques of the forty-niners. Word of gold strikes came from Nevada and Colorado in the 1850s, from Idaho, Montana, and Arizona in the 1860s, and from South Dakota in the 1870s. A surge of prospectors—Californians as well as "greenhorns" from the east—responded to each rumor. They flooded towns like Deadwood, South Dakota, or Tombstone, Arizona, made them proverbial for sin, violence, and high life, and then deserted them, all within a few years. Denver and some other mining towns did survive to become cities, but their growth was to be in the future. Stability and attendant dignity then sometimes demanded that the colorful past be disowned with a change of name; Last Chance Gulch, for instance, emerged as Helena, Montana.

More important and more permanent than the gamblers, bartenders, and whores who followed the prospectors were the mining corporations that moved in after the loose gold had been picked up. Corporations brought a more regular system of law and order than the rough justice that characterized early settlement. With hydraulic equipment and new smelting and refining techniques to recover ore from quartz, mining was only a hazardous job that paid inadequate wages, rather than an independent way of life for tough free-lancers. Minerals came more efficiently from the earth—in twenty years Nevada's Comstock Lode poured out more than $300 million in gold and silver—and this time the riches went to clean-shaven stockholders with uncalloused hands.

Further east, the earth yielded a different kind of wealth. The same grass that sustained the buffalo sustained the long-horned cattle that abounded in Texas. Before the Civil War, a few visionary cattlemen had attempted to drive stock to market in Illinois, but Indians and distance made the venture unprofitable. After the war, the railroad reached the legendary "cow towns" of Dodge City, Kansas, and Abilene, Texas. The steer that was worth three or four dollars in Texas brought ten times that at the rail head. This potential profit brought about the fabled cattle drives, the cowboys who tended them, and vicarious adventure for millions of city-born Americans for generations to come.

The task was more humdrum than legend suggests. Day followed bone-wearying day of riding; restless cattle and rugged terrain were more hazardous than rustlers and revolvers; boredom was the chief occupational hazard. For twenty years cowboys pushed cattle from Texas to Kansas, until a combination of drought, terrible winters, and falling prices in 1885 and 1886 put an end to the drives.

The cattle drives would have ceased soon anyway. They had been possible only because much of the range was in the public domain. Cattle moved through open grassland on the way to market; young cattle matured on free Texas range. A benevolent government permitted such use of the public lands, and cattle barons could operate with very little capital. But by the mid-1880s, a few shrewd cattlemen began to lease range and exclude their competitors or to buy and fence water holes and streams. Ranchers eventually protected pasturage by purchasing it, and cattle-raising became a settled business enterprise with heavy capital costs; cowboys were merely wage-earning employees.

Sheep were one encroachment that forced cattlemen to buy their own ranges, for cattle will not graze after sheep. More of an obstacle than sheep-herders, however, were ordinary dirt farmers who demanded surveys, fences, and boundaries. The farmer brought the law of private property to the plains and ended the open range. Cattlemen occasionally cut fences, burned barns, and even murdered particularly stubborn opponents. But the ubiquitous farmers kept coming, and the rancher became a variety of farmer himself and adopted traditional American agricultural ways.

The Great Plains

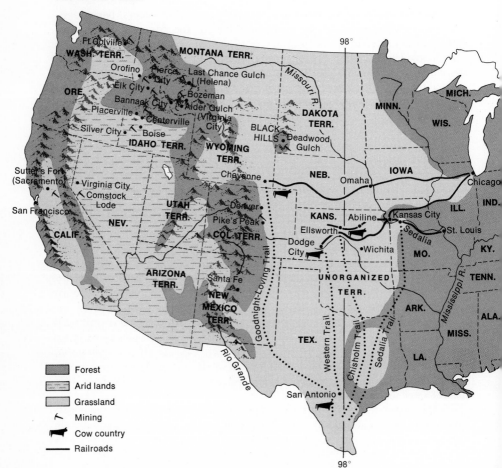

Forest
Arid lands
Grassland
Mining
Cow country
Railroads

Farmers overcame obstacles more formidable than obstinate cattle-men. The environment was forbidding and man's devices to tame it at first inadequate. Matted roots of virgin grass defied the plows that broke eastern sod until 1877, when James Oliver perfected a plow that could cut a deep furrow in the plains. Trees were scarce, but farmers found that damp sod houses served until timber could be imported, and barbed wire, which was readily available in 1880, permitted them to build fences without rails. A new variety of spring wheat, which came to the plains from Russia by way of Canada, proved more adaptable to the growing season than conventional varieties brought from the east. But homesteaders had no defense against grasshoppers and blizzards, which seemed alternately to sweep across the landscape and to bury everything in sight.

Even more than timber and a defense against snow and grasshoppers, the farmer needed water. Wells and windmills met the needs of people and livestock but were wholly inadequate for irrigating crops. Farmers developed a method of "dry farming" to conserve rainfall. They covered a deep furrow with pulverized earth to retard evaporation, and harrowed whenever there was rain. Because of the need for frequent cultivation, dry farming was expensive and, at best, unreliable. In 1877 Congress attempted to encourage irrigation with the Desert Land Act, which made up to 640 acres at twenty-five cents an acre available to farmers who would irrigate the tract within three years. After the land was irrigated, the farmer received clear title to the plot by paying an additional dollar per acre. But Congress could not create sources of water to fill irrigation ditches, and while some land was claimed under the act, there was more fraud than irrigation.

Like the farmers, Congress found the plains made past experience irrelevant. The basic land statute was the Homestead Act, which granted settlers 160 acres without charge. But while a quarter-section was an appro-priate unit in Iowa or Illinois, it proved inappropriate on the plains, for no homesteader could afford to plow, irrigate, and fence so much land. Yet both grazing and commercial agriculture required much more than 160 acres to turn a profit. Congress modified the system in 1873 with the Timber Culture Act, which permitted homesteaders to claim an additional 160 acres by planting trees on forty acres within four years. In 1878, in the Timber and Stone Act, Congress permitted the purchase at $2.50 per acre of quarter-sections whose chief resource was timber or mineral ores. Corporations, not farmers, were the chief beneficiaries of these changes in land policy. In general, settlers bought their tracts from railroads or from speculators, not from the government.

But buy land Americans did, and within twenty years after the Civil War the plains were peopled. In 1889 and 1890, Congress divided the north-western territories into six states, and when Congress decided that polygamy had been effectively outlawed in Utah, it too was admitted in 1896. The census for 1890 omitted the usual frontier line, for, the Superintendent of the Census announced, the line had effectively ceased to exist. The "unsettled area" had been "so broken into by isolated bodies of settlement" that the last frontier had vanished; the free land that had so long bolstered belief in economic opportunity had disappeared under a wave of settlers. In fact, there was still unsettled land; indeed, in the twentieth century more land has been distributed through the Homestead Act than was granted in the nineteenth. Nevertheless the realization that they had at last settled the continent roused both pride and anxiety in Americans.

Frederick Jackson Turner, a professor of history at the University of Wisconsin, noted the conclusion of the Bureau of the Census, and went on to some conclusions of his own in "The Significance of the Frontier in American History" (1893). It was the frontier, Turner argued, that transformed Europeans into Americans; the frontier converted European institutions into American institutions; the frontier made America democratic, energetic, and enterprising. Turner did not quite suggest that the end of the frontier meant that national character would deteriorate. But he did think it would change, and there was a touch of nostalgia in his final sentence: "And now, four centuries from the discovery of America, at the end of a hundred years of life under the Constitution, the frontier has gone, and with its going has closed the first period of American history."

But Americans did not stop moving, nor did they even cease to move west. Opportunity was, as always, somewhere else. Farm boys in Turner's own Wisconsin knew there was another frontier. And this one too called for imagination, enterprise, wit, and courage. The vegetation was different— smokestacks and cobblestones instead of trees and grass. More and more Americans thought the new frontier was in the cities.

THE WORKERS—
THEIR UNIONS, BATTLES, AND DREAMS

Even after sixty hours in a factory, many workers in those cities had not earned enough weekly wages to support a family. Yet most workers found the grim present tolerable and believed the future would be better. Social critics and prophets of other economic systems met chilling apathy; radicalism, and sometimes even reform, made no sense and had little appeal to American workingmen. Eventually they joined national labor unions and adapted to the new national economy, but before 1900, less than 5 percent of the labor force belonged to such organizations. Workers occasionally used strikes and pickets to influence their employers; very rarely did these disputes became violent. Labor parties, radicalism, unions, and violence were not characteristic of American labor's first response to industrialization. Most workers were passive instead.

Passivity was partly a product of the power of employers, for few employees had the resources or skills to bargain on equal terms with their bosses. In small plants and in small communities, some factory owners sympathized with their workers. Other employers insisted on offering employment on their own terms and made union membership cause for dismissal. Some workers believed that the political system made resistance futile by favoring "haves" over "have-nots." In labor disputes, for instance, courts seemed more responsive to property rights than to human needs.

Labor's inertia was also a product of the worker's state of mind.

Although most Americans were "laborers," they found the term distasteful. Earlier in the century, urban workers had called themselves mechanics or artisans. Clerks, school teachers, and other white-collar groups insisted that they were not "labor," even though they were employees who worked for a wage. Agricultural laborers were "farmers" or "tenants" or even "hands," but they resisted identification with "labor," which to them connoted urban grime and factory tedium. To the workers who composed American society, "labor" implied permanence—fixed occupation and inferior status; to become "labor" meant to surrender one's stake in the American dream, and to join a labor union was to quit short of success. "Work, work, my boy, be not afraid," ran a verse in one of William McGuffey's primers from which generations of American children improved their reading and absorbed approved social attitudes. "Look labor boldly in the face," the rhyme continued, "Take up the hammer or the spade / And blush not for your humble place." Hammer, spade, and labor, then, ordinarily indicated a humble station and provoked the blush of shame.

Even early unions seemed almost ashamed to be forthright labor organizations. The National Labor Union began among skilled ironworkers in 1866 and spread to other craftsmen such as coopers and shoemakers. But the NLU, with a peak membership of about 300,000 in a labor force of perhaps 18 million, could not dominate any one trade. Economic remedies would not secure the union's demands anyway, for they included such political objectives as the restriction of Chinese immigration, reform of the banking system, and full equality for women. The NLU wanted a working day of eight hours, but the route to that end, leaders held, lay through legislatures, not through strikes. William Sylvis, the ironworker who guided the organization until his death in 1869, thought cooperatives the most promising method of advancing labor's cause. Workers, in Sylvis' vision, would pool their capital, own the factories, market the product, and pocket the profits. Laborers, in short, would become employers; the success of the union would bring its own extinction. "By cooperation," Sylvis prophesied, "we will become a nation of employers—the employers of our own labor." The NLU did establish a few cooperatives, which, like the union itself, disappeared in the financial panic of 1873.

Uriah Stephens, the garment worker who founded the Knights of Labor in 1869, thought the craft union organization of the NLU too selfishly narrow. The Knights, by contrast, invited all to join except bankers, lawyers, distillers, and gamblers. Rich and poor, skilled and unskilled, black and white were alike welcome in this industrial union, where no lines of craft or class divided the members. The initiation, the semireligious ritual, and the membership lists were secret, partly to prevent reprisals by employers and partly to enhance the organization's appeal as a fraternal lodge, although Roman Catholic suspicion of secret ritual forced the Knights to drop it in 1882. By 1886 membership had reached a peak of about a million, at a time when the labor force numbered perhaps 25 million.

Appropriately for an organization that excluded virtually no one, the Knights preferred the boycott, which organized consumers, to the strike, which organized labor. Like the NLU, the Knights founded and mismanaged some unsuccessful cooperatives. Like the NLU also, the Knights appealed to legislatures to require the eight-hour day and to provide more currency through a reformed banking system. The Knights also asked for stricter safety regulations, the prohibition of child labor, and a graduated income tax. Arbitration, the union suggested, should settle industrial disputes.

In spite of official aversion to strikes, a local organization occasionally forced the Knights into one. In 1885 they struck Jay Gould's railway system. The strike, which the Knights had intended to avoid, was so successful that in fifteen months membership surged from 100,000 to 700,000 and the number of locals doubled. But a year later the spectacular growth turned into an equally spectacular tailspin. In Chicago a demonstration for the eight-hour day turned into a bloody melee in Haymarket Square. The Knights' reputation suffered, even though they were not responsible for the demonstration, for the strike with which it was connected, for the tension that set city, police, and workers on edge, or for the bomb that provoked the riot, in which seven policemen and four workers were killed. In a farcical trial, eight anarchists were subsequently convicted of inciting the riot, although their radical views were their only crime; four were executed and one cheated the state through suicide.

Precisely as the Haymarket riot boiled to bloodshed, Jay Gould provoked another railroad strike. The year before, the Knights had caught Gould in the middle of a speculative maneuver that forced him to settle on the union's terms; much better prepared for the strike in 1886, Gould crushed the union. Most Americans shrank from class warfare and usually reacted against labor when violence flared. Unjustly blamed for the Haymarket riot and badly beaten by Jay Gould, the Knights were virtually extinct before 1900.

Neither the NLU nor the Knights were labor unions by twentieth century standards, though both contained elements that later labor organizations elaborated. Both organizations theoretically rejected the strike and invoked the help of the whole society through politics, reform, boycott, and arbitration. While each included labor, neither was exclusively a labor organization.

Samuel Gompers and other officials of the American Federation of Labor had a different perspective. Their union, established just as the Knights lost momentum in 1886, was frankly a labor union, interested in programs that demonstrably and immediately improved the lot of the worker. Social critics, consumers, and politicians were welcome in the AFL, but they had to be laborers first. "Social reformers, like bumblebees," warned the journal of one AFL union, "are biggest when they are first hatched." But, like bumblebees also, they produced more noise than honey, and lacked "all the practical . . . qualities . . . for leadership." The best labor leader, the journal continued, was unconcerned about conditions in a utopia centuries in the future; he worried about "conditions here and now." The AFL, said one of its founders, had "no ultimate ends," but worked "from day to day" for goals that could be achieved "in a few years."

The goals were simple: higher wages, shorter hours, better conditions in the shop, recognition of the union as the bargaining agent for employees. The union's muscle was the strike, to be used sparingly and only when there was a reasonable chance of success. To enable members to endure strikes and to offer disability and death benefits most AFL unions collected high dues. Mounting bank balances made cautious union leaders more cautious. While locals, or sometimes even affiliated national unions, participated in politics or joined local reform movements, the AFL officially stayed aloof. Not until 1908 did the union formally support a presidential candidate. Labor's presidential candidate, William Jennings Bryan, ran on the Democratic ticket and finished a distant second, a result that did not encourage renewed partisanship. In 1924 the AFL endorsed Robert LaFollette, who ran on the Progressive ticket and finished a distant third. The AFL waited until 1952 before trying, and failing, again.

Like the NLU, the AFL consisted predominantly of skilled workers. Craftsmen had much more bargaining power than unskilled workers, who were too easily replaced. The AFL was in fact a national federation of unions of craftsmen—carpenters, masons, iron-moulders, printers, brewers, plumbers. By 1914 the organization claimed a total membership of more than 2 million, but since the labor force approached 40 million, the union could not speak decisively for American workers.

Radicals criticized Gompers for the AFL's failure to organize the unskilled, for its caution, for its refusal to support candidates of the Socialist party or other political groups of the left. Gompers held his union within the ideological limits of free enterprise and private property. Even if American society was not perfect, Gompers and his organization provided no other model. In 1900 an interviewer asked the labor leader whether the condition of workers was deteriorating, as was often charged. "Oh, that is perfectly absurd," snorted Gompers, who took some pride in the fact that wages then bought more than they had in the years before the AFL was founded. Gompers led labor in a struggle to acquire private property, not to abolish it. Workers had no grievance against industry, except that they were not receiving enough of its bounty.

Few employers before 1900 saw Samuel Gompers as a conservative bulwark of order. Indeed, most employers jealously guarded their right to pay what they pleased to employees of their own choosing; in the depression-wracked 1890s this determination collided with the rising confidence of labor organizations. The most publicized labor disputes of the decade involved Andrew Carnegie and George Pullman, prominent industrialists who thought their labor policy enlightened but did not intend to discuss it with unions.

In July, 1892, an AFL affiliate struck at the Carnegie steel mill in Homestead, Pennsylvania. Carnegie himself was in Scotland, but he fully agreed with his manager, Henry Clay Frick, who resolutely set out to break the union. Frick shut the mill down and summoned 300 Pinkerton guards to enable him to reopen with nonunion employees. Angry strikers fired on the Pinkertons as they approached Homestead on river barges, and before the workers had driven off the subdued Pinkertons, about a dozen people were killed. Eight thousand National Guard troops, sent by the Governor of Pennsylvania, proved more efficient than the Pinkertons, and the company gradually screened out union members and broke the strike.

The Pullman strike erupted two years later. Wages were reduced at the Pullman Palace Car Company, but rents and prices in the company town George Pullman had built to house his employees did not go down at all. Pullman fired those who protested the wage cut and provoked an angry strike. The American Railway Union, to which many of the strikers belonged, was a militant independent union headed by Eugene V. Debs, a fiery idealist who had become disenchanted with the conservative railroad brotherhoods. Debs ordered his members not to handle Pullman cars. The railroad companies discharged workers who followed Debs's instructions, but whenever one worker was discharged, others walked out too. Within a few days, several thousand workers were on strike and rail traffic had virtually stopped.

Since the strike was orderly, Governor John P. Altgeld of Illinois, who sympathized with labor, refused to summon the National Guard. President Cleveland, however, alarmed at reports of interference with interstate commerce and federal mail, sent two thousand federal troops into Chicago. Meanwhile, federal attorneys secured a court order that in essence forbade

Strikes were not popular.

KING DEBS.

Debs and other union officials to interfere with trains. In an attempt to keep the strike alive, Debs disobeyed the injunction and went to jail for contempt of court. While the union's leaders sat in jail, federal troops protected the trains and enforced the decree of a federal court that effectively broke the strike, the American Railway Union, and the morale of those laborers who wondered whom the government represented. Eugene Debs knew where he stood; in 1900, 1904, 1908, 1912, and 1920 he was the presidential candidate of the American Socialist party. But in his best year, less than 6 percent of the electorate voted for him. Even the dreams of the American workers were of free enterprise—of property, profit, and personal progress.

Nor was the dream beyond realization. Few laborers rose to affluence, but many, perhaps most, achieved modest gains in income, skill, property, and education for their children. The facts of social mobility do not match the fables, but American society was not static. Occasionally, laborers owned their own homes; more often, children of laborers became skilled or finished high school. For most Americans, that was enough to give substance to their dream.

THE URBAN FRONTIER

More and more often that dream had an urban setting. While the national population climbed sharply in the 1880s, numbers in many rural areas dropped. More than half the townships of Illinois and Iowa declined in population during the decade. That change came partly from consolidation of small farms into efficient, mechanized operations, for farms in Iowa and Illinois had gradually become agricultural factories after the Civil War. But New England farms were simply abandoned. However confining city life was, discouraged Yankees decided it was more profitable than trying to wrench a living from rocks and hills; three-fifths of New England's villages lost residents in the 1880s. Yet the population of the whole region rose about 20 percent as growth in New England's industrial areas more than replaced rural losses. By 1890 two of three residents in Connecticut, four of five in Massachusetts, and nine of ten in Rhode Island lived in what the census called towns.

Urbanization was a national phenomenon. Denver and Dallas quadrupled in population between 1880 and 1900; Los Angeles, Seattle, and Portland, Oregon doubled between 1890 and 1900. Industrial cities like Akron, Youngstown, Columbus, Cincinnati, and Cleveland dotted Ohio. And the nation's largest cities more than kept pace: Chicago's population increase in the 1890s was only slightly less than the total population of those five Ohio cities; New York's growth surpassed that sum.

When Lincoln became President, Chicago was a raw city on the edge of the frontier, with 100,000 citizens and big ideas. Ten years later, as the city became an important marketing center and the focus of the nation's railroads, the population jumped to 300,000. Stockyards, industry, the continued expansion of railroads, and the arrival of thousands of immigrants drove the population to 500,000 in 1880 and past 1 million in 1890. The

Population 1900

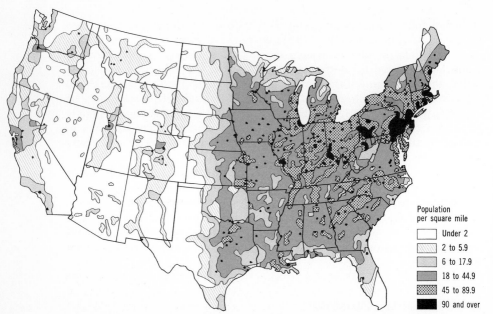

204.8
million

76
million

Population
per square mile

- Under 2
- 2 to 5.9
- 6 to 17.9
- 18 to 44.9
- 45 to 89.9
- 90 and over

1900

foreign-born residents of Chicago in 1890 equaled the total population of the previous decade. People came to Chicago, wrote one disapproving writer in 1895, "for the common avowed object of making money." In the making of money lay Chicago's "genesis, its growth, its end and its object"; few there were whose concentration wandered. In the headlong pursuit of cash, continued the critic, in rural idiom, "everyone cultivates his own little bed. . . ." But, he wondered, who looked "after the paths between," which were fast disappearing under "the weeds of rank iniquity. . . ."

Americans had long been accustomed to cities as centers of sin; urban iniquity was nothing new. But the size of cities increased the scope of evil, and uneasy Americans worried that the customs, values, manners, and morals of a healthy rural society might succumb to urban temptations. Whether or not prostitution, poverty, crime, drunkenness, and gambling were more prevalent in cities than in rural America, they were certainly more visible. And political and social institutions that had once curbed and controlled such behavior seemed to be breaking down under the assault of unprecedented numbers.

Urban families were often less cohesive than those on the farm. A father could not easily command the obedience of children whose earnings equalled or even exceeded his and whose education and command of the English language almost certainly surpassed his. Restaurants, packaged foods, ready-made clothing, and the pressure to get a job had changed the role of women. When the living room served also as the kitchen and perhaps the bedroom of a paying boarder, home was no place for family activity, leisure, or even love. When seven people lived in three or four small rooms, as they did in textile towns at the turn of the century, the stoop, the alley, and the street replaced the parlor, and the members of the family went their separate ways.

Protestant rural America suspected an urban culture that was often Catholic and sometimes Jewish. Proliferation of Catholic schools in the 1880s and 1890s seemed to wary Protestants evidence of a papal plot to avoid assimilation of American values and attitudes. The stereotype of the Jew as a devious, avaricious, and usually rich tradesman spread in hundreds of communities where Jews never lived.

Strange politics flourished in this urban environment of strange churches, strange tongues, and strange habits. Rural Americans decided that honesty had given way to corruption; graft seemed to be the ordinary method of conducting a city's business. Disgruntled reformers noted that education and ability were not automatic qualifications for public office and that membership in a prominent family seemed an almost automatic disqualification. Parties stood for patronage and spurned principle; party machines and bosses dealt in contracts, franchises, jobs, and votes. William Marcy (Boss) Tweed, who misgoverned New York City for several years around 1870, was only the most notorious of dozens of urban bosses who put city treasuries to personal political use.

Part of the payoff from fat contracts and municipal franchises went into partisan welfare work in an era before charity became a public responsibility. The unemployed laborer, needing a temporary job until the mill reopened, went to his precinct captain; a solicitous representative of the mayor helped the immigrant fill out his naturalization form and showed him how to mark the ballot; attached to the basket of food that stood on the thresholds of needy families at Christmas and Easter, and sometimes in between, was the card of the local alderman, who collected his return at the polls. Bosses or their flunkeys dignified wakes and weddings, feasts and

Boss Tweed, as seen by one of his most effective antagonists, the cartoonist Thomas Nast

funerals, with a few moments' presence and a few trite remarks. The personal touch in an impersonal city meant much more than self-righteous integrity. Bosses may not have governed cities very well, but many of them governed with self-serving compassion.

The cities seemed ungovernable anyway. Municipal charters, granted by state governments, often reserved to the state authority over the municipal taxes, facilities, and even appointments. American local government had evolved to meet the needs of small communities, where people knew and usually trusted one another. In anonymous cities that grew unexpectedly, such institutions were inappropriate, but changes, such as professional city managers, the city commission form of government, and less restrictive municipal charters, came predominantly in the twentieth century. The problems arrived in the nineteenth.

THE NEW IMMIGRATION

Some believed that a new flood of immigrants brought the problems. Although the shift had been under way for some time, Americans in the late 1880s and early 1890s awoke to this "new immigration"—Italians, Poles, Greeks, Russians, and Jews who far outnumbered the more traditional Irish, English, German, and Scandinavian migrants. In the 1890s about half of the nearly four million immigrants came from Southern and Eastern Europe; in the first decade of the new century, the proportion of "new immigrants" rose to almost two-thirds and the total to nearly nine million. The newcomers seemed more unlike native Americans than had their predecessors; they were not what Americans of the later nineteenth century were learning to call Anglo-Saxons. Nor did they all have light complexions and Protestant faith, and very few had much knowledge of, or experience with, self-government. Perhaps most of the new immigrants had been peasants; even more than American farmers who moved to the city, these immigrants found the change bewildering.

To protect themselves, to preserve a bit of the familiar in an unfamiliar world, immigrants in large cities clustered by nationality. Chinese or Italian or Irish neighborhoods had their own groceries, priests, and social and political organizations. Immigrants also clustered because they could afford only the cheapest, least desirable housing. Whole families lived in one tiny room; whole tenements used one water faucet and one toilet; whole blocks shared the same garbage and epidemics. The filth that frequently became part of an ethnic stereotype was more apt to be a product of crowding than of innate slovenliness. The stereotypes then picked up other characteristics: various groups were said to be clannish, stupid, radical, violent, drunken, illiterate, and lazy.

Before the stereotypes developed, American entrepreneurs had sought migrants as the bearers of prosperity. In the years right after the Civil War, transcontinental railroads, anxious to convert western lands to cash, advertised in Europe and offered reduced fares to immigrants who purchased railroad property. Until the contract labor law was repealed in 1868, manufacturers recruited European workers, paid their passage, and secured their labor for a specified period; one-third of the labor force in American factories in 1870 had been born abroad. In the 1860s and 1870s, two-thirds of the states took active steps to attract European settlement.

Well Americans might seek immigrants, for they added much more than cultural diversity. Because they brought a bit of property, because most of them immediately became productive members of society, and because they represented an important fraction of the American market, the Treasury estimated that each immigrant was equivalent to $800 in new capital. Andrew Carnegie thought the estimate too low: $1,500 would be closer. Whatever their cash value, Americans before 1880 wanted immigrants and were confident that they could be absorbed in this broad land with its expanding economy. Surely, like their predecessors, they would be assimilated through public education, vital political democracy, and unremitting hard work.

The immigrant did indeed work, often in the least skilled, most menial trades. Immigrant women worked in textile mills or as domestics in thousands of kitchens. Immigrant men wielded picks and shovels in mines, under city streets, and across the plains where the railroad was to go. Enterprising, often unscrupulous immigrants contracted to supply employers with groups of their unskilled countrymen at substandard wages. Called the *padrone* system, this device particularly victimized unskilled Italians; in 1883 one Italian laborer in Chicago had an annual income of $270 to support his family of five. The standard of living was so meager that the family survived on less income than many other Chicago laborers spent on groceries alone.

As immigrants became more numerous and more obtrusive, some

Sources of Immigrants, 1871–1910

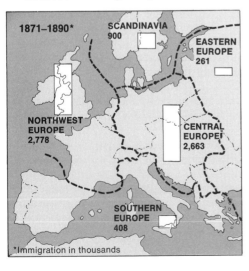

1871–1890*
SCANDINAVIA
900
EASTERN
EUROPE
261
NORTHWEST
EUROPE
2,778
CENTRAL
EUROPE
2,663
SOUTHERN
EUROPE
408
*Immigration in thousands

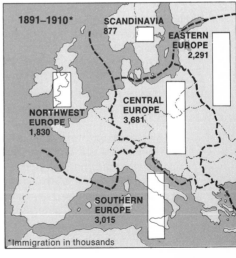

1891–1910*
SCANDINAVIA
877
EASTERN
EUROPE
2,291
NORTHWEST
EUROPE
1,830
CENTRAL
EUROPE
3,681
SOUTHERN
EUROPE
3,015
*Immigration in thousands

Americans worried about the apparent failure of new immigrants to assimilate. If the "melting pot" had ever existed, as Americans since colonial times had assumed, it was obviously producing a less homogeneous product in the late nineteenth century; many feared the alloy was inferior. Urban problems seemed inextricably related to unrestricted immigration. Immigrant neighborhoods often deteriorated into slums. Immigrants supported the political boss, who made a mockery of democracy and a fortune from corruption. Immigrants swelled the ranks of the poor for whose relief the resources of private charity were hopelessly inadequate. Immigrants gambled on the one chance of a windfall that might mean escape; from the bottle flowed another kind of escape. Reformers who wanted to do something about grime and graft and poverty and despair saw no reason to admit more immigrants who would only make insoluble problems greater.

Advocates of restriction proposed to select immigrants instead of permitting immigrants to select themselves. A substantial tax would keep out the poor; an examination by American consuls abroad might screen out Europeans of undesirable character. In 1882, the same year that Congress forbade all migration from China, another act required European immigrants to be certifiably sane, capable of self-support, and free of venereal diseases. In 1896 Congress passed an act to make literacy in some language a qualification for immigration. President Cleveland's veto slowed this attempt at restriction, which by 1897 claimed such varied supporters as the AFL and Henry Cabot Lodge, the conservative Republican Senator from Massachusetts. President Taft vetoed a similar bill in 1913 and President Wilson another one two years later. In 1917 Congress finally mustered enough votes to override Wilson's second veto, making the literacy test the first in a series of restrictive acts. After the First World War, Congress devised a new system of quotas based on the national origin of Americans who had already migrated. The old ideal that in the United States the poor and oppressed of Europe could be fused into a new, varied nation perished, like so many other ideals, in the slums.

Still, the immigrants not only survived; many of them prospered. Dismal as their wages were, one statistician estimated that an American immigrant earned about 40 percent more than his European counterpart. Some immigrants slipped through the slums and cities to the plains. The proportion of foreign-born in parts of Montana and the Dakotas was as high as in New England; Germans settled in Kansas, Nebraska, and California, and Scandinavians in Minnesota and Wisconsin. But isolation on a vast prairie could be as trying as loneliness in the frightful closeness of city quarters.

And, in some ways, that same isolation pervaded industrial America. The owner of a small business felt terribly alone as he faced an impersonal economic system that seemed about to dispense with his services. The anxious urban worker, trying to stretch his wage through periods of unemployment, and the frustrated farmer, who thought the whole world conspired to ruin him, also thought of themselves as isolated. Americans in an earlier, simpler age had gloried in being apart from their fellows, considered themselves self-reliant and independent, and rejoiced in their individualism. The new industrial society seemed to call for groups—for corporations, unions, granges, lodges, and for responsive political parties. Once Americans discovered organization, they recovered their optimism, organized with their proverbial energy, and allowed their new industrial plant to raise their standard of living.

Suggested Reading

Samuel P. Hays's *The Response to Industrialism, 1885–1914** (1957) and Robert H. Wiebe's *The Search for Order** (1968) are brief interpretive surveys that provide different insights into the period of industrialization.

Walter P. Webb's *The Great Plains** (1931) and Fred A. Shannon's *The Farmer's Last Frontier** (1945) are distinguished older works on farming and the frontier. Ole E. Rolvaag's novel *Giants in the Earth** (1927) provides a compelling picture of the life of an immigrant family on the plains.

Samuel Gompers' autobiography, *Seventy Years of Life and Labor* (1925), is the account of an urban immigrant. Gompers' version of urban life and union labor may be supplemented by Constance McL. Green, *The Rise of Urban America** (1965), Stephan Thernstrom, *Poverty and Progress** (1964), and Philip A. Taft, *The A. F. of L. in the Time of Gompers* (1957). Oscar Handlin's *The Uprooted** (1951) is a moving account of the immigrant experience, and John Higham's *Strangers in the Land** (1963) recounts the nativist response to immigration. Helen Hunt Jackson's outrage at the treatment of the Indians pervades *A Century of Dishonor** (1881). Dee Brown, *Bury My Heart at Wounded Knee* (1970), describes westward expansion from the Indians' point of view.

NOTE: See also works cited in *Suggested Reading* for Chapters 13 and 15.

*Available in paperback edition

CHRONOLOGY

1868   Presidential election: Ulysses S. Grant (Republican) defeats Horatio Seymour (Democrat)

1872   Presidential election: Ulysses S. Grant (Republican) defeats Horace Greeley (Democrat, Liberal Republican)

1876   Presidential election: Rutherford B. Hayes (Republican) defeats Samuel J. Tilden (Democrat) when a special electoral commission awards Hayes 20 disputed electoral votes

1878   Bland-Allison Act provides limited coinage of silver

1880   Presidential election: James A. Garfield (Republican) defeats Winfield S. Hancock (Democrat); Chester A. Arthur succeeds Garfield in 1881

1883   Pendleton Act begins federal civil-service appointment by merit

1884   Presidential election: Grover Cleveland (Democrat) defeats James G. Blaine (Republican)

1888   Presidential election: Benjamin Harrison (Republican) defeats Grover Cleveland (Democrat)

1890   McKinley Tariff
Sherman Silver Purchase Act

1892   Presidential election: Grover Cleveland (Democrat) defeats Benjamin Harrison (Republican) and James B. Weaver (Populist)
Populist party enters national politics; Omaha Platform

1894   Wilson-Gorman Tariff includes income tax

1895   *Pollock* v. *Farmers' Loan and Trust Co.* declares income tax unconstitutional

1896   Presidential election: William McKinley (Republican) defeats William J. Bryan (Democrat)

SCANDAL, SPOILS, AND SILVER:

POLITICS, 1870–1900

In the last three decades of the nine-teenth century, the pageant of American politics reflected the vitality and variety of American life but had curiously little to do with it. Campaigns were earnest and exciting, but in retrospect many of the issues seem trivial and most of the candidates nearly interchangeable. "Garfield, Arthur, Harrison, and Hayes . . ." mused Thomas Wolfe, the twentieth century novelist. "Which had the whiskers, which the burnsides: which was which?"

Wolfe might pardonably have lengthened his list. Although the era's leading statesmen differed, their differences were idiosyncratic, not fundamental. Some politicians were more honest than others, some more flamboyant or more stubborn or more successful. Few probed the questions that lay at the base of swirling political controversy. Did whites intend to accept blacks as unqualified equals? Did laissez faire in fact denote governmental impartiality? Would the nation's standard of living rise with rising industrial productivity? Could the traditional ethic of the church govern behavior in the counting house, the courthouse, or the Congress?

THE POLITICS OF DEADLOCK

Occasionally a party seeks control to carry out a program, in which case office may be a means to a greater end; but for Republicans and Democrats of the late nineteenth century, electoral victory usually seemed to be an end in itself. Before 1896 minor parties accurately charged that the two major parties were look-alikes, distinguishable only in detail. Neither had a conspicuously positive program; each opposed industrial regulation and inflated currency, and each even resisted attempts to curb corruption until an aroused public forced enactment of civil-service legislation.

Although the parties had similar platforms, their constituencies differed. Democrats built on the solid, white South and on northern, urban political machines. Both of these groups cared less about national than about local matters—the end of reconstruction and of black equality in the South, the control of patronage and of contracts in northern cities. Until 1896 Democratic presidential candidates usually came from New York, where respectable Democrats were as conservative as any Republican. Horatio Seymour, New York's Civil War Governor, lost to Ulysses S. Grant in 1868; Horace Greeley, the quixotic editor of the New York *Tribune*, lost to Grant in 1872; another governor, Samuel J. Tilden, lost when the disputed election of 1876 was awarded to Hayes; Grover Cleveland, mayor of Buffalo in 1881 and Governor in 1882, won the presidential elections of 1884 and 1892 and was narrowly defeated by Benjamin Harrison in 1888. None of these New Yorkers roused much enthusiasm on the plains, and the Democrats had little support among western farmers until William Jennings Bryan appeared from Nebraska in 1896.

Republicans counted on those midwestern farmers, on the veterans of the Grand Army of the Republic, and on the black vote in the South. The party's steadfast refusal to scale down the union debt appealed to bankers, fiscal conservatives, and the numerous federal bondholders. Republican advocacy of the protective tariff won many manufacturers and much of the labor force in their mills. Western orators reminded homesteaders of their debt to the Republican party, and northern candidates repeatedly charged that Jefferson Davis and his fellow Democrats had tainted the Democratic party with southern treason. Sanctifying every Republican claim was the lingering spirit of Abraham Lincoln.

The Republican party was a fragile alliance of at least three factions that devoted nearly as much energy to squabbling with one another as they spent defeating Democrats. The "Mugwumps"—independent, idealistic, honest—tried to prevent the party of Lincoln from becoming the possession of Grant's corrupt cronies. The other two factions, the "Stalwarts" and the "Half-Breeds," divided over booty and patronage. The Stalwarts, led by Roscoe Conkling, a cocky senator from New York and an accomplished spoilsman, cynically avowed their interest in graft and the public payroll. The Half-Breeds, who rallied around James G. Blaine, Speaker of the House, Senator from Maine, twice Secretary of State, and the party's presidential nominee in 1884, tried to disavow Grantism while angling for control of Grant's following.

Although this uneasy Republican coalition generally won presidential contests and controlled the Senate, Democrats won the House in eight of twelve elections after 1870. Political deadlock was the order of the day. From the time Grant retired until 1896, when William McKinley trounced Bryan, Tilden was the only presidential nominee to achieve a majority of the popular vote, and he lost the election. In 1880, James A. Garfield had a popular margin of four-tenths of 1 percent over Winfield Scott Hancock, the Union General whom Democrats had nominated in the vain hope of breaking the Republican monopoly on the veteran's vote; Cleveland's victory over Blaine in 1884 was even less decisive.

Elections turned on personalities more than principles, upon which voters and politicians of both parties apparently agreed. Until Bryan brought issues back to politics in 1896, political discourse consisted of charges of corruption and appeals to parochial prejudices or local interests. To the major parties, in good times and hard, reform meant electing honest men to office—the safe, drawing-room sort of men who went to Protestant churches and wore whiskers and stiff collars. "Undoubtedly the tariff is an interesting and important subject," said Carl Schurz in 1884; "so is the currency; so is the bank question. . . ." But the Republican party, he asserted, must face up to an "infinitely more important" matter: "the question of

William Jennings Bryan on the stump

honesty in government." Good government to such reformers was the ultimate objective; few of them meant to use government to bridge the growing
gulf between rich and poor, to enable the employee to meet his employer on
equal terms, or to reduce involuntary unemployment in the midst of industrial depression. Those who wanted to use government for such ends looked
at politics from the outside.

GRANT, GRAFT, AND CIVIL SERVICE

Ulysses S. Grant was the best-known and, in the North, the most-
loved American of his day. Later generations picture the Grant of caricature
—the soggy cigar, the slovenliness, the alcohol, the scandals. His contemporaries, however, thought of Vicksburg, Appomattox, and the restoration
of the union. A misfit at West Point, a failure in business, a poor judge of
the character of friends and family, Grant learned in the Army to rely on
efficient professionals and to ignore idealists and amateurs; he applied the
same principle to politics.

Profiteering, dishonesty, and political corruption neither began nor
ended with Ulysses S. Grant; scandal has been disturbingly constant in
American political life. But during the Grant era no one seemed to mind.
For a time Americans shrugged their shoulders at corruption, apparently
figuring that the self-made politician compromised himself no more than
the self-made industrialist, who made a fortune and became a folk hero.
Even when the politician and the industrialist joined forces, the popular
reaction seemed more often envy than disgust.

So a congressman from Massachusetts became the lobbyist for the
Crédit Mobilier and handed out the corporation's lucrative shares to prevent a potentially embarrassing investigation of the financing of the Union
Pacific. One of the members of Grant's Cabinet, William W. Belknap,
resigned hastily when Congress discovered that he had accepted bribes to
allow a favored Indian trader to retain his profitable post at Fort Sill; the
House impeached Belknap, but the Senate gave him a technical acquittal
because Grant had already accepted his resignation. Grant's personal secretary, Orville E. Babcock, obstructed the investigation of the "whiskey ring,"
a profitable enterprise that furnished distillers with cut-rate, counterfeit
revenue stamps; some of the proceeds financed Republican state campaigns.
By his acquaintance with Jay Gould and Jim Fisk, two notoriously unscrupulous speculators, Grant lent an air of respectability to their unsuccessful
efforts to corner the gold supply in 1869; the President's brother-in-law was
deeply involved in the project.

Scandal seemed the custom, but there were honest public servants.
The plans of Gould and Fisk collapsed because Secretary of the Treasury
George Boutwell, with Grant's knowledge, released $4 million in gold at a
strategic moment. Benjamin Bristow, another member of Grant's Cabinet,
uncovered the "whiskey ring." President Chester A. Arthur, who had cooperated with Republican spoilsmen in New York, turned out to be conscientious

in the White House. He insisted, for instance, that profiteering in the Post Office by "star route" constractors be stopped.

Arthur also signed the Pendleton Act, which inaugurated a federal civil service based on merit. Civil-service reform had been long delayed, and the Pendleton Act, passed in 1883, was but a small first installment. Grant had made ineffectual gestures toward establishing a merit system during his first administration. While Secretary of the Interior under Hayes, Carl Schurz had adopted civil-service procedures in his department, particularly in the corrupt Indian Bureau. Public support for civil-service reform mounted after a disgruntled office-seeker assassinated President Garfield in July, 1881.

The Pendleton Act established a bipartisan Civil Service Commission to administer competitive examinations and to regulate federal employment. Initially the act covered only about one-tenth of all federal employees, but subsequent Presidents were empowered to extend its provisions and many did so to protect their own appointees. Grover Cleveland, who succeeded Arthur, supported civil-service reform in principle and allowed merit to dictate many of his early appointments; after 1885, however, he used federal offices more often for partisan purposes.

LAISSEZ FAIRE IN PRACTICE

Legislation had but a slight impact on the industrial revolution of the late nineteenth century. Land grants to railroads, unrestricted immigration, a tax policy facilitating capital accumulation, and the protective tariff undeniably encouraged industrialization, but the root causes were not political. Similarly, early regulatory legislation brought little change in American industrial development. Later laws had to bolster the Interstate Commerce Act (1887) before the nation's railroads were effectively regulated. In spite of years of litigation, the Sherman Antitrust Act (1890) never became an entirely reliable weapon against monopoly.

With the exception of those two laws, political debate about industrialization centered on the tariff and the currency, staples of American politics familiar to both politicians and public. Demands for tariff reduction came partly because the public perceived protection as an industrial subsidy and partly because the Treasury was too full. By 1867 the average duty was about 47 percent. In 1883, after several intervening revisions, the average rate had declined to about 42 percent. Four years later, embarrassed by a mounting surplus in the Treasury, Grover Cleveland suggested further cuts. A federal surplus meant a smaller amount of currency in general circulation, a condition that tended to lower prices in a period when the nation's economy was already depressed. Congress preferred to eliminate the surplus by spending it for such politically inspired projects as pensions for Union veterans and "pork-barrel bills" authorizing federally financed construction with attendant contracts and jobs. Cleveland vetoed pension bills about as fast as Congress passed them. He suggested the existence of a direct link between tariff and trusts and summoned his party to battle for tariff reform.

The summons generated little enthusiasm and even less reform. The Mills Bill of 1888, which was Congress's answer, was most popular in the South and roused most hostility in such areas as Indiana, which Democrats could ill afford to alienate. The bill continued protection for southern sugar and rice and for iron and coal, which were produced beyond the South. But Congress cut tariffs on wool and woolens, lumber, and various manufactured goods. Tariff-reformers in the party advocated the Mills Bill with a fervor worthy of a better cause. They injected the issue into the election of 1888, although Cleveland's interest in tariff reform had cooled before the campaign began.

Republicans took Benjamin Harrison's narrow victory in the election to be an endorsement of protection. In 1890 William McKinley, chairman of the House Committee on Ways and Means, reported a new tariff that raised the average duty to a new high of nearly 50 percent. The McKinley Tariff unintentionally helped eliminate the surplus, for the new duties reduced foreign trade and customs revenue.

The Republican Congress also mounted a direct assault on the surplus. A Dependent Pension Act granted pensions to any disabled veteran no matter how his disability occurred. James Tanner, Harrison's Commissioner of Pensions and a former official of the Grand Army of the Republic, shouted "God help the surplus!" and proceeded to distribute it. The annual appropriation for veterans jumped from about $90 million to $157 million during the Harrison administration, and the number of pensioners from fewer than 500,000 to nearly a million. "Pork barrel" appropriations and the Sherman Silver Purchase Act (see p. 296) further reduced the surplus. When it adjourned, the Congress had spent $1 billion for the first time in the history of the republic.

But the voters decisively rejected the "Billion-Dollar Congress" in 1890 and Benjamin Harrison in 1892. Once more in the White House, President Cleveland again asked for tariff reform. In 1894 a bill making substantial reductions cleared the House, but the Senate restored many of the cuts and the disappointed President allowed the Wilson-Gorman Tariff to become law without his signature. More important than the very small reduction in duties was the income tax Congress included to replace an anticipated drop in customs revenue. Within a year the Supreme Court ruled in *Pollock* v. *Farmers' Loan and Trust Co.* that the income tax was an unconstitutional direct tax on personal property, not levied in proportion to population, as the Constitution required.

By 1895 neither the tariff nor the income tax caused nearly so much public interest as did the quantity and quality of the currency. The issue troubled American politics from the end of the Civil War until the end of the century, particularly during the depressions of 1873 and 1893. When Americans of the time talked about money, they revealed profound uneasiness as well as their inadequate understanding of industrial change. Proponents of panaceas and defenders of the status quo alike claimed more than their programs warranted. For money is but the measure of prosperity, not prosperity itself.

Yet many Americans thought their measure short. The amount of circulating currency did not increase with expanding population and expanding commercial activity. During the 1870s and 1880s, all three varieties of money—coined gold, national bank notes, and greenbacks—increased in value as commodity prices generally declined. Those who had contracted debts when prices and wages were high found themselves squeezed as currency contracted; the wheat farmer had to sell more bushels to service his mortgage, and the small businessman became anxious about his note at the bank.

Inflationists in search of a constant dollar first tried to use the greenbacks issued during the Civil War. These bills continued to circulate at a discount after the war, and advocates of inflation argued that greenbacks should be used instead of gold to retire the government debt. This scheme, called the "Ohio idea," would have substantially increased the amount of available paper currency. Although the Democratic platform of 1868 included the "Ohio idea," the nominee, Horatio Seymour, like most New York Democrats, opposed tinkering with the currency supply and repudiated the plank. President Grant, equally firm in his stand for sound money, signed an act in 1869 that pledged the government to redeem its obligations in gold. In 1870 the Supreme Court decided in *Hepburn* v. *Griswold* that depreciated greenbacks were not legal tender for a debt contracted in the more valuable currency of the period before greenbacks were issued. The decision caused considerable financial confusion until Grant appointed two new justices who provided the votes to reverse the decision the following year in *Knox* v. *Lee*. In 1875, at Grant's urging, Congress passed the Specie Resumption Act, which reduced the number of greenbacks in circulation and declared the government's intention of redeeming them at par in 1879. When the Treasury in fact started to exchange greenbacks for gold, the paper note was on a par with specie.

National bank notes, like greenbacks, increased in value and diminished in quantity. Between 1880 and 1890, almost half these notes went out of circulation. Banks had to recall their notes, which were secured by federal bonds, as the government paid off its debt. Since the government proposed to retire the debt, and since every bond a national bank sold required a proportionate reduction in national bank notes, the contraction of the currency seemed likely to continue.

When paper money became a lost cause, inflationists shifted to silver, which the federal mint had coined since the eighteenth century. But the legal ratio of sixteen ounces of silver to one ounce of gold overvalued gold after the California gold strikes of 1849 lowered its price. Since silver brought more on the open market than at the mint, the government actually coined little silver after 1850. Congress merely recognized this economic fact in 1873 when the silver dollar was omitted from the list of authorized coins. This omission—subsequently tagged the "crime of '73"—seemed to inflationists part of a deliberate plot to contract the currency. Their outrage grew during the depression that began in 1873. At the same time, discoveries of large silver deposits in Nevada and Colorado rapidly depressed the price of silver and the official ratio of sixteen to one soon overvalued silver. Advocates of inflation clamored for repeal of the "crime of '73."

Inflationists argued that more money would cure the nation's economic ills, that it would raise prices and wages, stimulate consumer spending, relieve the fretting debtor, and make credit more generally available. In 1876 the House responded with a bill providing for the free and unlimited coinage of silver at the ratio of sixteen to one, a measure that advocates claimed would produce a gentle, controlled inflation. The Senate, where inflation had fewer friends, amended the measure to permit the purchase and coinage of not less than $2 million and not more than $4 million worth of silver per month. Even this token appropriation offended the fiscal orthodoxy of President Hayes, but Congress overrode his veto, and the Bland-Allison Act became law in 1878. Yet the law brought little inflation because the Treasury purchased as little silver as possible and exchanged silver dollars for gold.

THE POPULIST PROTEST

In the three decades after the Civil War, the American farm became more efficient and immensely more productive. Between 1866 and 1880 the production of wheat and cotton nearly tripled; corn production more than doubled and tobacco nearly doubled during the same period. But while production jumped, prices fell. The bushel of wheat that brought more than two dollars in 1866 brought less than one in 1880; cotton prices dropped from about fifteen cents a pound to less than ten. By 1895 wheat brought fifty cents a bushel, corn twenty-five or less, and cotton sold at about six or seven cents a pound. Merely to maintain a constant income, the wheat farmers would have had to double production between 1880 and 1895, and the cotton farmer would have had to increase his by almost half. Puzzled farmers studied their increasing production, declining income, and rising burden of debt and decided that something was wrong with the system.

In fact, American farmers were caught in a competitive market. Egypt, India, and other warm areas had begun to produce cotton when supplies from the South dried up during the Civil War. The Russian government encouraged the export of Ukrainian wheat in order to obtain foreign exchange, and Argentina, Australia, and Canada also developed foreign markets for surplus grain. The prices American farmers received for their staples were world prices, and as supply rapidly mounted, world prices declined. In order to maintain their income, farmers grew more crops, which increased world supply and brought further reductions in price.

In a sense, then, overproduction caused distress on the farm, although hungry people unable to consume had a different perspective. More basically, the individual American producer of agricultural exports was simply too small to influence the competitive market in which he sold; he had no control of his price. Although economic reality was complex, and an immediate solution difficult to discern, anxious farmers viewed their plight in moral terms and grasped quick political solutions. What was happening to the farmer, his spokesmen cried, was unjust, and the government should root out injustice forthwith.

Initially rural reformers thought state control of railroad rates would increase the net income of farmers. Increasingly through the 1880s, however, when railroad regulation proved difficult to legislate and often ineffective when passed, farm organizations turned to inflationary measures. Chief among these proposals was the "subtreasury system" of the Southern Farmers' Alliance. The Alliance wanted the government to construct warehouses or grain elevators in which farmers could store crops. This stored produce was to serve as security for a loan in legal tender notes of 80 percent of the current price of the crop. The system would permit farmers to sell at peak prices, retire their loans, and pay the government a reasonable storage fee. Branches of the Farmers' Alliance outside the South advanced other inflationary measures, including the unlimited coinage of silver, and such reforms as a federal income tax, direct election of senators, and effective regulation or government ownership of railroads.

The demands were political and the Alliance went into active partisan politics. In 1890 Alliancemen won seats in midwestern and southern legislatures, and the wheat-raising states of the Great Plains sent several angry independent representatives to Washington. In 1891 delegates from the Alliance and other agricultural groups met with social reformers and labor-union officials to launch the People's party. In July, 1892, the party assembled in solemn convention at Omaha to announce Populist principles and nominate for President James B. Weaver, a dignified former Union general who had a long association with agrarian protest.

The Populist protest was more strident than dignified, and most Populists were not so calm and reserved as was James B. Weaver. From Kansas came "Sockless" Jerry Simpson and Mary Elizabeth Lease, who was widely reported to have advised the farmers to "raise less corn and more hell." From Georgia came Thomas E. Watson, a redheaded demagogue who already held a seat in Congress. And from Minnesota came Ignatius Donnelly, who wrote a fighting preamble for the party's platform clearly indicating that Populism was no ordinary political movement. "We meet," read Donnelly's preamble, "in the midst of a nation brought to the verge of moral, political, and material ruin." He ran down the nation's problems: corruption, censorship, bribery, fraud, and a growing rift between rich and poor. "From the same prolific womb of governmental injustice," the indictment continued, "we breed the two great classes—tramps and millionaires." Other parties were no help to a "plundered people"; they proposed to wage a "sham battle over the tariff, so that capitalists, corporations, national banks, rings, trusts, watered stock, the demonetization of silver and the oppressions of usurers may all be lost sight of. They propose to sacrifice our homes, lives, and children on the altar of mammon. . . ." Populists, Donnelly proclaimed, believed that "the powers of the government . . . should be expanded . . . as rapidly and as far as the good sense of an intelligent

Mary Elizabeth Lease: protest
from the plains

people and the teachings of experience shall justify, to the end that oppression, injustice, and poverty shall eventually cease in the land."

Therein lay the radicalism of the Populists. Those midwestern, southern, property-owning, Bible-quoting, old-stock farmers asked directly for the help of their government. No cant about laissez faire; no vows of rugged individualism—just a ringing statement that the government ought to help the poor and oppressed. Populism implied that economic individualism— the faith of Jefferson, Emerson, Lincoln, and Carnegie—no longer led to social improvement, however much it improved the lot of particular people. A system that provided the farmer with less income as he grew more cotton or that denied a willing worker employment, Populists held, was manifestly unjust. If the Gospel of Wealth, Social Darwinism, some other intellectual system, or even a series of laws condoned such conditions, then those creeds and codes too were unjust. The flat truism of one Populist orator wiped out much of the apology for laissez faire: "People," he said, "don't ask to be tramps."

Specifically, the Populist platform demanded that the government make land available directly to settlers instead of to railroads and speculators. The party advocated immediate expansion of the currency through the subtreasury system and the unlimited coinage of silver. Populists demonstrated their democratic faith by calling for the secret ballot, the initiative and referendum, and amendments limiting the President to one term and permitting the direct election of senators. Several resolutions showed the interest of predominantly rural delegates in a farmer-labor alliance. They favored the eight-hour working day and the restriction of immigration, sympathized with the Knights of Labor, and despised Pinkertons. Most importantly, Populists pledged themselves to secure a graduated income tax and government ownership and operation of railroads, telephone, and telegraph. The party itself, of course, secured neither measure. But the income tax has been the most important instrument for social and economic change in the twentieth century; and in calling for government ownership, Populists challenged economic individualism head-on.

Conservatives, particularly in the East, concentrated on the parochial rhetoric of Populism and on its simplistic view of agricultural distress and the measures that would relieve it. Populist spokesmen were ridiculed as hicks, harpies, and fanatics who dispensed rural nonsense out of a cracked pot. And Populists failed to secure the urban support they sought, partly because they seemed too radical. The party had a small eastern following, consisting mostly of gentle socialists led by Edward Bellamy. But wages and hours, not government ownership, concerned urban workers. Samuel Gompers, for instance, was no social critic and vehemently condemned reformers who diverted labor's energy from immediate objectives. The Populist orator was far more critical of industrial America than were most of those who claimed to speak for the worker.

Without an urban base, the People's party was doomed to political futility, but it created a stir before subsiding. In 1892 Weaver received more than a million popular votes and carried Kansas, Colorado, Nevada, and Idaho. Ten Populist congressmen and five senators took seats in Congress, and three governors and more than a thousand state legislators proved the party's local vitality. But sturdy Grover Cleveland won the election of 1892. Although his campaigners had occasionally promised reform in his name, inflation had no sterner foe than Grover Cleveland.

It was time for inflation, for as Cleveland took office in 1893, a sharp depression gripped the nation. New investments financed through stock issues dropped from $100 million to about $37 million with a resulting loss of new jobs. Nearly 500 banks failed in 1893, and another 350 went under during the rest of Cleveland's term; only about 200 had failed, by contrast, in the preceding Harrison administration. Railroads went bankrupt too, including such major lines as the Union Pacific and the Northern Pacific. President Cleveland called Congress into special session to alleviate the economic crisis.

The President believed the depression had a single cause and proposed a deceptively simple solution. He forgot the fact that farm prices had been depressed for years; he ignored speculation, economic conditions abroad, and various other factors that together contributed to business distress. The depression, the President said, was "principally chargeable to Congressional legislation touching the purchase and coinage of silver. . . ." He asked Congress to repeal the Sherman Silver Purchase Act, and implied that prosperity would promptly ensue.

Passed in 1890 as part of a political deal to secure support for the McKinley Tariff, the Sherman Silver Purchase Act required the Treasury to make monthly purchases of 4.5 million ounces of silver, an amount roughly equivalent to the domestic output. Because the market price of silver continued to decline, the Treasury's expenditure for silver did not differ greatly from that required by the Bland-Allison Act. Since the Treasury paid for silver in legal-tender notes and then redeemed the notes in gold, the Sherman Act brought no inflation. But by 1893 the policy of paying gold for notes secured by silver brought an alarming decrease in the Treasury's gold reserve, which sank below the $100 million minimum that sound-money advocates believed essential to maintain the gold standard.

The Democratic Congress resisted Cleveland's single-minded insistence on repeal of the Sherman Act. Even so conservative a financier as J. P. Morgan preferred a compromise to outright repeal. Congressional leaders offered Cleveland various schemes, but the President exerted every bit of executive pressure to secure repeal. Secure it he did, at the cost of a split that disabled his party and ended the effectiveness of his second administration before it had well begun. For the repeal of the Sherman Silver Purchase Act did not raise prices, restore confidence, bring prosperity, or even save the gold reserve. Cleveland had to authorize several bond issues to maintain gold stocks; one such issue, in 1895, brought Morgan and his syndicate a profit that, when exaggerated on the campaign trail, provided evidence for the charge of silverites that bankers and government had combined to fleece the public. A senator from North Carolina doubted that Cleveland could again win a single southern electoral vote. Ben Tillman, a salty South Carolinian who converted the state's Democratic party to Populist principles, compared Cleveland unfavorably to Judas Iscariot and promised to "prod" the President "in his fat ribs" with a pitchfork.

Seldom has a President been so rebuffed in an off-year election as was Cleveland in 1894; Republicans not only gained control of the House but secured a thumping margin of 140 seats. Twenty-four states sent no Democrats at all to Washington, and the party lost control of New York, Illinois, Wisconsin, and such Democratic strongholds as Maryland, Missouri, and North Carolina. Tom Watson exultantly likened the party's catastrophe to the "comprehensive, simultaneous, and complete smashup" of the Wonderful One Hoss Shay.

With the exception of some Republican politicians, no one could claim 1894 was a good year. Tobacco prices touched a new low for the decade, and cotton brought less than a nickel a pound. Freight loadings dropped sharply, indicating a widespread lull in economic activity. Although the number of strikes declined from earlier levels, unprecedented numbers of workers were affected. Estimates of the extent of unemployment ranged as high as one of every five urban workers.

Government at almost every level seemed resigned to let the depression cure itself, but in the West and South, silver orators held up the prospect of immediate inflation and instant prosperity. A little pamphlet called *Coin's Financial School* appeared in 1894 and spread the message more widely than any speaker. "You increase the value of all property by adding to the number of money units," said the imaginary Professor Coin to the imaginary students in his imaginary school. "You make it possible for the debtor to pay his debts; business to start anew, and revivify all the industries of the country, which must remain paralyzed so long as silver as well as all other property is measured by a gold standard." To fiscal conservatives, such promises were worse than misleading; they were immoral and anarchistic. But the lines gradually became firm: those who would do something about the depression favored the free and unlimited coinage of silver; those who would abide by the "immutable" principles of political economy favored unflinching support of the gold standard.

Cleveland did his part to eliminate alternatives and drive compromisers into one camp or the other. His use of troops in the Pullman Strike showed little inclination to let labor secure better wages through unions. When "armies" of unemployed men marched on Washington to file "a petition with boots" for federal relief, the administration jailed or dispersed the petitioners. Jacob Coxey, who led one of these groups, suggested that the unemployed be put to work constructing a system of roads financed by $500 million in legal-tender notes; Coxey was arrested for walking on the grass in front of the Capitol.

THE BATTLE OF THE STANDARDS

Jails, troops, and a hard heart—such, claimed opponents in Cleveland's own party, was the President's program. Through 1895 and 1896, Democratic silverites worked to control the convention and dictate the nominee in 1896. Before Democrats assembled in Chicago, Republicans nominated William McKinley, endorsed existing fiscal policies, and incurred the wrath of a few western silverites who stalked out of the party. Democratic silverites insisted on giving the voters a choice and wrote a platform that in effect disavowed Grover Cleveland. The platform specifically condemned the bond issues Cleveland had used to maintain the gold reserve and denounced the national banking system for good measure. The party pledged to restore the graduated income tax, to regulate railroads, and to establish more effective federal control of trusts. In the crucial plank, the platform demanded the free and unlimited coinage of silver at the ratio of sixteen to one.

Debate over the plank on money provided the party with its candidate. William Jennings Bryan, a young, handsome former congressman from Nebraska, mesmerized the convention with his speech for silver; before the spell wore off, he was the party's nominee. Bryan's economic ideas were no less primitive, however, than Cleveland's. Once "we have restored the money of the Constitution," Bryan proclaimed, "all other necessary reform will be possible; but until this is done, there is no other reform that can be accomplished." And Bryan's rhetoric showed his acceptance of the business ethic of his day.

> We say to you that you have made the definition of a business man too limited in its application. The man who is employed for wages is as much a business man as his employer; the attorney in a country town is as much a business man as the corporation counsel in a great metropolis; the merchant at the cross-roads store is as much a business man as the merchant of New York; the farmer . . . is as much a business man as the man who goes upon the Board of Trade and bets upon the price of grain; the miners . . . are as much business men as the few financial magnates who . . . corner the money of the world.

Bryan spoke to and, he fervently believed, for "this broader class of business men."

Bryan's nomination surprised Populists no less than it enraged Cleveland's followers. Populists had expected to wage the campaign on the silver issue, but to do so with their own candidate risked splitting the vote. To fuse with Democrats, on the other hand, risked the loss of a separate identity and the subordination or disappearance of other political objectives. Southern Populists were especially reluctant to merge with the conservatives who dominated the Democratic party in the South; Tom Watson termed such a retreat a return of "the hog . . . to its wallow." But so important had silver become to the public and to most Populist leaders that they preferred surrender disguised as compromise to a campaign that would surely divide the silver forces. The party endorsed Bryan for President, but substituted Watson for the unsatisfactory Democratic nominee for Vice-President. Win or lose, the Populists were doomed, for a victorious Bryan would have rewarded Democrats and a defeated Bryan did in fact leave Populists divided, bickering, and leaderless. Yet, in a sense, Populists had made their point. Their program had a prominent place in American political discourse for the next quarter-century, and the farmer whose interests they championed soon made good his claim to governmental attention. Bryan accepted Populist support, rejected his Populist running mate, and took to the stump with a vigor no previous presidential candidate had ever displayed.

William McKinley, a benign, gracious, courtly man, conducted a more traditional campaign from his front porch in Canton, Ohio. But the Republican campaign, directed by McKinley's close friend Mark Hanna, matched the Democrats' in energy. Political delegations arrived at Canton, conferred with McKinley, and shared his views with the press. The nominee favored a protective tariff and pointed out that as governor of Ohio he had enjoyed the support of many urban workingmen. McKinley probably reached more voters through the Republican press than Bryan did in 18,000 miles of speech-filled travel. Hanna efficiently shook down worried conservatives and amassed a campaign fund at least ten times as great as Bryan's. And in pamphlet after pamphlet, article after article, Republican publicists hammered the theme that Bryan was a dangerous lunatic if not a communist or anarchist revolutionary. McKinley carried California and Oregon, the northern Midwest, and the industrial East, where urban working people suspected that inflation was not a fundamental answer to their problems.

Bryan swept the Plains, the Rockies, and the South. But McKinley had 600,000 more votes than his opponent, and almost 100 more electors.

The "battle of the standards" was probably less important than the excited electorate believed in 1896; in the last analysis, prosperity did not depend upon silver and gold. But at least the campaign was the result of an honest effort to deal politically with economic questions—that much Bryan had accomplished. However superficial his solution, Bryan instinctively responded to the needs and fears of simple people, and he believed the

299

The Election of 1896

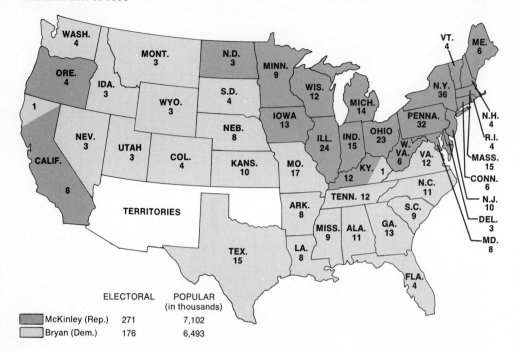

	ELECTORAL	POPULAR (in thousands)
McKinley (Rep.)	271	7,102
Bryan (Dem.)	176	6,493

government must do so too. The "Great Commoner" never moved to the White House, but he had more impact on American politics than any President between Lincoln and Theodore Roosevelt.

Prices took a turn for the better as McKinley assumed office, partly because the world supply of gold increased with new discoveries in Alaska and South Africa. Agricultural prices climbed from the troughs of the early 1890s, and industrial productivity resumed its upward course. Republicans nurtured prosperity with time-honored legislation. In the Dingley Tariff of 1897 they restored protective duties to record levels that averaged about 50 percent. In 1900 Congress passed the Currency Act, which established a gold reserve of $150 million and officially put the country on the gold standard. Conservatives thought it was a good way to close the books on the old century.

Suggested Reading

Matthew Josephson's *The Robber Barons** (1934) and *The Politicos** (1938) typify an older view of the post–Civil War years. More recent surveys of the period include John A. Garraty, *The New Commonwealth* (1968), Ray Ginger, *The Age of Excess** (1965), and a collection of essays edited by H. Wayne Morgan, *The Gilded Age** (1963).

The classic account of the Populists is John D. Hicks, *The Populist Revolt** (1931). Norman Pollack, *The Populist Response to Industrial*

America* (1962), sees the Populists as radicals, while Richard Hofstadter, *The Age of Reform** (1955), emphasizes their ties to the agrarian past. C. Vann Woodward's *Tom Watson** (1938) is a model biography of the southern Populist leader.

Paul W. Glad's *McKinley, Bryan and the People** (1964) is one of several accounts of the election of 1896. The best recent biographies of McKinley are Margaret K. Leech's *In the Days of McKinley* (1959) and H. Wayne Morgan's *William McKinley and His America* (1963). Paolo E. Coletta has written three biographical volumes on Bryan (1964, 1969). Horace S. Merrill suggests in *Bourbon Leader** (1957) that Grover Cleveland has been overrated in some respects. Irwin Unger's *The Greenback Era, 1865–1879** (1964) is an excellent study of financial policy.

NOTE: See also works cited in *Suggested Reading* for Chapters 13 and 14.

*Available in paperback edition

CHRONOLOGY

XVI

EXTENDING

AMERICAN INFLUENCE

"For three centuries," wrote one of the nation's foremost historians in 1896, "the dominant fact of American life has been expansion. . . ." Even as Frederick Jackson Turner wrote, this expansive energy thrust his country into the Spanish-American War and into the prevailing international scramble for colonial possessions. American enthusiasm for new territory quickly cooled; the drive to enlarge commercial opportunity and diplomatic influence, on the other hand, had begun well before, and endured long after, the Spanish-American War. Americans, as Turner remarked, agreed on expansion; they debated whether that expansion must include colonial control.

The policies of William H. Seward, Secretary of State in the 1860s, demonstrate the remarkable continuity of nineteenth-century American foreign relations. Seward's insistence on the Monroe Doctrine and on American predominance in the Caribbean recalled the ambitions of Thomas Jefferson and John Quincy Adams and anticipated those of William McKinley and Theodore Roosevelt. The possibility of an interoceanic canal attracted speculative adventurers in Seward's time, as it had at the time of the California gold rush and would until the oceans met in the twentieth century. Seward's attempt to enlarge American trade with Asia resembled Daniel Webster's efforts in the Tyler administration and those of Benjamin Harrison, Grover Cleveland, and William McKinley thereafter; the Asian market attracted industrialists and steamship captains as it had earlier tempted traders and clipper masters.

THE URGE TO EXPAND

Seward's contemporaries perferred to invest at home and to shoulder domestic racial problems before undertaking new ones abroad. But the arguments and circumstances that stalled Seward lost force as the century went on. Reconstruction ended, and with it doctrines of racial equality that might make heavier the white man's imperial burden. Some felt a renewed urge for free land as the census disclosed a disappearing frontier. The national Treasury, pledged in Seward's day to paying off the Union's war debt, brimmed embarrassingly full two decades later. Descendants of Civil War veterans, unlike their elders, had no haunting fear of conflict; instead they sought a chance to elevate the nation's patriotic and military spirit. Other countries, particularly England, which had been disillusioned with empire at midcentury, set an example of renewed acquisitiveness as the century waned. Capitalists and merchants needed a foreign outlet for investment and goods when domestic demand dipped during the industrial depressions that plagued the latter part of the century.

As restraints became less confining, positive support for expansion grew. Concern about foreign markets extended throughout the economy. Wheat farmers knew that domestic prices would sag even lower if markets abroad were closed. Exporters ordinarily sent more than half the tobacco and cotton crops overseas, and the fraction sometimes climbed to four-fifths. American steel, oil, and textile companies competed with European industries in all corners of the world. During the two decades after 1875 imports exceeded foreign sales in only two years, and the drive to secure yet larger foreign markets had formidable political support.

Walter Q. Gresham, a Republican who served as Cleveland's Secretary of State, believed commercial expansion essential to the nation's social and economic tranquility. Strikes and labor violence, socialism and income taxes, populism and inflated currency—these and other demagogic schemes, Gresham believed, would disappear if a waiting market absorbed what a healthy economy could produce. "Our mills and factories," Gresham observed, "can supply the [domestic] demand by running seven or eight months out of twelve." More foreign trade, the Secretary thought, would suffice; Americans did not need more territory. Yet not all who accepted Gresham's diagnosis of the nation's malaise were content with his limited prescription.

If the United States was to add colonies, they must be added quickly, for an all-out race for empire began late in the century. European colonization soon blotted out trade with Africa, which had caught the State Department's fancy during Chester A. Arthur's administration. A comparable decline in economic opportunity loomed in Asia. Russia, Germany, Britain, France, and Japan all coveted parts of China. Some Americans thought the United States should take official steps, including appropriate annexations, to assure continued access to the vast Chinese market. The renewed burst of European expansion did not trouble every American, but a persuasive minority of prominent citizens—college presidents, editors, merchants, and politicians—began to advocate imperialism.

A few cosmopolitan, ambitious young politicians saw expansion as the route to higher office, just as it had been earlier for James K. Polk. Theodore Roosevelt most notably linked enlarging the nation's domain with enlarging his own reputation. Henry Cabot Lodge, the junior Senator from Massachusetts, and Albert J. Beveridge, soon to become the Senator from Indiana, also promoted colonial expansion. Henry and Brooks Adams, descendants of Presidents, were not themselves politicians but advocated expansion in their writing and at the highest level of Washington society. John Hay, Abraham Lincoln's private secretary and William McKinley's Secretary of State, was an ardent expansionist, a close friend of the Adamses, and a social acquaintance of most of the Republican elite.

Protestant missionaries preached expansion too. They joined an international effort to bring Christianity to the world's heathen in a single generation, an effort that political control might hasten. American missionaries called the nation's attention to Hawaii and shaped policy in Korea. They gave eager audiences in churches all over the land a first-hand account of the hardships of thousands of misgoverned, backward pagans (or Catholics) who yearned for democratic government, American textiles, and Protestant Christianity. Contributions from the faithful discharged only part of the congregation's responsibility; Christians should also support a national policy that backed the Protestant gospel with American Marines. "God . . . is training the Anglo-Saxon race for an hour sure to come in the world's future," wrote Josiah Strong, a leader of the American Home Missionary Society. His *Our Country*, published in 1885, made expansion an American Christian duty.

Duty pervaded the imperial urge. Duty to the Deity dictated that His earth be efficiently used and His word be spread. Duty to mankind dictated uplifting inferior races with kerosene lamps, calico, schools, and elections. Duty to the Darwinian law of nature dictated competing with other nations to refine the American system and make it even more fit for future generations. Duty to the nation dictated raising the flag over outposts that protected our coastlines, our trade, and our strategic interests.

Protection of those interests rested primarily on the Navy. In the 1880s the American fleet was inferior not only to fleets of major European powers but even, Rudyard Kipling scoffed, to the Chinese navy, which, "if properly manned, could waft the entire American navy out of the water. . . ." The United States, continued the English poet, was "as unprotected as a jellyfish." In 1893, when Grover Cleveland ordered a warship to Nicaragua to strengthen his policy there, the vessel sank on the way and exposed the nation's embarrassing naval weakness.

The persuasive writing of Captain Alfred Thayer Mahan, a friend of Lodge and of Roosevelt, hastened construction of the modern American fleet. Congress had ordered four steel cruisers during Chester Arthur's administration, several years before Mahan's *The Influence of Sea Power Upon History* appeared in 1890. Mahan's argument that greatness came to nations that mastered the oceans helped persuade Congress to authorize twenty-five new vessels, including three new battleships. Because these coal-burning ships required fuel depots and naval bases, the nation's new navy not only protected colonies but also required them.

Earlier in the century a big navy and colonial expansion would have produced diplomatic friction with England, the major naval and imperial power in the world. But by 1890 English-speaking peoples had reached a tacit understanding that had survived diplomatic provocation and dozens of anti-British appeals for the Irish-American vote. Opportunities for diplomatic misunderstanding abounded: the United States resented England's failure to keep the Confederate raider *Alabama* in port during the Civil War; England resented episodic American eagerness to add Canada to the United States; American fishermen off Nova Scotia and Canadian seal-hunters off Alaska angered rivals who claimed exclusive rights in territorial waters. Yet successive British governments patiently tolerated frivolous American treatment. Changes in Europe, especially the threatening increase in German naval power, made Britain willing to overlook American diplomatic immaturity and to allow the United States to dominate areas like Central America, where American and British policies coincided. Gradually, an unspoken Anglo-American agreement joined the Monroe Doctrine as one of the guiding principles of American foreign policy. "I think," predicted Theodore Roosevelt in 1900, "the twentieth century will be the century of the men who speak English."

THE BEGINNING OF EMPIRE

In the 1850s, William H. Seward had exhorted the nation to "command the empire of the seas which alone is real empire." As Secretary of State a decade later, Seward retained his imperial vision. To protect a potential American empire in the Caribbean and to enforce the Monroe Doctrine, he opposed European intervention in the Western Hemisphere. Napoleon III had taken advantage of the American Civil War to install Maximilian, a Hapsburg prince, on the throne of Mexico, but in 1867 Seward's diplomatic pressure, the lack of French reinforcements, and the resistance of Mexican insurgents finished Maximilian's brief reign. Seward proposed annexation of Santo Domingo after yellow fever and the aroused inhabitants combined to end Spain's attempt to repossess it. Seward also asked for the purchase of the Virgin Islands from Denmark and of Alaska from Russia. Preoccupied with reconstruction, Congress passed over the beckoning Caribbean empire and almost refused Alaska. But Seward extolled the untapped Alaskan mineral wealth, modestly compared his real-estate bargain with the Louisiana Purchase, and suggested that the Aleutian chain "extended a friendly hand to Asia" that might grasp the Oriental market. Congress gave in and completed the deal in 1867.

Most of Seward's nineteenth-century successors in the Department of State believed, as he had, in expanding the trade and influence of the United States. Until the Spanish-American War, they ordinarily stopped short of expanding the nation's territory. "Our great demand is expansion," Secretary of State James G. Blaine proclaimed in 1890. But, he added immediately, "I mean expansion of trade with countries where we can find profitable exchanges. We are not seeking annexation of territory."

There were occasional exceptions. As Santo Domingo had tempted Seward, so it tempted President Grant, but he could not persuade either his Secretary of State or the Senate to share his enthusiasm. Cuban insurrections in the 1870s seemed to expansionists an invitation to annex the island. Politicians with Irish constituencies periodically proposed to raise the flag over Canada. The Navy wanted a base in Haiti. Eventually the Navy did secure two magnificent harbors in the Pacific: Pago Pago, on Tutuila in the Samoan group, and Pearl Harbor, in Hawaii, to which the Navy secured exclusive rights in 1887. In both cases, naval bases provided a step toward annexation.

Samoa also attracted British and German naval strategists, and for a dozen years the three nations tried various methods of sharing control. The United States insisted that Samoa remain at least nominally independent and refused to permit simple partition and annexation of territory. But if the United States did not absorb the Samoan outpost, neither did it permit others to do so. In 1899 the United States finally divided the archipelago with Germany and formally added Tutuila to the Pacific empire, which by that time also included the Philippines and Hawaii.

A reciprocity treaty, negotiated in 1875, gave Hawaiian sugar planters privileged access to the American market until 1890, when the McKinley Tariff awarded domestic producers a bounty and repealed the duty on imported sugar. Annexation would make Hawaiian planters, many of whom were of American extraction, eligible for the bounty. In 1893 they overthrew the native dynasty and established a republic under the presidency of Sanford Dole. John L. Stevens, the American minister in Honolulu, recognized the new government almost immediately and secured American Marines from Pearl Harbor to intimidate remaining supporters of Queen Liliuokalani. The republic quickly concluded a treaty of annexation and the exuberant Stevens raised the American flag.

Stevens' treaty arrived in Washington in the final weeks of the Harrison administration and by common consent was held for the new Congress and the new President. Cleveland sent James Blount, a former congressman from Georgia, to Hawaii to test the sentiment of the inhabitants. Blount reported that Stevens had acted imprudently and that most islanders favored independence. But the Queen resolutely promised to behead the members of Dole's government, who naturally refused to surrender control of the state.

Cleveland decided to let the Hawaiians resolve the impasse themselves, made a few partisan observations about Stevens' action, and withdrew the treaty. Lack of a formal agreement, however, did not break the close economic link with the islands or preclude naval control there. The President simply followed the traditional American policy of seeking the economic and strategic advantages of empire without assuming the political liabilities. Formal annexation of Hawaii, like that of Samoa, waited for 1898 and the Spanish-American War.

Cautious and deliberate in handling Hawaiian annexation, Cleveland was hasty and bellicose in 1895 when he stepped into a long-simmering dispute about the boundary between Venezuela and British Guiana. Britain, Cleveland thought, stubbornly held to an unjust position simply because Venezuela was weaker. He decided to redress the balance. He neither asked nor received the advice of the Venezuelan government before authorizing Secretary of State Richard Olney to dispatch a vigorous note to London. "To-day," Olney asserted, "the United States is practically sovereign on this continent. . . ." The Secretary followed this tactless premise with a demand that Britain either permit arbitrators to draw a frontier line or face war with the United States. The British government delayed for some months before denying Olney's assertions, rejecting his demands, and calling the administration's bluff.

But Cleveland meant what Olney had said. In December, 1895, without informing the Venezuelan ambassador, the President announced that the United States would appoint a commission, send it to Venezuela to determine the boundary, and then enforce the decision. War with Britain was possible, Cleveland warned, but "supine submission to wrong and injustice" would be worse than war. Once he had publicly revealed his inflexible determination, Cleveland permitted flexible diplomats to avoid the war he had invited. Partly because one war at a time seemed enough—and the Boers in South Africa were proving unexpectedly stubborn—Britain resolved that no colonial boundary was worth a war with the United States. This decision implicitly accepted the Monroe Doctrine, confirmed the developing Anglo-American diplomatic entente, and frankly acknowledged the admission of the United States to the fraternity of world powers. As an incidental result of Britain's decision, an international tribunal awarded most of the disputed territory to British Guiana, a decision the indifferent State Department placidly accepted in 1899.

THE SPANISH-AMERICAN WAR:
CUBAN INDEPENDENCE AND A PACIFIC EMPIRE

Although Cuba was a Spanish colony, the island's economy meshed with that of the United States. American tariff policy determined the prosperity of Cuban sugar planters, and the change in duties in 1894 was in part responsible for the rebellion that rocked the island in 1895. Americans had large investments in Cuba, including some in sugar plantations, and confidently expected to enlarge the American share of the island's commerce.

As the rebellion dragged on, and as demands for American intervention mounted, American businessmen became progressively more uneasy. Those who thought the election of 1896 had established fiscal sanity feared the inflation that invariably accompanied war. Taxpayers grumbled about the millions already spent in inefficient enforcement of the neutrality laws and dreaded the greater expenditures of war. Surveillance of the insurrection tied up American forces that might have inhibited frantic European efforts to establish spheres of influence in China. Uncertainty about the nation's foreign policy led to economic uncertainty, which threatened the first fragile signs of recovery from the recent depression of 1893. Although Henry Cabot Lodge predicted that an independent Cuba would be "a great market for the United States" and a great "opportunity for American capital," on balance American enterprisers preferred to nurse what prosperity they had.

Other groups were more bold. The AFL resolved in favor of intervention. Patriotic societies and veterans' organizations thought a war for Cuba would renew the nation's spirit and revive its glorious martial tradition. Republicans who had criticized Cleveland's hesitant course were unhappy when William McKinley's seemed no different. Protestant clergymen encouraged their congregations to take up the Cuban cause against Spain, which a Chicago Baptist minister called "Pope-ridden." As early as 1896, 1,200 hardy St. Louis volunteers offered to serve the cause of Cuban freedom, and a ten-year-old from Newark, New Jersey, stole a pair of pistols and started to hike to Havana. A shrewd politician—which William McKinley was—could hardly miss the signs.

But McKinley was also cautious. Presidential intimates announced, for instance, that McKinley would "use his powers to stop the bloodshed insofar as he can without involving the United States in war"—whatever that meant. For more than a year adroit variations on that ambiguous theme enabled the President to keep the simultaneous support of businessmen who opposed war and Republican "jingoes" who demanded it. His negotiations with Spain never came to anything. The Spanish government talked of reform in Cuba while its generals used concentration camps to discourage civilian support of Cuban guerrillas. McKinley proposed Cuban autonomy, as Grover Cleveland had, and looked into ways of purchasing Cuban independence. One by one, McKinley exhausted the alternatives to American intervention.

Two New York newspapers did their shrill best to exaggerate, or even create, Spanish atrocities and to encourage American intervention. William Randolph Hearst's *Journal* and Joseph Pulitzer's *World* engaged in a circulation race that required sensational headlines whether or not events justified them. One too scrupulous artist, sent to Cuba to cover the insurrection, was said to have wired Hearst that there was no war. "You furnish the pictures," was Hearst's reported response, "and I'll furnish the war." This "yellow journalism," in New York and elsewhere, certainly whipped up popular demand for war. But Hearst and Pulitzer did not single-handedly manufacture that demand. The public bought their newspapers because they contained what people wanted to read; the "yellow" newspapers catered to popular enthusiasm as much as they enhanced it.

But events in February, 1898, furnished copy that required little journalistic exaggeration. The Spanish Ambassador Enrique Depuy de Lôme belittled President McKinley in a private letter that became public in the Hearst press. The Ambassador questioned McKinley's willingness to stand up against popular opinion, which was about what Theodore Roosevelt was saying at the same time. De Lôme's letter caused a momentary stir that was soon forgotten in the excitement over the sinking of the *Maine*.

McKinley had sent the *Maine*, one of the nation's shiny new battleships, to Havana harbor to safeguard American lives and property. On

February 15 more than 250 American sailors died when the vessel blew up. The press, and the public, held Spain responsible for the explosion; the actual cause remains unknown. Perhaps insurgents torpedoed the vessel, correctly anticipating that the United States would blame Spain; perhaps an internal explosion sank the ship; perhaps Spanish agents did in fact blow up the *Maine,* although that now seems the least likely possibility. In any case, the resulting hysteria in the United States made McKinley's continued restraint more difficult than ever.

Yet, until McKinley sensed a united demand from the American people for a free Cuba, his restraint persisted. Those opposed to war gradually stilled their objections; by March, William Jennings Bryan had made the demand for intervention officially bipartisan. McKinley's cables to Madrid became more firm. The Spanish government backed down until in early April all that was left to concede was Cuban independence. And that step Spain would not take. On April 19, Congress authorized McKinley to use American troops to expel Spanish forces from the island. Before the declaration passed, Congress displayed the nation's unselfish zeal in the Teller Amendment, which explicitly stated that the United States would not annex Cuba. But Congress neglected to forbid other territorial additions, and the crusade against Spanish colonialism brought the United States a colonial empire.

When John Hay subsequently referred to the "splendid little war," he was not speaking for the ordinary trooper. The Army launched the crusade from an unsanitary staging area near Tampa, Florida, and in June inexpertly landed an invading force in Cuba. Confused lines of command linked regular units and volunteer regiments such as the Rough Riders, which Theodore Roosevelt had recruited. Soliders received woolen uniforms, spoiled rations, and inadequate medical support.

Spanish forces killed fewer Americans than did mosquitoes. The only major land engagement of the war took place at San Juan Hill near Santiago. And even that battle was probably unnecessary because the Navy had already blockaded the city. The Spanish fleet, holed up in Santiago harbor, eventually escaped to meet complete destruction in a running battle along the Cuban coast. One American sailor was killed in the encounter. Six more Americans were wounded in the most intense fighting on Puerto Rico, which American forces occupied in July.

Nor were casualties greater on the other side of the world, where the Navy added to the American empire before the army landed in Cuba. A week after the declaration of war, Commodore George Dewey's Pacific squadron destroyed the Spanish fleet in Manila Bay without the loss of one American ship or a single American life. The next day, McKinley ordered an expeditionary force to the Philippines; a few days later the Navy received instructions to seize Guam. Theodore Roosevelt, then Assistant Secretary of the Navy, sent the cable to Dewey that set off this chain of events, and although McKinley later professed surprise at Dewey's sudden appearance in Manila Bay, in fact the President had approved Roosevelt's instructions to the Pacific fleet. And the President did not order Dewey to leave Manila after the battle but instead sent troops to end Spanish administration in the islands. The decisions were conscious; the result intentional. In 1899 Senator Mark Hanna, the Ohio industrialist who was widely, if incorrectly, thought to be the brains behind McKinley, announced the nation's determination to secure "a large slice of the commerce of Asia." The United States had "better . . . strike for it," Hanna continued, "while the iron is hot." McKinley had done just that.

Within three months, the Spanish-American War was over. The President instructed his delegates to the peace conference to demand independence for Cuba and, after some hesitation to be sure the public favored annexation, the cession of Guam, Wake, Puerto Rico and the Philippines to the United States. Partly because American conquest of the Philippines was not complete, and partly to disguise seizure as purchase, the United States agreed to pay Spain a face-saving $20 million.

Righteous American senators put up stiffer resistance to the treaty than did defeated Spanish diplomats. The principles of the Declaration of Independence and the prospective problems of colonial administration combined to create an articulate minority in the Senate that threatened to block ratification. From whatever misguided motive, Bryan, who actually opposed annexation of the Philippines, persuaded a few wavering Democrats to vote for the treaty. Lack of an attractive alternative persuaded others to accept the islands rather than permit them to become parts of the British, German, or Japanese empires. Filipinos continued against the United States the insurrection begun against Spanish control, and the

William McKinley (left) watches the signing of the peace treaty with Spain, August, 1898

insult to the flag influenced those who cherished national honor. (It took three years, 70,000 troops, and many of the same antiguerrilla methods Spain had used in Cuba to convince the Filipinos of the benefits of American civilization.) McKinley took the public pulse on a speaking tour and became satisfied that the public favored annexation. When businessmen no longer balked at colonies, McKinley pushed ahead, and the Senate, by a narrow margin, agreed.

THE CHINESE MARKET: A CONTINUING FANTASY

"If it is commercialism to want possession of a strategic point giving the American people [a] . . . foothold in the markets" of China, Mark Hanna snapped, "for God's sake let us have commercialism." The Philippines, in short, were the warehouse; China was to be the store. But Russia, Germany, France, and Japan dreamed of dominating the China trade, to say nothing of Britain, which had nearly 80 percent of the market in the 1890s. All these countries were bringing diplomatic pressure on the feeble Chinese Empire, from which they hoped to extort exclusive trading privileges. American exporters feared that these spheres of influence would block American trade. John Hay, the new Secretary of State in 1898, did not know much about China, but he recognized a mounting pressure to enlarge the American share of the Chinese market.

William W. Rockhill, a career diplomat who advised Hay on Asian affairs, drafted the Open Door notes, which stated the basic American policy. In 1899 Hay formally asked the major powers with Chinese spheres of influence not to discriminate against traders from other nations. Since a sphere of influence was supposed to prevent the Open Door, Hay's notes met a cool reception in European foreign ministries. Britain conditionally agreed to the American request, and Japan, France, Italy, and Germany agreed subject to the full acceptance of all other powers. Russia returned a qualified refusal, which effectively released the other countries from their consent. Secretary Hay then correctly calculated that none of the powers would publicly avow reservations and boldly announced that all had endorsed the Open Door.

John Hay sent his second series of Open Door notes a year later, in the aftermath of the Boxer Rebellion. In their protest against concessions to foreigners, Chinese patriots, known as Boxers, had cut off the entire diplomatic community in Peking, which had to be rescued by a multinational force. When some of the affronted powers suggested territorial reprisal, Hay broadened American policy. The United States, Hay wrote, required not only the preservation of the trading rights he had mentioned in 1899, but also the preservation of "Chinese territorial and administrative entity."

The Open Door notes gave expansion the commercial connotation it had had before 1898. The bitter debate over the Spanish treaty, the insurrection in the Philippines, and the possibility of more trade in China combined to dampen lingering American desire for more colonies. To be sure, the United States added territory after 1898; but the popular urge to color the map had gone. Although Bryan tried to make the election of 1900 a referendum on empire, the electorate had already tired of the issue. A vote for William McKinley, who dealt Bryan his second crushing presidential defeat, was a vote to keep what we had and to drop the subject.

The Open Door was more easily stated than maintained. Indeed, two months after he had sent the second notes, Secretary Hay himself inquired about a naval base on the Chinese mainland at Samsah Bay. The Japanese government, with a nice sense of irony, suggested that Hay's request might infringe China's "territorial and administrative entity," and Hay did not pursue the matter further. A year later, when Japan asked if the United States planned any response to expanding Russian penetration of Manchuria, Hay confessed that the United States would not risk war to keep the door open. The Open Door policy expressed hope, not determination.

And the hope soon withered. Trade with China never developed, and investment opportunities went to those whose strategic control enabled them to extort concessions. Although the American China Development Corporation secured the right to build a Chinese railroad in 1898, for example, J. P. Morgan and the other directors decided to sell out before completing the project. Not even President Roosevelt could convince the company to change its decision. President Taft encountered chilling apathy when he tried to convince American capitalists to construct a Manchurian railway. American businessmen realized before their Presidents did that China was a market without purchasing power and that geography gave Russia and Japan advantages that the Philippines in no way offset. By 1907 Roosevelt admitted that the Philippines were "our heel of Achilles." To protect the islands, Roosevelt went on, would require enormous fortification and "a navy second only to that of Great Britain." Lacking both, Roosevelt and his successors sought a balance of power in East Asia to discourage excessive ambition by any single nation.

Russia, Roosevelt believed, most threatened the balance of Asian power. The Czar had secured control of Port Arthur and the right to link the port with the Trans-Siberian Railway; Russian intrigue in Korea was badly disguised. Both in Manchuria and in Korea Russian plans conflicted with those of Japan. Before confronting Russia directly, Japan signed an alliance with Great Britain in 1902 and secured Roosevelt's benevolent neutrality. Then, on February 8, 1904, without a declaration of war, Japan smashed the Russian Pacific fleet at Port Arthur. "Japan," Theodore Roosevelt wrote to his son, "is playing our game."

The game threatened to go on too long. Roosevelt hoped Japan would thwart Russian expansion but stop short of establishing its own hegemony in East Asia. Japan won impressive victories, both at sea and in Manchuria, but the economic drain led the Japanese cabinet to ask Roosevelt to mediate. Although the Russian armies had been soundly defeated, and in spite of strikes and demonstrations that merged in the Revolution of 1905, Czar Nicholas II at first resisted Roosevelt's overtures. The President patiently and skillfully brought Russian and Japanese delegates together at Portsmouth, New Hampshire, and kept them there until the Treaty of Portsmouth ended the Russo-Japanese War in 1905.

For his efforts Theodore Roosevelt won the Nobel Peace Prize and the ill will of both belligerents. The settlement at Portsmouth satisfied neither Russia, which gave up territory, nor Japan, which failed to secure the indemnity to which it felt entitled. Nor did the balance of Asian power, which Roosevelt's compromise renewed, ensure open access to the Asian market. The United States continued to pay lip service to the Open Door until the Second World War and reaffirmed the policy in several treaties and executive agreements. Yet, restating the American position did not make other powers respect it, and the Open Door was soon only slightly ajar.

In the Taft-Katsura memorandum of 1905, Roosevelt recognized a Japanese protectorate in Korea that ended the Open Door there. In 1908, in an exchange of notes between Secretary of State Elihu Root and Japanese Ambassador Kogoro Takahira, both countries ritualistically renewed their support of the Open Door. This Root-Takahira agreement also pledged Japan and the United States to respect each other's Pacific possessions, a promise the United States wanted in order to protect the Philippines. But another portion of the Asian market vanished in 1911, when Japan and Russia divided Manchuria into a northern sphere of Russian influence and a southern sector, where Japan predominated. In 1915 Japan took advantage of the preoccupation of European powers with the First World War and made the Twenty-One Demands on China, which, if conceded, would

Roosevelt with Russian and Japanese delegates, 1905

have permitted Japanese domination of China. Bryan, then Wilson's Secretary of State, protested, but Robert Lansing, who followed Bryan in the State Department, signed another executive agreement in 1917. The Lansing-Ishii agreement once more reaffirmed the Open Door and simultaneously admitted that Japan had "special interests" in China as a result of "territorial propinquity." The determination of strong rivals, particularly Japan, had forced a quiet American diplomatic retreat from East Asia; in 1909 the Navy abandoned plans for a primary Pacific base near Manila and concentrated on the development of Pearl Harbor. Without the fleet, American policy could not be enforced.

As if Russia, China, Manchuria, and the Philippines did not sufficiently complicate Japanese-American relations, California added another dimension. In 1906 a decision by the San Francisco Board of Education to educate Japanese-Americans in segregated schools brought outraged objection from the Japanese Foreign Ministry. While Roosevelt sympathized with Japan, the Constitution gave him little control over education in California. Eventually the President convinced the Californians to reverse their decision and the Japanese not to permit laborers to emigrate to the United States. But this Gentlemen's Agreement, completed in 1908, did not exclude all Japanese immigrants and did not satisfy California. In 1913 the state legislature outlawed Japanese ownership of land in spite of pleas from President Wilson and Secretary Bryan and protests from Japan.

THE WESTERN HEMISPHERE:
INFLUENCE AND INTERVENTION

Growth of American influence in the Western Hemisphere more than balanced gradual withdrawal from East Asia. As "territorial propinquity" made Manchuria a zone of Japanese influence, so the Caribbean became an American lake. Construction of the Panama Canal increased the strategic interest of the United States in all of Central America. But American policy-makers did not repeat their unfortunate Philippine experience; informal protectorates in Central America substituted for colonial control.

Barriers that for a half-century had prevented construction of a canal were gradually surmounted. Medical research controlled tropical diseases that had resisted earlier efforts. Improvements in locks enabled engineers to drop the unworkable plans of a French company for a sea-level canal. New York speculators bought control of the French company, so its exclusive Panamanian franchise would not hinder American efforts to complete a waterway. Following cordial discussions with the British ambassador Sir Julian Pauncefote, John Hay announced in 1900 that Britain had renounced the right, guaranteed in the Clayton-Bulwer Treaty of 1850, to

AMERICAN EXPANSION, 1857-1917

Dates of acquisition appear with place name

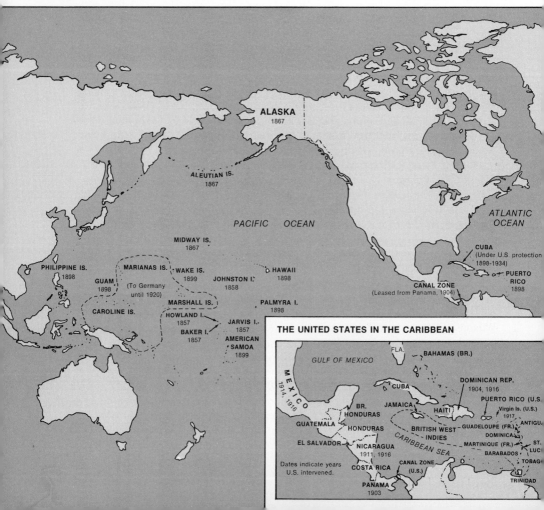

THE UNITED STATES IN THE CARIBBEAN

joint construction and control of any interoceanic canal. When in 1901 the Senate wisely refused to ratify the treaty unless it included permission to fortify the waterway, Hay and Pauncefote negotiated a second treaty, which removed that diplomatic block. In 1902 Congress authorized President Roosevelt to pay the American stockholders of the French company $40 million for its exclusive franchise. Tomás Herrán, Colombia's representative in Washington, obligingly granted the United States a ninety-nine-year lease on a canal zone in Colombia's Panama province in return for $10 million and an annual payment of $250,000.

But the Colombian legislature unexpectedly resisted Hay's financial inducement. Since the French company's rights reverted to Colombia in 1904, Colombia decided to delay a year in order to collect the company's $40 million too; the Colombian Senate consequently rejected the Hay-Herrán treaty. Roosevelt privately raged about the "Dagoes" of Colombia who perversely halted the progress of civilization. He stationed the U.S.S. *Nashville* off Colón to protect American rights in the isthmus. In 1903, when a Panamanian rebellion broke out, the *Nashville* prevented Colombian troops from disembarking; two days later Hay informally recognized the rebel regime. Within two weeks Hay concluded a treaty with Philippe Bunau-Varilla, a Frenchman and lobbyist for the French canal company, who coincidentally represented the new Panamanian republic in Washington. On the same financial terms that Colombia had rejected, Panama gave the United States a ten-mile-wide canal zone in perpetuity in the Hay-Bunau-Varilla Treaty.

With the right to build the canal the United States also acquired the resentment of much of Latin America. If Roosevelt had waited for the Colombian "bandits," construction would not have been delayed more than eighteen months, a lag that does not seem excessive when "civilization" had already waited more than fifty years. And Roosevelt's public delight in his accomplishment showed little sensitivity to Latin American pride: "If I had followed traditional, conservative methods," Roosevelt boasted in 1911, "I would have submitted a dignified State paper . . . to Congress and the debates on it would have been going on yet; but I took the Canal Zone . . . and while the debate goes on the Canal does also." Recognizing that Roosevelt's impetuous action rankled south of the border, the Wilson administration offered to pay Colombia $25 million, but Republican partisanship blocked any compensation until 1921.

Proud Latin American neighbors also resented the Roosevelt Corollary to the Monroe Doctrine, which the President announced in 1904. Monroe's pronouncement sheltered only those nations that kept order and paid their bills, Roosevelt remarked; "chronic wrongdoing . . . may . . . ultimately require intervention by some civilized nation." For Roosevelt, the "civilized nation" in the Western Hemisphere was the United States. The Roosevelt Corollary publicly avowed the protectorate policy already practiced in Panama and in Cuba, where the Cuban constitution granted the United States the right to intervene. Within the next few years, under the guise of preventing European debt collection, Americans landed Marines, took over customs houses, and reorganized the fiscal systems of the Dominican Republic, Haiti, and Nicaragua. The last of the Marines returned to the United States in 1934.

Roosevelt's immediate successors did not alter his policies. Without Roosevelt's vigor and without conspicuous success, William Howard Taft tried to encourage American investment abroad; when Latin American debtors proved sloppy about their obligations, the State Department brought diplomatic pressure to secure repayment. Woodrow Wilson criticized Taft's "dollar diplomacy" and assured the world in 1913 that the United States would "never again seek one additional foot of territory by conquest." Wilson's administration kept the letter of his pledge; the Virgin Islands, added in 1917, were purchased from Denmark, not conquered. But protectorates in Haiti, the Dominican Republic, and Nicaragua and Yankee armies in Mexico certainly seemed out of keeping with the spirit of Wilson's remarks.

Like Roosevelt, and like the progressive generation for whom both men were spokesmen, Woodrow Wilson acted on strong moral convictions. Wilson intensely disapproved of General Victoriano Huerta, one of a series of strong men who tried to master political and social upheaval in Mexico. Since Wilson believed diplomatic contact officially bestowed American approval on foreign governments, he refused to recognize Huerta's regime. Wilson thereby overturned a long-standing practice of exchanging representatives with whatever government was in power. The President also imposed an arms embargo in his determination to "teach the South American republics to elect good men." But every faction suspected his motives, and he twice blundered into armed intervention in troubled Mexico.

Conflict in the first instance was relatively brief. In April, 1914, Wilson abruptly ordered the bombardment and seizure of Vera Cruz to prevent delivery of German arms for Huerta's forces. The Mexican Army put up stiff resistance before leaving the port to American troops. Wilson's action may have benefited Huerta's Mexican opponents, but they denounced it no less vehemently than Huerta himself. A few days after the landings, Wilson eagerly accepted arbitration from Argentina, Brazil, and Chile, which led to evacuation of American forces during the following six months.

Wilson's second Mexican conflict occurred because Venustiano Carranza, Huerta's chief rival and successor, could not subdue Pancho Villa, a swashbuckling political maverick who never successfully distinguished between banditry and revolution. Perhaps because he thought an American invasion would discredit Carranza, Villa deliberately provoked a punitive expedition by American troops. In 1916 Villa's men abducted sixteen Americans from a Mexican train and shot them; in March Villa raided Columbus, New Mexico, and left nineteen dead Americans. With Carranza's grudging consent, General John J. Pershing led 6,000 American troops into Mexico to administer justice to Villa's raiders. The expedition never found Villa; instead it clashed with Mexican forces and nearly set off another war with Mexico. Finally, in January, 1917, as American participation in a bigger war across the Atlantic became more and more imminent, Wilson ordered Pershing back to Texas. The General soon found German armies in France less elusive than Mexican outlaws.

That war in France confirmed, for those who were unaware of what had happened in the preceding half-century, that the United States had progressed from regional to world power. This change was not the result of new possessions in the Caribbean or the Pacific, nor even the result of dismembering the Spanish empire and sinking its sorry fleet. Events at home were more responsible than events abroad for the nation's diplomatic eminence, which far-sighted leaders from Seward to Roosevelt had instinctively understood. The United States became a full-fledged world power when the American people realized that their industrial economy gave them diplomatic leverage in proportion to their enormous potential strength, and when they consciously decided to use that leverage.

Suggested Reading

Walter LaFeber's *The New Empire** (1963) is a stimulating survey emphasizing economic causes for American expansion. Ernest R. May's *American Imperialism* (1968) stresses the influence of the European example on American opinion-makers; see also his *Imperial Democracy* (1961). One opinion-maker, Alfred T. Mahan, argues the need for a strong navy and for island bases in *The Influence of Sea Power upon History** (1890). Julius W. Pratt's *The Expansionists of 1898** (1936) is still useful. Walter Millis' *The Martial Spirit** (1931) is another older account that points up the errors that eventually led to the Spanish-American War. Frank Freidel's *The Splendid Little War* (1958) is an extensively illustrated account of the Spanish-American War. In *Twelve Against Empire* (1968) Robert L. Beisner provides an important study of those who opposed expansion.

The foreign policy of Theodore Roosevelt is examined in Howard K. Beale, *Theodore Roosevelt and the Rise of America to World Power** (1956), and in Raymond Esthus, *Theodore Roosevelt and Japan* (1966), which may be compared with Charles E. Neu's study of Japanese-American relations, *An Uncertain Friendship* (1967). A. Whitney Griswold's *The Far Eastern Policy of the United States** (1938) remains useful. Robert E. Quirk examines one aspect of Wilson's Mexican policy in *An Affair of Honor** (1962).

*Available in paperback edition

CHRONOLOGY

1900   Presidential election: William McKinley (Republican) defeats William Jennings Bryan (Democrat)

1901   McKinley assassinated; Theodore Roosevelt becomes President

1902   Roosevelt intervenes to settle coal strike

1904   Supreme Court rules against Northern Securities Company
Lincoln Steffens' "The Shame of the Cities" published
Presidential election: Theodore Roosevelt (Republican) defeats Alton B. Parker (Democrat)

1905   Supreme Court rules against laws regulating maximum hours in *Lochner* v. *New York*, a precedent modified in *Muller* v. *Oregon* (1908)
Founding of Industrial Workers of the World

1906   Hepburn Act gives ICC power to set railroad rates

1907   Financial panic

1908   Presidential election: William Howard Taft (Republican) defeats William Jennings Bryan (Democrat)

1909   NAACP founded

1912   Presidential election: Woodrow Wilson (Democrat) defeats Theodore Roosevelt (Progressive) and William Howard Taft (Republican)

1913   Underwood-Simmons tariff reduces duties
Federal Reserve System established
Sixteenth Amendment (permitting income tax) ratified; Seventeenth Amendment (providing for direct election of Senators) ratified

1914   Clayton Antitrust Act and Federal Trade Commission Act complete Wilson's New Freedom program

1916   Wilson prods Congress to enact more social legislation
Presidential election: Woodrow Wilson (Democrat) defeats Charles Evans Hughes (Republican)

XVII

PRESIDENTS

AND PROGRESSIVES

The message Theodore Roosevelt sent to Congress in December, 1901, began appropriately with grief for his murdered predecessor and closed with sympathy for the British people on the death of their Queen. The passing of William McKinley and Queen Victoria marked the end of the nineteenth century; the presidency of Theodore Roosevelt symbolically opened the twentieth. Much of the old endured; in many respects, Theodore Roosevelt was as Victorian as the Queen. But he foreshadowed the future as well—the fifteen years Americans have called the progressive era.

These years were years of change or perhaps of the recognition that unassimilated change had already occurred. Most progressives knew the economic revolution of the recent past was responsible for conditions that made old axioms suspect. When Theodore Roosevelt left the White House in 1909, 1 percent of the nation's businesses manufactured 44 percent of the total output, and the richest 1 percent of the population owned nearly half the nation's property. These statistics challenged the economic maxims about free enterprise and the moral homilies about thrift and opportunity that Americans for generations had accepted without question.

Change had other dimensions as well. There were more Catholic churches and more Italian and Slavic names. Membership in the AFL

Theodore Roosevelt: progressive leadership

increased four times in a dozen years. Socialists elected mayors and legislators in Massachusetts, congressmen in Wisconsin and New York, and made an impressive showing in Los Angeles. Some painters experimented with nonrepresentational art, while others turned their talent to social purposes, with stark depictions of scenes from the slums. Sentimentality and rhyme disappeared from the work of many first-rate poets. Clergymen discovered social justice and preached the social gospel. And the nation optimistically set out to make everything right again.

Not everyone caught the fever. The weary, the old, the apathetic, the cynical, the disfranchised, the perpetually poor, the newly rich, and the contentedly immoral were impervious to the progressive impulse. But the energetic, the young, the optimistic, the educated, the urban professional with an active conscience, and the patrician with a comfortable inheritance poured their hopes into the progressive cause.

The movement was full of contradictions. It included such men as the agrarian fundamentalist William Jennings Bryan and the urban atheist Clarence Darrow; Socialist Eugene Debs marked the left boundary and the conservative Republican William Howard Taft perhaps marked the right. After scoffing at Populism in the 1890s, progressives proudly enacted much of the Populist program, including direct primaries, income tax, currency reform, and several curbs on the power of business. Progressives believed in both competition and industrial efficiency, which were often incompatible. They favored both economic individualism and social justice, which sometimes conflicted. And they advocated democracy, until the voters selected unprogressive men.

Progressives thought, as a matter of course, that good men made good choices, that all decent Americans behaved just like the progressives themselves. Their moral assumptions ordinarily formed the unexamined premises upon which their political and economic programs were based. Progressives worshipped a Protestant God and espoused an individualistic creed derived from John Calvin by way of Benjamin Franklin, Andrew Jackson, and Andrew Carnegie. They were sure that personal effort and thrift advanced both the individual and the society. They revered orderly procedure and respected the rights of property. William McKinley would have approved their fiscal policy and Horatio Alger their faith in social mobility. Their emphasis on competition may have owed something to Charles Darwin, and their stress on morality unquestionably owed much to Christianity.

Progressive reform was part of what the philosopher George Santayana called "The Genteel Tradition," and, as the phrase implied, such reform was tinged with condescension. A few of the more humble reformers understood that their proposals were *for*, rather than *of*, the people, all of whom did not share progressive preconceptions. But few reformers ever wondered, for instance, whether honest government really made ordinary voters happier, whether competition effectively met the economic needs of the whole population, or whether Anglo-Saxons in fact had an innate edge over everyone else. When, by progressive standards, people chose unwisely, reformers turned from choices to laws and wrote their moral assumptions and their versions of reform into the statute books. When black southerners voted for white conservatives, progressives helped to disfranchise the blacks and then rationalized their action as reform. When immigrants resisted Anglo-Saxon manners and creeds, progressives joined those who wanted to restrict immigration. When drinkers would not voluntarily abstain, progressives enacted prohibition. And when some Americans tried to use democratic procedures for "unprogressive" ends, progressives restricted political discourse as no one had since the Federalists. Progressives condoned forcing the correct choice in the service of a righteous cause.

LOCAL PROGRESSIVE ACTION

Progressivism was flourishing before Theodore Roosevelt discovered it. In thousands of communities respectable citizens united to do battle with the county political "ring" or with the boss who presided over a community's contracts and payroll. These local reform movements responded to local needs in demanding parks, schools, and public transportation, higher wages and shorter hours for municipal employees, municipal home rule and more democratic local government, municipal ownership of utilities or public regulation of their rates, more equitable taxation, assimilation of immigrants, and, above all, clean elections and respectable political leaders. Tammany Hall in New York, the nation learned, was only the most notorious machine; others in Pittsburgh, St. Louis, Minneapolis, and elsewhere were only less candidly corrupt. But in Cleveland, where Mayor Tom Johnson flamboyantly fought "the interests," in Toledo under

Mayor Samuel M. "Golden Rule" Jones, in Detroit, and in smaller cities across the land progressives happily attacked the status quo.

The status quo proved resilient and had several prepared lines of defense. As one frustrated reformer said: "When I was in the city council . . . fighting for a shorter work day, [my opponents] told me to go to the legislature; now [my fellow legislators] tell me to go to Congress for a national law. When I get there and demand it, they will tell me to go to hell." This buck-passing from one level of government to another drew progressives first into state governments, which enacted many progressive proposals, and then into national politics.

In Iowa, where Jonathan Dolliver challenged stand-pat Republicans, in Georgia, where Hoke Smith challenged stand-pat Democrats, in California and New Hampshire, where Hiram Johnson and Robert Bass challenged railroads, and in other states under other men, progressives gathered support. Robert F. Wagner, a German immigrant who represented part of New York City in the state senate, did not have the typical progressive's family background, but the bills he introduced made him part of the movement. He asked for the direct election of senators, direct primaries, the short ballot, and the vote for women; he proposed to regulate child labor and get minimum wages for women; he wanted to permit the cities to own utilities and the state to conserve water resources.

Robert M. LaFollette gave Wisconsin the driving leadership that made the state the "laboratory of democracy." For a quarter of a century LaFollette's magnificent voice was the voice of reform, and for longer than that his imprint remained on his state. LaFollette goaded Wisconsin into enacting a direct primary, conservation measures, regulation of railroads, banks, and lobbyists, and new tax laws, including an income tax that demanded more of corporations and railroads. The political organization that LaFollette built in Wisconsin was unquestionably a machine, but it unquestionably produced responsive, honest government for the people of that state and served as a model for reformers in the rest of the nation.

In 1906, the year that Wisconsin sent Robert LaFollette to Washington, progressive journalists had identified the Senate as the graveyard of reform. Earlier that year, David Graham Phillips had written a trenchant article entitled "The Treason of the Senate" that gave substance to the popular belief that a clique of millionaires and corporate lawyers ran the upper chamber as a gentleman's club. Phillips' article inspired President Roosevelt to denounce the "muckrakers" of contemporary journalism who proposed no constructive remedy for the sordid conditions they exposed. Characteristically, Roosevelt in the same speech also attacked manipulators of corporate securities, but his phrase about the muckrakers of reform lingered longer in the imagination of the public.

Muckraking had become by 1906 a phenomenal publishing fad. In 1903 the January issue of *McClure's Magazine* proclaimed open season on "the interests" with three articles exposing malfeasance in government, business, and labor. One article was an installment of the influential series called "The Shame of the Cities" by Lincoln Steffens. Another was part of Ida Tarbell's critical history of the Standard Oil Company, which

Suffragettes: Their amendment was finally ratified in 1920.

revealed the abuses of industrial competition and the overweening power that resulted from competitive survival. Ray Stannard Baker's article on "The Right to Work" condemned racketeering among labor union officials. S. S. McClure's editorial called attention to "the arraignment of American character" contained in the three articles and suggested that such conditions existed only on the sufferance of complacent citizens. While Steffens indicted corrupt politicians, Tarbell greedy businessmen, and Baker powerful labor barons, McClure blamed the public that permitted its own exploitation.

Other magazines—*Cosmopolitan, Munsey's, American*—copied McClure's successful formula. If the flurry of activity that greeted each new exposure was usually temporary and inconclusive, some of the literature brought results. Lincoln Steffens' assault on urban corruption stimulated reform movements in San Francisco and Kansas City, which Steffens had not even written about, as well as in Philadelphia and Kansas City, which he had. Upton Sinclair's *The Jungle*, a harrowing account of working conditions in the stockyards, and Charles Edward Russell's series of articles on the beef trust aroused popular concern that helped secure passage of the

Meat Inspection Act in 1906. But the Meat Inspection Act was not exactly what either had had in mind; Sinclair thought he was making a case for socialism and Russell's concern was economic power.

Ray Stannard Baker's *Following the Color Line* (1908) did not even produce an unintentional result. For the black was progressivism's forgotten man. Nice people, progressives believed, helped uplift dark-skinned people in the Philippines or the Caribbean, but equality for those on the other side of town was out of the question. The California progressive excluded the Oriental almost as ruthlessly as the southern progressive excluded the black. The racism of northern progressives was less visible and less conscious, but nonetheless present. Theodore Roosevelt ate lunch and discussed patronage with Booker T. Washington at the White House, but southern delegations to the Progressive party's convention in 1912 were lily white, and Roosevelt himself squelched demands that a pledge of racial equality be included in the platform. Woodrow Wilson permitted southern postmasters to drop blacks from the federal payroll and allowed segregation to become the rule in the federal civil service. Progressives not only accepted disfranchisement and segregation; they often wrote the laws themselves. Racism, Baker observed, was the white man's problem. The southern black was manifestly subject to the white man's whim; whites would construct twentieth-century southern society. And they did it, of course, by leaving the blacks out.

A few progressives of both races established the National Association for the Advancement of Colored People in 1909. To edit its journal, *The Crisis,* the NAACP hired W. E. B. DuBois, a brilliant young northern-born black with a doctorate from Harvard and several books to his credit, including the anguished autobiographical *Souls of Black Folk.* But neither *The Crisis,* nor its angry editor, nor the organization's legal efforts to secure

Roosevelt addresses Negro Business League. Booker T. Washington is seated at Roosevelt's left.

equality ruffled the white community, which preferred to keep the black firmly and quietly in his subordinate place.

COPING WITH CHANGE

Progressives sought reform partly to impose order on change that seemed incomprehensibly rapid. Wasteful lumbering methods, for instance, would soon strip the nation of timber unless intelligent conservation practices were adopted. The widening gap between rich and poor and the radicals who pointed to it endangered social stability. Orderly change would provide lumber for present and future building; moderate economic reform would disarm radicals and bring social harmony and political stability. Cautious reform was the progressive means; harmony and stability were the ends.

Economic rationalization—the process of efficiently organizing the economy instead of trusting the random disorder of competition—appealed to businessmen as a means of controlling change. The process was by no means complete in the progressive era, but economic rationalization had begun and the prophets were persuasive. Frederick W. Taylor used time-and-motion studies to determine the most efficient use of worker, machine, and plant; his system of scientific management was widely imitated. The creation of a Graduate School of Business Administration at Harvard University testified that business had become a profession for trained men, not a competitive jungle. Smaller manufacturers banded together in the National Association of Manufacturers to promote common interests through the press and the legislatures. Other industrialists joined with conservative labor leaders in the National Civic Federation, which advocated an early form of welfare capitalism and the arbitration of industrial disputes.

Theodore Roosevelt accepted the conventional wisdom of his day, which held that consolidation was the inevitable result of competition: "This is an age of combination," he remarked in 1905, "and any effort to prevent all combination will be not only useless, but in the end vicious. . . ." Yet the trusts must behave; they must not take advantage of their economic power to cheat the public. Roosevelt distinguished early between tolerable "good" trusts and "bad" trusts, which must be taken to court. Almost every progressive eventually made a similar judgment in order to restrict the power of business while preserving its efficiency. "I am for big business," said Woodrow Wilson, making Roosevelt's distinction in other words, "and I am against the trusts." The Supreme Court drew a similar line when it dissolved Standard Oil in 1911 with a decree that distinguished between "reasonable" and "unreasonable" restraint of trade.

The Court, like the other branches of government, found the pace of change confusing and had great difficulty separating the individual's economic rights from his social responsibilities. By the 1920s the justices had embraced laissez faire, but earlier decisions are less consistent. In 1898, for instance, in *Holden* v. *Hardy,* the Court held that Utah could legitimately set an eight-hour work day for miners and smelters. But in 1905, in *Lochner* v. *New York*, a law restricting bakers to a sixty-hour week was thrown out as an unjustifiable limitation on freedom of contract. Three years later Louis D. Brandeis presented a brief that relied on sociological statistics rather than legal precedent to demonstrate that long hours impaired the health of working women. In *Muller* v. *Oregon* (1908), the Court accepted Brandeis' argument and sustained a state law limiting women to ten-hour work days. Although the Lochner precedent was not mentioned, many constitutional authorities thought it had been superseded. Yet later, in *Adkins* v. *Children's Hospital* (1923), the Court brushed off the Muller precedent and cited Lochner in declaring unconstitutional a federal statute limiting the working hours of women in the District of Columbia. Evidently the Court was unsure of the proper role of the state in the economy.

The Court was, however, consistently opposed to labor unions. Although suspicious of the Sherman Act when corporations were on trial, the federal courts had no difficulty applying the statute to unions. In *Loewe* v. *Lawlor*, in 1908, the Court forbade the secondary boycott, the device whereby one union cooperated with another in withholding patronage or respecting pickets. Samuel Gompers and the AFL asked both parties to promise legislation to upset the decision, and the union endorsed the Democrats in 1908 when they responded. But Democrats did not win in that election, and neither, in general, did unions in the progressive era.

With the reluctant help of President Roosevelt, the United Mine Workers did win a partial victory in 1902. The anthracite miners, ably led by John Mitchell, walked out in the early summer. They demanded recognition of the union, substantial wage increases, reforms in the method of measuring their output, and other changes. As summer turned to fall and coal stocks dwindled, the railroads that controlled the mines held fast to the divine right of property. But Republican congressional candidates in the chilly East demanded a quick settlement, and Roosevelt stepped in. When management proved stubborn, Roosevelt invoked J. P. Morgan's aid, and the combination of government and Wall Street induced the owners to agree to a compromise settlement by arbitration. The arbiters awarded the miners a 10 percent raise but denied recognition of their union, and the strike ended.

REGULATION UNDER ROOSEVELT

Specific governmental action to prevent specific abuses, Theodore Roosevelt came to believe, served the public more effectively than indiscriminate competition. In his first message to Congress, following several reassuring remarks about the need for "calm inquiry and . . . sober self-restraint," Roosevelt had gingerly called for public protection from the predatory trusts and for additional regulation of railroads. Since regulation imposed order and reduced the number of imponderables that businessmen encountered in competitive enterprise, federal regulation was less abhorrent to many large businesses than the rhetoric of laissez faire suggested. And the alternative of state regulation, with dozens of different and perhaps conflicting codes, frightened any corporate executive interested in a national market. As the *Wall Street Journal* noted at the end of 1904:

> . . . as between governmental regulation by forty-five states and governmental regulation by the . . . federal government, there can be but one choice. . . . The choice must be that of a federal regulation, for that will be uniform over the whole country and of a higher and more equitable standard.

Besides, federal standards of quality or federal labor regulations might well reduce competition from marginal producers whose profit depended on selling a shoddy product or exploiting their workers. For competition remained in spite of consolidation. The share of the market held by United States Steel, for instance, dropped steadily between 1901 and 1920. Regardless of Standard Oil's market dominance, the number of major oil-refiners increased. Competition was the rule among telephone companies at the beginning of the century, and consolidations in copper-mining and meat-packing gradually lost in their effort to control their respective markets. Major meat-packers, indeed, apparently welcomed federal meat inspection as a way of protecting themselves from the competition of fly-by-night slaughterhouse operators. Before Congress passed the Meat Inspection Act in 1906, J. Ogden Armour, owner of a major Chicago packing firm, noted that *"No packer can do an interstate or export business without government inspection."* Inspection protected the public, but it also protected the large producer from unscrupulous competitors. The Pure Food and Drug Act, also passed in 1906, had similar advantages both for the public and for large producers.

Responsible railroad men had long understood the benefits of regulation. The Elkins Act, passed in 1903, forbade rebates as had the Interstate Commerce Act some years before. The practice was, however, more carefully defined so that the shippers who received rebates, as well as the railroads that paid them, were liable to punishment. Most railroads, no longer anxious to preserve their competitive right to give rebates, supported the bill.

The Hepburn Act, which Congress passed only after adept presidential intervention in 1906, was another matter. When a shipper complained, this law gave the Interstate Commerce Commission the power to set rates and forced the railroad to go to court to challenge them. The ICC also received regulatory jurisdiction over pipelines, express companies, and ferries and the authority to examine a corporation's financial records to establish equitable rates. To get the bill through, Roosevelt threatened conservatives with a reduction of the tariff and progressives with no legislation at all; he used Democrats when his own party balked. Progressives like LaFollette protested that unless the ICC had the authority to establish independently the value of a railroad's property, the right to set rates was meaningless. LaFollette's charge proved correct, and Congress soon had to remove the loophole. But Theodore Roosevelt settled for the measure that his sense of political timing told him he could get, rather than risk no legislation at all.

Roosevelt's efforts to strengthen the ICC indicated his reliance on governmental regulation to prevent the abuse of economic power. His failure to use the Sherman Act disclosed his lack of faith in competition. Paradoxically, Roosevelt gained an undeserved reputation as a trust-buster from one important case against the Northern Securities Company, the holding company that controlled the railroads of the Northwest. Behind the Northern Securities Company were some of the most important names in American finance: J. P. Morgan and Jacob Schiff of Wall Street and railroad tycoons E. H. Harriman and James J. Hill. When in 1904 the government won the suit, the Sherman Act and the power of the public seemed enhanced; the verdict confirmed that the public, represented by its agent, the government, had property rights too. The restatement of the public's rights had immense political significance, and the decree reasserted Washington's role in economic decision-making. But dissolving the company had little direct economic effect. The promoters of the monopoly went unpunished. Morgan and Schiff continued to cooperate with one another and even with Theodore Roosevelt, to whose presidential campaign in 1904 they contributed a total of $250,000.

Roosevelt understood politics; his knowledge of economics was rudimentary. When a sharp panic buffeted the nation's banks in 1907, Roosevelt was nearly as bewildered as the general public. Lacking a program and the theoretical means of formulating one, the President relied on the advice of men from Wall Street whom he considered trustworthy. Morgan and Judge E. H. Gary of United States Steel offered to purchase control of Tennessee Coal and Iron from a distressed firm in New York, an action they said would restore confidence and avert the failure of several important financial institutions. Roosevelt agreed not to invoke the Sherman Act, even though the acquisition of an important competitor certainly enhanced the dominance of Gary's firm in the steel industry. Subsequently the panic subsided, for reasons other than the merger, and Roosevelt's anxiety was relieved.

The President knew that economic distress meant political disaster, and his political sense was as acute as that of any other American of his day. While he deprecated professional politicians, his control of his party was the envy of all professionals, and his contact with most of them in Congress was cordial. He easily secured his own nomination in 1904 and dictated that of William Howard Taft in 1908. With exuberant overstatement and a superb talent for public relations, the President converted modest advances into momentous triumphs, for which he claimed, and duly received, public praise. He was, as a progressive social worker observed in 1912, "America's first publicity man." Cautiously at first, but with increasing assurance after he secured his own political mandate in 1904, Roosevelt publicized what he called "reform," which he made more fashionable than did any muckraker. In the process, of course, he drew attention both to himself and to his office. Roosevelt's tenure in the White House left the public accustomed to dazzling presidential leadership. The dynamic modern presidency, in which the chief executive serves as the political representative of all the people, as the initiator of legislation, and as the defender of the interests of the inarticulate public is a legacy of the progressive years.

Roosevelt and Taft, 1909

THE UNHAPPY PRESIDENCY
OF WILLIAM HOWARD TAFT

No one ever described Taft as dynamic. As Roosevelt's Secretary of War and all-purpose trouble-shooter, Taft had been a loyal, effective administrator. He was well educated, genial, placid, and pledged to continue Roosevelt's policies. He preferred seclusion and calm to the exhilaration of partisan politics. In his quiet way Taft registered a few presidential accomplishments. But the public was no longer accustomed to quiet presidential ways, and Taft's four years in the White House turned into a prolonged political uproar that drowned out an impartial consideration of what the President did.

Taft believed the Sherman Act was "a good law that ought to be enforced. . . ." In four years, his administration instituted twice as many anti-trust proceedings as had Roosevelt in eight. Taft's decision to use the Sherman Act against United States Steel in 1911 outraged his predecessor. In spite of Roosevelt's prior permission, the government asked the company to give up Tennessee Coal and Iron, an action that caused Roosevelt to declare unregulated competition as anachronistic as giving flintlocks to the army. Yet to the public Roosevelt was a trust-buster and Taft had an unmerited reputation for standing pat.

In railroad legislation also Taft thought he was advancing along the course Roosevelt had charted. The Mann-Elkins Act of 1910 once more expanded the jurisdiction of the ICC, this time to include telegraph and telephone lines. The Commission was also empowered to initiate rate schedules without requiring a prior public complaint; once the rate was established, the carrier had to prove the schedule unfair. The new law, like the Hepburn Act, provided no method of impartially evaluating the railroad's capital investment, which had an immense effect on costs and therefore on rates. But the Physical Valuation Act, passed three days before Taft left office in 1913, remedied that defect. Although the President quietly encouraged his own state to ratify the constitutional amendment permitting a federal income tax, progressives remembered instead that he had publicly opposed a tax before there was an amendment. Taft took no public position on the amendment permitting the direct election of senators, but by 1912, when Congress sent the proposal to the states, he was popularly supposed to oppose all progressive change.

This supposition, as the record indicates, was not correct, but Taft had no one to blame but himself. He shunned the public and had no gift for speaking. He managed ineptly almost all his contacts with politicians. When Taft sought the middle of the political road, he alienated progressives without reconciling conservatives. Roosevelt's path to political success led Taft straight to political purgatory.

It all began even before Taft was inaugurated. The rules of the House of Representatives permitted a Speaker to dictate the committees and nearly to shape the legislation as he chose. Joseph Cannon, usually called "Uncle Joe," a ruthless, cynical conservative from Illinois, used all the Speaker's powers. A group of Republican progressives led by George Norris of Nebraska proposed to strip the Speaker of some of his power when the new Congress opened after Taft's inauguration. Taft disliked Cannon and at first encouraged Norris' insurrection. But Roosevelt and Nelson Aldrich, who was Cannon's counterpart in the Senate, pointed out that the insurgents lacked the votes. If his administration opened with a disgruntled Speaker, Taft was told, his legislative program would be stillborn. Aldrich and Cannon promised the President their cooperation in his effort to reduce the tariff, and Taft let it be known publicly that he supported the Speaker's traditional powers. Two years later, when the question came up again, Taft once more backed Cannon. But this time Norris had enough support to change the rules and to remove the Speaker from the powerful Rules Committee. Cannon's defeat was also a defeat for the President.

Meanwhile, Taft had also lost the battle for a lower tariff. The Republican platform in 1908 had declared ambiguously for tariff reform, and the House reported a bill making significant reductions. But Senator Aldrich worked on the bill until more than 800 amendments made it more satisfactory to the party's eastern industrial constituents. Pressure from Taft improved the final Payne-Aldrich tariff, but it still outraged progressive Republicans of the Midwest. Taft's complacent remark that the law was "on the whole . . . the best tariff bill that the Republican party ever passed" did little to reconcile the insurgents.

Taft also alienated Theodore Roosevelt. Already uneasy about his successor when he retired to hunt African big game, Roosevelt came out of the bush in 1910 to find Gifford Pinchot bearing tales of Taft's betrayal. As Chief Forester, Pinchot had been one of Roosevelt's closest associates in his effort to conserve the nation's timber, water, and scenery. No achievement of his administration was closer to Roosevelt's heart than conservation. He had removed land from public sale, created national forests and parks, encouraged irrigation, sponsored dams, and held off the economic interests that wanted to convert public resources to private profits. Pinchot charged that Taft, abetted by Richard A. Ballinger, his Secretary of the Interior, had given up the cause.

In fact, the Ballinger-Pinchot controversy was not so simple as Pinchot claimed, and neither Taft nor Ballinger was a conspiring foe of conservation. But Ballinger had made available for sale public lands that had been withdrawn in the Roosevelt administration, and Taft had dismissed Pinchot's protests. Pinchot then took his case to Congress and to the press. A congressional investigation whitewashed Ballinger and Taft reluctantly fired Pinchot for insubordination, an action that neither Roosevelt nor conservationists forgave.

THE ELECTION OF 1912

Roosevelt, who had retired full of vigor, began to wonder whether Taft was, after all, the appropriate agent to carry out his policies. Robert La Follette, whom Roosevelt had never liked, was planning a campaign to commit the Republican party to progressive principles and to wrest the presidential nomination from Taft. Other progressives hesitated, hoping Roosevelt would lead the crusade. Roosevelt began speaking on political subjects in the summer of 1910, and what he said differed profoundly from what Taft had come to stand for. Progressives united behind Roosevelt when La Follette's health seemed to break in the midst of his exhausting campaign.

But as no one knew better than Roosevelt, Taft had a firm grip on the machinery of the Republican party. The President controlled the convention, received the nomination, gave his acceptance speech, and lapsed into almost complete inactivity for the rest of the campaign. To the strains of "Onward Christian Soldiers," Roosevelt's followers founded the Progressive party and made the Republican schism final. Roosevelt gave the new party a symbol with the remark that he was "strong as a Bull Moose." He began with characteristic élan to carry his New Nationalism to the country.

The "New Nationalism" was only a new slogan to describe what Roosevelt had been saying for some time. As President, he had suggested that regulation of big business was preferable to wholesale trust-busting. Regulation was the heart of the Progressive economic program, an emphasis that pleased George W. Perkins, the Morgan associate and industrialist who financed the campaign. Although some idealists resented the platform's omission of a pledge to enforce the Sherman Act, the rest of the document showed the influence of professional social workers and well-intentioned advocates of social justice in planks that demanded industrial safety, abolition of child labor, minimum wages for women, workman's compensation, and federal activity to improve the quality of rural life, to maintain the health of all citizens, and to preserve the beauty and resources of the nation.

The Republican split cheered the Democrats, who had lost four consecutive presidential elections. Convinced that Bryan could not win in

1904, the party had turned the nomination back to conservative eastern Democrats. But Alton B. Parker, a colorless New York judge, had been a poor match for Theodore Roosevelt, and almost by default Bryan had been nominated again in 1908, when he lost to Taft. The elections of 1910 brought a crop of new Democratic governors and control of the House of Representatives for the first time since 1892. Nineteen-twelve looked like a Democratic year.

It took forty-six ballots to find the candidate, but, in selecting Woodrow Wilson, Democrats chose well. A southerner by birth and upbringing, a northerner by education, an educator by trade, an upright Calvinist by conviction, conservative on economic matters but acceptable to Bryan and Democratic progressives, Wilson had impressive credentials. What he lacked was political experience, personal warmth, and the capacity to see the point of view of anyone else. In 1910 Woodrow Wilson had resigned from the presidency of Princeton to run for governor of New Jersey. As governor, he survived a widely approved fight with the bosses of his party and convinced the legislature to enact controls on railroads and utilities, to institute workman's compensation, and to adopt the direct primary. In 1912 his New Freedom was the major alternative to Roosevelt's New Nationalism.

On close inspection, the New Freedom looked quite like the old laissez faire. Roosevelt dismissed Wilson's program as "rural Toryism." Wilson responded that Roosevelt's notion of regulating business would end with business in control of government instead of the reverse; only competition, secured through enforcement of the antitrust laws, Wilson argued, would preserve economic democracy. He branded Progressive demands for more government as paternalistic assaults on personal freedom. Not government but the self-reliant individual, Wilson held, created social justice.

The election of 1912 justified change, although precisely what kind of change was not clear. Taft, the most conservative man in the field, won about 3.5 million votes and carried just two states. Nearly a million voters went to the other extreme and voted for the Socialist candidate, Eugene V. Debs. Roosevelt won over four million votes and 88 electoral votes from six states. Woodrow Wilson won the rest—over 6 million popular votes, a landslide victory in the electoral college, and a solidly Democratic congress.

WILSON'S FIRST TERM

Like Wilson himself, many of those Democratic congressmen went to Washington because the opposition had divided. Dozens of the legislators were new to Congress, and the party's congressional leadership had little experience directing a majority. The President filled the void. He was as active a President as Roosevelt had been and more of a legislative leader. He declared himself the people's lobbyist, and for the first time since John Adams, the President went to Congress to deliver his message in person.

He asked for a new tariff and a new banking system. In response the House produced the Underwood Bill, which lowered the general tariff level, ended protection of many items altogether, and added a small income tax

The Election of 1912

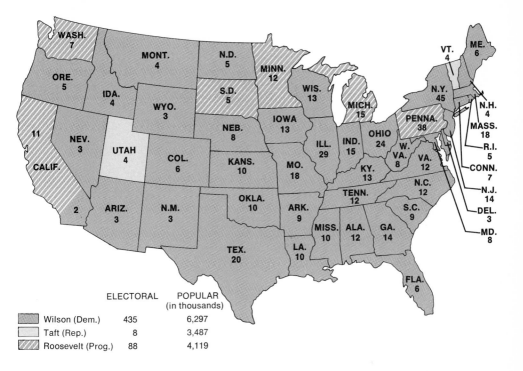

	ELECTORAL	POPULAR (in thousands)
Wilson (Dem.)	435	6,297
Taft (Rep.)	8	3,487
Roosevelt (Prog.)	88	4,119

to replace lost revenue. But tariff reform had come from the House before, only to die in the Senate. This time Wilson cajoled, pleaded, and invoked public support, and the Senate actually improved the Underwood tariff with additional reductions and a higher tax rate on larger incomes. Wilson finally signed the bill late in 1913; he had undertaken what Roosevelt had refused to undertake and succeeded where Taft and Cleveland had failed.

The panic in 1907 had shown the need for banking reform. The existing system was not sufficiently responsive to the demand for more currency to meet credit requirements in an expanding economy. In addition, a few Wall Street banks held the reserves of too many of the nation's smaller banks; these funds gave New York institutions great power and transmitted any tremor in the city's banking business to the rest of the country. The panic in 1907, for instance, began with a run on New York's Knickerbocker Trust Company. A commission headed by Senator Aldrich and a House committee whose chairman was Louisiana Democrat Arsène P. Pujo began investigating banking reform before Wilson's election. The Aldrich Commission recommended establishment of a new, privately managed central bank not too different from that of Alexander Hamilton or Nicholas Biddle. The Pujo report revealed that financial power was already too concentrated and recommended legislation to prevent further consolidation through interlocking directorates or the direct control by banks of insurance companies and industrial concerns.

The party of Andrew Jackson could not reestablish Biddle's bank, although the banking system did remain in private hands as the Aldrich

Commission had recommended. The Federal Reserve Act created twelve regional Federal Reserve banks, owned by the private banks of the district. To ensure stability, private banks had to keep a percentage of their assets on deposit in the Federal Reserve. The Federal Reserve banks issued legal-tender notes, which were an obligation of the United States government but were secured partly by gold and partly by the short-term commercial and agricultural loans made by member banks. This arrangement permitted expansion of the currency as the demand for credit increased, and the regional division permitted response to local conditions. A Federal Reserve Board, appointed by the President, gave central direction and public control. The rediscount rate—the charge made by the Federal Reserve for exchanging currency for the secured paper of member banks—was expected to help control fluctuations in the business cycle. In addition, the Federal Reserve could expand the supply of currency quickly by buying large quantities of federal bonds with Federal Reserve notes or take currency out of circulation by selling bonds and withholding the currency used to purchase them.

When the Federal Reserve Act passed in December, 1913, Woodrow Wilson thought his presidential mission virtually complete, for neither the New Freedom nor its author had set the government the task of securing social justice. Wilson refused in 1914 to support a child-labor bill and opposed measures to ease agricultural credit and to eliminate the injunction in strikes, because such bills were "class legislation." He did sign the La Follette Seaman's Act in 1915, which greatly improved working conditions for merchant sailors, but the administration merely accepted, rather than supported, the measure.

Wilson did not even have much interest in the "trusts," to which he had devoted so much campaign oratory in 1912. The administration lost enthusiasm for the Clayton Antitrust Act before it passed in 1914. The bill had been intended to strengthen the Sherman Act and at the same time exempt labor unions from antitrust prosecution. But the compromise that finally passed effectively did neither, even though Samuel Gompers chose to pretend that labor had won a political victory. The Wilson administration instituted even fewer antitrust suits than did the subsequent administrations of Presidents Harding and Coolidge, neither of whom was known as a trust-buster.

Instead, Wilson turned, as Roosevelt had, to regulation. Congress replaced Roosevelt's Bureau of Corporations with the Federal Trade Commission in 1914. The FTC was empowered to investigate corporations and to issue "cease and desist" orders to prevent unfair competitive practices. The Commission, Wilson's Secretary of Commerce wrote, was "a counsellor and friend to the business world," and not "primarily a policeman to wield a club over . . . the business community." Wilson appointed conservatives to the FTC (as he did to the Federal Reserve Board), and through consultation with concerned businessmen, the Commission helped provide efficiency and, in some cases, less competition among entrepreneurs.

The FTC resembled the New Nationalism rather more than the New Freedom. As the election of 1916 approached, Wilson borrowed several other items from Roosevelt's platform and appealed to former progressives

Child labor in a cannery

with an extraordinary year of legislative activity. In 1916, for the first time, Wilson responded to the demands of working people. Although he had opposed earlier attempts to prohibit child labor, he signed the Keating-Owen Act, which outlawed interstate shipment of goods produced by children. In 1919, after the Court, in *Hammer* v. *Dagenhart*, had declared the Keating-Owen Act unconstitutional, Wilson signed another law that attempted to prevent child labor with a confiscatory tax, which the court in turn struck down after Wilson left office. The Workman's Compensation Act (1916) insured federal employees against some of the hazards of accidents for the first time. Under the threat of a nationwide railway strike, Congress provided in the Adamson Act for an eight-hour day on the nation's interstate railroads. The President also pleased reformers by appointing Louis D. Brandeis to the Supreme Court and by withstanding the wave of conservative criticism that greeted the appointment.

Democrats also had to pacify farmers in 1916, particularly Bryan's followers who thought the Federal Reserve Act had done them less than full justice. Earlier, the Smith-Hughes Act (1914) had furnished funds to provide county agents to advise farmers on new agricultural techniques. In 1916 two acts made agricultural credit more readily available. The Warehouse Act was the old Populist subtreasury scheme under another name; it permitted farmers to use deposited crops as collateral for loans. The Farm Loan Act used federal funds as initial capital for twelve regional banks that were to finance farm mortgages at reasonable rates.

Wilson's record was remarkable and just barely good enough. He attracted some of Roosevelt's following when the Rough Rider's consuming interest in the European war led him to abandon the Progressive party with the suggestion that it nominate Henry Cabot Lodge, the thoroughly traditional senator from Massachusetts. Instead, the Progressive party collapsed. Republicans nominated Charles Evans Hughes, an associate justice of the Supreme Court who had been an able, progressive Governor of New York. The raging European war haunted the campaign, and by linking the moderate Hughes with the bellicose Roosevelt, Wilson appealed to the electorate's overwhelming desire for continued neutrality. Narrow margins in Minnesota and California provided the President's small majority in the electoral college; his edge in the popular vote was about 600,000 ballots. As his first term closed, Wilson had selected well from progressive proposals for social justice; in his second term, the effort to create a better society at home yielded to an attempt to make the world safe for democracy.

PROGRESSIVISM IN RETROSPECT

Progressives did not achieve either democracy abroad or social justice at home. They did make the domestic political process more democratic, and they curbed some of the worst excesses of selfish interests. They also left economic power largely undisturbed and perhaps even accelerated consolidation. And they clung so closely to traditional American values that they rejected out-of-hand those who suggested that self-reliance, for instance, might be a self-serving doctrine of the "haves" in an industrial society, and not an eternal truth.

Lawrence, Massachusetts, in 1912 was a community in need of social justice. Most of Lawrence's nearly 90,000 inhabitants were immigrants or the children of immigrants; 30,000 of them worked in the mills of the city, and fully two-thirds of the population was directly dependent on the textile industry. The average weekly wage of a textile worker in 1912 was $8.76, an amount that the Commissioner of Labor declared "entirely inadequate to sustain a family." An hour's labor bought a pound of hamburger or perhaps four eggs in the city's grocery stores. The census showed that on the average seven people lived in four or five rooms in Lawrence's tenements, and many families took in boarders to help pay the three-dollar weekly rent.

Under progressive pressure, the Massachusetts legislature reduced the standard industrial work week from fifty-six hours to fifty-four. But to the surprise of progressives, when the new law took effect, Lawrence's textile workers walked out spontaneously. Although less than 10 percent of the employees belonged to unions, workers of a dozen nationalities maintained a united front for two months. Police and inexperienced militiamen patrolled the city as social tension mounted and fear became almost tangible. The Industrial Workers of the World, a radical organization whose goal was the end of capitalism, heightened fear by taking over the strike and threatening to take over the mills and perhaps to take the city apart. Management eventually met almost every one of the strikers' demands.

The strike in Lawrence shows progressivism in a harsh light. The progressives who legislated a reduction in hours assumed that workers wanted leisure, as middleclass citizens did. But two hours less work meant two hours less pay, and the textile workers in Lawrence, already on the edge of subsistence, needed money more than leisure. Most progressives did not know the people for whom they thought they were acting any better than the Lawrence city missionary, a Protestant who lived in a plush suburb, knew the thousands of Catholic immigrants he was supposed to serve; his reaction to social conditions in Lawrence was surprise at how well the poor managed. The progressive was sympathetic and well intentioned. But the world of the immigrant industrial worker was simply not his.

And when the people progressives wanted to help tried to help themselves or rejected ready-made programs, the sympathy of progressives grew strained. They did not much like strikes and labor unions, for instance, or neighborhoods with strange music, foreign food, and strong drink, or bloc voting for Catholics, or any suggestion of socialism. Real unity among working people in Lawrence frightened the progressives of Massachusetts more than all the corporate capital in the East. The progressives did not want to redistribute wealth except among nice, middleclass people; they wanted to lift the worthy poor into the middle class. When working people had reservations about temperance, or remained loyal to a political boss, or when they were tainted with economic radicalism, the affronted progressive, as is the American way, advocated laws to curb such obstinacy. The disillusioned prewar progressive often turned into a staid supporter of the postwar status quo.

Suggested Reading

John M. Blum has written two outstanding brief, interpretive studies of progressive Presidents: *The Republican Roosevelt** (1954) and *Woodrow Wilson and the Politics of Morality** (1956). Elting E. Morison has edited eight volumes of the *Letters of Theodore Roosevelt* (1951–1954); Arthur S. Link is the chief editor of a similar project to publish the Wilson papers on a more extensive scale. Link has also written five volumes of biography of Wilson* (1947–65). Henry F. Pringle perhaps overstates the case for Taft in *The Life and Times of William Howard Taft* (1939).

Two complementary surveys of the progressive years are those of George E. Mowry, *The Era of Theodore Roosevelt** (1958), and Arthur S. Link, *Woodrow Wilson and the Progressive Era** (1954). In *The Age of Reform** (1955), Richard Hofstadter argues that the loss of status impelled progressives to reform, while Gabriel Kolko suggests in *The Triumph of Conservatism** (1963) that reform was minimal. Robert H. Wiebe has also studied the interaction of the reform movement and the business community in *Businessmen and Reform** (1962). Charles B. Forcey's *The Crossroads of Liberalism** (1961) is a study of the progressives who founded the *New Republic*. Henry F. May, *The End of American Innocence** (1959), examines the ideas of many progressive intellectuals.

*Available in paperback edition

CHRONOLOGY

1914   Outbreak of war in Europe.

1915   German U-boat sinks *Lusitania*
William Jennings Bryan resigns as Secretary of State, replaced by Robert Lansing

1916   *"Sussex* pledge" given by Germany

1917   Germany renews unrestricted submarine warfare; United States declares war
Railroad Control Act gives government right to operate American railroads
Espionage Act (amended in 1918 by Sedition Act)

1918   Overman Act grants President authority to mobilize economy
Wilson announces Fourteen Points
Republicans win congressional election
Armistice signed in Europe, November 11

1919   Negotiation of Treaty of Versailles
Wilson suffers stroke
Senate rejects Treaty

1920   Senate refuses consent to Treaty a second time

XVIII

THE GREAT WAR

AND THE LOST PEACE

Progressives conducted foreign policy with the same moral assurance that distinguished their assault on domestic social ills. "When properly directed," Woodrow Wilson once remarked, revealing at once the condescension, the self-righteousness, and the faith of progressives, "there is no people not fitted for self-government." As progressives were sure every decent American shared their aspirations, so they assumed that people of other, less fortunate, nations aspired to "the American way." And as progressives were sure every decent American shared their value system, so also they assumed that the values of the world's enlightened peoples coincided. The same confidence that led progressive politicians to seek the New Jerusalem in state legislatures led progressive diplomats to sign treaties to stop war. When the treaties failed, progressives fought a great war, that man might never have to fight another.

That Great War ended a century in which international conflicts had been limited. And it ended much more: dynasties, capital accumulated in the sweat of generations, a complacent faith in human progress, the conviction that civilization centered in Western Europe, and millions of lives. The First World War reduced Europe's economic and military edge over the rest of the world, sapped the vitality of Western democratic institutions, and snuffed them out completely in Russia. The war brought disillusionment that paralyzed postwar reform, economic   instability that precipitated a worldwide depression, and political upheaval that resulted in modern totali-tarianism in Germany and the Soviet Union. And the war's unsatisfactory peace made inevitable a rematch in the Second World War.

EUROPE'S WAR

Europe was ready for war before it came. Two alliance systems —Germany and Austria-Hungary arrayed against England, France, and Russia—ensured that no conflict would long remain local. And opportunities

to fight multiplied in the decade before 1914: Germany's drive for naval parity threatened England; British and French efforts to thwart German expansion annoyed Germany; Russia and Austria quarreled about the Balkans; every power watched for territorial opportunity in the decaying Turkish empire; trading concessions anywhere stirred jealousies throughout the continent. In the end, an assassination that grew out of Balkan rivalries sparked the explosion. Serbian nationalists killed the heir to the Austrian throne. An Austrian ultimatum demanded concessions Serbia thought humiliating. When the Czar backed the Serbs and the Kaiser backed the Austrians, the great powers could not halt the fatal progression. Russia ordered mobilization. In response Germany invaded France to eliminate Russia's Western ally. The campaign against France began with Germany's occupation of Belgium, whose neutrality Britain had guaranteed for nearly a century. So, in August, 1914, most of Europe found itself at war.

Few foresaw the costs. Every government expected to win a short offensive war before winter. German troops looked forward to leave in Paris, while Russian and French soldiers planned a gay rendezvous in Berlin. No one foresaw the way trenches, barbed wire, and machine guns would keep the world's most powerful armies penned in a small patch of French real estate for four bloody years. The war in Eastern Europe devastated more territory and reaped the same monotonous human harvest. The expected quick and glorious triumph became a sour stalemate from which no belligerent could gracefully retire.

Americans took sides in the struggle, although Woodrow Wilson's initial proclamation of neutrality had asked for absolute impartiality "in thought as well as in action." Some took sides because of sentimental or family ties with the "old country"; Irish-Americans, for instance, favored the Central Powers because any enemy of England was a friend of Ireland. Skillful Allied propagandists persuaded some Americans that Britain and France were defending humanity and civilization against German atrocities. Economic interest probably convinced some industrialists, investors, and bankers that virtue, as well as profit, was on the Allied side. Woodrow Wilson had long admired British scholarship and British parliamentary government; he personified the cultural link among English-speaking peoples. Members of the diplomatic corps understood that American security rested in large part on the British fleet. As a result, the United States had a strategic interest in maintaining the European balance of power that Germany intended to upset. In addition, the State Department had a tacit understanding with Great Britain that had grown since the Spanish-American war; German policies, on the other hand, had irritated American diplomats in discussions about Samoa, the Philippines, the Monroe Doctrine, and tariff reductions.

Whatever their prejudices and whatever their ethnic heritage, Americans vehemently opposed participation in Europe's war. They did not realize that a colonial empire and an industrial economy made obsolete the foreign policy devised for an isolated, agrarian nation. They believed their security, guaranteed since independence by two oceans, remained intact. Americans did not understand that submarines required a redefinition of the traditional rights of neutral nations. And most Americans did not even know that their defense budget had become among the largest in the world, a fact that every foreign ministry on the continent had to take into account. When they finally went to war, the American people naively assumed that their allies shared the aims and beliefs of progressive Americans: legal procedure, orderly progress, social justice, human decency. No nation ever went to war with more honorable intent; no nation ever made peace more selflessly; no nation ever calculated the designs of both friend and foe so badly.

AMERICA'S ATTEMPT TO STAY OUT

As signs of a coming conflict multiplied during the decade before the war, all the powers made gestures to strengthen the fabric of international peace. Theodore Roosevelt helped end the Russo-Japanese War in 1905 and used diplomatic pressure in 1906 to bring Germany and France to a conference at Algeciras that compromised their conflict over Algeria. With Secretary of State Elihu Root, Roosevelt supported international conferences at The Hague, which attempted to codify neutral rights and to devise automatic procedures for referring dangerous disputes to impartial settlement. Root himself negotiated twenty-four bilateral treaties, with every major power except Russia and Germany, that referred legal disputes to arbitration.

William Jennings Bryan thought the effort insufficient. "I believe that this nation could stand before the world today," Bryan proclaimed in 1910, and declare "that it did not believe in war, . . . that it had no disputes that it was not willing to submit to the judgment of the world." Three years later, as Wilson's Secretary of State, Bryan began to commit the country to that creed. He negotiated Treaties for the Advancement of Peace with thirty nations. These agreements automatically referred disputes to an investigatory commission. To permit a thorough investigation, neither party would increase armaments or resort to war for twelve months. Bryan's long public career gives no more apt illustration of his progressive faith in human reason:

> When men are mad, they talk about what they can do. When they are calm, they talk about what they ought to do. And it is the purpose of this plan to provide a time for passion to subside, for reason to regain its throne.

In August, 1914, no "cooling-off period" permitted reason to subdue passion, and Europe went to war. The initial public reaction in the United States was surprise, then panic, then a surge of Allied sympathy, and finally a fervent belief that neutrality best served American interests. Surprise came from a decade of false alarms and a rather general belief that humanity had outgrown tantrums and violence. Panic pervaded the financial centers, for 1914 was already a bad year, and the war threatened to interrupt international commerce. Without shipping, American goods could not reach foreign markets; without imports and the duties on them, the government lost about 40 percent of its revenue in 1914 and 1915. Sympathy for the Allies came from trade and tradition, and also from the German Chancellor's tactless dismissal of a broken treaty as a mere "scrap of paper." Yet neutrality was not only the safest policy—it was the most practical one as well, for the United States was not yet ready to dedicate its military capacity to a more resolute alternative.

Perhaps in a short war neutrality might have served. But as the war dragged on, the strategic needs of the belligerents and the economic interests of the United States combined to require constant diplomatic discussion. Traditionally, neutrals might sell, but not deliver, military equipment to belligerents; neutrals could use the sea only for commerce that did not directly contribute to the war machine of a belligerent; neutral citizens and ships had the right to a warning before attack, to legal process before confiscation, and to rescue if a vessel provoked hostility.

In practice, belligerents, not traditions, determine the rights of neutrals. A neutral nation has no appeal, short of abandoning neutrality altogether. Diplomatic initiative, then, lay in London and Berlin; Washington simply reacted. When Woodrow Wilson asked Congress to declare war in April, 1917, the responsibility for the decision rested as directly on the German Emperor and his government as it did on the President and his Cabinet.

SINKINGS BRING WAR

For more than two years before 1917, German strategists and diplomats had argued with one another and with Americans about the use of the submarine. Submarines simply could not abide by traditional rules for belligerent behavior; U-boats were too fragile to risk warning even lightly armed merchantmen and were too small to rescue survivors. Submarines could not establish blockades as surface vessels did. To be effective, undersea craft had to rely on stealth, which violated what Americans believed were their neutral rights.

Yet Germans, with considerable justification, argued that the American interpretation of neutral rights favored Great Britain. The British blockade effectively kept American goods from German markets, while the German effort to keep goods from Britain generated outraged protest in the United States. Germany charged that the British had violated American rights by confiscating products not previously defined as contraband and by interdicting the sale of food.

As the conflict became a war of attrition, Britain tightened the blockade and mined the North Sea; neutrals could secure a pilot who provided passage through the minefields only by opening cargoes to British inspection. British officials also examined American mail to trace German-American trade. The government published a blacklist of American companies doing business with Germany; to boycott these firms became an Englishman's patriotic duty. This blacklist was a tactless mistake, but

Britain made few others in probing the limits of American toleration. When the Cabinet prohibited the shipment of cotton to Germany, for instance, Britain offered to buy the entire American crop, if necessary, to sustain the price and to retain the good will of southern congressmen.

Eventually Germany's dilemma was reduced to its simplest form: unrestricted use of submarine warfare would bring American intervention. The German government decided to run the risk. In February, 1915, Germany declared that submarines would sink, without warning, vessels in the waters surrounding the British Isles. The State Department protested this abridgement of American rights for which Germany would be held to "strict accountability." In April one American was killed when a British vessel went down; on May 1 an American tanker was torpedoed. That same day the German embassy placed advertisements in New York papers advising Americans of the risk of travel on belligerent vessels, and American passengers boarding the British liner *Lusitania* received telegrams and subsequent oral warning of the dangers of travel in the war zone. On May 7, eighteen minutes after a torpedo had crashed into the *Lusitania*, she went to the bottom of the Irish Sea, taking 4,500 cases of ammunition and nearly 1,200 people with her, 124 of whom were Americans. It was a deed, the *Nation* charged, "for which a Hun would blush, a Turk be ashamed, and a Barbary pirate apologize." A

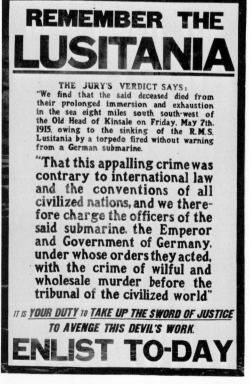

people that condoned such warfare had become "wild beasts against whom society has to defend itself at all hazards."

Shock, horror, anger, and incredulity—these were the popular responses to the tragedy. But in spite of the first moments of rage, the demand for a revenging war never came. "We must," one Baptist editor wrote, "protect our citizens, but we must find some other way than war." Secretary Bryan thought Wilson asked Germany to concede too much and resigned rather than sign a protest he thought too forceful. James W. Gerard, the American Ambassador to Berlin, wondered whether American tourists might not as conveniently sail on neutral ships to avoid diplomatic complications.

But Wilson and Robert Lansing, who succeeded Bryan, persisted in protracted negotiations to secure the full measure of neutral rights. Germany met most of Washington's demands with an apology, an indemnity, and secret instructions to submarine commanders not to attack passenger liners. In spite of this secret order, the British liner *Arabic* was torpedoed in August, and two American passengers died. Under diplomatic pressure from Wilson, Germany publicly promised not to sink unresisting passenger ships. In May, 1916, after a torpedo crippled the French steamer *Sussex*, endangering the twenty-five Americans aboard, Wilson prodded the German government to a promise to warn merchant vessels before attack. The condition of this *"Sussex* pledge" was that the United States require Great Britain to be equally scrupulous in observing the rights of neutrals. Wilson accepted the pledge, ignored the condition, and secured a lull of several months without submarine incidents. Although the Kaiser reversed himself early in 1917, Wilson had temporarily deprived Germany of the full use of a major weapon.

Wilson's persistence in holding Germany to his interpretation of international law contrasted with his forbearance in the face of Britain's failure to observe neutral rights. Historians have blamed one-sided economic commitment, British propaganda, and the Anglophile sentiment of the President and his advisers for this apparent favoritism. In fact, trade did flow predominantly to the Allies; trade and loans to the Central Powers between 1914 and 1917 totaled less than $250 million, while the Allies received more than $10 billion in credit alone. British propaganda may well have increased the enthusiasm of those who favored the Allies. Woodrow Wilson did indeed prefer the Allied side, and his administration, especially Secretary Lansing and Walter Hines Page, the Ambassador to England, were hardly neutral "in thought"; Lansing believed that German domination of Europe would be a diplomatic disaster for the United States. But Wilson's Anglophilia did not entirely determine his policy, for the "peace without victory" he hoped to secure did not coincide with Britain's ambitions. Moreover, Wilson did keep his nation neutral until Germany knowingly provoked intervention. Since there never was a possibility that the United States would ally with the Central Powers, Wilson's neutrality was the best Germany could hope for and about as impartial a posture as the United States could assume.

While Wilson attempted to keep successive crises from tugging his countrymen into war, he simultaneously launched a long-term effort to end hostilities and thereby prevent American intervention. Colonel Edward M. House, Wilson's closest adviser on foreign affairs, spent much of 1915 seeking a formula for mediation. In 1916, House and British Foreign Secretary Sir Edward Grey initialed a memorandum stating that the United States would "probably" join the Allies if Germany spurned a peace conference, but no belligerent was ready for the negotiated compromise Wilson had in mind. In December, 1916, Germany offered peace in return for annexations along the Baltic, domination of Poland, cessions from France and Belguim, and reparations—conditions that were entirely unacceptable to the Allies. Undaunted, Wilson tried once more to find an area of agreement to start negotiations. But at the end of January Germany renounced the earlier restrictions on submarine warfare. Wilson's peace efforts were obviously finished, his mediation firmly rejected.

MOBILIZATION AND WAR

The United States learned remarkably little from the war that raged in Europe for two years. That war clearly demanded mobilization of the whole nation, efficient use of industrial resources, psychological preparation for trench warfare, and new equipment—airplanes, gas masks, radios, armor. Yet no fact better indicates the nation's neutrality than its lack of preparation. When informed in 1916 that the army had begun to plan for American participation, President Wilson curtly told Secretary of War Newton D. Baker, "I think you had better stop it." Partly in consequence, a month after the American declaration of war the army still had no plan for moving American units to France and no strategic concept of what to do with them when they got there. The Army Reorganization Act of 1916 authorized a larger National Guard and a gradual increase to 200,000 men for the regular army; a year later, the army needed 200,000 *officers*, and had only about 9,000 in uniform. In 1916 the Signal Corps possessed precisely two radios and the Infantry 285,000 rifles. The Army's Chief of Staff was an authority on the languages of American Indians, which suggests that his combat experience was closer to the frontier than to French trenches. Three weeks after the declaration only 32,000 men had enlisted, a number far short of the million the administration wanted.

Wilson had decided to rely on conscription even before the first apathetic response to his call for volunteers. The President and Secretary Baker believed conscription was the most equitable way to recruit an army, and then went ahead in spite of the opposition of Champ Clark, the Speaker of the House. After the Selective Service Act passed in May, more than 24 million men registered, of whom about 3 million eventually served with nearly 2 million others who volunteered. Before the Armistice, more than 2 million Americans had landed in France.

Secretary Baker, General John J. Pershing, and General Peyton C. March successfully improvised in the absence of advance planning. Pershing, commander of the American Expeditionary Force, went to France in 1917 without strategic guidance, tactical plans, or soldiers. He insisted on inten-

General Pershing (hand on hip, left) insisted on trained troops.

sive training of American troops before committing them to battle and on adequate numbers before replacing embattled Allied organizations with American units. His estimate of the importance of training was correct, as was his decision to hold Americans out of major engagements until he had enough force to make a significant impact, for drooping morale in some Allied battalions might have infected American replacements.

Early in 1918, Pershing's growing forces met the enemy in the spring campaigns north of Paris. By late in the summer, 1 million Americans had come ashore in France; more than 250,000 were engaged in an Allied counter-offensive that eliminated a threatening German salient along the Marne River. In September Pershing took over the southern sector of the front near Verdun and began the first independent American operation of the war with an offensive in the Argonne Forest and along the Meuse River. The operation lasted a month, caused more than 100,000 American casualties, but forced the Germans to retreat and contributed significantly to their decision to seek an armistice in November. On November 11, 1918, when the Armistice was signed, the American army had occupied its own sector for just sixty days. The American contribution to victory on the Western Front was significant, but brief.

The United States Navy, in conjunction with the British fleet, whipped the submarine menace and deposited American troops in Europe without the loss of a single doughboy. The U-boat failed in part because of the addition of American vessels to those already hunting undersea craft. Probably more important than the additional ships themselves in saving lives and equipment was the convoy system that Admiral William S. Sims persuaded the British Admiralty to try. Military escorts, Sims correctly maintained, could protect merchantmen from marauding submarines. The convoys ensured the almost uninterrupted arrival of American troops and supplies and proved even to Germans the folly of their expectation that submarines could win the war.

American Operations on the Western Front, 1918

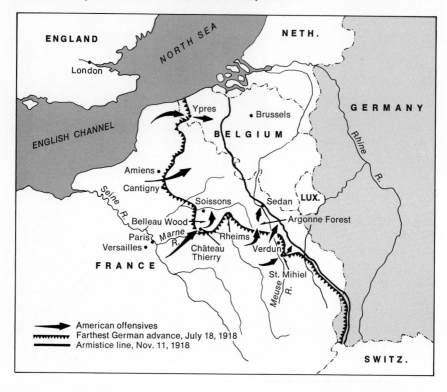

American offensives
Farthest German advance, July 18, 1918
Armistice line, Nov. 11, 1918

Preceding the military success in France there was a triumph of organization at home, a triumph that, like the one abroad, was secured only after false starts and at considerable cost. The army's procurement system, unable to adjust leisurely habits to more frantic times, bogged down in red tape. American quartermasters had no helmets; consequently British steel shielded American heads. Less than 500 of 3,500 artillery pieces in American batteries in France came from American arsenals; of the nearly 9 million shells those guns fired, about 8,400 were made in the United States. The American Expeditionary Force (AEF) received 7 million tons of supplies from home, and purchased 10 million tons in Europe, a statistic that suggests the Allies had not reached the last ditch when the United States entered the war.

Although the Armistice came before America had completed industrial mobilization, Wilson had found a way to harness the economy by 1918. The Lever Act of 1917 created federal agencies to raise production and control distribution of food and fuel. Under the direction of Harry Garfield, the son of the assassinated President, the Fuel Administration increased coal and oil supplies and incidentally encouraged the consolidation in both industries that inhibited postwar competition. The Food Administration, given imaginative leadership by Herbert Hoover, encouraged cultivation of "Victory Gardens" to give civilians a sense of patriotic participation. (President Wilson even grazed a few sheep on the White House lawn.) Hoover secured voluntary observance of wheatless Mondays and meatless Tuesdays to conserve staples. The Food Administration guaranteed the price of wheat, thereby bringing into production thousands of marginal acres that have since produced the surpluses which perplex agrarian economists.

Industrial mobilization demanded more than voluntary measures. Late in 1917, when the nation's railroads proved unable to cope with the tremendously increased volume of freight, Wilson ordered Secretary of the Treasury William G. McAdoo to run them. Three months later Congress passed the Railroad Control Act, which authorized federal management and fixed the compensation stockholders would receive. A National War Labor Board, approved by Samuel Gompers, recognized labor's right to bargain collectively but denied the right to strike in wartime. To organize American industry, Wilson turned to a successful Wall Street operator named Bernard Baruch. Wilson delegated to Baruch's War Industries Board the extraordinary regulatory authority that Congress conferred upon the President in the Overman Act of 1918. Baruch streamlined the American economy, allocated strategic materials without waste, and in the long run, reduced competition in the interest of industrial efficiency. Progressives had never dreamed of economic regulations on such a scale. Several thousand government agencies testified to the loss of individual liberty that accompanied the war effort.

DEMOCRACY AT HOME

Radicals, pacifists, and misfits felt that loss of liberty most acutely. The President's warning of June, 1917, was stern: "Woe to the man or group of men that seeks to stand in our way in this day of high resolution. . . ." War, as Wilson remarked on another occasion, demanded "force to the utmost, force without stint or limit." The steamroller state, with Wilson at the controls, flattened the domestic nonconformist with the same inexorable discipline and determination that General Pershing displayed in France. Unless a critic was of the stature of Theodore Roosevelt, whose criticism of Wilson was shrill and unchecked, he ran afoul of the Espionage Act of 1917 and the Sedition Amendment to that act, passed a year later. State statutes also promoted loyalty, and various unofficial agencies enforced their own brand of patriotic conformity.

The federal legislation outlawed disrespectful language about the flag, the government, or the armed forces and prohibited speech or action that interfered with the conduct of the war, conscription, or the sale of bonds. Congressional sponsors promised that these provisions would not stifle legitimate criticism, but even so enthusiastic a war hawk as Henry Cabot Lodge thought the act unnecessary. Lodge pointed out that the statute would not trap "a single spy or a single German agent," but rather was "aimed at certain classes of [domestic] agitators. . . ." He voted against the bill, which soon became the basis for the Attorney General's boast that ". . . never in its history has this country been so thoroughly policed."

Public pressure put an end to the performance of German music, instruction in the German language, and the careers of a few people with Germanic names. Patriotic policemen and prosecutors, with and without legal authority, hounded those whose patriotism seemed wanting. A New Yorker went to jail for circulating copies of the Declaration of Independence with the concluding question: "Does your government live up to these principles?" A Sacramento newspaper demanded dismissal not only of those teachers it believed disloyal but also of those who were "apathetic" toward the war. Automobiles belonging to pacifist Mennonites were seized, auctioned, and the proceeds used to purchase Liberty Bonds. Raids in Pennsylvania, Texas, Missouri, and California harassed Jehovah's Witnesses. Conscientious objectors faced military courts, military prisons, and physical abuse. A District Attorney in Los Angeles suppressed a film entitled "The Spirit of '76" because it showed British atrocities during the American Revolution and thereby criticized an ally; needless to say, another film called "The Beast of Berlin" passed his test. Yellow paint—on houses, automobiles, store fronts, and people—became a standard method of identifying wartime "slackers."

Less than a week after Wilson asked for the declaration, the Socialist party officially proclaimed the war a result of the international rivalry of predatory capitalism and pledged "continuous, active, and public opposition" to the struggle. Many Socialists promptly left the party. Those who remained and took their platform literally found judges ready to impose stiff sentences; whether sedition or economic radicalism provoked the sentences was never entirely clear. Eugene Debs opposed conscription, as did any number of congressmen, but a ten-year sentence in the Atlanta Penitentiary effectively removed the Socialists' best known speaker and candidate. Without a warrant, the government seized the party's national headquarters, rifled the files, and then indicted five members of the executive committee for conspiracy, all of whom eventually received twenty-year sentences. Although the Supreme Court ordered a new trial and none of the defendants actually went to jail, their conviction left the party without direction at a time when direction was sorely needed. When Milwaukee elected Socialist Victor Berger to Congress, the House refused to permit him to sit. When Socialists presented periodicals at the Post Office, federal officials declined to distribute them. When peace came, the comatose Socialist Party did not revive.

The Industrial Workers of the World never thought much of Socialists anyway. The radical union charged that Socialists were too full of talk and too reluctant to take action against capitalists and their industries. Most numerous in the mines, forests, and fields of the Pacific coast, the "Wobblies," as the members of the IWW were called, thought the war with Germany furnished a splendid opportunity to escalate their war with capitalism. It was a war the IWW lost, for the government moved swiftly to end the organization once and for all. A long federal trial removed the union's national officers. State prosecutors hustled strikers across borders to avoid legal process and penned other Wobblies in barbed-wire enclosures. Quasi-official lynchings occurred here and there along the Pacific coast. For a few concerned conservatives, the elimination of the Wobbly menace provided a silver lining in the dark cloud of war.

In addition to making dissent dangerous through sedition legislation, the government endeavored to stir positive support for war. The Committee on Public Information contrasted the unselfish American crusade with the German threat to Western civilization. Through the Committee's propaganda efforts, an extensive international audience read Woodrow Wilson's idealistic speeches. The CPI also furnished American journalists with guidelines that enabled them at once to promote the war and to avoid prosecution through "voluntary" censorship.

The editor of a black newspaper in San Antonio was not sufficiently discreet. Following a racial incident in Houston, for which military authorities hastily hanged thirteen black soldiers, the San Antonio *Inquirer* suggested that perhaps death in defense of black Texans was better than fighting in Europe "for a liberty you cannot enjoy. . . ." The judge awarded the editor two years for attempting to promote mutiny among the 360,000 blacks in the nation's service.

The migration of southern blacks to northern cities, which was to flood during the Second World War, began during the First. Northern employers lured southern sharecroppers from worn-out cotton land to dreary northern slums. But the blacks discovered that old prejudices persisted in new locations, and racial tension soon erupted into riots, of which the most prolonged took place in 1917 in East St. Louis, Illinois. The burning and killing along the Mississippi was less organized than along the rivers in France, but not less brutal. One outraged observer reported that black citizens endured atrocities "worse than anything the Germans did in Belgium."

The "war to make the world safe for democracy" did nothing for democracy at home. Racial equality, which blacks naively took to be a component of northern democracy, failed to materialize in segregated slums. The pressing demand for wartime efficiency submerged the progressive dream of economic individualism. In the administration of a Jeffersonian Democrat born in Jefferson's own state, freedom of speech did not include the right to question the President's judgment; among a tolerant people, religious toleration did not extend to those who took seriously the sixth commandment. The progressive crusade to crush tyranny abroad evidently required tyrannical conformity at home.

WILSON'S BLUEPRINT FOR PEACE: THE FOURTEEN POINTS

Woodrow Wilson thought permanent international peace worth its cost in temporary domestic compromise. He subordinated his progressive faith in individual liberty to the great end of the Great War. He asked the world to swear allegiance to the noblest elements of the Anglo-American tradition, to make a peace that secured every people an "equal right to freedom and security and self-government and to a participation upon fair terms in the economic opportunities of the world." So great was his belief in man that it survived successive disappointments as the French, the Italians, the Japanese, the British, and even his fellow countrymen persisted in protecting their national interest instead of doing their international duty.

The President disclosed his blueprint for peace in an address in January, 1918. Wilson's Fourteen Points showed that American belligerence had not altered his hope of securing a generous peace through personal mediation. The allied nations did not challenge some of Wilson's propositions, such as the evacuation of Belgium and the return of Alsace-Lorraine to France. Other propositions, such as the re-creation of Poland and the establishment of new nations from the remnants of the Austro-Hungarian empire, derived from Wilson's progressive belief in national self-determination. Tariff reduction and uninhibited commercial use of the oceans would reduce economic privilege and bind the nations together through trade. Finally, "a general association of nations" would preserve the peace Wilson's martyred generation had won.

Even as the President enumerated his fourteen idealistic points, Germany was dictating peace terms to Russia that were softened by no lingering idealistic scruple. The price of peace that Germany offered Lenin's new Russian regime was high and unnegotiable. Failure to halt the grinding war had already undermined the short-lived liberal government that had succeeded the Czars in March, 1917; to secure peace in March, 1918, Lenin agreed to give up territory that included most of Russia's iron and coal deposits, one-third of its industry, and one-fourth of its population. The Allies, however, refused to accept either the Russian Revolution or the peace that released thousands of Germans for duty at the western front. When diplomatic persuasion failed to keep Russia in the war, the Allies maintained thousands of troops in the Soviet Union. These forces protected Allied war materials, secured harbor facilities, and offered comfort and occasional aid to domestic (and presumably democratic) opponents of the Bolsheviks. After the Russians made peace, Wilson reluctantly agreed to small American expeditions to Murmansk and Siberia, a half-hearted and ultimately ineffective intervention that dragged on for nearly two years.

THE TREATY OF VERSAILLES

The Russian Revolution was a constant reminder of the incalculable cost of military exhaustion and political default, conditions that by mid-1918 prevailed in much of Central and Eastern Europe and were not unknown in the West. In October the German High Command decided to abandon the struggle and asked Wilson for an armistice based on the Fourteen Points. The President preferred to discuss peace with a representative government, a preference that was in part responsible for the creation of the fragile new German republic that had to complete the shameful capitulation. The Armistice of November 11 was in fact a disguised German surrender, for Wilson's terms deprived Germany of the capacity to renew the war. But German civilians greeted their returning veterans as heroes because no Allied armies had sullied German soil and because the Fourteen Points guaranteed an honorable peace.

Wilson's guarantee, a postwar generation of bitter Germans argued, was a high-sounding fraud. The proposed universal disarmament turned out to be German disarmament. National self-determination meant residence for thousands of Germans in Italy, Czechoslovakia, and Poland and precluded forever a union of Austrian Germans with their northern kinsmen. The equitable adjustment of colonial claims gave Japan the German possessions in the North Pacific and divided those in the South Pacific between Australia and New Zealand. Although Wilson had promised consideration of the interests of colonial inhabitants, the interests of the great powers clearly predominated; Britain and France, for instance, received control of the oil-rich areas of the Middle East.

As angry, helpless Germans discovered, the Treaty of Versailles was not entirely Woodrow Wilson's handiwork. Allied delegates worked in haste to provide a settlement that would isolate the Bolshevik menace: "Better a bad treaty today," ran conventional wisdom in Paris, "than a good treaty four months hence." Bolshevism was the backdrop for the peacemakers,

The "Big Four": (left to right) David Lloyd George (Britain), Vittorio Orlando (Italy), Georges Clemenceau (France), and Wilson

but the need of France for guaranteed security shaped the actual negotiations. In successive generations, German troops had twice overpowered their French opponents; only an extraordinary coalition had saved Paris the second time. Georges Clemenceau, the tough octogenarian Premier of France, meant to make sure that Germany had no third opportunity. Clemenceau raised no objection to Wilson's idealism until it inhibited French supremacy on the continent; at that point, Clemenceau became unyielding.

Under the circumstances, Wilson probably did about as well as any man could have. But to the distress of the Germans, he compromised on the Fourteen Points. To the distress of the ambitious Italians, he refused to regard as binding the Treaty of London, which had promised Italy the South Tyrol and territory at the head of the Adriatic. To the distress of the Japanese, Wilson appeared to keep a declaration of racial equality out of the Treaty, although he did not vote against it himself. To the distress of the French, Wilson blocked their possession of the mines of the Saar and their permanent occupation of the strategic Rhineland. To reassure Clemenceau, Wilson and the British Prime Minister David Lloyd George signed a security treaty that promised military assistance to counter future unprovoked German aggression. Germany had to confess responsibility for the war and assume unlimited financial obligation for damages. Wilson modified national self-determination in order to give Poland access to the sea, to satisfy Japan's economic demands in China's Shantung Peninsula, and to give Czechoslovakia defensible frontiers. Nevertheless, the terms of the Treaty of Versailles, and the subsequent treaties with the other Central Powers, were less severe than the promises the Allies had made to one another in their secret wartime agreements. Whatever his compromises, Wilson believed he had also created the agency to correct all the hasty mistakes of Versailles and of fallible statesmen to come. For the one point Wilson would not yield was the fourteenth; he wrote the Covenant of the League of Nations into the Treaty, and those who would accept the peace must accept the new association of nations that, Wilson fervently hoped, would keep it. Although the League lacked its own military force, Article X, which Wilson called "the heart of the Covenant," committed members to respect the political independence and territorial integrity of other members and to protect them from external aggression.

THE SENATE REJECTS THE TREATY

Fervent American nationalists like Henry Cabot Lodge and Theodore Roosevelt, both of whom had once had kind words for international peace-keeping, feared that Wilson's League would impair American sovereignty. No international body, warned the Treaty's opponents, could regulate American immigration, set American tariffs, limit American markets, send American troops into battle, or modify the Monroe Doctrine. Irish-Americans denounced Wilson's failure to press for Irish independence, and Italian-Americans, German-Americans, and Polish-Americans resented various territorial compromises. The President did little to disarm his domestic critics. While he accomplished many of his diplomatic objectives at Versailles, political blundering at home undid his achievement.

The mistakes began even before he sailed for France. Progressive ideology and Wilson's conception of the presidency required an appeal to the electorate to overcome partisan obstruction. But Wilson's last-minute plea for a Democratic Congress in 1918 brought only humiliation when his Republican foes won control of both houses. Resentment of presidential intervention probably cost the Democrats fewer votes than did prohibition, inflation, and pervasive war-weariness. But the President unwittingly converted a routine election that his party was likely to lose into an apparent vote of no-confidence in his own foreign policy.

Nor did Wilson conciliate either the Senate or the Republicans in selecting delegates to accompany him to Paris. He passed over the entire Senate, and only Henry White, a retired career diplomat, was even nominally a Republican. The President himself led the delegation, an unprecedented decision that personalized the Treaty. Secretary of State Lansing, Colonel House, and General Tasker Bliss, who had combined military and diplomatic assignments during the war, completed the group. A boatload of specialists advised the official delegation; after arrival in Paris, the advice of the specialists was seldom asked and even more rarely taken.

Wilson also ignored the counsel of House and Lansing, both of whom feared the President was failing to heed portents of the Senate's displeasure. In March, 1919, Senator Lodge, Chairman of the Committee on Foreign Relations, published a "round-robin" letter in which more than one-third of the Senate declared the Covenant unacceptable. Negotiators at Versailles, at Wilson's insistence, made gestures to relieve the Senate's apprehensions about tariffs, immigrants, and the Monroe Doctrine. To a suggestion that he permit further revision, Wilson peevishly responded that "the Senate must take its medicine."

Had the Senate acted quickly, Wilson might have had his way. Lifted by the President's rhetoric and elated by their military victory, most Americans probably approved the Treaty when Wilson submitted it to the Senate. Lodge waited for this initial enthusiasm to subside while opponents of the Treaty advertised its deficiencies. He packed the Foreign Relations Committee with Senators who advocated amendments, read the Treaty, line by tedious line, to the committee's stenographer, listened patiently to anyone with an objection, however trivial, and organized a campaign from the platform and in the press to alert the public to the need to "Americanize" (and "Republicanize") Woodrow Wilson's peace.

There was no love lost between Woodrow Wilson and Henry Cabot Lodge. Personal antipathy may have strengthened the President's resolve to resist compromise and the Senator's determination to amend the Treaty. But politics were more important than pique in setting Lodge's course. A split in his Republican party had permitted Wilson to become President. Disagreement among Republicans over the Treaty might renew that split and continue the party's exclusion from the White House. About a dozen Republicans, many of them veterans of the Progressive schism, opposed the League of Nations in any form. One of these "irreconcilables," Senator Hiram Johnson of California, was actively seeking the Republican presidential nomination; another, William E. Borah, threatened to bolt the party if Lodge did not commit the Republican majority to the defeat of the League. A dozen Republicans supported Wilson's treaty with slight modifications. And the remainder, among whom Lodge counted himself, favored attaching "strong reservations" to the Treaty to limit what they called Wilson's delegation of American sovereignty. Only a few Democrats, on the other hand, thought amendments necessary. Most of Wilson's party saw things Wilson's way.

The division of the Senate lent itself to several political strategies, but the President was unyielding. He would not compromise, although he needed two-thirds of the Senate and his own supporters numbered less than half. He would not accept even minor explanatory reservations to the Treaty, although he himself had prepared amendments that might have attracted enough Republican votes to carry the Treaty. He would not permit Democrats to support Lodge's more stringent reservations, although that course of action would almost certainly have resulted in ratification.

Lodge's reservations did not fundamentally alter the Treaty. But their phrasing and the name "Lodge" attached to them annoyed the President. Most of the reservations—including one on the Monroe Doctrine, one reserving to Congress the right to declare war, and one specifying exclusive national control of tariffs and immigration policy—could have been incorporated without modifying Wilson's objectives. Another reservation formally excepted the Shantung clauses from the Senate's approval, partly because those provisions were misunderstood to give Japan sovereignty in the area. Lodge permitted politicians with Irish constituencies to stand up to Great Britain with a gratuitous proclamation of American support for Irish independence. The most serious of the Lodge Reservations undermined Wilson's attempt to coerce future aggressors with international boycotts; Lodge's amendment would not promise automatic American support for economic sanctions.

Whatever the content, the tone of the Lodge Reservations was suspicious and grudging. Wilson believed that the American people supported the Treaty wholeheartedly. True to his progressive ideals, the President planned a whirlwind speaking tour to rally the nation and save the Treaty from mutilation. The tour would have taxed a young and vigorous statesman. Wilson was no longer young and eighteen months of wartime decisions, an exhausting round of negotiations in Paris, a slight stroke, and blinding headaches resulting from arteriosclerosis had all combined to deplete his vigor. His tour began without evoking much response but picked up momentum and support as he worked his way westward across the continent. And then, when he seemed on the verge of success, he collapsed in Pueblo, Colorado, and had to cancel his speeches for the rest of the trip. About a week after his return to Washington, Wilson suffered a disabling stroke that precluded all activity for three weeks and left him partially paralyzed for the rest of his life. The isolation of the sick room hardened his resolve, and he brusquely dismissed all suggestions of compromise as the Treaty neared a decision in the Senate.

In November, 1919, Lodge presented the Treaty with his reservations. Democrats and irreconcilables combined to defeat Lodge's motion, fifty-five to thirty-nine. Subsequent parliamentary jockeying in effect provided a vote on the Treaty with mild Democratic reservations, which lost, fifty to forty-one, when irreconcilables joined Lodge's forces. Finally, fifty-three senators voted not to consent to the Treaty as negotiated, and only thirty-eight stood up for Wilson's unamended document. The Treaty did not even achieve majority support, let alone the two-thirds of the Senate required by the Constitution. The Senate's action was not conclusive, however, and the Treaty came up for reconsideration in March, 1920. About half the Democrats decided that a treaty with reservations was better than no treaty at all; they joined twenty-eight Republicans in support of the Lodge Reservations. The remaining Democrats dutifully followed Wilson's demand to be counted for principle; they joined the irreconcilables. The forty-nine senators who supported the amended Treaty were seven votes short of the necessary two-thirds. And this time the question was closed.

THE END
OF THE PROGRESSIVE CRUSADE

The President's progressive faith survived even the shock of the Senate's vote. The people, he believed, would overturn the verdict in the coming presidential election, a "solemn referendum" on the League. Bryan, who knew better from his experience in 1900, remarked that the notion of conducting a presidential election as a referendum on foreign policy was quixotic. But Woodrow Wilson seems not to have realized that progressivism as he understood it had perished in the Great War. He wrote progressivism into the Covenant of the League of Nations, and his own people did not respond. He carried his crusade to those people, disabled himself in the process, and apparently changed not a single vote in the Senate. Although he kept pulling up a dry bucket, Woodrow Wilson still believed the well brimmed with public support.

The mistaken belief that he had public support had lured Wilson into serious political blunders in his second term. He assumed that the rest of the world shared his view of the war, whereas other people had simply used his magnificent phrasing to avoid deciding what the war was about. He mistook the adulation of throngs in Italy and France for support of his idealistic peace; in fact, the crowds cheered in anticipation of the rewards of military triumph. Not even his own people wanted a peace without victory; their version of a settlement was one that would make the world safe for the United States, whether or not the rest of mankind approved. Wilson overestimated the sophistication of his American audience, which preferred the comforting fantasy of isolation and diplomatic independence to his harder message of the collective responsibility of all great nations to preserve the peace for all mankind.

And, like many other progressives, the President misjudged the persuasive force of causes he believed morally right. Self-righteous himself, he failed to reckon with the power of political, economic, and diplomatic self-interest. Entrenched political bosses, corporations, and isolationist senators had resisted the progressive assault remarkably well. The military establishments of other nations, their economic interests, and their territorial ambitions also survived Wilson's onslaught. He had summoned the world's peoples to a moral crusade; they settled for bigger boundaries, punitive reparations, and what they thought was national security.

Because the United States was unready to accept the international role that Wilson envisioned, the decision to stay out of the League probably made little long-term difference. One more grudging great power in Geneva would not have prevented the Second World War. As it turned out, Britain and France converted the League to a quasi-alliance in defense of the status quo, and American policy in the interwar years would not have markedly changed the League's direction. The League never dealt with the unfulfilled national aspirations of Japan and Italy, with the legitimate desire of Germany for relief from an absurd burden of reparations, with the tensions caused by keeping the Soviet Union an international outcast, with the economic trauma of the great depression, or with the diplomatic trauma of renewed aggression. In an age of rampant nationalism, Woodrow Wilson unsuccessfully preached international cooperation; in an acquisitive time, he appealed to forbearance. He would not compromise, nor did he gladly suffer fools, foes, or inferiors. Such is the stuff of prophets, but prophecy is only one element of political leadership.

Suggested Reading

Arthur S. Link's brief, interpretive *Wilson the Diplomatist** (1957) is supplemented in his multivolume biography of the wartime President. Ernest R. May studies Wilson's policies in the years of American neutrality in *The World War and American Isolation, 1914–1917** (1959). Daniel M. Smith's *The Great Departure** (1965) covers much the same material in a balanced survey.

Edward M. Coffman gives the military history of the war a personal dimension in *The War to End All Wars* (1968). The assault on individual liberties at home is the subject of *Opponents of War, 1917–1918** (1957) by Horace C. Peterson and Gilbert C. Fite. Two volumes by George F. Kennan, *The Decision to Intervene** (1956) and *Russia Leaves the War** (1958), discuss the impact of the Russian Revolution on American policy.

Thomas A. Bailey has written two studies of Wilson's diplomacy: *Woodrow Wilson and the Lost Peace** (1944), which deals with the negotiation of the Treaty, and *Woodrow Wilson and the Great Betrayal**

(1945), which is critical of Wilson's political tactics and judgment. John M. Keynes criticizes the Treaty's economic provisions in *The Economic Consequences of the Peace* (1919). Ralph A. Stone's study, *The Irreconcilables* (1970) is dispassionate and definitive. John A. Garraty's *Henry Cabot Lodge* (1953) is the best biography of Wilson's formidable opponent.

*Available in paperback edition

CHRONOLOGY

XIX

CONFUSION AND CHANGE

IN THE 1920s

The legend persists that the American people forgot their cares in a swinging orgy of sin and speculation in the decade between Versailles and the Crash. Bathtub gin blurs not only the nation's memory, but even the history of the 1920s, and the flapper, the flask, the fast buck, and F. Scott Fitzgerald have become the symbols of an age.

They were symbols at the time, to be sure, but then they were not representative. Most women, even most young women, were not flappers, but rather clerks or coeds or housewives whose knowledge of high life came from the movies and whose knowledge of Freud was filtered through the *Ladies Home Journal*. Although sophisticates sneered at prohibition, more people obeyed the law than broke it. If the stock market became a national fixation, only perhaps a million Americans were involved in the bubble that burst in October, 1929. And not all the nation's intellectuals took off for Paris to become "sad young men" preoccupied with their own disillusionment. The majority of Americans retained their illusions; the decade, indeed, was full of illusions. Most Americans apparently believed that a simple statement and a few signatures would make international peace perpetual; most Americans apparently believed that endless, almost

Stereotyped symbols of the decade

effortless, prosperity was the nation's destiny. And most Americans probably believed in—and ordinarily acted on—such old-fashioned truths as tolerance, thrift, and temperance. Nonconformists gave the decade its character, but humdrum conformity was more characteristic of the generation Gertrude Stein called "lost."

RETURNING TO NORMALCY: WILSON, HARDING, COOLIDGE

Republicans dominated the politics of the decade, but it began with a Democrat in the White House. The postwar Woodrow Wilson, paralyzed by his stroke and politically bankrupt after the struggle over the League, was not the Woodrow Wilson of the New Freedom. Executive leadership vanished; Woodrow Wilson was the first of the decade's presidential practitioners of laissez faire. The President evidently had no plan for demobilization and for conversion to peacetime production; the failure to foresee and react to a dynamic economy was to become characteristic of Wilson's immediate successors. Such economic legislation as Congress passed favored the business community, whose power Wilson had once eloquently opposed. And, with tacit presidential consent, Wilson's Attorney General presided over an hysterical hunt for subversives that both outraged

364

and intimidated the people who had once thought Wilson their prophet. His last two years in office were years of reaction.

This reaction was visible partly in legislation that awarded the spoils of peace to business groups. The Merchant Marine Act (1920) restricted foreign shippers and subsidized American companies with federal loans, profitable mail contracts, and favorable terms for purchase of the merchant fleet the government had built during the war. The Esch-Cummins Transportation Act (1920) authorized the return of the railroads to private ownership and increased the regulatory power of the ICC. But the legislation did nothing to conserve the gains in efficiency achieved during the war, and in effect, increased the competitive advantage of those systems that least needed help.

As important as what the Wilson administration accomplished was what it failed to do to ease the transition to a peacetime economy. The War Department shelved a plan to coordinate demobilization and employment and simply released men as quickly as possible. Wartime industries found their orders abruptly canceled; government construction almost stopped. The federal government was too anxious to balance its budget to curb rising unemployment; Wilson suggested that perhaps local governments might undertake public works projects.

Labor organizations tried to preserve high wartime wages in a series of strikes in 1919. At the President's orders Attorney General A. Mitchell Palmer served an injunction that sent disappointed coal-miners back to the pits. Steelworkers, who struck to secure a forty-eight hour week, found federal troops protecting strikebreakers in Illinois; the steel industry remained unorganized. So did the police in Boston, where municipal and state authorities ended the walkout on their own terms with federal approval but without federal intervention.

Alerted by European Communist activity that followed the Russian Revolution of November, 1917, some Americans saw the strikes of 1919 as the American proletariat's first stride toward power. In fact there were no great conspiracies and precious few Communists, for labor's demands were traditional: recognition of the union, better wages, shorter hours. But beginning in 1918 and on into 1920, the nation looked for radicals who were supposed to be plotting the nation's postwar distress.

At its worst, popular hysteria denied free speech, free press, and the protection of ordinary judicial procedure. Aroused legislatures forbade the display of red flags and made membership in radical organizations a criminal offense. These criminal syndicalism laws officially harrassed the Industrial Workers of the World, whose unofficial suppression had started during the war with lynching and vigilante activity. The House of Representatives and the New York state legislature refused to seat duly elected Socialist representatives. Attorney General Palmer ordered a series of raids in 1920 that took several thousand people into custody, including many who just happened to be in an area where radicals were thought to congregate. Eventually about 500 aliens, not entitled to the constitutional protection of due process, were deported.

And then, before Woodrow Wilson left office, the Red Scare was over.

The results of the frantic search were ludicrously out of proportion to the energy expended: an occasional Wobbly, a few aliens whose radicalism was nostalgic habit rather than a response to American conditions, and an occasional native nonconformist. Charles Evans Hughes, whose conservatism and patriotism were equally unimpeachable, denounced the New York legislature's exclusion of its Socialist members. Humorists pointed to the incongruity of a mighty nation's debilitating fear of a few frustrated misfits. In New York, in December, 1919, a teary would-be bride told reporters and a church full of disappointed guests that Reds must have abducted the missing groom. A day or two later, the sheepish young man surfaced, complete with a previous wife and family, and the "red menace" was suddenly a joke.

One haunting remnant lingered. In May, 1920, two Italian anarchists were arrested and charged with robbery and murder in South Braintree, Massachusetts. More than a year later, after a trial many observers thought a mockery, both defendants, Nicola Sacco and Bartolomeo Vanzetti, were

The Passion of Sacco and Vanzetti, by Ben Shahn

sentenced to death. Liberals argued that execution would make the two men martyrs for their political radicalism and their Southern European origin. Others, including most of respectable America, held that the trial had been fair, and that the defendants were undesirable anyhow. Whatever the truth—one recent opinion is that Sacco was guilty and Vanzetti innocent—the nation wrangled interminably about the two rather pathetic principals in the case even after their execution in 1927.

The Red Scare was bipartisan. Yet if the election of 1920 had an issue, it was "Americanism." Just what "Americanism" meant was not clear, but it was clear that Warren G. Harding, the Republican nominee, was for it, and it was clear, as Senator Boies Penrose predicted, that it would "get a lot of votes." Harding's phrase that the country needed "not nostrums, but normalcy" caught the nation's mood and defined "Americanism" as precisely as anyone needed. Although James M. Cox, the Governor of Ohio, had not been closely associated with Wilson, he and his Democratic running mate, Franklin D. Roosevelt, seemed Wilson's heirs. The voters obviously wanted a change, for Cox held only the South and Harding received an unprecedented 60 percent of the popular vote.

Wilson had proclaimed the election a solemn referendum on the League of Nations, and in a sense it was. Harding had followed the lead of Henry Cabot Lodge while the treaty was before the Senate and during the campaign had indicated continued personal opposition. A few Republicans who favored the League argued that a vote for Harding was a vote for the League, but the argument displayed more ingenuity than accuracy, and the American for whom the League of Nations was the primary issue probably voted for Cox. And there simply were not enough. "Americanism" and "normalcy" meant a placid nationalistic foreign policy and an unruffled government at home. Warren G. Harding, whose inclination was inaction, was admirably qualified to preside over both.

The personal qualities that secured Harding's nomination ensured his failure as President. Harding became the Republican nominee because he was utterly dependent upon other people for direction, because he was enthusiastically responsive to the call of party and personal loyalty, because he was handsome and one of the boys, and because he was ordinary. He was never master of his own administration. His cronies and his party abused his confidence and had virtually no program except their own advancement. His short, unhappy tenure in the White House proved that ordinary men make wretched Presidents.

Harding's Cabinet combined three eminent Republicans with others unqualified for public office and unworthy of public trust. Charles Evans Hughes was a dignified Secretary of State; Herbert Hoover turned the somnolent Commerce Department into a hive of innovation; Andrew Mellon was an honest, if extremely conservative, Secretary of the Treasury. On the other hand, Harry Daugherty, Harding's political mentor and Attorney General, Edwin M. Denby, the Secretary of the Navy, and Albert B. Fall, the Secretary of the Interior, were all implicated in the Teapot Dome scandal, which was exposed after Harding's death in 1923. Fall was convicted of taking a bribe from oilmen who wanted to tap the Navy's underground reserves at Teapot Dome in Wyoming. Some of Harding's subcabinet appointees were equally unscrupulous. Charles Forbes, the chief of the Veterans Bureau, systematically enriched himself at the expense of the veterans he was supposed to serve. The President knew his friends had betrayed him, but he was incapable of any action sterner than privately deploring the situation. While Harding himself did not share the booty, the cynical air of easy morality extended to the White House, where poker, bootleg whiskey, and a presidential mistress gave a dubious distinction to Harding's brief lease.

Harding died in August, 1923, before the scandals of his administration were fully known. And Calvin Coolidge, who had a knack for being in the right place at the right time, took the presidential oath from his father in the candle-lit parlor of the family's farm house in Plymouth, Vermont. The ceremony gave Coolidge an aura of rural simplicity that he was at pains to preserve as an antidote for the easygoing good fellowship, the cigars, the alcohol, and the scandals that were soon associated with Harding. Fresh from rural Vermont, radiating rural virtue, came the honest hayseed Calvin Coolidge, who never did anything that anyone could call convivial. Harding and Coolidge differed little on policy, but personally they differed profoundly. Harding's scandals blew over without exacting a political price from the Republicans; indeed those who persisted in investigating Teapot Dome, like Senators LaFollette and Walsh, were sharply criticized for their pains.

THE ECONOMICS OF NORMALCY

The stock-market crash of 1929 altered the economic perception of those who lived during the 1920s. By comparison with the depression that followed, the 1920s seemed fabulously prosperous, an impression that was only partly accurate. The stock market did of course climb to unprecedented levels and some shrewd operators made speculative fortunes. New consumer-goods industries sparked real economic growth in the decade. An eager market absorbed automobiles, refrigerators, radios, and motion pictures. Widespread use of automobiles brought a burst of highway construction, billions in new investment, and expanded output among suppliers of oil, glass, steel, and rubber. The market for refrigerators and radios depended upon wide distribution of electricity, which in turn required heavy investment in copper, rubber, and other basic industries. The movies whetted consumer appetites and prescribed fashion for Americans, who were increasingly concerned with what they wore and owned.

But an improving standard of living was not a universal experience in America. A brief, but severe, postwar economic crisis left nearly 5 million people unemployed and reduced the national income by 10 percent. Close to 100,000 bankruptcies and nearly a half-million farmers who lost their farms testified to the breadth of the disaster. Wholesale prices and industrial production plummeted. Agricultural prices remained depressed throughout the decade. Wheat that had brought $2.50 in 1919 sold for less than $1.00 in 1921; a bushel of corn dropped from $1.88 to $.42. Although most of the economy pulled out of the depression in 1922, profitable farming reappeared only with the Second World War. A prudent Minnesota Swede bought a good farm in 1912, improved it, and paid off half his mortgage by 1920. In 1925 prices had fallen to the point where his net income for long days of hard work and his return on a large investment amounted to half what his eighteen-year-old daughter received for typing in a downtown office. In 1929 the Swede could not meet his interest payments; three years later he rented the farm that had been his from the insurance company that had foreclosed his mortgage.

Farmers, textile workers, coal miners, and others whose industries lagged in the decade could not sustain the continued consumption upon which prosperity depended. Congressmen from rural areas were particularly sensitive to rumbling discontent. Since the Presidents took no action, legislators from farm states organized loosely in a "farm bloc" to secure redress for their constituents. Two acts in 1921 regulated marketing practices in the stockyards and speculation in the grain exchanges. The Capper-Volstead Act of 1922 exempted agricultural cooperatives from antitrust laws. Those acts, along with an Emergency Tariff in 1921 and the more permanent, more protective Fordney-McCumber Tariff of 1922, which raised rates nearly 25 percent above the Underwood schedule, almost completed the legislative record of the Harding administration.

None of this legislation met the farmers' immediate need for more purchasing power. In 1924 the McNary-Haugen Bill, a measure designed to raise agricultural prices, was introduced. The bill proposed a protected domestic market for American farmers and authorized the disposal of surplus production abroad at the world price. Farmers were to make up with an "equalization fee" the difference between the depressed world price and the protected domestic price. Since the nation consumed more farm produce than was exported, the measure, the farm bloc claimed, would raise rural income. But representatives from nonfarm areas proved hard to persuade, and when the bill finally passed in 1927, President Coolidge vetoed it. The bill had so many defects, Coolidge said, that he could not "state them all without writing a book." Coolidge held the proposal unconstitutional, labeled it an unjustifiable subsidy to one segment of the population, and correctly argued that it contained no mechanism for controlling surplus production, which was at the heart of the problem. Congress modified the bill somewhat in 1928, but Coolidge vetoed it again.

The presidential veto was Coolidge's substitute for a legislative program. In 1928 he vetoed Senator George Norris' bill authorizing the government to operate the nitrate plants and electrical generating facilities constructed in the Tennessee Valley during the First World War. Coolidge suggested that the complex be sold to private investors instead. The President also vetoed a bill in 1924 to pay World War veterans a bonus, but the veterans secured enough congressional support to override that veto.

Neither Coolidge nor his predecessor furnished the initiative for administration policies. In both cases, the fiscal policy was that of Andrew Mellon, who had made his fortune in aluminum and banking, and whom his contemporaries knew as "the greatest Secretary of the Treasury since Alexander Hamilton." Mellon believed that high corporate and income taxes penalized resourceful businessmen and discouraged private investment. He repeatedly urged Congress to reduce wartime taxes, and Congress responded by repealing the excess profits tax in 1921 and by cutting the surtax on large incomes in 1924. But legislators simultaneously raised the estate tax and added a gift tax. Finally in 1926 Mellon's program passed without qualification: the surtax on large incomes dropped from 40 to 20 percent; the gift tax was repealed; the estate tax was reduced by half; a variety of excise taxes disappeared completely. Senator Norris, who opposed Mellon's program, charged that it saved Mellon himself more than "the aggregate of practically all the taxpayers in the State of Nebraska."

Senator Norris also charged that Harding and Coolidge had in effect repealed progressive legislation by appointing men who undermined the purposes of regulatory agencies. Attorney General Daugherty had advertised his willingness to ignore antitrust statutes. One of Harding's appointees to the Tariff Commission had edited *The Protectionist*. William E. Humphrey, designated by Coolidge to head the Federal Trade Commission, had once called that body "a publicity bureau to spread socialistic propaganda." With Humphrey at the helm, the FTC ceased to stimulate competition and helped reduce it.

Nor did Secretary of Commerce Herbert Hoover believe competition an unmixed blessing. He dedicated his department to developing greater national efficiency through industrial cooperation under governmental auspices. Hoover encouraged the proliferation of trade associations that exchanged economic information, such as prices and data on cost accounting. The Commerce Department collected statistics, subsidized technological innovation, and suggested ways of improving efficiency. Later, during his presidency, Hoover was identified with the outdated economic orthodoxy of laissez faire; yet his ideas about competition and about the place of government in business owed more to Henry Clay and Alexander Hamilton than to those who demanded an inactive state. Hoover's direction of the Commerce Department rested on the assumption that a benign government, without itself controlling the economy, could help business create a higher standard of living for the nation.

The Supreme Court, however, held to the rules of laissez faire. The Court used the Fourteenth Amendment, the usual judicial instrument for striking down regulatory and welfare legislation, twice as often in the 1920s as in the decade preceding. Congress could not, held the Court, use the power to tax to keep children out of the mills (*Bailey* v. *Drexel Furniture Co.*, 1922). Whatever the Clayton Act said, the justices decided in *Duplex Printing Press Co.* v. *Deering* (1922) that courts could prevent unions from using secondary boycotts, and the antitrust laws hampered union activity throughout the decade. In 1923 the Court revived the Lochner doctrine and ruled in *Adkins* v. *Children's Hospital* that Congress could not set minimum wages for women working in the District of Columbia. In harmony with its legal constituency, with the other two branches of government, and probably with the American people as well, the Court stood squarely for unfettered private enterprise.

AN URBAN NATION

Americans in the 1920s found themselves poised between an exciting, uncertain, urban future and a rural past that seemed in retrospect more secure. They prided themselves on being up-to-date when they sipped a forbidden cocktail at the country club, read James Joyce or Sigmund Freud, or contemplated divorce. But most Americans avoided speakeasies and did not think that really good books included four-letter words. And most Americans intended to go right on repressing their libido, whatever Freud said, nor did they know any nice people who were divorced. They associated modernity with the city—and they wanted it; they associated morality with the farm—and they wanted that too. Calvin Coolidge seemed the resolution of the paradox: he was the embodiment of rural simplicity while presiding over modern, urban America, the taciturn prophet of prosperity, the symbol of thrift in an age of installment buying, the picture of serene certainty in a frantically uncertain era.

Uncertainty accompanied change. The urban prosperity of the 1920s rested on mass production of consumer goods, which in turn required mass consumption. Suddenly all the resources of advertising, one of the nation's newest big businesses, battered such frugal maxims as "use it up; make it do." Even if the old car did still run, the smart driver bought a new one now and got head of the Joneses. Saving was unnecessary; self-indulgence was good business.

As advertising advanced materialism, so too broad acceptance of natural and social science encouraged a secular outlook, which eroded the certainties of traditional religion. Americans continued to go to church, but they were only slightly embarrassed about skipping a service for a Sunday drive. Religious doctrine, particularly that of Protestantism, became less demanding, and many churchgoers went less to worship than because "it was the thing to do." Although fundamentalists held out, most Christians conceded that modern science made impossible a literal acceptance of the book of Genesis. The 1925 trial of John Scopes, a Tennessee schoolteacher who had used Darwinian insights in his classes, succeeded in finally discrediting fundamentalism for much of the nation, even though Scopes lost his case. Candid discussion of sexual habits in psychological or scientific terms made sex less a matter of religious dogma than a matter of casual conversation. The abject failure of prohibition to prohibit discredited the churches and religious leaders that had promised a dry millenium. Yet Americans clung to their religion and often preserved the shell without the substance. "I believe these things," remarked a midwesterner about Christianity, "but they don't take a big place in my life."

Traditional patriotism, like traditional religion, seemed under seige; those who mistrusted change rallied to the flag as well as the church. Woodrow Wilson's internationalism, which persisted through the decade in his small but articulate following, implied a loyalty to humanity that transcended loyalty to nation. But nationalism triumphed in the debate over the Treaty, in the several debates over membership in the World Court, and in the hearts of most Americans in the towns and small cities where most Americans lived. Members of veterans' organizations, particularly the American Legion, shifted from the defense of the nation from foreign powers to the defense of the nation from domestic threats, which were sometimes imagined. Patriotism became a staple of instruction in the public schools.

Ethnic diversity, especially in the urban neighborhoods that resisted assimilation, seemed an affront to those who believed that a unified nation required a homogeneous, Protestant, white, English-speaking population. One way to limit ethnic diversity was to curtail immigration, which an act in 1921 limited to an annual total of 357,000. In addition, the act held annual immigration from any one nation to 3 percent of Americans of that national origin enumerated in the Census of 1910. Congress found the act insufficiently restrictive and in 1924 reduced the annual quota to 150,000 (to take effect in 1929), and the quota for each nation to 2 percent of the census of 1890. Changing the base for the quota from 1910 to 1890 effectively reduced Catholic and Jewish immigrants from Southern and Eastern Europe.

Preserving the nation from foreign influence did not satisfy those concerned with the domestic threat to American institutions. The Ku Klux Klan revived its crusade for Americanism in the 1920s and defined the doctrine as white Protestant domination. The Klan became as powerful in parts of the North as it was in the South, where the black population generally remained cowed. Blacks had left the South for jobs in northern cities during the war and continued the migration in the postwar decade. Economic competition and racial tension over housing and public facilities brought race riots in Chicago, Omaha, and Knoxville, and more than seventy lynchings in 1919 alone. The Klan spread among northern whites, who for the first time encountered blacks in numbers large enough to make them more than a curiosity.

The Klan also spread among Americans who feared a Roman Catholic threat to Protestantism. Alfred E. Smith, the Governor of New York and the nation's most eminent Catholic politician, became the Klan's most important political target. Smith was brought up on New York's Lower East Side, and his association with Babylon was lifelong. He apologized for none of his urban idiosyncrasies; indeed, disapproving rustics thought he betrayed an unseemly pride in his church, his city, and his opposition to prohibition. His political record showed a genuine interest in helping working people although it did not reveal much accomplishment toward that humanitarian end. His administration was efficient, honest, and rather conservative.

But many Americans had long believed New York the source of the nation's sin. And in 1924 the urban and rural wings of the Democratic party were so split that neither Smith nor William Gibbs McAdoo, the Californian who bore the colors of Bryan's still loyal supporters, could secure the presidential nomination. In a close vote the convention defeated a resolution that specifically condemned the Klan. The weary, divided Democrats eventually awarded their nomination to John W. Davis, a conservative corporation lawyer, whom Calvin Coolidge ignored during the campaign and trounced in the election.

Robert M. La Follette summoned progressives of all parties to support his presidential candidacy in 1924. His platform contained familiar planks: conservation, political democracy, collective bargaining, tariff reduction, subsidized agricultural credit, and that progressive staple, increased regulation of railroads. La Follette's campaign aroused some initial enthusiasm and the endorsement of the American Federation of Labor and of the American Socialist party. But the new Progressive party had few local candidates, little organization, and almost no money. Organized labor soon cooled on the effort, and important union leaders, such as John L. Lewis of the United Mine Workers, supported Coolidge. Republican orators tagged La Follette as a radical, but so uninspiring was Davis that La Follette carried his own Wisconsin and ran second to the triumphant Coolidge in several western states, including California.

After the disaster of 1924, Democrats could not deny Smith the nomination in 1928. But Smith could not overcome Herbert Hoover's appeal to Protestant, rural, dry America. Hoover lost the electoral votes of only eight states, and he carried such traditional Democratic bastions as North Carolina, Florida, Texas, and Oklahoma. But in urban America Smith ran well. He carried the nation's largest cities and established the Democratic party as the political arm of urban liberals. Smith's urban gains proved more enduring than Hoover's success in the Democratic South.

Small-town America could reject Al Smith more easily than it could

Spectators watch illegal beer go down the gutter.

the urban culture that he symbolized. For the city advanced on the country-side not only by growing in area and population but also by more subtle means. The radio, one of the decade's glamorous new toys, sent the tastes, jokes, and polish of New York into the most remote corners of the nation. The movies brought the dazzling and thoroughly urban world of Hollywood to the most provincial cinema. Books and magazines, published in cities and written by city people, portrayed the city as the refuge of civilized man. Farmers, once the personification of virtue, became instead rubes. And city slickers, once considered unfortunates who could not escape the crowded centers of vice, came to symbolize intelligence, sophistication, and success.

H. L. Mencken, by general consent, was the voice of this urban sophistication. Mencken turned the Scopes trial into a monkey show; Mencken's reporting made religious fundamentalism a national joke. In the *Smart Set*, the appropriately named magazine he edited for those who wanted to seem cosmopolitan, and in the *American Mercury*, Mencken provided an outlet for aspiring writers of the 1920s. They made fun of the "booboisie" and "debunked" Puritanism, national heroes, and other beliefs that those who were "in the swim" thought outmoded.

Intellectuals of the progressive era had revealed the serpent in the American Eden in order to get rid of serpents. Intellectuals in the 1920s thought getting rid of serpents the height of folly and sometimes made them the most interesting part of the literary garden. The American small town, previously the object of sentimental reverence, became in Sherwood Anderson's *Winesburg, Ohio* or Sinclair Lewis' *Main Street* parochial, confining, and intolerant. Ernest Hemingway's novels, particularly *A Farewell to Arms*, challenged the idealism and morality of the progressive generation. For the characters in the novels of Scott Fitzgerald high life was the route to happiness; not every reader perceived that Fitzgerald's route never seemed to reach its destination. T. S. Eliot made emptiness the theme of *The Waste Land*, the most admired poem of the decade.

A few intellectuals, notably the philosopher John Dewey, remained incorrigibly optimistic about man's ability to improve himself. But the ordinary American, buffeted by change, found little consolation and not much guidance in what he read. Old landmarks—small towns, friendliness, sobriety, self-denial, optimism, Protestantism, and even patriotism—seemed to be disappearing in the name of progress. And instead of pointing new ways to familiar goals, the nation's intellectuals led those who denied that ways existed and that the goals were worth striving for. Lacking new landmarks and afraid to lose familiar ones, most Americans somewhat half-heartedly hung on to old ideals.

Intellectuals, for the moment, gloried in their rootless lack of ortho-doxy. But a society needs an orthodoxy, and even though many Americans had lost faith in the one they had, they kept it for lack of anything more satisfying. The replacement—urban liberalism, which combined an active government and new economic ideas in an idealistic vision of a better, more prosperous society—became the new orthodoxy in the next decade. In advocating an active government, urban liberalism showed its ancestry in progressivism of the earlier years of the century. But the political base of the later movement was entirely different. Progressives relied on the genteel, Protestant, upper and middle classes; urban liberals, often under patrician leadership, rallied the swarthy, swarming, and sweaty city dwellers that most progressives had feared.

Outside the cities, as La Follette's effort in 1924 attested, progressivism survived during the 1920s. Congressional progressives blocked, delayed, and modified probusiness legislation, although they could rarely enact their own proposals. Progressivism hung on too in prohibition, restriction of immigration, suspicion of labor unions, and other illiberal manifestations of the progressives' soured discovery that the masses did not share such values as temperance, Protestantism, and competitive individualism.

THE DIPLOMACY OF ISOLATION

While the First World War had not made the world safe for democracy, Americans were quite sure the world had become safe for the United States. Two oceans offered more protection than collective security; isolation seemed desirable and attainable. But isolation did not preclude traditional diplomatic activity in the Western Hemisphere, continued concern about the Open Door in Asia, or the economic interest roused by American investment in Europe. Isolation was a wistful faith that the rest of the world would understand the purity of American intent and permit the United States to do as it pleased. Like so many of the nostalgic ideals of the 1920s, isolation proved impossible to achieve.

"We seek," announced Warren G. Harding in his inaugural address, "no part in directing the destinies of the world," a remark that ended any hope for American acceptance of the League of Nations. For some months Secretary of State Hughes did not open correspondence from League functionaries for fear of implying recognition. Eventually Hughes opened his mail, and his successors even sent unofficial observers to sessions of the League in Geneva. No offical relationship, however, was proposed or contemplated. In lieu of signing a treaty with the Central Powers, Congress in 1921 formally terminated the war with a joint resolution that reserved to the United States all the rights of the victorious allies. Nothing was said about responsibilities.

One of the legacies of the war was armament, which virtually all Americans hoped to reduce in order to hold down world tension and domestic taxes. In December, 1920, Senator Borah urged that an international conference consider the naval arms race. In 1921 President Harding invited diplomats to meet in Washington, where Secretary Hughes amazed them with an opening speech proposing that the principal naval powers scrap more vessels, as one observer remarked, "than all the admirals of the world had destroyed in a cycle of centuries." The United States, for instance, was to sink thirty ships of more than 845,000 tons. Hughes sought parity for the American and British fleets and a somewhat smaller navy for Japan. Negotiations less public than Hughes's first proposal resulted in the

Five Power Pact, which fixed a ratio of 5 : 5 : 3 : 1.6 : 1.6 for tonnage of capital ships of the United States, Britain, Japan, France, and Italy. The diplomats could not find a formula for restricting vessels smaller than battleships and aircraft carriers.

The Washington Conference also considered naval bases and fortifications in the Pacific. In the Five Power Pact, Britain, Japan, and the United States agreed to construct no new facilities in their possessions in the western Pacific. The agreement in effect made the Japanese fleet dominant in the area, for without fortified bases, the American and British navies could not effectively challenge Japan in its home waters. Britain, Japan, France, and the United States also guaranteed one another's Pacific possessions, and all four nations agreed to consult in the event of a threat to the status quo in the Pacific. This Four Power Pact formally replaced the Anglo-Japanese Alliance of 1902, which had become a source of embarrassment to Great Britain and of concern to the United States. Finally, in the Nine Power Pact, to which China, Portugal, Belgium, and the Netherlands agreed in addition to the signatories of the Five Power Pact, the Open Door became a multilateral agreement. The document guaranteed the "independence and . . . territorial and administrative integrity of China," but the other agreements of the Washington Conference eliminated the military means of holding the Chinese door open.

Subsequent attempts (in Geneva in 1927 and in London in 1930) to extend naval restrictions to submarines and other support vessels were fruitless. Italy under Mussolini was building rather than reducing its navy; France wanted an Anglo-American guarantee of French security in return for concessions; Japan had expansive ambition and intended to preserve the naval means of gratifying it. In retrospect, the Washington Conference may seem to have conceded too much to Japan. But in 1922 Americans thought the treaties a resounding success for American diplomacy and a welcome relief for the world's taxpayers. The Senate ratified the results, specifying only that the Four Power agreement did not commit the United States to any international effort to retain the Pacific status quo.

In 1928 American diplomats went beyond disarmament and solemnly agreed to outlaw war as an instrument of national policy. The multinational Kellogg-Briand Pact crowned the efforts of American pacifist groups who had persuaded Senator William E. Borah to support their effort to renounce war. Aristide Briand, the Foreign Minister of France, proposed that the United States and France join in a "mutual engagement tending, as between these two countries, to outlaw war." Secretary of State Frank Kellogg, who had succeeded Hughes in 1925, suggested that all nations be invited to subscribe to Briand's proposal. In August, 1928, the first fifteen nations, including the United States, formally agreed to use peaceful means to settle international disputes. The Senate consented by a vote of eighty-five to one, but many Senators knew the treaty was, as Virginia's respected Senator Glass said, "worthless but perfectly harmless." Enforcement of the Kellogg-Briand Pact rested on international collective action, for which the treaty itself made no provision; if automatic sanctions had been included, the Senate would doubtless have withheld its ratification. For the goal of

American policy was not international cooperation to end international war; the goal was rather an end to international war so that the United States could remain safely isolated.

Yet the expanding American economy made isolation difficult. American enterprise, unimpaired by the war, dominated postwar international trade, and the nation had a vital interest in the prosperity of its primary markets. The United States had long had a favorable balance of trade; after the war, America became an international creditor as well, with extensive foreign investments. But protective tariffs excluded foreign goods, which were the only means other countries had to pay for American goods and credit. American loans temporarily furnished the exchange necessary for continuing international trade. Near the end of the decade, however, when domestic speculation seemed more profitable, loans dropped, and the American tariff again complicated international trade.

The related questions of German reparations and interallied war debts also troubled international economic relations. Germany did not intend to meet the reparations payments imposed at Versailles and perhaps could not have done so. Although the United States never admitted any link between reparations and the debts owed the United States by Britain, France, and other European allies, these debtor states fully expected to pay their American bills with German cash. Indeed the Allies thought the United States ungratefully grasping for insisting on repayment at all. Most of the borrowed money had been spent in the United States for American goods and had stimulated American industry. In addition, the Allies argued, the war effort had been a common cause; if America had lent money, they had shed blood, which ought to even the transaction. But neither the government nor the taxpayers would forgive the debts. Coolidge summed up American policy by observing simply, "They hired the money, didn't they?"

Yet the question was not simple. Early in 1923 Germany defaulted on reparations payments. Before the end of the year, inflation had ruined the German currency and threatened the French franc. An international commission headed by Charles G. Dawes, an American banker, scaled down reparations payments. The Dawes Plan provided for loans, largely from the United States, to restore a sound German currency and to revive the economic activity that had to precede reparations payments. In effect, the United States lent money to Germany, which paid reparations to the Allies, which then paid their debts to the United States. Like many another economic expedient, the Dawes Plan collapsed in the depression that closed the decade.

Isolation as a diplomatic ideal never extended to the Western Hemisphere. The 1920s opened with American marines in Nicaragua, Haiti, and the Dominican Republic and with the Roosevelt Corollary as the operative American policy. Not all the marines had come home a decade later, nor had all the American restrictions on the sovereignty of Cuba, Panama, and other Latin American republics been abrogated. But in 1930 the Roosevelt Corollary was formally renounced, and the United States was irrevocably committed to a course another Roosevelt would call "the policy of the Good Neighbor."

Mexican-American relations revealed the new direction. The social revolution that began in Mexico during the Wilson administration brought constitutional changes that vexed important groups of Americans. Mexican law decreed that subsoil rights belonged to the nation and not to the individuals who owned the earth's surface. American oil companies refused to accept this ruling and expected diplomatic help from the State Department. The Mexican government also nationalized the property of the Roman Catholic Church, prohibited religious instruction in primary schools, and curtailed the number of priests per province. American Catholics, angry at what seemed official persecution, urged the government to intervene on behalf of religious liberty.

In retrospect, neither dispute seems crucial. Yet the combination created diplomatic friction. In 1927 Dwight Morrow, whom Coolidge appointed Ambassador to Mexico, began to persuade the Mexicans rather than bully them. With tact and a keen sense of public relations, Morrow secured the confidence of the Mexican government and worked out a compromise that permitted American companies once more to pump oil and Mexican churches once more to hold mass. Morrow's solutions were not final, but his quiet method of seeking them replaced the habit of sending marines.

Before his inauguration in 1929, President-elect Hoover dramatized American interest with a tour of Latin America. To be sure, he sailed on a battleship, but while in Argentina he promised that the United States would not intervene in the internal affairs of other American republics. This pledge became official policy, apparently by inadvertence, when the Clark Memorandum was published in 1930. The Memorandum pointed out that the Monroe Doctrine had initially protected Latin American republics from foreign intervention but that Theodore Roosevelt's interpretation had brought constant American intervention and outraged proud, independent peoples. The new American policy still did not permit European interference in the hemisphere, but at least American control was to be more subtle.

The activity of the State Department—negotiations, treaties, a different hemispheric policy—indicates that isolation was one of the myths of the 1920s. Yet in another sense, isolation was a fact, for it was never a policy so much as a state of mind. And after Versailles the United States certainly intended to reject the rest of the world. The difficulty was that the nation renounced only responsibility while forcefully demanding the perquisites of power.

Suggested Reading

As the 1920s closed, Frederick Lewis Allen wrote *Only Yesterday** (1931), an account of that decade that retains its charm. William E. Leuchtenburg's *The Perils of Prosperity** (1958) has the advantage of perspective. Another survey, David A. Shannon's *Between the Wars**

(1965), is especially useful for its emphasis on Wilson's last years in the White House. Arthur M. Schlesinger, Jr., is critical of Republicans and their policies in *The Crisis of the Old Order** (1957), the first volume of his study of Roosevelt. The first three volumes of Frank Freidel's biography of Roosevelt (1952, 1954, 1956) carry FDR to the presidency.

George E. Mowry has edited a useful collection of sources entitled *The Twenties** (1963); another collection, *The Aspirin Age** (1949), edited by Isabel Leighton, overemphasizes the bizarre but is worthwhile. Alfred M. Kazin's *On Native Grounds** (1942) treats the literature of the "lost generation." *Red Scare** (1955) by Robert K. Murray chronicles the harassment of radical dissenters.

The foreign policy of the period may be followed in two works by Robert H. Ferrell, *Peace in Their Time** (1952) and *American Diplomacy in the Great Depression** (1957), and in Elting E. Morison's *Turmoil and Tradition** (1960), an excellent biography of Henry L. Stimson.

*Available in paperback edition

CHRONOLOGY

1929   Agricultural Marketing Act
Stock market crash

1930   Hawley-Smoot Tariff

1932   Reconstruction Finance Corporation chartered
Presidential election: Franklin D. Roosevelt (Democrat)
defeats Herbert Hoover (Republican)

1933   The "hundred days" of the New Deal:
     Bank "holiday"; Emergency Banking Act
     Tennessee Valley Authority (TVA) established
     Agricultural Adjustment Act (declared unconstitutional in 1936)
     National Industrial Recovery Act (declared unconstitutional in 1935)
     Federal Emergency Relief Act

1935   The "Second New Deal":
     Works Progress Administration (WPA) established
     Wagner-Connery Labor Relations Act (upheld in 1937)
     Social Security Act
Founding of Congress of Industrial Organizations (CIO)

1936   Soil Conservation and Domestic Allotment Act
Presidential Election: Franklin D. Roosevelt (Democrat)
defeats Alfred M. Landon (Republican)

1937–38   Roosevelt unsuccessfully attempts to "pack" the Supreme Court

XX

TWO PRESIDENTS,

ONE LONG DEPRESSION

The late 1920s are replete with contrasts. It was a time of pervasive optimism and of retribution that came as suddenly as the punishment for blasphemous pride in Greek tragedy. The United States, rich and expansive, plunged from the euphoria of prosperity to the prolonged despair of the most persistent depression any industrial nation has ever endured. President Herbert Hoover, whose reputation had rested on his humanitarianism, his efficiency, and his economic genius, became the symbol of numb bewilderment in the face of human despair. Time, Incorporated, announced the forthcoming publication of *Fortune* just as fortunes vanished in the nation's stock exchanges. (Those stocks and bonds were, ironically, called securities.) Even as businesses toppled, one businessman after another adorned the cover of *Time* itself, including, on successive weeks surrounding the debacle on Wall Street, Ivar Kreuger and Samuel Insull, two as yet unrevealed corporate manipulators whose empires would soon disappear and leave thousands of angry, defrauded stockholders.

"Given a chance to go forward with the policies of the past eight years," Herbert Hoover prophesied as he accepted the Republican nomination in 1928, "we shall soon with the help of God be in the sight of the day when poverty will be banished from this nation." At his inauguration the following March, President Hoover proclaimed that he had "no fears for the future of our country," for, he held, it was "bright with hope." Presidents are apt to exaggerate on such occasions; it was Hoover's misfortune that his hyperboles were believed, and that events so quickly made his phrases seem foolish. Some Americans never believed Herbert Hoover again; the next President had to restore their faith in national leaders.

The policies of the "last eight years," in which Hoover declared his faith, were partly responsible for his undoing. For the Republican party and the public, awed by the nation's wonder-working businessmen and bankers, permitted them to gain a disproportionate share of the prosperity of the 1920s. At the base of the boom were the new industries that produced consumer goods—automobiles, refrigerators, radios, motion pictures. Mass production requires mass consumption, which the rich alone cannot provide. And Republican fiscal policy did more to encourage the rich to invest than to enable the poor to consume.

Nor was all the investment sound. Twice in the 1920s a speculative fever gripped the nation and temporarily blurred economic reality. For a few months in 1925 and 1926 Florida real estate was the magic carpet to riches. Developers bought, subdivided, and sold lots at a furious pace; a brisk market in unimproved property sprang up among northern speculators, many of whom had never seen the area they so vividly described. Soon impatient traders bought and sold purchase agreements, a device that reduced the immediate investment to 10 percent of the agreed price. Since the purchaser expected to sell his agreement at a quick profit, the ultimate price was nearly irrelevant. Advertising and shrewd promotion forced the pace; William Jennings Bryan, for example, sat under an umbrella and discoursed on the health-giving qualities of the Florida climate. Everyone heard about the lot that once sold for $25 and was subsequently resold several times at prices eventually reaching $150,000. Streets, utilities, and sometimes even the land itself did not exist; surveyors discovered that oceanside lots were occasionally underwater. The market began to fall in the summer of 1926; in the autumn a massive hurricane took more than four hundred lives and destroyed the remnant of the Florida land boom.

The speculation in Florida served as spring training for the stock-market season that opened in 1927. Gradually, but inexorably, stock prices climbed. Loans to brokers, an index of speculative activity, grew from $2.5 billion to $3.5 billion during the year, a total more than twice the usual annual figure before 1925. Nineteen twenty-eight was better than 1927; nearly twice as many shares changed hands, and such favorites as Montgomery Ward, du Pont, and Radio Corporation of America advanced spectacularly. RCA, for instance, which had yet to pay its first dividend, zoomed from 85 to 420; even for 1928 that increase was fantastic, but other stocks also improved sharply. Brokers' loans climbed past $5 billion before the end of the year.

The market boiled on through the first months of 1929. The whims of buyers changed; Montgomery Ward and RCA advanced at a slower pace than in 1928, while General Electric, Westinghouse, and other issues became speculative favorites. Through the summer of 1929, in spite of rising interest rates, brokers' loans mounted at the rate of $400 million per month; the total soon approached $7 billion. September 3, 1929, marked the apex of the great bull market. For the rest of the month and in early October the market was uncertain. On Thursday, October 24, the investing public had a preview of the abyss, for prices broke sharply and for a few hours panic ruled the Exchange. But some of the nation's financial leaders, led by Thomas Lamont of the Morgan firm, pledged to support the market and authorized Richard Whitney, a vice-president of the Exchange, to act. Whitney ordered large blocks of key stocks at prices well above their depressed levels and the market stabilized. A few issues even showed a net gain for the day. On Friday and Saturday the market was active and prices held firm.

But panic began anew on Monday, and no support came from the bankers. On Tuesday, October 29, a decade ended. More than 16 million shares were sold, most at immense losses. Since those shares, some of which were well on their way to worthlessness, were also collateral for brokers' loans, loans had to be liquidated too. And the crash in October was only the beginning. Throughout the rest of 1929 and through 1930, 1931, and 1932 the market sagged.

A DEEPENING DEPRESSION

The crash only wiped out speculators; most sober Americans were just interested spectators. Perhaps as many as a million people were actively trading stocks in 1929, and by no means all of them became destitute overnight. *Time* suggested that the panic was a brilliant coup of shrewd market operators; no one worried aloud that the economic illness might spread beyond Wall Street. But slowly the nation's business atrophied. A vital economy might have shrugged off even such a serious setback as the rout in the market, but the American economy in 1929 was less vital than it appeared. The banking system, tied to the market through brokers' loans, reeled with other speculators. The nation's political and economic leaders, who believed that the market had to correct itself, allowed their economic theories to render them helpless while paralysis spread. The panic oozed from the market to the rest of the economy and became an interminable depression.

President Hoover first attributed the crash to a failure of business confidence. Superficially, Hoover's interpretation was appealing: the speculative cycle was, after all, a psychological as well as an economic phenomenon; stock prices bore no clear relationship to economic reality; the market did not respond to such economic checks as increased interest and rediscount rates, for speculation reached its height when interest on brokers' loans was more than 10 percent and occasionally reached 20 percent. If the boom had been built on confidence, perhaps confidence would also remedy the depression. With this outlook, Hoover almost had to act as if the depression were a myth; he could hardly acknowledge its presence lest confidence be further shaken. So the President issued cheery statements proclaiming that the economy was fundamentally sound. He also invited prominent business executives to confer with him at the White House, and they jointly issued statements reiterating their faith in the economy. But the economy itself refused to be coaxed back to prosperity. In 1930 the Chairman of the Republican National Committee charged that someone was rigging the stock market to discredit the administration. "Every time an Administration official gives out an optimistic statement," he complained, "the market immediately drops."

As the depression deepened, as some Americans approached a second winter without employment, as charities and states ran out of funds for relief, as newspapers reported that people were foraging in dumps and

"Hooverville"

garbage heaps, and as malnutrition and exposure came to public attention, Herbert Hoover became the nation's scapegoat. His optimistic statements were packaged with the fatuous pronouncements of the nation's economic seers in an irreverent little book called *Oh, Yeah!* Villages of shacks, invariably called "Hoovervilles," sprouted in New York's Central Park and other, much less desirable locations. Though the complacent cliché maintained that "No one has starved," a few people did in fact starve, and many people went hungry as unemployment climbed with the same eerie monotony that had once characterized the stock market: 4 million at the end of 1930; 7 million by October, 1931; 11 million when the nation voted to replace Hoover with Roosevelt; perhaps 14 million when Roosevelt took office.

And while unemployment mounted, everything else fell. New investment dropped from $10 billion to $1 billion between 1929 and 1932. Industrial production in the same years declined more than 50 percent. The average wage of factory workers went down 60 percent, and only the fortunate few had jobs at any wage. National income slumped from $81 billion in 1929 to $41 billion in 1932. Eighty-five thousand businesses and 5,000 banks failed; and with each failure of whatever size, more of the nation's capital assets disappeared.

Every statistic masked real people with blighted dreams, pressing needs, and choking anxieties. There was the midwestern widow who lost twenty years of savings and her husband's insurance when the local bank failed. For a few moments she screamed in front of the bank's closed doors; then her screams turned to sobs and she went home, where she sat, mute and uncomprehending, in the middle of her kitchen, until she was taken to an asylum for the insane. And there was the Oregon sheepherder who killed his whole flock and left 3,000 sheep to rot in a canyon because it would cost him $1.10 to ship each one to market, where it would sell for a dollar. Since he could not afford to feed the animals through the winter, he slaughtered them. About the same time, on the other side of the continent, police stumbled on the secluded spot where a young couple, without food for days, had gone to die quietly together.

HOOVER ACTS

The President was sensitive to the nation's distress. When confidence showed no sign of an early return and when the economy showed no sign of improvement, Hoover''s sensitivity overcame his economic scruples. The President began to use more than words to combat the depression. By comparison with Franklin Roosevelt's New Deal, Hoover's action was tentative and grudging. But he did take steps to support agricultural prices; he provided federal credit to steady staggering banks; he tried to prevent unemployment from spreading, although he did little to relieve the condition itself; and in 1932 he acknowledged that the government might have to assist those at the bottom of the economy who most needed help.

Before the crash Hoover had called Congress into special session to consider the chronic depression in agriculture. The Agricultural Marketing Act of June, 1929, established the Federal Farm Board to work with cooperatives in marketing agricultural commodities. Congress appropriated $500 million from which the Board made low-interest loans to marketing cooperatives. The administration hoped that cooperatives could stabilize the market through their purchases. But since the board did not control production, bumper crops continued to depress agricultural prices; in 1931 the effort was abandoned.

Hoover also asked the special session to raise rural purchasing power through a revision of the tariff. Congress did not complete the measure until 1930, and when passed, it did little to help the farmer. The Hawley-Smoot Tariff made duties that were already protective even more so. The new law raised duties on 70 agricultural commodities and on 900 industrial products, but it did not protect farmers from a surplus that was domestically produced. And the new tariff provoked retaliatory legislation abroad that reduced foreign markets for American produce. One thousand economists signed a statement outlining the probable damage to international trade and vainly urging a presidential veto.

International trade was none too vigorous before the tariff. American loans to European countries, especially to Germany, had fallen off when investment in the stock market became more attractive; with the depression, loans practically ceased. The crisis also aggravated continuing friction over war debts and reparations. Early in 1929 an international committee headed by Owen D. Young, an American businessman, reduced Germany's reparations payments. The depression, however, made the Young Plan and the rest of the tangled controversy over war debts and reparations almost irrelevant. Payment of both debts and reparations slowed, and by 1933 ceased almost completely. At the Lausanne Conference of June, 1932, the European powers made a virtue of economic necessity and canceled nearly all of Germany's obligation.

But Hoover did not, and perhaps politically could not, forgive the war debts. Instead, after the failure of a major Austrian bank in May, 1931, he proposed a one-year moratorium on both reparations and inter-allied debts. Before French assent was secured, the financial panic had spread to German banks and, soon after, to other European institutions. Delay robbed Hoover's moratorium of whatever economic lift it might have given. In retrospect Hoover thought the wave of European bank failures had set back American recovery just as his program for restoring confidence began to work. The depression after 1931, he wrote later, was a European import, a comforting interpretation that absolved innocent Americans of any responsibility for the depression itself and thus of the responsibility for initiating a program to alleviate it. The belief was naive. For the depression was longer and more severe in the United States than it was in Europe; nor was the nation on the way to renewed prosperity in 1931, as Hoover bravely hoped.

The congressional election of 1930 indicated that the voters did not respond to Hoover's inaction. Although the Republicans retained a slim edge in the House, the Senate became Democratic. The election results, the dismal economic outlook, and the crisis in European banking all seemed to demand more than presidential exhortation. During 1931 and 1932 Hoover outlined programs to combat the effects of the depression. Guiding the President's policy was his fixed faith in the gold standard, the balanced budget, and governmental economy. If action were required, he would help important private banks and industrial concerns to revive private investment and employment, rather than have citizens directly dependent upon their government.

In October, 1930, Hoover had promised federal leadership for a state and local campaign of voluntary self-help, apparently a euphemism for charity. In 1932 the administration blocked an appropriation of $375 million for relief, but made loans available to local governments in increasing amounts. Hoover asked Congress in 1931 for more funds for the Federal Land Bank, an agency for rural credit established in 1916; Congress responded with $125 million, and in July, 1932, added another $125 million for homeowners threatened with foreclosure. Both measures provided immediate currency for banks whose assets were sound but not readily negotiable. Early in 1932 Congress fulfilled another of Hoover's requests by chartering the Reconstruction Finance Corporation, a federal lending agency that within six months lent over a billion dollars to banks, insurance companies, and other financial institutions. Many of these loans went to the nation's financial elite, including a bank in Chicago of which former Vice-President Charles G. Dawes was an officer. Only a month before the loan to his bank was approved, Dawes had been president of the RFC; his resignation did not silence critics who contrasted the administration's haste to help beleaguered bankers with its unwillingness to help the ordinary people.

The RFC was also Hoover's instrument to help these people. In 1932 the RFC was empowered to lend $1.5 billion to local authorities for the construction of public works, such as highways and housing that would eventually return in tolls and rents the money advanced. And the RFC might lend $300 million to communities whose relief funds were exhausted. Neither of these authorizations was vigorously administered; the RFC lent only about $30 million for relief and somewhat less for public works before Hoover left office.

And all the indexes continued to go down while unrest mounted. A few intellectuals turned to Marx, a few farmers resorted to violence to forestall foreclosure, and a comparatively few veterans marched on Washington to lobby for immediate cash payment of the veteran's bonus that Congress had established in 1924. The Bonus Expeditionary Force (BEF) of perhaps 12,000 or 15,000 unemployed veterans camped for a few days in shacks and unoccupied federal buildings on Washington's Anacostia Flats. In June, 1932, the House passed a bill to pay the bonus in unbacked paper currency, but the measure died in the Senate. The disappointed veterans accepted the Senate's action, demonstrated their continued patriotism by singing "America" on the steps of the Capitol, and about half of them accepted the government's offer to lend money for the trip home. The other half, with-

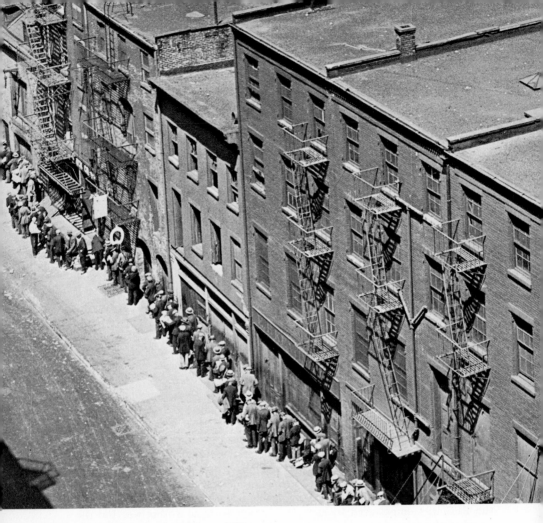

Manhattan bread lines, 1932

out any reason to return or any home to return to, stayed on in the encampment, to the increasing anxiety of the administration. In late July Hoover ordered the army to disperse the BEF and clear Anacostia Flats. The Chief of Staff, General Douglas MacArthur, personally supervised the operation of four infantry companies and four troops of cavalry, which employed tear gas, tanks, and machine guns to rout the BEF. The veterans scattered; the shacks on Anacostia Flats burned; and the nation correctly refused to believe the administration's assertion that the ragtag BEF spearheaded a revolution.

FDR TRIUMPHS

The nation's bankruptcy was more than economic; it was theoretical as well. Businessmen and bankers, on whose advice the nation had relied, offered homilies about thrift, hard work, and faith or, more forth-rightly, they simply confessed complete bewilderment. And as the election of 1932 approached, the major political parties offered little clear direction. Republicans listlessly renominated Hoover on a platform no more advanced than that of William McKinley. The party called for reduced government expenses and a balanced budget, a protective tariff, restricted immigration, and unspecified changes in the prohibition statute.

Nor did the Democrats seem an alternative, for their record had been as financially conservative during the 1920s as that of their rivals. Like the GOP, the Democratic party in 1932 advocated reduced spending and a balanced budget. But Democrats also suggested change: their platform promised the farmer a market where he could recover more than his cost of production and called for a lower tariff, a program of unemployment and old-age insurance, reform of banking practices, regulation of stock exchanges, and repeal of prohibition. The delegates to the convention in Chicago knew any platform they wrote would serve and any candidate they chose would win.

They chose well. Franklin Delano Roosevelt's background of inherited wealth, tutors, a posh prep school, and Harvard College was no barrier to his understanding of human misery. Bored by the practice of law, he eagerly entered politics when local Democratic bosses offered him the nomi-nation for the New York Senate in staunchly Republican Dutchess County in 1910. Once elected, Roosevelt became known as a progressive when he actively opposed Tammany Hall's candidate for the United States Senate. Like most Democratic progressives, he worked for Woodrow Wilson's nomi-nation, and when Wilson won, Roosevelt became Assistant Secretary of the Navy, the same position once occupied by his distant cousin Theodore Roosevelt. He made a respectable effort as the party's vice-presidential nominee in 1920. In the summer of 1921 infantile paralysis crippled Roose-velt; crutches, braces, and pain became a part of his routine; he never again walked unaided. In 1924 he briefly reclaimed the political spotlight with a felicitous nominating speech for Al Smith; in 1928 he again nominated Smith and became himself the party's nominee for Governor of New York. Elected in 1928 and again in 1930, Roosevelt was the odds-on Democratic candidate for the presidency when the convention opened. Two congres-sional veterans, John Nance Garner of Texas and Cordell Hull of Tennessee, and the still hopeful Smith were Roosevelt's major opponents. On the fourth ballot, Garner's supporters, assured that the Texan would have second place, voted for Roosevelt and completed the ticket.

Roosevelt's governorship foreshadowed more of the program he was to call the New Deal than did the campaign for the White House. He had collected a varied staff of advisers, some as orthodox as Hoover and others who were contemptuous of orthodoxy. He had seen New York's rural dis-tress and had publicly discussed methods of achieving agricultural parity, that is, of raising the buying power of farmers to the level of urban resi-dents. He had spent state funds for public works. In 1932, he had asked for, and been refused, $20 million to be used for direct relief where necessary and for useful public works where possible. "One of the duties of the State," Roosevelt said, "is that of caring for those of its citizens" whom circumstance prevented from caring for themselves. This responsibility extended, he added, to times of massive unemployment.

On the campaign trail, Roosevelt was less candid. He accused Hoover of presiding over "the greatest spending Administration" in peacetime history; Roosevelt promised to reduce spending by 25 percent. His farm program was at best confused. He opposed the expansion of bureaucracy and federal controls, while he proposed programs that would expand both. In one speech he suggested that the country had built too much productive capacity, that the government and business must plan together for a mature economy; in another he echoed the competitive creed of optimistic progressives. Herbert Hoover thought the campaign "a contest between two philosophies of government" and charged Roosevelt with proposing changes that "would destroy the very foundations of our American system." But Hoover overestimated both the danger and the consistency of his opponent. In the campaign, as later in the White House, Roosevelt was trying out ideas, not making solemn pledges.

Roosevelt need not have campaigned at all if his only object had been to win the election, for that was won before the campaign began. But Roosevelt's obvious energy, his buoyant welcoming of responsibility, his infectious enjoyment in seeing people and talking to them enhanced popular confidence, which in turn made Roosevelt's leadership more effective. In November, 282 counties that had never before supported a Democrat voted for Franklin Roosevelt. He carried all but six states and swamped Hoover by nearly 12 million popular votes.

It was the occasion, the tone of voice, the mood, and not the words that made Roosevelt's inaugural address memorable; preceding the alphabetical agencies and preeminent in the New Deal was FDR himself. The most famous line in the speech—"the only thing we have to fear is fear itself"—echoed a platitude that provoked derision when Hoover had used it; coming from Roosevelt, the assurance seemed more authoritative. Roosevelt outlined national needs but was seldom specific in his prescription for meeting them. Yet the whole tone of his address confirmed his intention to do something. The speech bristled with allusions to war: the American people "must move as a trained and loyal army willing to sacrifice for the good of a common discipline"; Roosevelt himself "unhesitatingly" assumed "the leadership of this great army"; and he promised that if the crisis continued he would ask Congress for "broad executive power to wage war against the emergency," just as he would in the event of a foreign invasion.

Action he had pledged, and action the country got. The actions were not always coherent, and it sometimes seemed that the New Deal's left hand repaired damage done by the right. Roosevelt's critics accused him of instituting a planned economy, but the New Deal was more spontaneous than planned. Roosevelt knew better what his goals were than what his programs were. The goals were pragmatic: he wanted to restore prosperity and to reform the economic system in such a way that a similar disaster would never again overtake the American people. The President was impatient with ideologies and comprehensive schemes; all he wanted was results.

The legislation of the New Deal came in bursts, the first one in a special session called the "hundred days," from March to June, 1933, and the second in 1935. Even the lulls were productive, by ordinary legislative standards, until 1938, when the New Deal as a creative force was finished. Throughout the New Deal, programs for economic recovery were mingled with more permanent programs for reform. The New Deal began as a gigantic effort to do something for everyone, but as the depression wore on, Roosevelt increased the proportion of help for the underprivileged and curtailed aid to business. In this respect, the "second New Deal" of 1935 and after showed that Roosevelt had drifted to the left. Yet the National Recovery Administration (NRA), the keystone of the first New Deal, and the Tennessee Valley Authority (TVA), created in 1933, were as abrupt departures from traditional American political and economic principles as anything that came in the second New Deal.

THE NEW DEAL AND THE ECONOMIC CRISIS

The banking crisis demanded the new President's immediate attention, for when he first took office and for some days thereafter, not a bank in the nation opened for business. Beginning in October, 1932, governors had proclaimed temporary "holidays" to prevent runs on banks; by the following March precautionary closing had occurred in nearly half the states, and Treasury officials urged the other half to follow suit. Roosevelt issued a proclamation making the holiday national and official and then called Congress into special session to ratify his action and to provide legislation to end the emergency. The Emergency Banking Act, passed only a few hours after Congress assembled, required most banks to have an authorization from the Treasury before reopening, permitted the RFC to make immediate loans to banks the Treasury found to be sound, and allowed the Federal Reserve system to issue notes based on the assets of strong banks. Most banks began to function again after a few days, but the Treasury refused immediate licenses to more than 1700 shaky banks, some of which eventually consolidated their assets and reopened. On March 12, 1933, Roosevelt made his first "fireside chat," an informal radio report to the nation in which he assured Americans that the newly licensed banks were secure. Within three weeks bank deposits increased more than a billion dollars, and that crisis was over.

The Home Owners Loan Corporation, established a few weeks later, was another device to take the pressure off both banks and their debtors. The HOLC refinanced urban mortgages, thus relieving the anxiety of those whose homes were in danger of foreclosure and at the same time providing the banks with liquid assets that were essential. Foreclosures soon declined from the rate of a thousand per day in the first months of 1933; when the HOLC wound up its affairs, it had refinanced one of every five nonfarm mortgages in the nation.

Having met the emergency, the administration moved to prevent a recurrence. The general prosperity of the 1920s had hidden the failure of nearly 7,000 banks, most of which were small ones located in areas dependent upon depressed agricultural staples. The Glass-Steagall Act, passed in June, 1933, required the separation of commercial and investment banking and enlarged the Federal Reserve Board's authority, which the Banking Act of 1935 increased still further. The Glass-Steagall Act also guaranteed bank deposits up to $2,500 through the Federal Deposit Insurance Corporation (FDIC). These reforms provoked some grumbling in the financial community but were much less extensive than nationalized banking, which had been seriously proposed. Moreover, they worked: the nation had fewer bank failures between 1933 and 1940 than had occurred in any single year of the 1920s.

Two related statutes subjected stock exchanges to federal supervision. The "Truth in Securities" Act of 1933 required corporations to file with the Federal Trade Commission sworn statements about their financial condition before new stock could be issued. In 1934 Congress established the Securities and Exchange Commission (SEC) to regulate trading and prevent unscrupulous manipulation of stock prices. The government did not, of course, guarantee investments; but it did insist that the investor have accurate information on which to base his decision and a fair market in which to trade.

The Emergency Banking Act in effect took the country off the gold standard, a step that Congress confirmed officially in April, 1933. About the same time, Senator Elmer Thomas sponsored an amendment to the New Deal's primary agricultural legislation that empowered the President to inflate the dollar by changing its gold content, by coining silver at any ratio to gold he chose, and by issuing $3 billion in greenbacks, which the President decided not to print. Although the Thomas Amendment gave Roosevelt authority he did not particularly want, the administration did try to induce inflation by manipulating the price of gold and silver. For a few months in 1933 Roosevelt regularly raised the price of gold, thereby making the dollar worth less, in the vain hope that other prices would rise in response. A similar program to buy the entire domestic output of silver at an inflated price helped the politically influential silver interests (which were economically less important than the chewing gum industry) but did not improve general price levels. When neither program generated the expected inflation, Roosevelt turned from currency experiments to other methods of curing the depression.

Financial reform and inflated currency were useless without vitality in the nation's industry and agriculture, without employment, without a flow of goods in response to consumer demand. In the National Industrial Recovery Act (NIRA) of June, 1933, Congress wove together several proposals designed to restore business prosperity and to permit workers to share the expected benefits.

The most orthodox provision of this act appropriated more than $3 billion for construction of roads, bridges, buildings, and other public works. Roosevelt assigned Secretary of the Interior Harold L. Ickes, a gruff, honest, former Bull Mooser, to administer the Public Works Administration. Although the need was for immediate spending, Ickes conscientiously scrutinized blueprints and proposals to make sure the public received full value, and the PWA did not inject large amounts of money into the economy until the middle of the decade. Ickes' integrity secured worthwhile projects at minimal expense, but his failure to spend more rapidly may have delayed recovery.

Much less orthodox was the National Recovery Administration, which Hugh Johnson, a stormy, salty former general, ran with gusto. During the First World War Johnson had worked with the War Industries Board, and the NRA showed the effect of that earlier cooperation between business and government. In its reliance on industrial self-regulation, the NRA derived from the trade associations that Herbert Hoover had encouraged while Secretary of Commerce. Under the sponsorship of the NRA, representatives of industry, labor, and government (the spokesman for the consumer) assembled and drew up codes to cover a particular business. When approved by the President, these codes had the force of law and regulated production, competitive practices, and less effectively, wages and hours. Theoretically, the codes would produce a "planned economy," whose benefits employees, producers, and the public would share. In fact, it soon became apparent that the plans were often those of the dominant firms in an industry, to which such benefits as there were accrued through price fixing. Although the NIRA prohibited monopolistic practices, the codes suspended the anti-trust laws. And instead of stimulating production, the NRA tended to permit restricted production and thinly veiled price stabilization.

Franklin Roosevelt launched the NRA with all the panoply of a crusade. General Johnson designed a stylized blue eagle bearing the bold legend "We Do Our Part" to symbolize the effort. The blue eagle, indeed, had to enforce the codes, for Johnson, fearing that the law might not survive a court case, could punish those who did not enlist in his crusade, or those who deserted, only by depriving them of their right to display the blue eagle. The first response to the NRA was disappointing, but General Johnson's frantic efforts, which culminated in a mammoth parade down New York's Fifth Avenue, generated public support. Yet, the codes, proclaimed with such enthusiasm, proved difficult to draft, more difficult to administer, and nearly impossible to enforce. Such a prominent manufacturer as Henry Ford refused to have anything to do with the NRA. Disillusion with the program was early and pervasive. By 1934 a National Recovery Review Board, which Roosevelt asked the noted lawyer Clarence Darrow to run, was already critically evaluating the NRA. Darrow's report accused the agency of promoting and protecting monopoly; these findings brought on a polemical exchange between Johnson and Darrow that did not advance the NRA, public policy, or recovery. In 1935 the Supreme Court, in *Schechter Poultry Company* v. *United States,* unanimously struck down the NIRA as an unconstitutional delegation of legislative power to code-making bodies and as an unjustifiable expansion of the commerce clause to include intrastate businesses. Publicly outraged, the President was privately relieved. General Johnson had promised more than the NRA could deliver; it was a political liability and a failure as well.

By 1935 business had become disenchanted with FDR, and the administration proposed no comprehensive replacement for the NRA. The Robinson-Patman Act of 1936 and the Miller-Tydings Act of 1937 helped protect smaller businesses by outlawing unreasonably low prices and by permitting "fair-trade" laws, which required standard prices on nationally distributed retail goods. The Guffey Coal Act (1935) reenacted parts of the NRA code for that sick industry. But otherwise the New Deal turned from helping business to regulating it. The Public Utility Holding Company Act (1935) authorized the Federal Power Commission, the Federal Trade Commission, and the Securities and Exchange Commission to regulate various branches of electrical and gas utilities. The act did not quite provide a "death sentence" for holding companies, as angry power lobbyists claimed, but it did require that holding companies demonstrate that efficiency or something other than profit required their continued control of operating utilities. In 1938, prodded by Ickes and other former progressives, Roosevelt attacked the continued economic consolidation that had brought 5 percent of the nation's corporations nearly 90 percent of the nation's corporate assets. Congress established the Temporary National Economic Committee (TNEC) to investigate concentration of economic power and the Justice Department began to enforce the Sherman Act. So the New Deal, which began by suspending antitrust statutes, ended by reviving them.

THE PROGRAM FOR AGRICULTURE

The agricultural policy of the New Deal was an amalgam of proposals as old as those of the Grangers with the brand new notion of controlling production. Proposals to make the nation's rural areas profitable as well as bounteous came from college professors like M. L. Wilson and Rexford G. Tugwell, from Democrats like Senator Elmer Thomas of Oklahoma, whose monetary theory came straight from William Jennings Bryan, from farm-equipment manufacturers like George Peek, from life insurance companies burdened with too many overdue mortgages on too many unprofitable farms, and from editors of farm newspapers like Henry A. Wallace, who became Roosevelt's Secretary of Agriculture and second Vice-President. Packed in one legislative bundle in 1933, these proposals emerged as the Agricultural Adjustment Act, to be administered by the Agricultural Adjustment Administration (AAA).

The act came none too soon. Farmers had endured the declining prices of the 1920s, the apparent indifference of Calvin Coolidge, and the hesitant, ineffective programs of Herbert Hoover; in 1932 patience had given way to anger in some areas. In Iowa, Milo Reno's militant "farm holiday" movement tried to keep crops off the market in order to raise prices. Foreclosed farmers marched to Washington demanding a moratorium on forced sales. In parts of the Midwest, foreclosures and sheriff's sales became farces when armed friends of victims intimidated judges and creditors. Yet prices continued to drop. By 1933 the farmers' purchasing power was 40 percent below that of 1929, which by any other standard was a bad year.

The AAA paid farmers direct subsidies in return for decreased production. The cost of the subsidy was passed on to the consumer through a tax paid by processors of agricultural produce. The act carefully catered to rural sensitivity by requiring the farmers themselves to approve production agreements and by using local farmers to administer the program where possible. In order to reduce the already planted crop of 1933, farmers had to destroy some growing cotton and slaughter 5 million pigs before they became marketable. No one was happy about destroying potential food and clothing when millions of people lacked both; Norman Thomas, the perpetual spokesman for America's few socialists, tartly congratulated the New Deal for removing the paradox of poverty in the midst of plenty by eliminating plenty. Wallace and his advisers saw no alternative. At least superficially, the AAA seemed to work. Agricultural production declined while prices and farm income went up, sharply in the case of cotton growers. Even so, more intensive cultivation of fewer acres continued to produce more crops than forecasts called for, and farm prices did not reach parity.

After the harvest in the fall of 1933 the AAA established the Commodity Credit Corporation to hold surpluses off the market. Rather like the subtreasury scheme of the Populists, the CCC used crops as security for loans. To qualify, farmers had to agree to reduce production the following year. The New Deal also found other ways of extending credit to farmers faced with foreclosure and tax sales. The Emergency Farm Mortgage Act, passed as part of the Agricultural Adjustment Act, permitted Federal Land Banks to refinance farm mortgages. The Farm Credit Act, administered by Henry Morgenthau, Roosevelt's friend and later Secretary of the Treasury, made more credit available to more farmers; within seven months Morgenthau had lent nearly $100 million to keep farmers on their farms. But the problem persisted, and in 1934 Congress passed three separate acts dealing with farm credit, one of which, the Frazier-Lemke Farm Bankruptcy Act, made foreclosure so difficult that the Supreme Court declared the statute unconstitutional.

In a six-to-three decision in 1936, the Court also declared the processing tax provision of the Agricultural Adjustment Act unconstitutional and by taking away its source of funds rendered the AAA ineffective. The decision was strained; the dissent was unusually sharp; the President was furious, partly because the election of 1936 would occur just after the next harvest, when prices would be still fresh in the minds of farmers. Congress put the AAA in a new wrapper by substituting for the processing tax a direct payment to farmers who adopted such soil-conservation practices as not planting the staple crops that were in chronic surplus. The Soil Conservation and Domestic Allotment Act was less effective in reducing production than a drought that hit the farm belt in the mid-1930s. The drought, plus strong winds and the effect of years of plowing, created the dust bowl and sent thousands of displaced "Okies" from Oklahoma, Kansas, Texas, and other parched states off to California in search of nonexistent jobs.

When the drought ended, Secretary Wallace proposed new methods of holding down production, and Congress enacted them in the second Agricultural Adjustment Act of 1938. The statute permitted the Secretary of Agriculture to impose marketing quotas and acreage allotments to reduce surpluses. To achieve parity, the act authorized the Commodity Credit Corporation to lend money on the security of nonperishable staples at slightly less than parity. The presence of stored surpluses promised what Wallace called an "ever-normal granary" in the event of natural disasters and at the same time kept prices from rising very far above parity. For if the market improved, farmers would sell their stored crops, pay off their loans, and drive prices down to parity levels. The war prevented a test of the "ever-normal granary," since surplus food had many wartime uses.

None of these programs improved the lives of the most destitute rural residents. Benefit payments went to landowners, not to farmhands, tenants, sharecroppers, and migrant laborers. The Soil Conservation Act diverted a portion of the benefit payment to sharecroppers, but poverty, pellagra, and hookworm continued to be their lot. In 1935 Roosevelt put Rexford Tugwell in charge of the Resettlement Administration, which was empowered to undertake a variety of projects to enable both rural and urban poor to escape to new communities and presumably to new opportunities. Battered by congressional criticism, the RA actually resettled few families and was absorbed in 1937 by the Farm Security Administration. The FSA enabled agricultural laborers to purchase farms with government credit; in spite of the poverty of the borrowers, there were few defaults on these loans.

The New Deal perhaps transformed rural life most with one of the least noticed, least controversial programs. In May, 1935, Roosevelt established the Rural Electrification Administration to help make power available to isolated farms. The REA encouraged the establishment of cooperatives, lent them money to build distribution facilities, and advised them about marketing power. Electricity not only eased the tasks of farming but also removed many of the differences between urban and rural life.

THE POOR AND THE UNEMPLOYED

Probably the most comprehensive measure of the entire New Deal was the program to improve the Tennessee Valley, an area where living standards had long lagged behind those of most of the rest of the nation. The act establishing the Tennessee Valley Authority (TVA) successfully concluded Senator Norris' prolonged effort to have the government develop a complete plan for the valley. The three-man directorate of the TVA was to plan nothing less than a total rehabilitation of the region, to control its rivers and convert their energy to electricity, to replace eroded gullies and naked hills with productive farms and growing forests, to diversify the economy and bring prosperity to parts of seven states.

The TVA built more than 20 dams, which transformed the rampaging Tennessee River into the tamest stream in the world, and made an inland waterway more than 600 miles long. The agency introduced new

Wheeler Dam, part of the multipurpose TVA

crops and new techniques to improve fertility and prevent erosion. And by the end of the 1930s, the TVA produced and distributed electric power, thereby providing what FDR called a "yardstick" to measure the costs of private utilities. Although competition decreased the price of privately produced electricity by about 70 percent, utilities discovered that increased volume pushed their profits up. Nevertheless, private utilities, led by Wendell Willkie, the dynamic president of the largest holding company in the area, attacked the TVA's power operation both in court and in public. The attack in court failed, but the public attack was more successful, for Congress ignored subsequent attempts to apply TVA techniques to other river valleys. To be sure, as opponents of the TVA have argued, the taxes of the whole nation raised the economic level of one region. But the Tennessee Valley has probably repaid the nation with income taxes that would never have been paid if the area had continued in its depressed pre-TVA condition.

The Tennessee Valley in 1933 was not the only depressed area in America. In 1931 West Africans had taken a collection for starving New Yorkers; two years later, hunger had increased beyond relief through private charity. Before the end of March, 1933, the administration combined the need for relief with an interest in conservation and chartered the

Civilian Conservation Corps. The CCC employed as many as a half-million young men in reforestation, flood and erosion control, and maintenance of national parks. FDR had an almost Jeffersonian faith that fresh air and hard work would transform the temporarily unemployed into sturdy, self-reliant citizens. If the CCC did not work wonders of individual regeneration, it did at least keep some young men off the job market and it planted more than half the trees set out by man since the nation began.

With millions of unemployed Americans requiring help in 1933, the CCC was hardly a start. In May Congress established the Federal Emergency Relief Administration (FERA), and Roosevelt appointed Harry Hopkins, a young social worker, to direct the agency. No scruples about budgets troubled Hopkins; it was need that stirred him. The legislation permitted him to allot money to states for direct relief. Within hours of its passage Hopkins had granted several million dollars. But he disliked direct relief nearly as much as did Hoover. Hopkins preferred to provide the needy with employment, if necessary under federal sponsorship, and he persuaded FDR to his view. In November, 1933, Hopkins established the Civil Works Administration to employ about four million jobless on projects that required little equipment and much labor, such as leaf-raking and street-sweeping. The CWA enabled many families to survive the winter of 1933–1934 before the program expired in the spring.

But unemployment did not abate. Federal relief programs continued until 1935, when Roosevelt made a distinction between the unemployed, for whom the federal government assumed responsibility, and the unemployable, whose welfare was left to state and local authorities or to private charity. The Works Progress Administration, of which Hopkins was the chief, employed as many as 3.5 million people on a host of projects. The WPA not only built roads, bridges, public buildings, airports, and parks; but also sponsored symphony concerts, hired artists to paint murals, established a federal theater, commissioned unemployed writers to produce a series of guide books to the states, and through the National Youth Administration (NYA), provided employment for college students. Hopkins believed the WPA must do more than employ people; it must also preserve their morale and their skills, which the nation would some day need again. Some of the agency's projects were not very useful—"boondoggling" the critics said—and the various arts projects were particularly vulnerable because some of them seemed to promote radicalism. But before it ended in 1943, the WPA had saved the dignity, and perhaps the lives, of millions of Americans.

The WPA was a response to depression; Social Security was a permanent program to cure the curse of unemployment in an industrial society. Drafted by a group under the direction of Secretary of Labor Frances Perkins, the Social Security Act of 1935 combined unemployment insurance with a program to provide annuities for the aged or dependent survivors of workers. A tax on payrolls, paid by employers and employees, provided funds. Unemployment-insurance benefits, administered by the states, would mitigate the effect of economic cataclysm and might prevent the spread of unemployment by making continued consumption possible. Annuities for the aged might enable this growing segment of the population to leave the job market without imposing a financial burden on their families. By comparison with the politically potent appeal of Dr. Francis Townsend, whose Townsend Plan proposed to grant $200 per month to every citizen over 65, provided only that the money was spent before the next check arrived, the New Deal's Social Security seemed conservative. Initially the grants were small and many Americans were not included in the program, but so successful has it been that political debate since 1935 has centered on the degree of desirable expansion.

WORKERS AND THEIR UNIONS

Before 1933 organized labor had been nearly as suspicious of Presidents as Presidents were of unions. Neither Theodore Roosevelt nor Woodrow Wilson, for instance, had anything resembling a labor program. Nor, in the beginning, did Franklin Roosevelt. Indeed, the New Deal's labor legislation owes relatively little to the President and a great deal to congressional friends of labor, such as Senator Robert F. Wagner of New York. In the late 1930s, the labor movement, displaying a new zeal, organized industries that had for decades resisted. For the first time, national unions were capable of bargaining on equal terms with the nation's bigger industries. The New Deal sponsored that growth.

In Section 7(a) the National Industrial Recovery Act required all codes to guarantee the right of workers to bargain collectively and forbade employers to discriminate against union members. The NRA codes bound employers to abolish child labor and to pay a minimum wage, initially set at thirty or forty cents an hour (depending upon location), for a forty-hour week. To enforce these provisions, the act created the National Labor Board, which Roosevelt appointed Senator Wagner to head. The NLB attempted to mediate industrial disputes, but it was only partially successful. Organized labor, encouraged by the law and by public opinion, which had swung decisively against business during the depression, embarked on an organizing drive that employers determined to thwart. A wave of futile strikes in 1934—in textiles, automobiles, steel, and a general strike in San Francisco—convinced Senator Wagner that new legislation was required. When the Supreme Court invalidated the NIRA in 1935, the administration no longer had a labor program, and FDR accepted the substitute Wagner had prepared.

The Wagner Act of 1935 forbade several "unfair labor practices" and created a National Labor Relations Board (NLRB) to enforce its provisions. "Unfair labor practices" included domination of company unions, discrimination against employees because of union membership or activity, and refusal to bargain collectively with any union chosen by the workers at an election. The act specifically made a union designated in this way the exclusive representative of all workers in the plant. Apparently relying on the Supreme Court to declare the legislation unconstitutional, some employers flouted it. But in 1937, in *NLRB* v. *Jones and Laughlin Steel Co.,* the Court upheld the NLRB, and employers had to learn to live with unions.

The Wagner Act contained no standard of wages and hours, which earlier NRA codes had included. Replacing these provisions was tricky, for the Supreme Court had apparently limited the power of legislatures. The Walsh-Healy Act of 1936 empowered the Secretary of Labor to establish minimum wage levels that all government contractors must meet, specified a forty-hour week, and prohibited child labor. Finally, in 1938, Congress passed the Fair Labor Standards Act, which, although exempting agricultural labor and several other groups, established a minimum wage of twenty-five cents per hour for workers engaged in interstate commerce. The forty-four hour week permitted for three years was to drop to forty thereafter. Congress has subsequently raised the minimum wage and extended the number of people to whom the law applies several times.

Legislation was less important in improving the standards of working people than were the unions themselves, especially the Congress of Industrial Organizations. The CIO began as a federation of industrial unions inside the American Federation of Labor but soon found itself outside. John L. Lewis of the United Mine Workers and David Dubinsky and Sidney Hillman of the garment workers had urged the AFL to stop arguing about craft jurisdiction and to organize the mass-production industries in industrial unions. At a rowdy convention in 1935, livened by a fist fight between Lewis and William Hutcheson, president of the Carpenters' Union, the AFL turned down the industrial form of organization. Lewis and his followers walked out of the convention and out of the AFL.

While the CIO continued to feud with the older labor union, it had energy to spare for employers. In 1936 the CIO set aside $500,000 to organize the steel industry; in March, 1937, United States Steel signed a contract with the United Steelworkers without a strike. The attempt to organize smaller steel-producers resulted in pitched battles that the union lost during the summer of 1937; "little steel" was not unionized until 1941. Henry Ford used a strong-arm security force to blunt the drive of the United Auto Workers. But in 1937, after a rash of "sit down" strikes, General Motors and Chrysler capitulated to the UAW. Sit-down strikers simply refused to leave the plants; they were orderly, but they barricaded themselves in the shop, and at least by implication, they held building, tools, and equipment hostage for a favorable settlement.

By 1939, then, labor-management relations were far different from those of a decade before. Tough unions battled employers on more equal terms; even many unorganized workers had the protection of minimum wages and maximum hours. But the framework remained industrial capitalism—private corporations, independent unions. The government had fostered the growth of unions, to be sure, and thereby affected the process; but the government did not write the contracts or own the industries. The result of the New Deal was about what Samuel Gompers had wanted nearly a half-century before.

THE POLITICS OF THE NEW DEAL

Franklin D. Roosevelt was one of those commanding political figures to whom no man was indifferent. Those who admired him did so with a devotion that bordered on reverence; those who disliked him did so with a passion that bordered on monomania. And some went from one extreme to the other in the same year. Some thought he had delivered them and the country from destitution; others thought he had changed, and perhaps destroyed, the American way of life.

Whatever else the New Deal changed, American politics never again ran the predepression course. The central government, once committed to stabilizing the national economy, has not withdrawn. Several interest groups whose needs government previously had ignored—organized labor, for instance, and farmers—had a voice in government that sometimes seemed louder than that of the business groups, which had previously been more clearly heard. Prepared for active Presidents by Theodore Roosevelt and Woodrow Wilson, the nation was accustomed to executive initiative and to presidential dominance in a more active, more powerful government in Washington. And the party of Lincoln, which had dominated

Franklin D. Roosevelt

national politics since 1860, gave way to the party of FDR. Between 1860 and 1933 Democrats simultaneously occupied the White House and organized both houses of Congress for only eight years; since 1933 Republicans have simultaneously organized both the executive and legislative branches for only two years. One of the changes the depression brought was a new majority party.

And the party had new dominant groups. Briefly during the early New Deal, the Roosevelt administration and the business community managed to hide mutual suspicion because each thought it needed the other. But as early as 1934 the rift was visible, and it grew wider until the Second World War. By 1935 Roosevelt had intuitively broadened the base of the Democratic party. To the South and the cities, which Al Smith had captured, Roosevelt added organized labor, midwestern farmers, middleclass intellectuals, Catholics, Jews, women, and a good many Republicans who had once followed another Roosevelt. FDR fused rural Bryan Democrats with urban Cleveland-Smith Democrats, and added Progressives who had supported Wilson and Theodore Roosevelt. The coalition proved formidable and enduring.

Roosevelt's Democratic party, like all political coalitions, was shaped partly by its opponents. In 1934 a group of financiers, industrialists, and such disgruntled Democrats as Al Smith, formed the American Liberty League, which shrilly accused the administration of replacing a free economy with a regimented one. In a similar vein, Herbert Hoover charged in 1934 that "those who appear to merit political power" had snatched control of the economy from those whose ability entitled them to manage. Since the business elite, which Hoover favored, had left the economy in rather a mess, Democrats must have hoped fervently that Herbert Hoover would keep talking. And in the congressional election of 1934 Roosevelt's party increased its margin in both houses.

For a time Democrats had to compete with several political splinter groups that advanced deceptively simple cures for the depression. Support for the Townsend Plan rolled east from California, for neither professional economists, who pointed out that the plan would place 60 percent of the national income at the disposal of less than 10 percent of the population, nor the Social Security act, blunted the fervor of Dr. Townsend's followers. From Detroit, Father Charles Coughlin, the "radio priest" who received even more mail than the President, beamed his weekly message that only remonetizing silver would bring inflation. If his proposals were otherwise vague, Father Coughlin's enemies were clear, including at various times bankers, Communists, Jews, "internationalists," and FDR. Neither the physician nor the priest had the political sensitivity of the shrewd, ambitious, and formidably able Senator from Louisiana, Huey P. Long. By 1934 Long's "Share Our Wealth" program promised to make "Every Man a King," with an immediate capital grant of $5,000 and a guaranteed annual minimum income of $2,000, all of which would be obtained with a capital levy on large fortunes. Pensions, higher education, more leisure, and a variety of other fringe benefits added to the attractiveness of Long's pitch.

Politics, not ideology, molded the program, for Long boasted that he never "read a line of Marx or Henry George or any of them economists." Socialists and Communists, who did read their economists, made almost no impression on the electorate; in 1936 the Socialist presidential candidate received fewer than 200,000 votes, the Communist less than half that. The other dissidents, robbed of their most attractive candidate when Long was assassinated, rallied discordantly behind Congressman William Lemke and the Union ticket, which polled nearly 900,000 votes. Roosevelt, by contrast, had the support of almost 28 million voters.

The only important issue in 1936, Roosevelt remarked with pardonable exaggeration, was Franklin Delano Roosevelt. Republicans unwisely cooperated by attacking the President and his program from the campaign trail. Yet the Republican platform betrayed a curious ambivalence: the preamble proclaimed "America is in peril," but the promises that followed sounded suspiciously like imitations of programs the Democrats had already enacted. A similar ambivalence disarmed the Republican candidate, Alfred M. Landon of Kansas. Landon eventually thundered conservative rhetoric, but it sounded odd in the mouth of a governor whose record had been rather progressive. Roosevelt conducted an apparently desultory campaign, and pundits thought the election might be close. Just before the election Roosevelt took the offensive in a New York speech in which he met his conservative critics head-on:

> Never before in all our history have these forces [of reaction] been so united against one candidate as they stand today. They are unanimous in their hate for me—and I welcome their hatred.

> I should like to have it said of my first Administration that in it the forces of selfishness and lust for power met their match. I should like to have it said of my second Administration that in it these forces met their master.

Roosevelt never entirely conquered American selfishness, but he certainly conquered Landon. James A. Farley, Roosevelt's Postmaster General and political deputy, predicted that the President would lose only the 8 electoral votes of Maine and Vermont. In the end, FDR did in fact win the other 523 electors.

Roosevelt understandably thought his triumph a mandate. Congress, where Democratic majorities rose again, was apparently his to command. But the Supreme Court, dominated by conservative justices who seemed nearly immortal, was apparently oblivious to political majorities. The *Schechter* decision of 1935 had ended the NIRA with a decision so restricted in its interpretation of the commerce clause that Roosevelt feared any economic legislation was jeopardized. A year later Justice Owen Roberts, for the majority of the Court in the *United States* v. *Butler,* declared the AAA's processing tax unconstitutional because it was a device to redistribute income instead of a bona fide tax. Justice Harlan Fiske Stone filed an incisive dissent, implying that the majority opinion was "a tortured construction of the Constitution," and reminding his judicial brethren that "courts are not the only agency of government that must be assumed to have capacity to govern." Although the Court upheld the TVA in the *Ashwander* decision (1936), the case did not settle the agency's right to distribute power. New Deal agencies did not always meet defeat in Court, but the victories were ordinarily limited, and the defeats swept away major portions of Roosevelt's program.

Early in 1937, without consulting congressional leaders, Roosevelt sent Congress a bill to reorganize the judiciary. Seizing on the fact that several justices were over seventy years old, Roosevelt proposed that he be empowered to appoint, to a total of six, an additional justice for each superannuated one on the bench. The proposal was clearly designed to pack the Court, and opponents of the New Deal, who had previously been divided, united in rousing defense of the separation of powers. All of Roosevelt's prestige and political magic availed him nothing. Following a prolonged debate that split his party, the Senate killed his bill. And Roosevelt was never again able to use the party as an obedient instrument. When the President intervened in several Democratic primaries in 1938, voters handed him a humiliating series of defeats, and Republicans scored impressive gains in the following general election. The Democratic party broke into components—liberals, conservatives, unions, southerners, bosses, and a host of other factions. Roosevelt himself survived the party's division, but the innovation of the New Deal was over.

Although the flood of legislation diminished sharply, at least the Court ceased to condemn earlier New Deal measures. In 1937, during the storm over court-packing, the justices discovered flexibility in the Constitution. In *West Coast Hotel Co.* v. *Parrish*, the Court held that states could establish minimum-wage laws. The narrow definition of interstate commerce in the Schechter decision was apparently reversed in the *NLRB* v. *Jones and Laughlin Steel Co.*, in which the Court accepted the Wagner Act. In two other cases in 1937 the Court ruled that the Social Security program was within federal power. A year later the Court repulsed an attempt to prevent the TVA from selling electricity. The form of the Constitution, the prestige of the Court, and most of the program of the New Deal survived the contest.

The depression was a trauma in the national experience perhaps comparable only to the Civil War, and few aspects of American life escaped change. Political issues, parties, and styles of leadership were profoundly altered. The government assumed part of the regulatory role of the mythical pre-1929 "impersonal market." Yet the depression did not disappear. In 1938 almost 10 million Americans lacked jobs; in 1940 the total was still 7 million. The New Deal had neither spent the nation into the poorhouse, as Roosevelt's detractors charged, nor boosted it to prosperity, as some Keynesian economists had hoped. John Maynard Keynes, the noted British economic theorist, had argued that governmental deficit spending could effectively be substituted for private investment to produce prosperity. But as Keynes himself knew, Roosevelt followed Keynesian precepts no more than he did any other theoretical percepts. The depression jolted not only what had been economic orthodoxy but also such traditional American values as thrift, prudence, and hard work and such naive beliefs as the inevitability of American prosperity and the innate superiority of the nation's institutions.

Many of those values and most of the nation's institutions survived the depression. However slowly, the American political system produced reform and continued to inspire confidence and hope. However dreary the present, Americans did not reject their past; they even overlooked the follies of the 1920s and gave the decade a posthumous pizzazz. The nation that finally emerged from the depression differed remarkably little from predepression America.

Suggested Reading

William E. Leuchtenburg's *Franklin D. Roosevelt and the New Deal** (1963) is an excellent piece of scholarship as well as a brief, judicious synthesis of other works on the New Deal. Harris G. Warren's *Herbert Hoover and the Great Depression** (1959) is critical of Hoover's policies, but more sympathetic than John Kenneth Galbraith's *The Great Crash** (1955). David A. Shannon has edited a collection of documents in *The Great Depression** (1960) that gives an individual dimension to the economic statistics of the Depression years.

Edgar E. Robinson sees Roosevelt as exercising too much power in *The Roosevelt Leadership* (1955). James M. Burns's interpretation, *Roosevelt: The Lion and the Fox** (1956), is more influential. The second and third volumes of the study of the New Deal by Arthur M. Schlesinger, Jr., carry the narrative through the election of 1936: *The Coming of the New Deal** (1959) and *The Politics of Upheaval** (1960). Samuel Lubell's *The Future of American Politics** (1952) is also useful for the politics of the period. In *An Encore for Reform** (1967) Otis L. Graham finds that the young progressives did not always mature into New Dealers.

The New Dealers themselves wrote extensively. Thurman Arnold's *The Folklore of Capitalism** (1937) is more interesting than most of the memoirs, and John M. Blum's three volumes of *From the Morgenthau Diaries* (1959–67) are more comprehensive than most of the biographies. David E. Lilienthal describes one of the New Deal's most comprehensive programs in *TVA** (1953).

*Available in paperback edition

CHRONOLOGY

1931   Japan occupies Manchuria

1932   Stimson Doctrine announces American refusal to recognize territorial transfer through conquest

1933   United States recognizes the Soviet Union
Montivideo Conference: United States renounces right to intervene in Latin America

1935–39   Congress passes neutrality acts

1935   Italy invades Ethiopia

1936   Germany reoccupies the Rhineland

1937   Japan invades China; American gunboat *Panay* bombed in Yangtze River

1938   Munich Conference

1939–45   The Second World War:
September, 1939: Germany invades Poland; Britain and France declare war
April–June, 1940: Germany occupies Norway, Denmark, Low Countries, France
March, 1941: Lend-Lease Act passed
June, 1941: Germany invades Soviet Union
August, 1941: Atlantic Conference
December, 1941: Japanese bomb Pearl Harbor; United States enters war
November, 1942: Allied invasion of North Africa
September, 1943: Allied invasion of Italy
June, 1944: Allied invasion of France
October, 1944: American invasion of Philippines
February, 1945: Yalta Conference
May, 1945: Germany surrenders
August, 1945: Japan surrenders after atom bombs destroy Hiroshima and Nagasaki

1940   Presidential election: Franklin D. Roosevelt (Democrat) defeats Wendell L. Willkie (Republican)

1944   Presidential election: Franklin D. Roosevelt (Democrat) defeats Thomas E. Dewey (Republican)

1945   Harry S. Truman succeeds Roosevelt in April

ISOLATION

AND INTERVENTION

The 1930s were years of depression in the United States. Elsewhere in the world the decade was marked by renewed war, by the loss of national independence or the threat of such loss, and by the acceptance of totalitarian dictatorship that promised instant national greatness, painless industrialization, or more of the earth's surface. Preoccupied with their own economic paralysis, ordinary Americans weighed events abroad more for their economic promise than for their effect on national security. Even if isolation was never achieved, it was the ideal to which most Americans probably aspired. Until the end of the decade, Franklin Roosevelt worried more about his New Deal than about Adolf Hitler's New Order; although the toll of Chinese civilians killed in the Japanese bombing of Shanghai shocked official Washington, these numbers were, on the whole, less disturbing than unemployment statistics from Chicago.

The depression helped remove a few disputes that had plagued diplomats in the 1920s. In 1933 the lure of the Russian market made diplomatic recognition of the Soviet Union seem less dangerous than it had appeared in the previous decade. The United States had steadfastly refused to exchange ambassadors with the USSR because the Communist government had repudiated the Czarist debt, encouraged subversive propaganda, and harassed Russian Christians and Jews. After the Russians promised to curb propaganda in the United States, formal diplomatic contact was renewed. But recognition fulfilled neither the best hopes of its proponents nor the dire predictions of those who had opposed it. Propaganda did not cease, trade did not climb, and wholesale subversion did not ensue.

Economic distress also effectively ended international squabbling over war debts and reparations. Token payments unofficially prolonged until 1934 the moratorium that Herbert Hoover had officially proclaimed in 1931. As depression deepened, debtor nations, with the exception of Finland, abandoned even the pretense of payment. Congress formally ended the vexatious dispute with the Johnson Act of 1934, which forbade future loans to nonpaying nations and tacitly acknowledged default of their debts.

But the depression did nothing to reduce other international tensions and probably exacerbated some of them. The disruption of international trade was partly responsible for Japanese demands for political and economic change in East Asia. Economic dislocation in Germany enlarged the receptive audience for Hitler's demagogic promises to junk the Versailles settlement and redraw the map of Europe. The failure of the Italian economy to keep pace with Mussolini's grandiose vision drove him to seek colonial outlets for what he called "surplus population." Economic distress in Western Europe gave Stalin the security his diplomats had failed to provide and permitted him to turn the Soviet Union's entire national energy to the rapid development of an industrial plant, with diplomatic consequences that lasted well beyond the decade.

Not all these changes were understood at the Geneva headquarters of the League of Nations, where debate, like the dress of the diplomats, was ordinarily dignified and stiffly formal. The United States remained aloof, as it had since a proud President and a stubborn Senate had refused to compromise. Yet the world's statesmen at least pretended that the League was important, until the Japanese delegation shattered the pretense by stalking out early in 1933. Within months the Germans followed. The League continued to talk about international problems, but few delegates believed that it could actually do anything. National intransigence and international depression had smashed the Versailles settlement.

Not many Americans mourned. Whatever enthusiasm there had once been for Woodrow Wilson's peace dissipated in the decade after he left the White House. Historians, journalists, and novelists spread the word that munitions merchants, bankers, propagandists, and Anglophile politicians had drawn the United States into the First World War to increase their profits and bail out their friends; idealism, these revisionists asserted, had been the sugar coating on a noxious pill. Disillusionment with the struggle rubbed off on the peace, which few Americans in 1933 defended as just. Yet any modification of that peace, Americans believed, must come in an orderly manner and must not disturb their national interest.

This unwillingness to stand firmly for the status quo, coupled with an unwillingness to permit the changes that other ambitious powers demanded, produced hesitant American policy in the 1930s. On the one hand,

Americans were aware that changes in the power of Japan and Germany required a new diplomatic stance; on the other hand, American policymakers clung to the Open Door and half-heartedly opposed Hitler's demands. On the one hand, Americans wanted desperately to stay out of European entanglements that seemed almost certain to bring another world war; on the other hand, Americans generally despised Fascism, totalitarianism, and Nazism, and the country needed allies in the impending struggle to check these evils. On the one hand, Americans wanted the domestic benefits of economic nationalism, and on the other, they preached the virtues of improving international amity through international trade. These ambiguities plagued and virtually paralyzed American foreign policy, except in Latin America, where Yankee strategic and economic power overawed potential rivals.

THE POLICY OF THE GOOD NEIGHBOR

"In the field of world policy," said Franklin Roosevelt as he took office, "I would dedicate this nation to the policy of the good neighbor...." The President then explained that the good neighbor kept his obligations and stayed in his own yard, a definition that effectively ruled out substantial international change. The phrase "Good Neighbor Policy" soon described only diplomatic contact in the Western Hemisphere, for some of the neighbors in Europe and Asia undertook to enlarge their share of the neighborhood.

No nation's foreign policy is entirely altruistic, and the Good Neighbor Policy was no exception. The United States appeared to give up unilateral action in the hemisphere, but renouncing Theodore Roosevelt's Corollary and making enforcement of the Monroe Doctrine a hemispheric responsibility in fact made little practical difference. Most Latin American republics were economically tied to the United States, which was their best market for oil, sugar, coffee, copper, and bananas. Even combined, the southern republics lacked the military capacity to resist the United States, and local jealousies prevented their ever getting together. With more or less grace, then, Latin America had to follow the lead of the United States.

It was, therefore, tactful of American policy-makers to stop flaunting Yankee supremacy. President Hoover had begun to draw the velvet glove over the steel fist; Roosevelt and Cordell Hull, his Secretary of State, completed the process. In 1933, at a Pan-American conference in Montevideo, Uruguay, Hull signed a treaty that denied the right of any state "to intervene in the internal or external affairs of another." The Montevideo agreement implied American willingness to give up the Platt Amendment, which had permitted American intervention in Cuba since 1901. In 1934 the State Department announced the formal abrogation of the amendment and in 1936 negotiated a treaty with Panama that gave up the right to intervene there too.

In return, the Latin American republics joined the United States in an attempt to seal off the Western Hemisphere from the troubled other half of the globe. In Buenos Aires in 1936, the American states promised to consult one another if an international war seemed to "menace the peace of the American hemisphere." Two years later, at Lima, Peru, the pledge to consult was strengthened by a pledge to resist "all foreign intervention." When war broke out in Europe, the Declaration of Panama of 1939 warned all belligerents to stay well outside the territorial waters of American states. In 1940, after the Nazis had overrun Western Europe, the Act of Havana proclaimed the hemisphere's unwillingness to permit the transfer of possessions from one European power to another. The Monroe Doctrine had become a hemispheric policy, not just a pronouncement of the United States.

While apparently making concessions, the United States in fact gave up nothing at all. For the Latin American republics simply joined in sponsoring a policy that the United States had previously championed. The Good Neighbor Policy was designed to make diplomatic contact less strained and to bring increased hemispheric trade, which might stimulate the depressed Yankee economy. However loose the diplomatic leash seemed to be, Latin Americans could usually be brought to heel by a tug on the economic chain. The Good Neighbor Policy was a good-will gesture that cost the United States next to nothing.

STAYING NEUTRAL

The depression reinforced pervasive American disgust with world politics. Convinced that Europeans had tricked the United States into one great war, bungled the peace settlement, and then declined to pay their bills, many Americans swore off Europe along with grand international causes. After 1933 they found an outlet for their remaining idealism in the New Deal.

While the New Dealers attempted to transform America, depression and dictators transformed Europe. Democratic institutions disappeared not only in Germany but also in Poland, Spain, and Austria; constitutional monarchies vanished in Italy and Greece; neither Britain nor France displayed democratic vitality at home or zeal in defense of democracy elsewhere. As early as 1934 American newspaper-readers knew that barbed wire, short rations, and numbing terror prevailed in German concentration camps and, not long after, in those of the Soviet Union as well. As early as 1936 Nazi bureaucrats told American newspaper editors that extermination was the only satisfactory long-term answer to what was euphemistically called "the Jewish problem."

Americans did not like dictators or their so-called ideologies. Although the depression convinced a few Americans that capitalism was finished, the Communist party rallied few converts and the Communist underground fewer still. Although Hitler succeeded in making anti-Semitism both official and respectable in Germany, American anti-Semitism remained the preserve of cranks and bigots. The German-American Bund drilled storm troopers in rural hideaways; enterprising native Nazis like William Dudley

Pelley organized imitation fascist bands and aped Hitler's rhetoric and mannerisms. But neither the Bund nor the native *Führers* attracted so much attention as they did contempt.

However firm the rejection of domestic totalitarianism, Americans rarely advocated diplomatic action to curb it abroad. However vigorously Americans disapproved of Stalin's purges, Hitler's concentration camps, or expansion by militarists from Italy or Japan, the United States' diplomatic response was ordinarily no more than a note of protest, and sometimes not even that much. Isolation, the dominant public mood, eclipsed the disapproval of dictatorship.

Since 1941 isolation has had a bad press, and even many one-time isolationists have renounced their previous faith to adopt collective security, the "internationalist" alternative. Yet, if some isolationists were naive in the 1930s, and if some were Communists or anti-Semites, most were decent Americans as well informed and as intelligent as those with whom they disagreed. Isolationists included pacifists, Anglophobes, and people who could see no moral choice between spineless Britain and blustering Germany. Many isolationists believed that bankers and businessmen had hoodwinked a gullible public and witless politicians into participation in the First World War, a national error that must not be repeated.

The isolationist position had a reputable heritage from Washington and Jefferson and rested squarely on respected concepts of neutral rights and international law. Isolationists blended national humility with pride in the nation's power. They rejected the arrogant assumption that the United States had any business telling other people how to organize their lives, and they boasted that the United States could stand alone. Isolationists feared that traditional institutions and ancient liberties, already rocked by depression, might disappear in another war. They foresaw that such a war would require alliances and end the American habit of nonentanglement. Undoubtedly the isolationists underestimated the danger to Western values that Nazism and militarism posed, but they also correctly predicted some of the consequences of a war to end those evils.

Isolation found legislative expression in the neutrality acts that Congress began to pass in 1935. The first neutrality act, a hasty and temporary measure, prohibited the sale of arms to belligerents upon presidential proclamation that a state of war existed. The act went on to give up one of the rights of a neutral nation that President Wilson had most stubbornly upheld: Congress gave the President authority to prohibit Americans from traveling on belligerent ships. Subsequently, in 1936, Congress forbade loans to any belligerent, and early in 1937 Congress extended the provisions of previous neutrality acts to cover all civil wars. New legislation in May, 1937, repeated all the earlier prohibitions and gave the President discretionary authority to prohibit sale of anything at all to belligerents unless the purchaser paid cash and carried the goods away in his own ships. After the European war began in September, 1939, Congress permitted the sale of arms on the same "cash and carry" basis, a concession that, because of the British fleet, favored Hitler's foes.

By that time Hitler's foes needed help, for each of the neutrality acts had been a response to deteriorating conditions abroad. Late in 1935 Italy invaded Ethiopia, and Roosevelt imposed the embargo on arms sales required by the 1935 Neutrality Act. Britain and France publicly deplored Mussolini's aggression while privately informing the Fascist Duce that they would not interfere. With its two strongest members self-disarmed, the League imposed an ineffective embargo on arms, camels, and rubber, but not on steel, trucks, and oil. The United States continued to supply Italy with the petroleum products that eventually enabled Fascist armies to overrun Ethiopia.

While Mussolini was mopping up in Ethiopia, Hitler sent troops into the Rhineland, from which the Treaty of Versailles had barred military bases. British and French policy, in disarray after Ethiopia, could not stop Hitler; even the protests from London and Paris were muted. Later in 1936 both Hitler and Mussolini took advantage of the civil war in Spain to test their troops and equipment in support of General Francisco Franco's Fascist coup. The Spanish Republic rallied support from the Soviet Union and an extra-legal "Abraham Lincoln Brigade" of American liberals. But Stalin soon turned to purging his own followers, American liberals were too few and too late, and the Spanish Republic collapsed.

In the spring of 1938, over the weak protests of the Western powers, Hitler rode in triumph to Vienna as his troops occupied Austria. Less than six months later, following some hurried, unconventional, and undignified negotiation at Munich, Britain and France in effect forced Czechoslovakia to cede Hitler the Sudetenland, a substantial slice of western Czechoslovakia that included a large minority of German-speaking inhabitants. In March, 1939, in spite of solemn promises made at Munich that the Sudetenland had been the last demand, Hitler annexed the rest of Czechoslovakia. In August, Hitler purchased Soviet neutrality with the Baltic states and eastern Poland, a price the Western Allies had refused to pay. The Nazi-Soviet pact clearly signaled the end of Poland, whose independence Britain and France had sworn to support. A week after the Nazi-Soviet agreement, the German blitzkrieg began in Poland; two days later Britain and France declared war on Germany and the Second World War was formally under way.

THE END OF PEACE IN ASIA

Like other industrial nations, Japan felt the impact of the depression. Economic distress, the ambitions of military leaders, and nationalism combined in a scheme to surround the Japanese Asian market with Japanese frontiers. Within this Greater East Asia Co-prosperity Sphere, Japan was supposed to supply manufactured goods in return for the raw material and agricultural produce of other lands.

Some Asian peoples resisted Japanese mercantilism. Chinese and Japanese economic interests clashed, most notably in Manchuria, an area nominally under Chinese political control, where Japan had secured economic concessions by treaty. In September, 1931, Japanese troops used an explosion on the South Manchurian Railway as an excuse to overrun the entire province. The Japanese garrison in Manchuria was more belligerent than its civilian superiors in Tokyo, and the occupation may even have been contrary to the intent of the Japanese Cabinet. But once Manchuria was secured, Japan would not budge; both Chinese protests and resolutions of the League of Nations were ignored. After threatening sterner action, the League appointed an investigating commission, which in 1932 reproved China for its attempt to interfere with legitimate Japanese interests in Manchuria but more sharply condemned Japan for the rash use of entirely too much force. Japan soon walked out of the League and established a satellite regime in Manchuria, which was renamed Manchukuo.

Japan paid no more attention to American protests than to those from Geneva. The United States regarded the occupation of Manchuria as a violation of the Kellogg-Briand pact renouncing war, and as a breach of the Nine Power agreement to maintain the Open Door. Although Henry L. Stimson, Hoover's Secretary of State, could not formally cooperate with the League, he favored stern international action to roll back the Japanese advance. He got no cooperation, either in Washington or abroad. President Hoover also disapproved of Japan's use of force, but in 1931 and 1932 he had too many pressing domestic problems to undertake an active Asian policy. The American public was understandably skeptical of the assertion that any vital national interest was at stake. Although European diplomats agreed with Stimson in principle, they thought Manchuria too remote and too unimportant to justify the massive effort that would apparently be required to undo Japanese conquest. The frustrated Stimson, after consultation with the President, was reduced to announcing American policy in a letter to William E. Borah, who headed the Senate Committee on Foreign Relations. The United States, Stimson wrote, would insist on its treaty rights in Manchuria. He hoped that other nations would join the United States in refusing to recognize territorial settlements imposed by force, a formula that became known as the Stimson Doctrine.

The Stimson Doctrine, like the resolutions of the League, confessed impotence. Japan had seized Manchuria by force; short of similar force, nothing Stimson or the League could do would make Japan give up Manchuria. An embargo of strategic materials, especially oil, might have hurt Japan, but Stimson could not interest the President or any other nation in imposing such a ban. The Stimson Doctrine indicated, for those who wanted to read the moral, that appeals to conscience and reliance on international agreements would not stop any nation bent on violence.

And violence spread in Asia. In 1932 Japanese troops occupied Shanghai following the first major air assault directed against a civilian population. Statesmen talked of outraged world opinion, but when the Japanese withdrew a few months later, they did so for their own reasons, not from any sense of guilt. In 1937 a full-scale Japanese invasion rapidly took over much of coastal China, from which Japan did not withdraw until peace returned to the Pacific more than eight years later. President Roosevelt refused to call the struggle a war, a decision that permitted Americans to evade the neutrality legislation and lend money to China. When the United States inquired about the Open Door, Japan curtly replied that the policy was no longer relevant. When Japanese aircraft in 1937 sank the *Panay,* an American gunboat, in the Yangtze River, the State Department and the public promptly accepted Japan's apology. It would take more than a shattered gunboat to dispel American isolation.

WAR ENDS DEBATE

However much Americans favored China or Poland or Britain or France, and however wicked they thought Japanese militarists and Nazi storm troopers, the first response was to avoid conflict, as the neutrality legislation demonstrated. Franklin Roosevelt had not objected to the neutrality acts as they passed, but in 1937 and 1938, when the world seemed headed for war, he discovered that the legislation made him almost powerless to check Japanese aggression in China or to thwart Hitler's designs in Europe. Roosevelt tried to achieve European security and a "quarantine" of aggressors through private diplomacy and public addresses. Neither method proved successful.

In the spring of 1940 the Nazis abruptly turned west, and by the end of June they had smashed resistance in Scandinavia, the Low Countries, and France, and had the British wondering when invasion of their island would come. Hitler's rapid advance convinced isolationists that the United States should concentrate on its own defense, not dissipate its strength abroad. The America First Committee, the most active isolationist organization in the months before Pearl Harbor, stressed the dangers of diplomatic entanglement and the advantages of "fortress America"—an armed, alert nation separated from the rest of the world by two broad oceans. The America First Committee reached a national audience through an active press campaign and through the speeches of Charles A. Lindbergh, the aviator-hero of the 1920s.

But the Nazi success in Europe gradually broke the spell of American isolation. William Allen White, a Republican newspaper editor from Kansas, became the national chairman of the Committee to Defend America by Aiding the Allies (an unwieldy title that was usually shortened to the White Committee), which countered isolationist arguments. By inclination an internationalist, Roosevelt nevertheless let White and others carry the running debate with the isolationists. The President's caution was partly political; much of the debate coincided with his campaign for reelection in 1940. But Roosevelt also hoped that events abroad would unify the country, for no responsible democratic statesman wants angry domestic controversy to divide a nation at war.

The split was deep. In 1938 Congress had narrowly refused to debate the Ludlow Amendment, which would have required a national referendum to declare war. Roosevelt's successful effort to modify the neutrality acts in 1939 required all his political skill and still embittered his relationship with Congress. As late as August, 1941, isolationists in the House came within a single vote of blocking selective-service legislation that military authorities argued was crucial.

If the debates were bitter, isolationists usually lost and internationalist successes became more frequent. The Republican National Convention of 1940 passed over well-known isolationist senators, like Robert Taft of Ohio and Arthur Vandenburg of Michigan, and selected the internationalist dark horse Wendell Willkie. Willkie's nomination took some of the partisanship out of foreign policy, for he criticized the execution of American policies, rather than the policies themselves. When British Prime Minister Winston Churchill renewed his pleas for American destroyers to supplement the British navy, Roosevelt indirectly consulted Willkie before completing the "Destroyer Deal," which swapped fifty old American destroyers for 99-year leases on British bases on Newfoundland, the West Indies, and British Guiana. Since the trade strengthened "fortress America," Roosevelt blunted isolationist criticism, although supplying warships to a belligerent obviously violated the canons of conventional neutrality.

Yet isolation refused to die. Antiwar sentiment tempted Roosevelt into an unwise end-of-campaign pledge not to send American "boys ... into any foreign wars." After he won reelection, losing only ten states, Roosevelt took steps that made his pledge seem opportunistic vote-catching. In January, 1941, he recommended to Congress a program of "lend-lease," which empowered the President to buy war materials and give them to countries whose defense he thought vital to American security. Roosevelt defended his proposal with the analogy of one neighbor lending another his garden hose to fight a fire; when the fire was out, the hose was returned, and there was no need to keep books on the transaction or create debts and future disputes. Isolationists saw lend-lease somewhat differently: it was, observed Senator Burton K. Wheeler of Montana, "the New Deal's triple-A foreign policy," which would "plow under every fourth American boy." Again the debate was bitter, and again the isolationists lost; the bill and an initial appropriation of $7 billion passed in March. Shipments to Britain began at once, and after Hitler invaded the Soviet Union in June, the Red Army also received American war material.

Supply logically included safe delivery, and step by inexorable step, the United States moved into the Atlantic, which German submarines in 1941 made hazardous. Hitler specifically ordered his U-boat commanders not to molest American vessels, even after they began protecting convoys halfway across the Atlantic. American occupation of Greenland and Iceland increased military traffic in the North Atlantic, and American naval forces began to cooperate with British antisubmarine units. The U.S.S. *Greer*, for instance, tracked a German submarine and radioed its position to pursuing British aircraft. The U-boat eventually fired on the American ship, to which Roosevelt responded with an order to shoot on sight any hostile submarine. The United States was informally at war in the North Atlantic several months before Pearl Harbor.

Roosevelt and Churchill meet at sea, 1941.

Indeed, the United States even announced its war aims before official entrance. In August, 1941, Roosevelt and Churchill met at sea off Newfoundland and issued the Atlantic Charter, which was, in effect, a joint statement by a belligerent and a technically neutral power of their mutual hopes for the postwar world. The Charter blended Wilson's Fourteen Points —national self-determination, freedom of the seas, and reduction of armaments—with Roosevelt's New Deal—freedom from fear, freedom from want. The document was the bland public result of the conference; privately Roosevelt and Churchill also discussed Japan's aggressive expansion in the Pacific. After France collapsed, Japan had occupied French Indo-China, and in 1941 Japan threatened to expand into Thailand, Malaya, Burma, and eventually to the Dutch East Indies. Churchill pressed Roosevelt for a promise to defend Dutch and British possessions in Southeast Asia, especially the British base at Singapore. Although the President subsequently warned Japan against an attack, he gave Churchill no binding promise. Roosevelt was not ready for a final confrontation with Japan and sought peaceful means of halting Japanese aggression.

But methods short of war were running out. Early in 1940 the United States allowed a trade treaty to lapse and gradually reduced shipments of strategic goods to Japan. In September, Japan signed an alliance with Germany and Italy to secure their support against the United States. In July, 1941, when Japanese troops moved into southern Indochina, Roosevelt froze Japanese assets in the United States, a step that made further commerce difficult. A few weeks later Fumimaro Konoye, the Japanese Premier, proposed a meeting with Roosevelt to discuss diplomatic differences between the two nations. Although Joseph C. Grew, the American Ambassador to Tokyo, thought the proposal should be accepted, Roosevelt disagreed. In October a more aggressive Japanese cabinet, under General Hideki Tojo, took control of Japanese foreign policy. Both nations made a show of negotiating thereafter, but they were really just swapping unacceptable demands until Japanese pilots ended the charade at Pearl Harbor on December 7, 1941.

Japan won an important tactical victory at Pearl Harbor. Surprise was complete; five battleships and fourteen other craft were at least temporarily put out of action; more than 2,000 Americans died. But for millions of Americans, intently listening to the incredible news on their radios that Sunday afternoon, the debate was over. The attack in Hawaii proved the foe's lack of scruples and showed that only force could stop wanton aggression. The nation united. On December 8, Congress declared war on Japan, and three days later, following declarations of war by Italy and Germany, on Japan's European allies as well.

Since that December afternoon, Americans have tried to explain the disaster at Pearl Harbor. A congressional investigation recorded thirty-nine volumes of conflicting testimony; a presidential commission blamed military leaders for failure to have the base alert; some historians have charged that Roosevelt provoked the attack to unify the country for war. The plot, however, was laid in Tokyo, not in the White House, and official bungling in Washington was at least matched in Hawaii. "Surprise," as Thomas Schelling has written, "when it happens to a government, is likely to be a complicated, diffuse, bureaucratic thing."

> It includes neglect of responsibility, but also responsibility so poorly defined or so ambiguously delegated that action gets lost. It includes gaps in intelligence, but also intelligence that, like a string of pearls too precious to wear, is too sensitive to give to those who need it. It includes the alarm that fails to work, but also the alarm that has gone off so often it has been disconnected. It includes the unalert watchman, but also the one who knows he'll get chewed out by his superior if he gets higher authority out of bed. It includes the contingencies that occur to no one, but also those that everyone assumes somebody else is taking care of. . . . It includes, in addition, the inability of individual human beings to rise to the occasion until they are sure it *is* the occasion—which is usually too late. . . . Finally, as at Pearl Harbor, surprise may include some measure of genuine novelty introduced by the enemy, and possibly some sheer bad luck.*

THE WAR EFFORT

The war opened with a disaster and promptly got worse. In the first months of 1942 Japanese troops swept through Southeast Asia, overran

---

* Thomas C. Schelling, "Foreword," in Rebecca Wohlstetter, *Pearl Harbor: Warning and Decision* (Stanford, Calif.: Stanford University Press, 1962), p. viii.

the Philippines, occupied islands in the Aleutian chain and in the Dutch East Indies, and even threatened Australia. At the same time, German submarines were sinking allied shipping faster than it could be replaced. And across the Atlantic the advance of Germany's *Afrika Korps* threatened to turn the Mediterranean into an Axis lake, while the blitzkrieg invasion of the Soviet Union sealed off Leningrad and reached the outskirts of Moscow.

But even before 1942 was over, signs of allied initiative increased. Although strategic planners had decided to press the European war first and to fight defensively in the Pacific, the American fleet won important engagements in the Coral Sea and near Midway Island. American marines landed on the beaches of Guadalcanal and hung on grimly, an offensive operation that marked the end of Japanese expansion. American carrier-based aircraft bombed Tokyo in April, which boosted American morale but had little military significance.

Convoys, radar, covering aircraft, and improved techniques in the shipyards enabled the Allies to begin winning the battle of the Atlantic.

The War in Europe

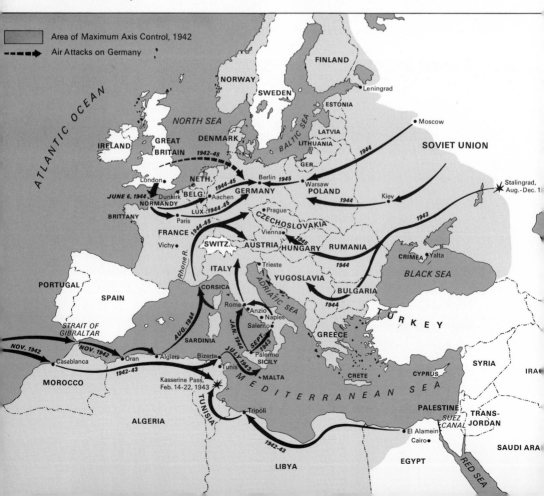

Increased aircraft production put thousands of bombers over Europe in constant strategic missions that harassed, though they did not cripple, the German war effort. Russian troops held Moscow, won at Stalingrad, and began the counteroffensive that was to end in 1945 in the courtyard of Hitler's private bunker amid the rubble of Berlin. British troops in Egypt held the *Afrika Korps* and then began to push it back across Libya. In November, Anglo-American landings in Morocco and Algeria trapped German forces between two allied armies. Much destruction and many casualties lay ahead; but the tide had turned.

419

Shipping out: A black regiment headed for duty handling wartime shipments

In part, the tide turned because the factories of the foe could not match the productivity of American industry. Massive American output was a result of careful organization as well as of fortunate location beyond the range of enemy attack. A second generation of alphabetical agencies allocated resources and manpower, controlled prices and priorities, regulated transportation, and systematically applied scientific research to military technology. By any measure, the result was staggering. A year after Pearl Harbor, American munitions factories were outproducing those of the enemy. Aircraft production increased 24-fold between 1939 and 1942, and then doubled again before the end of the war so that nearly 100,000 new planes a year came off the assembly lines. In 1941 construction of a freighter had taken nearly a year; by the end of 1942 shipyards were launching the same ships in less than two months.

The remarkable increase in production required a remarkable increase in the federal budget. Income taxes rose to a maximum of 94 percent and accounted for about 40 percent of the total cost of the war. The national debt climbed from about $50 million in 1941 to more than $250 million in 1945. But the money was spent with remarkably little corruption. A Senate Committee chaired by a peppery Missourian named Harry Truman doggedly exposed bungling, excess profits, and potentially wasteful schemes, thus reassuring most people that the government usually got its money's worth.

In addition to war production, American industry met most of the demands of civilians, who for the first time in a decade had money in their pockets. Rationing, of course, limited civilian consumption of shoes, meat, sugar, coffee, canned goods, gasoline, and tires. Other products, such as automobiles, disappeared from the market, as cuffs disappeared from men's trousers, copper from pennies, and aluminum saucepans from hardware stores. Americans crammed themselves into uncomfortable temporary quarters near factories or military installations, but most were housed better than the rest of the world's population, and many improved on the way they lived during the depression. And although they had to drink less coffee, without sugar, Americans still ate better than most other people, and many ate better than they had a few years before.

The civilian population produced the goods that sustained the troops. Students harvested crops, suburbanites turned their lawns into "victory gardens," and whole communities collected scrap metal to aid the war effort. More important, the nation went back to work in mill and factory. Most of the prospering labor forces invested part of each paycheck in victory bonds, a practice that built a reservoir of savings that pushed the postwar economy to the longest period of sustained prosperity and growth in history.

With American industry fully mobilized in 1943, the United States and its allies took the offensive in both theaters of war. From North Africa, Allied troops invaded Sicily, and from Sicily, Italy, where Mussolini's decrepit dictatorship fell within a week. But German troops rushed into the peninsula and slowed the Allied advance to a crawl: Rome did not fall until June, 1944, only two days before the long-awaited invasion of France. On June 6 General Dwight D. Eisenhower gave the order that sent an initial wave of nearly 200,000 men to the beaches of Normandy. In August, landings in southern France threatened to envelop German forces, which withdrew in haste toward the Rhine. In the winter of 1944–1945 Nazi armies mounted a last-gasp counterattack that became known as the Battle of the Bulge. But the bulge was contained, and American and British troops moved inexorably toward their rendezvous with the Russians in Berlin.

The Russian advance was no less rapid than the Anglo-American parade through Western Europe. An offensive in 1943 became a steamroller in 1944 as the Red Army moved through the Caucasus and the Ukraine, into Poland and smashed the eastern defenses of the Third Reich. His armies crushed, his capital besieged, his thousand-year Reich in ruins, Hitler took his own life on April 30, 1945. Germany surrendered on May 8.

Instead of mounting costly invasions of successive Japanese outposts, General Douglas MacArthur developed a strategy of island-hopping that took advantage of American naval control in the south Pacific and minimized American casualties. MacArthur simply by-passed some Japanese island bases as he moved north. The American Navy isolated these bases and prevented interference with MacArthur's progress. In the fall of 1944 MacArthur led American forces back into the Philippines while the Navy simultaneously provoked an engagement at Leyte Gulf that knocked the Japanese fleet out of the war. Manila fell early in 1945, and American forces advanced, with extremely heavy losses, to Iwo Jima and Okinawa, which were to serve as bases for launching the massive air raids before the final invasion. These bases, as it turned out, were not required, for the planes carrying the atomic bombs for Hiroshima and Nagasaki took off from fields on Tinian. On August 10, 1945, four days after Hiroshima, the day after Nagasaki, and even before the quarter-million casualties of the bombing had been counted, Japan asked for peace.

The war caused American casualties too—more than 400,000 dead and 600,000 wounded out of 16 million uniformed Americans. American losses were smaller than those of China, Germany, or the Soviet Union. But American casualties had mounted alarmingly as offensive operations approached Japan; President Truman's decision to use the atomic bomb was based partly on military estimates that an all-out invasion of Japan would cost at least a million additional American casualties.

The decision was President Truman's to make because, in a sense, Franklin Roosevelt was the nation's most prominent wartime loss. Roosevelt ran for a fourth term in 1944 almost as a matter of course; the voters elected him the same way. Republicans had turned down Wendell Wilkie in the primaries and nominated Thomas E. Dewey, the smooth, dynamic Governor of New York. Roosevelt dropped Henry Wallace, the avid New Dealer who had been Vice-President, in favor of Harry Truman, a New Dealer more acceptable to conservative Democrats. Roosevelt and Truman carried thirty-six states and ran about 3.5 million popular votes ahead of Dewey. But the President lived only three months after his fourth inauguration. On April 12, 1945, in Warm Springs, Georgia, he died of a cerebral hemorrhage.

DIPLOMACY OF THE GRAND ALLIANCE

Roosevelt managed the war from the White House. His executive agencies directed mobilization and parceled out materials. Harry Hopkins, who had once administered the New Deal's relief programs, became an unofficial Department of State and represented Roosevelt in London and Moscow and in conferences with military authorities. General George Marshall, the able, self-effacing Army Chief of Staff, and Henry L. Stimson, the Republican who became Secretary of War in 1940, were effective, loyal subordinates. Frank Knox, also a Republican, and Admiral Ernest J. King were Roosevelt's chief subordinates in the Navy, where the President himself had served as Assistant Secretary during a previous world war.

And Roosevelt personally conducted diplomacy at the highest level, from the prewar Atlantic Conference with Churchill to the Yalta meetings with Stalin and Churchill a few weeks before the President's death. Two weeks after Pearl Harbor, Churchill arrived in Washington to confer with Roosevelt about strategy and supply. The meetings continued and drew in other Allied leaders as the war progressed toward victory.

But the course of Allied diplomatic contact was not smooth. Only the Nazi menace fused the foreign policies of the United States, the United Kingdom, and the Soviet Union. Within the alliance, there was disagreement about strategy, suspicion that part of the team was loafing, and diverging ambition about the postwar world. Desperate for relief in 1942, the Soviet Union urged an immediate invasion of France to draw German troops from the eastern front; the Russians were contemptuous of the North African substitute. The British, for their part, resented Russian refusal to recognize the Polish government-in-exile and suspected that the Soviet Union meant to dominate Central Europe. The United States, especially in 1943 and 1944, suggested that the Soviet Union make a more positive effort in the war against Japan, a notion that Stalin resisted. Roosevelt needled Churchill about outdated imperial pretensions, and Churchill thought Roosevelt soft-headed in his negotiation with Stalin.

In addition, less powerful nations required diplomatic attention. Roosevelt insisted that China be numbered among the great powers, a notion that Chinese military futility belied and both Stalin and Churchill thought naive. Perhaps Roosevelt intended to build up Chinese prestige to fill the obvious power vacuum that would occur in the Pacific once Japanese might was destroyed. But China was so divided that not even the Japanese invasion could make the government of Chiang Kai-shek work with the rebelling Communists of Mao Tse-tung. American advisers, especially General Joseph W. Stilwell, pointed out that Chiang's inefficient, unpopular government could not become the peace-keeper of Asia. But Roosevelt and Churchill had to work with Chiang, and together in 1943 they defined Allied war aims for the Pacific area in the Cairo Declaration. Japan was to give up most of its outlying islands, though the fate of all of them was not specified because the United States was not sure which might be required as bases. Manchuria and Formosa were to revert to China, and Korea was to become independent "in due course."

France also pretended to world-power status and occasionally annoyed Allied statesmen. The United States maintained diplomatic relations with the French government of German-occupied France, which had its capital at Vichy. In an attempt to expedite the North African landings in 1942, Americans had even acknowledged the political authority of Admiral Jean Darlan, whose connection with the Nazis was embarrassingly close. Free French forces abroad disavowed Darlan, opposed Vichy's control, and looked to unbending General Charles de Gaulle for leadership. De Gaulle's was only one of several governments-in-exile, usually located in London, whose paper existence offered inspiration to people in occupied Europe and sometimes created difficulty for the wartime alliance.

Poland was the most vexing difficulty. Britain's stake in Poland was sentimental: England had promised before the war to preserve Polish independence and had gone to war to redeem that pledge. The American stake was political: the Polish vote was an important ethnic bloc located in politically important states. The Soviet stake was strategic: twice in the twentieth century Poland had been the pathway for invading German troops, and Stalin did not mean to expose his country once again. Stalin eventually recognized the Communist-dominated group called the Lublin government as the official spokesman for Poland, while London and Washington recognized the London government-in-exile. Diplomats could not resolve the impasse, but the Red Army made argument futile when it occupied the area and manifestly intended to stay.

Poland and other questions about the shape of the postwar world appeared on the agenda for the Yalta Conference, the first of the "Big Three" meetings devoted largely to peace-making. The meeting early in February, 1945, was badly timed for the Western Allies. The Battle of the Bulge had not yet been decisively won, while the Russians were rolling through Eastern Europe. American forces in the Pacific were advancing, but pessimistic planners estimated that Japanese surrender might still be years away. The atomic bomb was an untested hope. After twelve years in the White House and a fourth inauguration Franklin Roosevelt was weary, not well, and idealistically convinced that he could win and hold Stalin's friendship and Soviet cooperation. Although later charges of a sell-out at Yalta were exaggerated, in fact the United States seemed to approve of arrangements that certainly violated the spirit of the Atlantic Charter. But short of turning on the Russians, there was little that even a cynical, healthy Roosevelt could have done to deny Stalin his ill-gotten gains.

The expectation of victory that prevailed at Yalta made negotiation more taxing. Fear of Nazi Germany had held the Allies together and a crumbling Nazi Germany foreshadowed a ruptured alliance. The Polish dispute was papered over with an agreement to enlarge the Lublin faction by adding a few members from the London cabinet; "free elections" were eventually to provide a new, democratically chosen government. The homogenized cabinet was a farce, and the elections were not free. The Yalta conferees awarded part of Eastern Poland to the Soviet Union and appropriated part of eastern Germany to compensate Poland, which soon became a Soviet satellite.

The negotiators at Yalta carved what remained of Germany into zones of occupation and, from the British and American shares, awarded one to France. After much debate, $20 billion became the basis for future discussion of reparations, of which half would be paid to the Soviet Union. The question of access to divided Berlin, which was to plague postwar relations between Western occupation forces and the Soviets in eastern Germany, apparently never arose.

Stalin repeated at Yalta his earlier pledge to enter the Pacific war, within ninety days, he said, after German capitulation. With this assurance went Soviet demands: Outer Mongolia must remain a Soviet satellite and not return to Chinese control; Russian influence in Manchuria and access to ports on the Yellow Sea must be established; Japan must cede the Kurile Islands and the southern half of Sakhalin Island to the Soviet Union. Roosevelt undertook to persuade Chiang Kai-shek to accept these arrangements, and Stalin agreed to recognize Chiang's regime, a step that implied Soviet disavowal of the Chinese Communist movement.

Finally, the "Big Three" agreed on some fundamental principles for inclusion in the charter of the United Nations. In 1943 both houses of the American Congress had indicated their willingness to commit the United States to an international organization. In 1944 delegates from the United States, Britain, China, and the Soviet Union had begun to draft a charter but could not resolve questions that divided the great powers. At Yalta Roosevelt agreed that the Ukraine and Byelorussia should be represented in the UN Assembly in return for Stalin's pledge to support an American demand for three votes if Roosevelt felt them necessary. In addition, the wartime allies ensured their own postwar control of the UN Security Council by permitting a veto by France, China, or any of the three powers represented at Yalta. The veto provision meant that the UN would be ineffective in dealing with matters on which the great powers disagreed. Such issues were not far in the future.

WARTIME AMERICA

The Second World War lacked the zealous romance of most earlier American wars. Ernie Pyle's matter-of-fact reporting and Bill Mauldin's magnificent Willie and Joe cartoons show inventive, determined GIs, not crusaders. Although the Third Reich was incomparably more bestial than Imperial Germany had been a generation before, the German language did not disappear from academic curricula, and Germans never became "Huns" in common speech, as had happened during the First World War. Americans thought of the Second World War as a disagreeable job that had to be done. They did their share.

"My, Sir—What an Enthusiastic Welcome!"

©1944 by
United Features Syndicate, Inc.
Reproduced by
courtesy of Bill Mauldin

"Relocation center" for Japanese in America

The worst example of wartime hysteria came early. Surprise at Pearl Harbor and the subsequent series of quick disasters in the Pacific made many Americans suspect a plot. In part, the fear of conspiracy rested on a racial arrogance that could not admit defeat by Orientals; emphasis in the press on subversion and sabotage enhanced national unease. Americans of Japanese ancestry who lived on the Pacific coast were the victims. To prevent imagined sabotage, the President agreed to the Army's request that Japanese-Americans be moved to "relocation centers" in Colorado; they might more candidly have been called "concentration camps." Profiteers took advantage of distress sales of the property of internees as they tried to conclude their business before relocation. In 1943 and 1944 the Supreme Court upheld relocation as a legitimate exercise of the war power. Yet the danger of Japanese-American subversion was a fantasy. And in the Italian campaign, an Army unit recruited in relocation centers gave a splendid account of itself and demonstrated the continuing loyalty of Japanese-Americans in spite of their shabby treatment.

Japanese-Americans were forced to move, and a great many other Americans moved voluntarily. Booming wartime industries were located not only in Detroit and Akron, but in Oak Ridge, Tennessee, and in Hanford, Washington, and all over California. These new industries, with their higher wages, accelerated the increase in urban population that had begun more than a century earlier. The westward movement was also accelerated, and housing shortages were especially acute in the Southwest, the Northwest, and California.

Part of this internal migration was black. Nearly a million blacks, many from the old South, served in the still segregated armed forces; not all returned to the South after discharge. Some blacks, seeking a larger share of wartime prosperity, moved to northern and western cities, where restricted housing and mounting population combined to produce ghettoes. Although Congress passed no civil-rights legislation, in 1941, when black leaders threatened a mass march on Washington to dramatize discrimination, Roosevelt ordered defense contractors and federal agencies not to discriminate in their hiring practices. The Fair Employment Practices Commission that Roosevelt established did not of course bring instant economic equality, but the war itself probably encouraged American blacks to demand equality and probably increased the willingness of many American whites to concede it. The presence of many more blacks in the North made race relations a national problem, not a southern peculiarity, and revealed the hollowness of the pretense of northern equality. The gas chambers of Auschwitz exposed to all humanity the sickness of racial hatred. Not everybody learned the lesson, but some did.

Another important, if less striking, migration occurred during the war when millions of American housewives left their kitchens. Women joined all the armed services and worked not only as nurses but also in dozens of noncombatant jobs. Factories hired women as they had not since the earliest New England textile mills recruited the daughters of nearby farmers. The legendary "Rosie the Riveter" was unusual only in the rigor of her task; women worked on most of the nation's assembly lines.

The fact that women worked unquestionably loosened family bonds, especially in those families where the husband was at war. Children grew up with less supervision and more money. Prosperity, economic opportunity, and the local draft board all acted to pull families apart. Furlough marriages made in haste contributed to a rising divorce rate that formally called attention to family disintegration.

The most obvious wartime change was also the most welcome: prosperity returned to the nation. Consumer goods remained scarce, and a few dour economists predicted an early return to peacetime depression. But returning veterans did not become statistics on unemployment charts, and pent-up consumer demand bought out everything from stockings and steak

Women at war

to station wagons and ranch houses. With full wallets, three-shift work-days, and victories on the battlefields, the national confidence, shaken by a decade of depression, returned. Americans once again decided that what-ever the task, they would manage.

The Serviceman's Readjustment Act, usually called the GI Bill of Rights, provided time for the economy to absorb the demobilized veterans and supplied funds for their education. Former servicemen were eligible for a year of unemployment compensation; those who wanted education were entitled to tuition, books, and allowances for their dependents while studying, whether the course led to certification in plumbing or a doctorate in philosophy; the government guaranteed low-cost loans for those who wanted to establish small businesses or to build or purchase housing. The GI Bill was the product of the nation's earnest wish to pay the troops more than the minimal salaries they had collected while on active duty; it was the product also of congressional concern for khaki-clad voters and their dependents; and it was a hedge against recurring depression, for the various benefits kept veterans off the job market, stimulated basic indus-tries such as housing, and prevented economic desperation among the unemployed.

The GI Bill was also responsible in part for the enormous postwar American investment in education. The investment was not only in the bricks and mortar that piled up on the nation's campuses but also in the aggregate hours that the population spent learning. Americans as a whole became better educated, an undramatic fact perhaps, but one that is at the base of delayed social changes that are just beginning to rack American society and whose end is beyond present calculation.

Postwar prosperity prolonged the euphoria of victory. But if the nation had subdued the Axis and the depression, other tasks loomed. The United States had yet to determine the diplomatic consequences of the destruction of Germany and Japan, and of the weakness of Britain, France, and China. The nation had yet to probe the technological and moral conse-quences of the use of atomic energy. Americans had yet to distribute equitably the enormous output of their economic system. Racial justice had yet to be achieved. But surviving a war and a depression had been the tasks of a generation, and survival, for the moment, seemed assured.

Suggested Reading

Selig Adler's *The Isolationist Impulse** (1957) is more extensive chronologically than Manfred Jonas' *Isolationism in America** (1966), a convincing treatment of the period after 1935. Wayne S. Cole, *America First* (1953), focuses on the major isolationist pressure group.

Two volumes by William L. Langer and S. Everett Gleason defend American policy: *The Challenge to Isolation* (1952) and *The Undeclared War* (1953). Cordell Hull's *Memoirs* (1948) is useful for the views of the Secretary of State. More critical of American policy, especially of rela-tions with Germany, is Arnold Offner's *American Appeasement* (1969).

Two books by Robert A. Divine, *The Illusion of Neutrality** (1962) and *The Reluctant Belligerent** (1965), are reliable and brief. James M. Burns's *Roosevelt: The Soldier of Freedom* (1970) is excellent.

Dorothy Borg, *The United States and the Far Eastern Crisis of 1933–1938* (1964), reveals the complexity of the situation in Asia. Charles C. Tansill, *Back Door to War* (1952), oversimplifies in his argument that Franklin Roosevelt plotted American entry into the war. Rebecca Wohlstetter's *Pearl Harbor: Warning and Decision** (1962) is the best book on that disaster.

A. Russell Buchanan's *The United States and World War II** (1964) is useful, as is Gaddis Smith's brief survey, *American Diplomacy During the Second World War** (1965). Other works on wartime diplomacy include Winston S. Churchill's six-volume narrative, *The Second World War** (1948–53), Robert E. Sherwood's *Roosevelt and Hopkins** (1948), and any of a half-dozen titles by Herbert Feis, including *The China Tangle** (1953) and *Churchill, Roosevelt, Stalin** (1957). Samuel E. Morison has written fifteen volumes to chronicle the role of the fleet: *History of United States Naval Operations in World War II* (1947–60). The war of the ordinary GI is depicted in Bill Mauldin, *Up Front** (1945).

*Available in paperback edition

CHRONOLOGY

1945   Harry S. Truman succeeds Roosevelt
San Francisco Conference; UN Charter signed
Potsdam Conference

1947   Truman Doctrine
Taft-Hartley Labor Relations Act
George Kennan outlines containment policy in *Foreign Affairs* article

1948   Marshall Plan
Truman orders end of segregation in armed forces
Presidential election: Harry S. Truman (Democrat) defeats Thomas E. Dewey (Republican) and J. Strom Thurmond (States' Rights)

1948–49   Berlin airlift

1949   Truman proposes Fair Deal
NATO alliance established
Chiang Kai-shek abandons mainland China

1949–50   Alger Hiss case

1950–53   Korean War:
    1950: Chinese intervene
    1951: Truman recalls General Douglas MacArthur

1952   Presidential election: Dwight D. Eisenhower (Republican) defeats Adlai E. Stevenson (Democrat)

THE FAIR DEAL

AND THE COLD WAR

In January, 1953, a few days before his retirement, President Harry Truman sent his last annual message to Capitol Hill. The President looked back over nearly eight years in the White House and pronounced them good. The enemies of the Second World War had finally submitted; the American economy boomed; the administration had thwarted greedy private interests and extended the social gains of the New Deal. Truman was also proud that racial barriers, battered by "a great awakening of the American conscience," had begun to fall.

Truman's retrospective review had some conspicuous gaps. In his presidency the cold war began, warmed, and flared into a very hot war in Korea. Eastern Europe and China, Truman's critics claimed, "fell" to the Communists while he watched helplessly. A frustrated, divided nation began seeking scapegoats, and neither the President's sarcasm nor his reassurance ended the witch hunt. Truman's boasted prosperity, warned traditional economists, depended on inflation, constant federal deficits, enormous governmental budgets, and other unwise fiscal practices. Modest progress toward racial equality hardly justified complacency. Finally, some of the President's friends developed elastic consciences, and embarrassing scandals cropped up toward the end of his tenure.

Harry Truman had none of Franklin Roosevelt's oratorical skill, none of Dwight Eisenhower's genuine charm, and a political apprenticeship inferior to that of Lyndon Johnson. Captain Harry Truman had seen tough service with a Missouri artillery unit during the First World War and had returned to establish a haberdashery in Kansas City that promptly went bankrupt in the postwar depression. He became a respectable candidate for the notoriously unrespectable Pendergast machine and progressed through minor state offices to the United States Senate in 1934, where he remained until elected Vice-President a decade later. He was never part of Franklin Roosevelt's inner circle; in the year before Roosevelt's death, which included the convention and their campaign, the two men had seen each other on about a half-dozen occasions.

Truman's unexpected presidency began in shock, doubt, and hesitation, revealing the contradictory advice of bickering subordinates. The new President was quite an ordinary man—blunt, scrappy, impulsive, with an instinctive sympathy for other ordinary people. He used crisp Missouri vernacular to upbraid a music critic, who panned his daughter's talent, and the Foreign Minister of the Soviet Union, who obstructed the formation of the United Nations. He surrounded himself with cronies in some ways reminiscent of Warren Harding's "Ohio gang." His speeches were uninspired and his appearance uninspiring. Action, not reflection, and combat, not compromise, were Harry Truman's instincts. Since his presidency was a succession of crises, the action and the combat rarely subsided.

THE END OF A WAR—AND ANOTHER BEGUN

Franklin Roosevelt's vision of the post-Nazi world had assumed the close cooperation of the wartime allies. But old acquaintance did not deter Stalin from seizing new territory in borderlands. Winston Churchill was using the phrase "iron curtain" in correspondence with Truman before the war in the Pacific ended. In the United States, Admiral William Leahy, Roosevelt's Chief of Staff, Senator Arthur Vandenberg, the Republican spokesman on foreign policy, and James F. Byrnes, a former senator and justice of the Supreme Court who had been one of Roosevelt's most trusted trouble-shooters—these men suspected that the Soviet Union's postwar ambitions menaced American plans for peace. Leahy gave Truman a daily briefing on military matters; after the election of 1946 Vandenberg headed the Senate's Committee on Foreign Relations; in 1945 Byrnes became Truman's Secretary of State. The nation's foreign policy soon reflected the views of these presidential advisers.

The cold war began without public recognition and perhaps without official realization. The Soviet Union and the United States had disagreed on wartime strategy and on the shape of the postwar world. Although the Roosevelt administration had responded to Great Britain's request with a large loan for postwar reconstruction, a similar Soviet request received dilatory consideration and was never carried out. Harry Truman learned at first hand of Soviet-American disagreement when Foreign Minister

Vyacheslav Molotov stopped in Washington a few days after Roosevelt's death. In their conversation Truman alluded to apparent Russian unwillingness to carry out the spirit of the agreement made at Yalta concerning Poland; Molotov denied the President's charge, and the conversation became undiplomatically sharp. Molotov went on to California to sign the UN Charter, but relations between Moscow and Washington had perceptibly chilled.

In the following month, under pressure from Congress, Truman stopped lend-lease shipments to the Soviet Union, even though he was at the time pressing Stalin to enter the war against Japan. With some justification, however, Congress feared that American supplies were serving Soviet political purposes in Europe and were not awaiting military use in the Pacific.

This diplomatic friction was worrisome but not critical when the last of the wartime conferences assembled at Potsdam, near Berlin, in July, 1945, to plan the future of defeated Germany. Truman had replaced Roosevelt; before the conference ended, Clement Atlee replaced Churchill as the result of a British election; only Stalin remained of the wartime coalition. Preoccupied with military matters, Truman urged Stalin to enter the Pacific war. Truman's impatience with political questions suggests that neither the President nor the Department of State had done much long-range planning for the postwar world. The conference put off final decisions on such critical matters as the shape of post-Nazi Germany. The foreign ministers were to meet later, hammer out peace treaties, and do something about the Polish frontier. Meanwhile, the allies decided that trials of German war criminals at Nuremberg might proceed and that Russians might confiscate German capital equipment as an installment on the reparations debt. Occupation zones, the new "Big Three" agreed, should not become frontiers, nor interfere with German economic unity.

Truman's concern about the Japanese war persisted even after he heard at Potsdam of the successful atomic test in New Mexico. No one could predict the strategic consequences of the new weapon, nor was Truman assured of its reliability. His military advisers believed an amphibious campaign in Japan would cost at least a million casualties; the President wanted to be sure that Stalin had his share of those losses. Stalin kept his Yalta promise to the letter when he sent the Red Army into Manchuria, on August 8, ninety days after Germany's surrender and two days after Hiroshima.

The Hiroshima raid may have convinced Stalin to make good on his Yalta pledge in order to be sure the Pacific war did not end without Russian participation. On the other hand, Truman may have used the bomb as a first shot in the cold war, an attempt to end the struggle in the Pacific before the Russians could claim a place at the peace table. Although atomic weapons were indeed important in the eventual cold-war strategy of the United States, their use at Hiroshima and Nagasaki was probably more a function of the effort to defeat Japan than of the incipient effort to contain the Soviet Union.

Neither Franklin Roosevelt nor Harry Truman provided the idealistic

General MacArthur (left) at Japan's surrender

trappings for the Second World War that had distinguished Woodrow Wilson's leadership in the first. Yet Americans did assume that other people shared their faith in liberal political institutions, the rule of law, and free access to a free market. Russians especially refused to behave as Americans had expected. The lack of the gratitude that seemed due the United States for its aid in the common effort, resistance to American suggestions about democracy in Eastern Europe, and the obvious Soviet suspicion of American diplomatic intent revealed hostility for which the public was unprepared. Never one to back away from a scrap, Harry Truman answered mistrust with mistrust, which soon hardened into belligerence on both sides. In 1947, Americans remembered their half-forgotten conviction that you never could trust a Communist. By that time, the cold war had been going on for some months.

While the cold war was getting under way, the United States merrily dismantled most of its defenses. Although the Truman administration planned a gradual reduction in the swollen armed forces, the scheme promptly broke down under the irresistible political pressure to "bring the boys home." A year after the Japanese surrender, most of the boys were home, and only a skeletal force remained abroad, too small, the experts said, to meet the nation's military responsibilities. Never before had the nation undertaken such global commitments: the American navy patrolled more widely than had the British fleet in the best days of the empire; American troops occupied Japan, parts of Germany, and bases extending from Okinawa to the British Isles. But the public was mentally demobilized. Americans entrusted peace-keeping to the UN; if not the UN, the American atomic monopoly would surely intimidate any potential foe.

In 1947 a presidential commission alerted the nation to its decayed defenses. The commission recommended that the armed services be reorganized in a new Department of Defense, that the Strategic Air Command be enlarged and modernized, and that all eighteen-year-olds serve a year of compulsory military training. Congress refused to enact universal military training and extended the draft instead. But the National Security Act of 1947 did create the Department of Defense, and Congress soon pro-

vided more money for military purposes, particularly for the development
and production of aircraft. The build-up for the cold war was under way.

RECONVERSION IN A BOOMING ECONOMY

Meanwhile, veterans of the other war discovered that things
had changed in their absence. Boosted by overtime, wages were double
prewar levels; gross national product had also doubled; the labor force,
with the addition of women, teen-agers, and previously unemployable older
workers, stood at a new high; more than $130 billion in personal savings
awaited builders, manufacturers, brokers, and hucksters. The nation's
economic leaders feared that unplanned rapid demobilization might bring
mounting unemployment and another depression. At the same time, the
easy availability of money and the absence of consumer goods threatened
to produce rampant inflation. Truman had developed plans for the gradual
conversion of the economy to civilian production. He wanted to relax price
controls slowly, to raise the minimum wage, to prepare federal programs
to ensure full employment, and to encourage the construction of new housing. The Employment Act of 1946 formally announced the government's
intent to promote full employment, but Congress would go no further. Massive lobbying introduced so many loopholes in a bill that purported to
extend price controls that the President vetoed it. Prices promptly took off.

Inflationary pressure came also from the unions. Labor had made
wartime gains that union leadership did not mean to lose when war-induced
overtime schedules ended. Most unions had postponed their demands
during the war, although John L. Lewis' intransigence had led to strikes in
the coal mines and a vague public feeling that labor was unpatriotic. Union
officials took one look at the great markets awaiting peacetime production
and brought out new and fatter contracts. Strikes loomed in virtually every
industry, and in 1946 they came—in the stockyards, the automobile plants,
the mines, and the steel mills. When the railway brotherhoods threatened
to shut down every one of the nation's trains, Harry Truman became angry.
He wrote, but did not deliver, an indignant speech accusing John L. Lewis
of calling "two strikes in war time . . . that were worse than bullets in the
backs of our soldiers." Truman did ask Congress for authority to draft
strikers if their refusal to work endangered national security. Although
Congress passed no legislation, the President's request alone forced the
brotherhoods to a sullen settlement without a strike. After the miners
walked out later, Truman used federal courts, an injunction, and a massive
fine to get Lewis' followers back on the job.

When the political heirs of Franklin Roosevelt went to court for an
injunction against a labor union, it was a sign that the political climate
had changed. The Taft-Hartley Act of 1947 was another manifestation of
that changed mood. The act required union officers to take a non-
Communist oath and their organizations to allow a sixty-day "cooling-off
period" before beginning a strike. In the event a dispute threatened national
health or safety, the President might secure a court order postponing a

strike for eighty days. The act outlawed the closed shop and empowered states to enact "right to work" laws to forbid contracts that made union membership a condition of employment. If the law was neither "completely contrary to the national policy of economic freedom," as Truman alleged in his crisp, but futile, veto message, nor a "slave labor law," as union leaders claimed, the Taft-Hartley Act certainly was a change from the Wagner Act that it replaced.

In domestic affairs, as in foreign policy, the first months of the Truman administration lacked direction. His economic policy vacillated. Although he favored unions and vetoed a bill designed to check them, he had himself called public attention to the inordinate power of labor organizations. It was not a record to inspire confidence and Mr. Truman inspired little. "To err is Truman," people snickered. Republican strategists put it another way: "Had enough?" they asked in the congressional campaign of 1946. The voters had. For the first time since 1928, Republicans controlled both houses of Congress. And for the first time since 1932, Republicans could look forward to a presidential election without Franklin Roosevelt at the top of the Democratic ticket.

THE COLD WAR

Gradually the administration found a foreign policy. The growing debate inside the government became public late in 1946 when Secretary of Commerce Henry Wallace deplored the hard line Secretary of State Byrnes was taking in his contact with the Russians. Wallace thought the United States should woo the Soviet Union with friendship and claimed to have had Truman's approval before he spoke. Byrnes, on the other hand, was developing the policy of containment first outlined by George F. Kennan, a scholarly official in the embassy in Moscow. Truman fired Wallace, thereby siding with the State Department, which summoned Kennan to Washington to head the planning staff.

In July, 1947, *Foreign Affairs* published the famous "Mr. X" article, widely and correctly attributed to Kennan, that unofficially put the containment policy before the world. The United States, Kennan argued, must be capable of blocking each expansive Soviet threat. Stalemate would end the myth of inevitable Communist success and might produce internal friction to plague the Soviet Union, particularly when power had to be transferred to another generation. This containment policy was a formula for a tense world, where the foe had the initiative and no one had the satisfaction of immediate victory. Kennan's policy envisioned a constant war of nerves that in the long run would produce changes in Soviet policy, and, for the present, the stability of deadlock. The world might not be better, but at least it would survive.

A specific American action to sustain anti-Communist movements in Greece and Turkey foreshadowed the general policy. In February, 1947, the British Ambassador notified the State Department of his country's inability to bear any longer the expense of forces that were struggling with Greek

Communist guerrillas. In addition, the Soviet Union was putting diplomatic pressure on Turkey, which seemed unlikely to hold out if Greece became a Soviet satellite. In March, 1947, the President went to Congress for authorization to help Greece and Turkey retain their independence. His speech went beyond the immediate crisis to outline what was soon called the Truman Doctrine, which Truman himself later interpreted as a pledge "to support the cause of freedom wherever it was threatened." He asked for an appropriation of $400 million for economic aid to combat the misery from which Communism grew. Although fiscal conservatives grumbled about a global New Deal, Congress approved Truman's request with surprising speed.

Greece and Turkey were only the first steps. The Western European democracies, devastated during the war, could not develop enough economic momentum to blunt the Communist political effort. Communist movements in France and Italy increased alarmingly; economic disaster threatened even victorious Britain. In May, 1947, Undersecretary of State Dean Acheson suggested that the United States hasten economic recovery by financing European purchases of American goods. A month later, Truman's new Secretary of State, George C. Marshall, unveiled the European Recovery Program, soon known simply as the Marshall Plan. It was, Winston Churchill remarked, "the most unsordid act in history."

Without economic stability, Secretary Marshall said, there would be no political stability. Europe's economic needs would for some time exceed its ability to meet them, and Marshall suggested that the United States simply cover the deficit. He encouraged Europeans to work together to set priorities, and he did not exclude the Communist bloc: "Our policy," Marshall said pointedly, "is directed not against any country or doctrine but against hunger, poverty, desperation, and chaos."

European economic experts assembled promptly, without the Soviet Union, which chose not to participate, and without the satellites, which were told not to. The economists put together a shopping list that exceeded $22 billion, a massive injection of American capital that would dramatically raise production. The administration cut the request to $17 billion; the program eventually cost about $12 billion over four years. In those four years, the economic growth of participating countries climbed more than 50 percent; in West Germany, the economy grew a staggering 312 percent. Such a recovery in Germany, if unaccompanied by economic vigor elsewhere, might have caused alarm. But the general return of economic health and the multinational cooperation that the Marshall Plan required allayed some national jealousies. The program, on the whole, was a magnificent success.

Like the hasty effort to shore up Greece and Turkey, the Marshall Plan relied heavily on economic aid. Both were positive programs to restore Europe's economic vitality and political self-confidence. But the Truman administration sold both measures to a reluctant Congress and an uninformed public as ways of defeating communism. When communism did not in fact weaken, and the Kremlin raised its demands, instead of moderating them, simple economic aid appeared to some American planners inadequate for containing communism. Military aid to friendly powers seemed a more direct method, more comprehensible to the impatient public, and cheaper to the economizing Congress. George Kennan protested that containment need not require an arms race, a ring of bases around the Soviet Union, or constant American intervention to put down rebellions. Rather, as Kennan saw it, containment meant helping other nations to develop the prosperity and internal strength that would make communism irrelevant for them.

The drift toward reliance on military power began almost immediately after the Marshall Plan was enacted. Unable to reach agreement with the Soviets about German unification in March, 1948, the Western foreign ministers announced plans to unify at least the Western zones in the Federal Republic of Germany, which would receive aid under the Marshall Plan. The Soviet Union opposed first the creation and then any strengthening of West Germany. A dispute over new German currency served Soviet authorities as a pretext for stopping all surface traffic from West Germany to West Berlin. President Truman ordered a massive airlift that supplied the city for nearly a year until the Russians decided to call off the futile blockade. Since no agreement on access routes was reached, the first Berlin crisis ended without any long-term settlement.

During the airlift the United States joined eleven other North Atlantic nations in a binding military alliance. The North Atlantic Treaty, of April,

Foes become friends: the Berlin airlift

1949, declared that an attack on any of the signatories would "be con
an attack against them all" and established the North Atlantic Trea._
Organization (NATO) to coordinate defensive efforts. Since American military spokesmen testified that the United States did not expect to send
additional American troops to Europe, NATO's land forces would apparently remain inferior to the Red Army. Western Europe's chief military
defense, then, was the same American nuclear force that had defended the
continent before the alliance. The treaty did consolidate the conventional
forces of several nations against the day when the risk of Soviet atomic
retaliation might inhibit quick resort to the American nuclear stockpile. A
multinational force also reassured France and other nervous European
states that otherwise could not have tolerated German rearmament. And
the creation of NATO, together with the subsequent signing of the Warsaw
Pact by the nations of the Soviet bloc, revealed the military dimension
of the cold war.

Once, in 1949, President Truman tried to break out of the cold-war
mold. The fourth point in his inaugural address promised a "bold, new
program for making the benefits of our scientific advances and industrial
progress available for the improvement and growth of underdeveloped
areas." Technical assistance encompassed new agricultural and medical
techniques, for example, or the discovery and development of mineral
resources, or improved methods of fishing and plumbing—more than 200
projects in more than thirty countries in the last two years of Truman's
presidency. The Point Four program was a linear ancestor of the Eisenhower administration's more limited People to People program and of
John Kennedy's Peace Corps.

POLITICS AND THE FAIR DEAL

Although the nation's cold-war policy was bipartisan, partisanship on domestic issues continued unabated. If the President had developed
some grasp of foreign policy, his handling of unions, price controls, and
agricultural policy seemed fumbling to much of the electorate. Some
discouraged Democrats made an effort to draft General Dwight Eisenhower
to head the party's ticket in 1948, a notion that Eisenhower firmly squelched.
Sensing victory, Republicans again nominated New York's Governor
Thomas E. Dewey for President and teamed him with Earl Warren, the
progressive Governor of California.

Two other parties entered the campaign. Henry Wallace's Progressive
Party tried to persuade the electorate to abandon the cold war. Wallace
denounced the "Martial Plan" and hoped to reawaken Soviet-American
friendship. But the active participation of American Communists in Wallace's party certainly impaired his appeal. The Progressive campaign,
launched with great fanfare, ended with about a million votes.

Southern Democrats formed the other new party in opposition to
Truman's attempt to secure a measure of equality for blacks. Liberal
Democrats, led by Hubert Humphrey, the ambitious Mayor of Minneapolis,

won inclusion of a civil-rights program, including endorsement of a Fair Employment Practices Commission, in the party's platform. Unreconciled southerners, soon dubbed "Dixiecrats," walked out of the convention and formed the States Rights party, which nominated South Carolina's Governor Strom Thurmond for President. The defection proved less damaging than Republicans had hoped, however, when Thurmond carried only four states in November.

Dewey conducted a dignified campaign, said nothing to excite or to anger, and gave the impression that he was already providing mature presidential leadership. After the conventions, Truman called Congress into a blatantly political special session that he knew would produce no new legislation. The sterile congressional session gave Truman an opportunity to run against the "do-nothing Republican Congress" and to arouse popular fear that a Republican administration might repeal the New Deal. The President took his message on a headlong campaign rush around the country to the cheer "give 'em hell, Harry!" He warned his audiences that Dewey would bring back the good old days of Herbert Hoover. Although he often ran behind local Democrats, Truman won most of the black voters in crucial industrial states, impressive and unexpected support from the nation's farmers, and—by a margin of about two million votes—the election.

Truman's victory, however, did not give his domestic program the boost he had expected. His Fair Deal, outlined in the annual message of 1949, tried to extend the New Deal and to establish new programs for the nation's farmers and for growing numbers of old people, students, and blacks. The innovations in the Fair Deal almost invariably failed to clear Congress. Medicare, fair employment practices, federal aid to education, the Brannan Plan to support farmers' incomes instead of crop prices— these measures became the staples of subsequent Democratic platforms and the legislation of subsequent Democratic congresses. During the Truman administration Congress extended existing programs like Social Security and rural electrification, made larger appropriations for public power and federal housing, and raised the minimum wage. The Fair Deal probably also served as a threat that convinced hesitant conservatives to institute pensions, hospitalization insurance, and other private welfare programs to forestall public action.

No administration since Reconstruction had done so much to secure racial justice. If Truman's accomplishment was less than was needed and less than he had promised, he did at least call the nation's attention to the gap between profession and practice; he broke the conspiracy of silence and forced the issue into national politics. A presidential commission outlined the problem in a report in 1946 that suggested laws to produce equality in housing, education, and employment. Early in 1948, in a message that prepared rabid southern Democrats to defect, the President asked Congress for a permanent Commission on Civil Rights, legislation to make the ballot available to all citizens, abolition of discrimination in interstate travel, and, once more, a commission to enforce fair employment practices. The message evoked a torrent of oratory and nothing more, for Congress did not share the President's concern. Truman vetoed a measure that would have encouraged segregation in schools on military reservations and used executive authority in mid-1948 to order integration in the military services. Military segregation did not end overnight, but by mid-1950 black and white draftees were training together on military posts throughout the nation.

ASIAN COMMUNISM: CHINA AND KOREA

The wartime expectation that Chiang Kai-shek's China could keep the postwar peace in the Pacific was never realistic. Even before the end of 1945 Americans in China had warned the State Department of the sagging popular support for Chiang Kai-shek's government. The United States tried to shore up Chiang's regime, and the Soviet Union tried to strengthen the Communist faction led by Mao Tse-tung. The Soviet Union made captured Japanese arms available to the Communists, and the United States furnished transportation for Chiang's forces and eventually made military supplies and money available as well. In spite of American and Soviet aid, the struggle remained fundamentally a Chinese conflict, as it had been for more than a decade. When the conflict continued to disrupt China after the war with Japan ended, Truman sent General Marshall to China to assess the situation and, if possible, to mediate.

Hostility, Marshall reported, was too fundamental to remove by mediation. Neither side trusted the other; each preferred to gamble on victory. Chiang made a few half-hearted attempts to broaden his popular base, but in mid-1946 his grip on the country was manifestly slipping. In August, 1946, Truman wrote Chiang of American concern "that the hopes of the people of China are being thwarted by militarists and a small group of political reactionaries. . . ." Unless, Truman continued, "convincing proof is shortly forthcoming that genuine progress is being made toward a peaceful settlement of China's internal problems," he would have to redefine American policy. It was a tough letter, and it made no difference. General Marshall returned home with nothing to show for his effort.

After the civil war in China became overt, American military observers reported that Chiang's forces were well supplied and numerically superior. But they were ineptly led and lacked the will that their Communist opponents had in abundance. In 1947 General Albert Wedemeyer told Truman that military effort alone would never stamp out Chinese communism and that aid to Chiang would be nearly useless because his incompetent subordinates could not effectively manage a program like those established under the Truman Doctrine. Paradoxically, Wedemeyer then recommended increasing military assistance and sending military advisers to improve Chiang's campaign against Mao's forces. Truman's response was as confused as his advice. Although the administration believed Chiang could not win, it accepted a $500 million appropriation to help him do so.

To no avail. In 1949 Chiang and his forces left the mainland for the island of Formosa, which they converted to a fortress and which for more than two decades the United States recognized as the Republic of China.

Truman's opponents blamed his policy for the "loss" of China. This "China lobby," which included influential Republicans and important publishers, charged that Democratic administrations had helped Stalin more generously than they had Chiang and that American diplomats in China had underestimated Chiang's ability and support, as well as the menace of communism.

Past mistakes there had certainly been, many of which were Chiang's. And the need for a new policy based on new facts was evident in the State Department, where, in 1949, Dean Acheson had succeeded General Marshall. In January, 1950, Acheson unveiled the administration's revised Asian policy. As the State Department saw it, the great force for change in Asia was nationalism, not communism, and Acheson suggested that nationalism was anti-Soviet as well as anti-American. The Secretary doubted that military action would block subversion or solve any of the domestic difficulties that plagued Asian governments, but he tried to clarify the military responsibilities of the United States in the area. American forces would, he said, defend a perimeter extending from Japan through the Philippines. The first reliance of people beyond that line, an area that included Formosa, Korea, and all of mainland Asia, must be "upon the commitments of the entire civilized world under the Charter of the United Nations."

After Communist North Koreans invaded South Korea in June, 1950, Acheson's legion of critics claimed that his speech had invited the attack. If North Korean strategists had indeed read Acheson's words as an invitation, they misread them as badly as did the Secretary's domestic opponents. For when the attack came, the United States responded quickly to the resolutions of the United Nations, which was precisely the course Acheson had outlined.

Neither the Communist North nor the Republic of Korea to the south regarded the thirty-eighth parallel as a permanent boundary. Both halves of the country hoped to become the dominant partner in a unified nation. The Communists jumped first, with overwhelming numbers that almost immediately broke South Korea's armies. The diplomatic counteroffensive began at the UN, where a self-imposed absence cost the Soviet Union a chance to stop action with a veto. The Security Council called on the membership for military aid and later designated General Douglas MacArthur Commander of United Nations forces in Korea. Sixteen other nations contributed to the "police action," which was never a declared war. American troops, numbering about half of the UN forces, knew that "police action" meant war, and the American general, whose orders came directly from the Pentagon, knew that his designation as UN commander was a polite fiction.

President Truman had moved even more quickly than the UN to commit forces to the defense of Korea. Two days after the invasion Truman stationed the Pacific fleet off Formosa to prevent either China from attacking the other; he ordered American aircraft to support South Korean forces; then, in response to the UN resolution, he ordered MacArthur and two divisions of occupation troops from Japan to try to stem the North Korean advance. Truman's decisive response was partly instinctive; he was

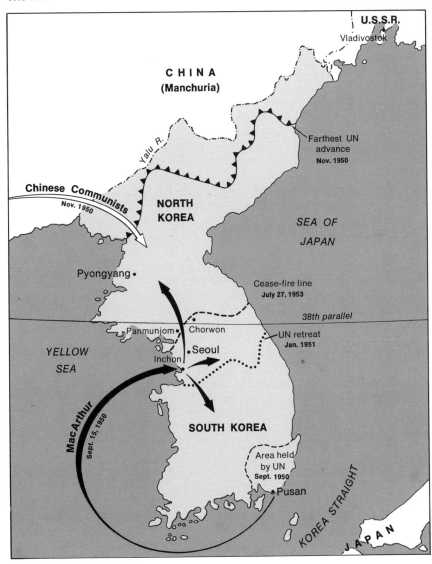

of the generation for whom appeasement was anathema. The President also responded decisively because the National Security Council had previously evolved, and the President had already approved, a world-wide strategy of "hold-the-line." When the time came, the President put the strategy into operation.

No act of Truman's second administration was so popular. The Korean War, which eventually became a political albatross, initially had almost unanimous support. Prompt military action to check aggression heartened American allies and supporters of the United Nations. Shaken by the expansion of communism in Eastern Europe and China, many

Americans were glad to strike back, to substitute the satisfaction of action for the frustration of containment. Senator Robert Taft, perhaps the most respected Republican in the nation, had been critical of Truman's foreign policy, but he reluctantly and publicly approved the Korean intervention. The American people found the minimal national sacrifice tolerable, for the country's astounding productivity amply supplied the troops while the domestic standard of living continued to advance.

For the first months, the war went badly. American troops retreated with the outnumbered forces of the Republic of Korea to the southeastern corner of the peninsula, where they established a defensive perimeter. Then, in mid-September, MacArthur sent an amphibious expedition ashore at Inchon and nearly trapped the entire North Korean force, which fled toward the north in disorder. The UN hastily authorized MacArthur's troops to pursue the foe into North Korea. As the UN armies came within striking distance of the Yalu River, which marked the Chinese frontier, a unified, democratic Korea seemed imminent, and MacArthur said he thought the American forces should be home for Christmas.

But they were not, nor for two Christmases thereafter. At the end of November, 1950, Chinese forces, whose entry MacArthur had not expected, split the UN Army, and another retreat to the south began. Early in 1951 the UN forces dug in near the thirty-eighth parallel, where for the next year and a half the war dragged on. General MacArthur had no stomach for stalemate. With the political support of administration critics, he suggested a blockade of Chinese and Manchurian ports, requested authority to bomb Chinese bases, and advocated use of the forces of Nationalist China. "In war," MacArthur said emphatically, "there is no substitute for victory."

The administration saw things differently. As MacArthur used the word, "victory" was not the goal; American strategists did not intend to "defeat" Communist China, but only to hold the line in Korea. The objective was limited and the war correspondingly limited. MacArthur and his host of supporters neither accepted nor understood such a policy. When he could not convince the administration to change, MacArthur went around it. His press releases complained of official restraints on his freedom of military action; his correspondence with Republican critics of American policy supplied them with material for fresh attacks. In March, 1951, Truman told MacArthur to make no major advance into North Korea that might upset negotiations for a settlement. MacArthur replied with a public demand that the foe surrender, a statement that temporarily stymied Truman's effort to open peace talks. Less than two weeks later MacArthur again called for a larger war in a letter that Joseph W. Martin, the Republican leader in the House, made public. Within the week the President dismissed the general and set the country off on an emotional binge.

For a moment, MacArthur expressed the nation's unhappiness that the simple old rules no longer governed the complex new world. MacArthur stood for victory, service, and patriotism, against compromise, containment, and communism. After MacArthur's appearance before an unusual joint session of Congress, one Congressman emerged, tears streaming down his face, and announced to waiting cameramen that he had just heard the voice of God.

A congressional inquiry probed both Asian policy and MacArthur's abrupt dismissal. One by one the Joint Chiefs of Staff testified that global strategy, especially the situation in Europe, dictated decisions about Asian policy. MacArthur's proposed war with Communist China, General Omar Bradley suggested, would have been "the wrong war, at the wrong place, at the wrong time, and with the wrong enemy." Such laconic common sense diminished MacArthur's martyrdom. His successor in the field, General Matthew Ridgway, proved able to conduct the war within the limits the President set. In July, although fighting continued, peace talks began, which would conclude early in the Eisenhower administration. After three years of warfare and the loss of more than 33,000 American lives, the boundary dividing the Korean peninsula stayed at 38°.

THE SEARCH FOR COMMUNISTS WITHIN

Some Americans believed the Communist menace centered in Washington, not in Berlin, Moscow, Peking, or Korea. Any Communist success abroad, these people believed, was the result of espionage, sabotage, or subversion in the American government. In 1950 Senator Joseph R. McCarthy, an accomplished demagogue from Wisconsin, began to lead the anti-Communist crusade, and the press labeled the growing national obsession with loyalty McCarthyism. For about three years, Red-hunting flourished. Even before McCarthyism became a national virus, President Roosevelt had instituted regular investigatory procedures among federal employees. In 1945 and 1946 President Truman had learned that an extensive Communist espionage operation in Canada had had an American counterpart. In 1947 Truman established a Federal Employee Loyalty Program that eventually found grounds for "reasonable doubt" of the loyalty of about 1 in 10,000 government employees and no proof whatsoever of espionage.

Senator Joseph McCarthy
(right) with aide Roy Cohn

Ironically, those results only encouraged the Red-hunters, who thought Truman's investigation must be covering up the extent of Communist infiltration. Communist agents, it was said, had blocked American aid that might have prevented Mao's triumph in 1949; spies, it was said, had sped the development of Russian atomic weapons, an accusation that seemed well founded after the confession in 1950 of Dr. Klaus Fuchs, a British scientist who had indeed turned classified nuclear information over to the Soviet Union. Then Whittaker Chambers, a journalist who claimed to have been a member of the Communist underground, charged that the spy network had included Alger Hiss, once a bright young New Dealer and in 1949 the President of the Carnegie Foundation for International Peace. The Hiss case became a symbolic battleground for progressives and conservatives, internationalists and superpatriots, intellectuals and anti-intellectuals, and for philosophical relativists and those who clung to what they claimed was "the American way." The accusing Chambers was plain, dumpy, God-fearing; the accused Hiss was urbane, handsome, and very Ivy League. With Chambers stood the House Committee on Un-American Activities, goaded by a freshman California congressman named Richard M. Nixon. A bipartisan galaxy of character witnesses from the field of international relations, led by Dean Acheson and his Republican successor in the Department of State, John Foster Dulles, testified for Alger Hiss. The President of the United States dismissed the whole business as a "red herring."

As was his habit, Harry Truman spoke too quickly and too tartly. From a hollow pumpkin, Chambers melodramatically produced evidence to support his accusation that Hiss had been a spy. Hiss sued Chambers for libel, and the government prosecuted Hiss for perjury, since the statute of limitations precluded a charge of espionage. When the first jury could not agree, the case had to be tried anew. Over and over again the accusations paraded across the front pages of the nation's newspapers. Early in 1950, when Hiss was convicted of lying about his associations and activities in the 1930s, much of the American public apparently leaped to the conclusion that Communist spies abounded in the government of the 1950s.

The junior Republican Senator from Wisconsin did his best to encourage that conclusion. After four lackluster years in Washington, Joe McCarthy muscled his way to the leadership of the anti-Communist cause with his unsurpassed willingness to make unsubstantiated accusations. He chased Communists in the State Department, who numbered more than 200, or 57, or 81, depending upon which of McCarthy's undocumented allegations one believed. Eventually the Senator named just one name, that of Owen Lattimore, a professor of Asian history whom the State Department had occasionally consulted, and who, McCarthy said, was the "top Soviet espionage agent" in the country, a charge for which there was no basis in fact. Indeed, a Senate committee solemnly investigated all McCarthy's statements and concluded that there was no evidence for any of them. The undaunted McCarthy campaigned against Millard Tydings, the respected Maryland Democrat who had headed the investigation, and helped end his long political career. No reputation was immune: in 1951

McCarthy called General Marshall a front man for the international Communist conspiracy.

The public responded because McCarthy offered a comprehensible explanation of the blighted American hope for a stable world. When other nations did not enthusiastically adopt "the American way," it was because Communists duped them. When American foreign policy failed to attain its objectives, Communists were responsible, just as they had subverted the heroic efforts of Chiang Kai-shek and General MacArthur. The Communist agent or "sympathizer" at home was at once deviously clever at disguising himself and readily identifiable because of his rejection of American values. He was, in McCarthy's rhetoric, a phony intellectual whom the decent plain people of the country instantly recognized. "It has not been the less fortunate or members of minority groups who have been selling this nation out," McCarthy said in 1950, "but rather those who have had all the benefits that the wealthiest nation on earth has had to offer—the finest homes, the finest college education, and the finest jobs in Government we can give." The anti-Communist tended to be anti-Establishment, anti-New Deal, and anti-intellectual.

Before the spy scare ended in the Eisenhower administration, McCarthy took his show on the road and sought Communists in government agencies abroad, in defense plants, in universities, and in the Army. A corps of misguided civil servants supplied him with a constant stream of undigested and unproved accusations. He inspired fear throughout the federal bureaucracy, uneasiness among his colleagues in the Senate, and a batch of two-bit imitators. And he caught not one Communist before the Senate finally condemned him in 1954 for insulting a general and making unfounded statements about the Army's security procedures.

Popular suspicion that Communists lurked in high places was one element in Republican campaign strategy for 1952. Truman's failure to hold popular support for his Korean policy and the nation's inability to end the conflict also enhanced Republican prospects. Corrupt practices or, at best, dubious judgment by some of the President's appointees, added to the Republican picture of a "mess in Washington" that only a new administration under a different party could clean up.

But the candidate, rather than any one issue, was the key to Republican victory. After a divisive preconvention campaign and a bitter procedural battle at the convention, the party passed over Senator Taft and nominated General Dwight D. Eisenhower, whose winning smile and personal warmth more than compensated for his lack of elective experience. Eisenhower seemed less rigid on foreign policy than Taft and slightly more progressive on domestic matters, but the nominee was well within the traditional limits of Republicanism.

Adlai Stevenson, the Governor of Illinois who reluctantly accepted the Democratic nomination, was a witty and eloquent opponent for the general. Neither literary grace nor a vigorous attack on the conservative Republican platform sufficed. Stevenson was unable to escape his role as Truman's political heir. The electorate believed that it was time for a

The Republican ticket in 1952

change but that Eisenhower would not let change become uncomfortable. Stevenson carried just nine states, all in the traditionally Democratic South.

Through Stevenson, in a sense, the voters rejected Harry Truman, for the election was a rough referendum on his presidency. Yet Truman's accomplishments were considerable. Even though most of the Fair Deal never reached the statute books, it extended welfare capitalism and made economic and social reform the permanent province of the federal government. Truman at least glimpsed the dimension of the social problems caused by crowding black people into deteriorating urban centers. Abroad, the Marshall Plan brought Western Europe from depression and despair to prosperity and confidence. The Korean War demonstrated both the nation's determination to resist aggression and its capacity to wage limited war.

But Truman's decisions, predicated on the irreconcilable hostility of the Communist bloc, separated the world into two armed camps; the cold war was the joint legacy of Truman and Stalin. The cold war, in turn, brought escalation of a red scare at home that aggravated social rifts among the American people and undermined their faith in government. Harry Truman never gave them new confidence, never developed for them new goals to replace discarded ones, never convinced them that he was right, even when he was. Truman's presidency was not a failure of vision, but of political leadership, which is the first prerequisite for domestic policy. He left a divided nation in a divided world when he left the White House.

Suggested Reading

Harry Truman defends nearly all his actions in two volumes of *Memoirs** (1955, 1956). Cabell Phillips, a Washington reporter, looks back with some perspective in *The Truman Presidency* (1966). Barton J. Bernstein and Allen J. Matusow have edited *The Truman Administration: A Documentary History** (1966). Earl Latham's *The Communist Conspiracy in Washington** (1966) is about as dispassionate as literature about Joseph McCarthy gets. Another of Truman's domestic problems is examined in R. Alton Lee's *Truman and Taft-Hartley* (1966). Richard E. Neustadt uses Truman's presidency for several illustrative examples in *Presidential Power** (1960).

Gar Alperovitz charges that American policy provoked the Cold War in *Atomic Diplomacy** (1965). John A. Lukacs' *A History of the Cold War** (1961, 1965) is less strident. Walter LaFeber's *America, Russia, and the Cold War** (1968) is a satisfactory survey, as is Paul Y. Hammond's *The Cold War Years** (1969). The memoir of former Secretary of State Dean Acheson, *Present at the Creation** (1969), is urbane and informative. *The United States and China** (1958) is the work of a foremost American student of China, John K. Fairbank. Other specialized works on foreign policy are Robert A. Divine's *Second Chance* (1967), a study of the shift to internationalism; John W. Spanier's *The Truman-MacArthur Controversy and the Korean War** (1959); and David Rees's *Korea: The Limited War** (1964).

* Available in paperback edition

CHRONOLOGY

XXIII

THE MODERN REPUBLICANS

Dwight Eisenhower and Harry Truman, born a few years and a few hundred miles apart, grew up in similar circumstances. Sons of ordinary folk in Kansas and Missouri, both learned early the moral truths of midwestern Protestantism. Eisenhower expressed those beliefs in the first public speech of his political career. Reliance on "the simple virtues," said candidate Eisenhower in 1952, "integrity, courage, self-confidence, an unshakeable belief in the Bible" would help the nation solve its most intractable problems.

Eisenhower's campaign seemed a pledge to repeal the entire Truman administration and perhaps that of Franklin Roosevelt as well. With some distaste the General allied with Senator Joseph McCarthy and other conservative Republicans in the common crusade to root fuzzy liberal Democrats out of Washington. A genial, well-advertised conference with Senator Robert Taft reassured Republican regulars that the nominee would curb the spreading federal government and introduce sober fiscal policy. Eisenhower's promised journey to Korea suggested that he would find a way out of "Truman's war." Republican campaigners implied that "Ike's" election would reverse the whole dreary course of American foreign and domestic policy.

Many of those campaign promises went unkept. Continuity with the policies of the Truman administration was more remarkable than the striking contrast in tone. Unlike the combative Truman, who at intervals irritated almost everybody and thoroughly ruffled the nation, the placid Eisenhower soothed. And that was almost the extent of the difference; the net record of the new administration showed only slight change. McCarthy soon declared another open season on federal employees. A succession of unbalanced budgets frustrated the determined efforts of every fiscal conservative in the party. And the containment doctrine, which Republicans had once labeled "sterile," remained the core of the nation's foreign policy.

Republicans did keep the critical campaign promise: they negotiated an end to the Korean War. To speed the protracted peace talks, Eisenhower and his Secretary of State, John Foster Dulles, threatened more force. In December, 1952, on the way back from his postelection visit to Korea, the President-elect mentioned that continued delay at the peace table might begin to cost the Communists heavier casualties. In the late spring of 1953, through Indian intermediaries, Dulles let Communist China know that American restraint in the use of nuclear weapons might not endure indefinitely. Within a month negotiations gathered momentum; in July the shooting stopped. A demilitarized zone and a UN truce team separated the two hostile halves of the country. Frontier incidents periodically reminded Americans that the cease-fire never became a final settlement, but a fragile truce was better than none.

Perhaps the death of Stalin had more to do with the Korean truce than did the atomic threat. The old Bolshevik died in March, 1953, and for a while his successors seemed intent on reducing international tension. Cold-war mistrust plagued both the Soviet initiative and the American response. Premier Georgi Malenkov proved his good faith by diverting revenue from arms to consumer goods, but he simultaneously brandished his new hydrogen bomb to demonstrate that he was negotiating from strength. Influenced by the prevalent McCarthyite attitude that even discussion with the wily Russians was treasonous, Eisenhower warily replied that an Austrian peace treaty, disarmament policed by UN inspection, and free elections in both a unified Korea and a unified Germany might convince the administration of a changed Soviet attitude. Negotiation in fact produced an Austrian treaty in 1955, and the Korean War did stop. But the cold war did not.

"DYNAMIC CONSERVATISM" AT HOME

Eisenhower was the prophet of modern Republicanism, a creed he vaguely defined as "dynamic conservatism." Eisenhower himself subordinated dynamism to conservatism; he shared an aversion to active leadership with his Cabinet, which was composed of businessmen, corporate lawyers, and a lone union official who resigned before a year was out. George Humphrey, a steel executive who became Secretary of the Treasury, communicated his passion for a balanced budget to the President and dominated domestic policy. The new Secretary of Defense, Charles E. Wilson, economized by seeking "more bang for the buck." The first Secretary of the new Department of Health, Education, and Welfare, Oveta Culp Hobby, spent her small appropriations carefully.

The end of the Korean stalemate permitted the President to unveil his modern Republican program, which on inspection turned out to be Herbert Hoover's program wrapped in a shiny, new verbal package. To free the market, Eisenhower dropped the last wartime wage, price, and rent controls. He signed a bill that gave jurisdiction and revenue from offshore oil deposits to the adjacent states, a symbolic act that enhanced state rights. The administration attempted to check the expansion of TVA, which the President cited as an example of "creeping socialism," by contracting with a private utility to supply power to TVA customers. But a Senate inquiry uncovered a conflict of interest that stalled this Dixon-Yates contract until the city of Memphis decided to build the necessary facilities. The embarrassing Dixon-Yates contract was then canceled. Advocates of public generation of electricity lost when the Federal Power Commission awarded the prized Hell's Canyon site on the Snake River to a private utility. The Revenue Act of 1954 gave more tax relief to the wealthy than to those in lower brackets. Ezra Taft Benson, the Secretary of Agriculture, wanted farmers to enjoy the benefits of free competition, but farmers and their congressmen raised such an outcry that the administration settled in 1954 for "flexible" price supports, which were to vary between 75 and 90 percent of parity. When agrarian discontent threatened the Republican hold on the farm states, Eisenhower proposed a "soil bank" in 1956 that paid farmers to withdraw land from cultivation in order to reduce agricultural surpluses.

Modern Republicans scored their social advances where political controversy had already waned. At the administration's request, Congress extended the benefits and coverage of Social Security. The Housing Act of 1954 enlarged the effort to encourage new construction and introduced a program of "urban renewal." In 1955 the statutory minimum wage was raised from seventy-five cents to a dollar. The Federal Highway Act of 1956 authorized the planning and building of 41,000 miles of interstate highway, the largest such program ever undertaken. After the Soviet Union fired the first man-made satellite into orbit in 1957, the argument against federal aid to education abated, and Congress passed the National Defense Education Act in 1958. The act made loans available to students and funded programs to improve the teaching of mathematics, science, and foreign languages.

The President had no civil-rights program when he took office. Eisenhower apparently believed that government could never end racial discrimination, but the Supreme Court demanded that government try. Speaking unanimously through Earl Warren, whom Eisenhower had just appointed Chief Justice, the Court held in *Brown* v. *Board of Education of Topeka* (1954) that segregation in public schools denied equal rights guaranteed by the Fourteenth Amendment. The "separate but equal" test established more than a half-century earlier in *Plessy* v. *Ferguson* was discarded;

School integration: Little Rock, 1957

separate facilities, the Court said, were inherently unequal. Subsequent decisions manifested the Court's determination to end segregation in parks, swimming pools, interstate transportation, and other public facilities.

Resistance focused on the schools, where in 1955 the Court ordered integration to proceed "with all deliberate speed." Southern whites sought refuge in publicly supported "private schools" in order to evade the Court's ruling. White Citizens' Councils, which sprang up throughout the region, were less subtle. These organizations brought political pressure on local school boards to delay integration and when time ran out resorted to economic coercion and terror to maintain segregation. In a few areas, school systems simply shut down.

The judicial process could not keep pace with the various evasions of the intent of the *Brown* decision. Although the President effectively carried out the integration of the armed forces, he showed little inclination to make a more inclusive effort or even to lend his prestige to enforcement of the Court's decision. Eisenhower's indecisiveness may have encouraged extremists to think the Court might safely be defied.

While he blinked at evasion, the President did not tolerate defiance. When the schools of Little Rock, Arkansas, opened in 1957, Governor Orval Faubus used the National Guard to keep order and also to keep nine black students out of the high school where a federal court had ordered them admitted. After prolonged and inconclusive discussion with the President, Faubus withdrew the Guard, but a hysterical mob barred the blacks from the school. Eisenhower finally sent federal troops to Little Rock to enforce the Court's decree and to demonstrate to the Deep South the folly of a direct confrontation with federal authority.

Federal authority was soon to become more extensive. As the crisis in Little Rock got under way, Congress completed action on the first civil-rights legislation since Reconstruction. The Civil Rights Act of 1957 created a permanent commission on civil rights to investigate discrimination and disfranchisement. Another act in 1960 authorized court-appointed officials to protect the voting rights of Negroes. The President made only a nominal effort to help congressional proponents of either bill overcome entrenched southern opposition. Senator Lyndon Johnson and Speaker Sam Rayburn, the two Texans who led the Democratic majority, supported the legislation and guided it toward the White House.

Some southern blacks were well ahead of the glacial pace toward integration that the President seemed to favor. For almost a year, beginning late in 1955, Martin Luther King, Jr., led the black population of Montgomery, Alabama, in a boycott of the city's buses to force changes in the seating arrangements. King, a Montgomery clergyman, stressed black

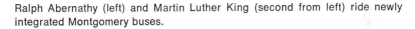

Ralph Abernathy (left) and Martin Luther King (second from left) ride newly integrated Montgomery buses.

solidarity, nonviolence, and the persuasive power of demonstration. His influence grew when a federal injunction ended the boycott on the blacks' terms. And the entire nation was soon to hear more of this eloquent new voice for equality.

The next round of protest belonged to the young. To the black students in Greensboro, North Carolina, who politely declined to leave the lunch counter that had refused to serve them and thereby set off an epidemic of sit-ins. To the small black children who walked to newly integrated schools through the invective and the spittle and the white, hate-distorted faces. To the northern students who actively supported racial equality by marching or by tutoring, either in the South or increasingly in nearby urban ghettoes. Exposure to northern ghettoes led to a growing realization that racism extended beyond the South.

Although the President's personal grasp on the electorate never loosened, the voters chose a Democratic Congress after 1952. Even in 1956, when Eisenhower overwhelmed Adlai Stevenson a second time, Congress remained Democratic. Two years later Democrats enlarged their congressional margin by nearly fifty seats in the House and a whopping thirteen in the Senate. While Eisenhower made most of the gestures expected of a party leader, he did so without partisan zest. He allowed other Republican officeholders to go their own way and rarely used patronage to twist congressional arms. Much of his party remained blithely untouched by the "modern" version of the Republican creed.

In the end, modern Republicanism became little more than an obsession with the balanced budget. In fact, most of Eisenhower's budgets were in the red, and the 1959 deficit of over $18 billion was the largest in peacetime history. But the President and his party kept trying to match income and expense. To the nation's chagrin, the administration pared research and development expenditures just as the Russian sputnik inaugurated the space age. To the disgust of Republicans in farm states, the President defended most of Secretary Benson's attempts to hold down the government's agricultural appropriations. Dissident generals claimed that reduced conventional military forces eliminated the nation's capacity to wage small wars and gave strategists no alternative to the big bomb. Quick reduction of government spending after the Korean War unquestionably contributed to a recession in 1953 and 1954, when an alarming increase in unemployment took place. Although the economy soon bounced back, other economic slowdowns in 1957 and 1958 and again in 1960 and 1961 caused individual hardship and social uneasiness. Keynesian economists argued that government spending should be increased in times of distress, but every drop in the economic index merely made the Eisenhower administration more sure that unbalanced budgets marked the way to economic perdition.

CONTAINMENT CONTINUED

As the domestic new Republicanism turned out to resemble the old, so "new directions" in Republican foreign policy resembled containment, which Dulles had once denounced as "negative, futile, and immoral."

At various times Dulles and other Republicans promised to repudiate "the sell-out at Yalta," to "liberate the captive nations" of Eastern Europe, to "unleash" Chiang Kai-shek so that he could reconquer the mainland, and to go to "the brink of war" to achieve results.

The deeds never matched the speeches. To the outrage of the Republican right wing, Eisenhower sent Charles Bohlen, Roosevelt's translator at Yalta, to Moscow as ambassador. The administration used all its prestige to defeat a constitutional amendment proposed by Senator John Bricker of Ohio that would have made executive agreements, like those at Yalta, subject to the Senate's approval. The iron curtain remained across Eastern Europe even when the "captive peoples" themselves made strenuous efforts to lift it. And when the President "unleashed" Chiang by moving the fleet out of the Formosa Strait, the result was nearly calamitous: Britain and France fretted that the United States would blunder into a debilitating war in Asia; Red China stirred up a decade-long tempest over the Nationalist-held islands near the Chinese coast; and the "unleashed" Chiang could take no advantage of his new freedom.

The Korean truce had stopped only one of Asia's wars. At one stage of the negotiations, Dulles tried to barter a cease-fire in Korea for another in French Indochina, where the hit-and-run tactics of native guerrillas were exhausting French forces. Dulles soon gave up his attempt to link the two wars, but the United States did help France. By 1954, when Indochinese troops surrounded the French garrison at Dien Bien Phu, the United States was paying about three-fourths of France's military expenses in Indochina. Without American military intervention at Dien Bien Phu, it was said, the investment would be lost. The President compared Southeast Asia to a row of dominoes and pointed out that if the Communists pushed over the Indochinese domino, others in the row would certainly tumble too. The Secretary of State told the Cabinet that, except for France, our European allies did not share his view that the United States must act: "If we take a position against a Communist faction within a foreign country, we have to act alone," Dulles reported. "We are confronted by an unfortunate fact— most of the countries of the world do not share our view that Communist control of any government anywhere is in itself a danger. . . ." Admiral Arthur Radford, Chairman of the Joint Chiefs of Staff, was willing to use atomic weapons to relieve Dien Bien Phu; Vice-President Nixon remarked that American troops could do the job.

But the prospect of another Asian war dismayed Congress. Prime Minister Anthony Eden of Great Britain also adamantly opposed any wider war in Indochina. General Matthew Ridgway, who had returned from Korea to become the Army's Chief of Staff, strongly advised against intervention. In the end, Eisenhower let events in Indochina take their course. After Dien Bien Phu fell in May, 1954, an international conference convened in Geneva to make an official end to the war. The conference divided the peninsula at the seventeenth parallel and made arrangements for elections in 1956 to unite the new country, now called Vietnam. The elections were never held, and the war soon turned into a struggle between north and south.

Shortly after the Geneva conference adjourned, Communist China announced its intention of acquiring Taiwan, and in September, 1954, as an apparent first step, began to shell Quemoy and Matsu, two Nationalist-held islands just off the Chinese coast. Once more, Admiral Radford was ready with nuclear weapons; once more the administration responded more calmly. In December the United States formally promised to defend Taiwan, and in January, 1955, Congress passed the Formosa Strait Resolution, which empowered the President to defend the islands between Taiwan and the mainland if the attack was part of an invasion of Taiwan itself. The resolution did not promise to protect the offshore islands, but the Chinese decided against a test of American intent. The shelling stopped in the spring of 1955.

To counter the expansion of Asian communism, Secretary Dulles induced Britain, France, Australia, and New Zealand to join the United States, Thailand, Pakistan, and the Philippines in the Southeast Asia Treaty Organization (SEATO). The new agreement, Dulles said, in effect proclaimed any "intrusion" into Southeast Asia ". . . dangerous to our peace and security." Modeled on NATO, SEATO did not create a comparably effective mutual defense system, in part because such Asian nations as India, Indonesia, and Burma would not participate. The signatories extended their protection to the new states of the Indochinese peninsula, but SEATO was manifestly a Western organization in a region dedicated to ending Western control.

Dulles tried to complete a worldwide defense system with the Baghdad Pact of 1955, which linked Turkey, Iraq, and Iran with Great Britain and the United States, and with SEATO through Pakistan. Less successful even than SEATO, neither the Baghdad treaty nor the subsequent Central Treaty Organization (CENTO) provided the basis for a stable American policy in the volatile Middle East. Like the other defensive alliances concluded in the decade after the Second World War, CENTO was supposed to thwart communism, which was not the major cause of instability in the region. Although the Soviet Union had an active interest in the Middle East, Arab nationalism, oil, and the irreconcilable enmity of Israeli and Arab caused more uproar than did communism.

Gamal Abdel Nasser, the Egyptian Premier, was the chief Arab nationalist, the chief foe of Israel, and the focus of Soviet attempts to gain influence in the Middle East. Nasser's grand design for the modernization of Egypt required the construction of a multipurpose dam on the Nile at Aswan. Both the Soviet Union and a Western consortium set up by the State Department agreed to finance the project. Meanwhile, Nasser undertook to purchase arms from Czechoslovakia, which alarmed American Jews, and recognized Communist China, which outraged the "China lobby." Southern congressmen discovered that the proposed new dam would irrigate thousands of acres of competitive cotton. Secretary Humphrey kept harping on the need for a reduced and balanced budget. Dulles' monetary advisers said that the Soviet Union could not finance the dam anyway. In July, 1956, Dulles abruptly and tactlessly withdrew the American offer.

Within a week Nasser nationalized the Suez Canal to provide his own capital. Egypt now stood squarely across the route by which most of the

Middle East's oil reached the European market. Britain and France favored seizing the incident as an excuse to overthrow Nasser. To gain time to find a peaceful way out, Dulles pacified Paris and London with promises of tankers, financial grants, and subsidized pipelines. When Dulles did not keep his pledges, Britain and France, in concert with Israel, reverted to their earlier policy. In October, Israel invaded Egypt; British and French forces joined the Israelis two days later.

The invasion brought consternation and anger in Washington. It came without prior consultation and just as the presidential campaign was drawing to a close. The United Nations immediately urged peaceful settlement. More importantly, the Soviet Union threatened to come to Egypt's aid with every weapon in the Russian arsenal. The United States brought great diplomatic pressure on Britain, France, and Israel, and the war ended within a week.

With it ended Anglo-French influence in the Middle East. The United States improvised to fill the gap. In March, 1957, Congress empowered the President to use American forces to defend any independent Middle Eastern country from a Communist coup, a policy called the Eisenhower Doctrine. In the next month, the President moved the Mediterranean fleet to bolster King Hussein's control in Jordan. In the summer of 1958, when the friendly government of Lebanon requested American help under the Eisenhower Doctrine, the President sent 70 ships and more than 400 aircraft to the area, and he ordered 14,000 men ashore, including a rocket battalion with atomic capability. The troops enabled the Lebanese government to survive the crisis and then gradually withdrew. In both Jordan and Lebanon the threat came from dissident Arabs. not Communists, but in the interest of preserving stability and of keeping the oil flowing, the administration overlooked that technical difficulty.

Crises in the Middle East and in Southeast Asia emphasized the new complexity of the cold war. The world no longer split neatly into partisans of the United States and satellites of the Soviet Union. A "third world"— the emerging nations of Asia and Africa—wanted no place in either camp but hoped to borrow technical skills, industrial processes, and money from both. However disagreeable he was, Nasser was no Communist; nor did the leaders of India, Indonesia, or Yugoslavia fit the cold-war pattern. Although the administration perceived the change, it did little to educate either the public or the Congress; it distributed military aid and enunciated the Eisenhower Doctrine in the name of stopping the advancing Communist menace.

Even in Latin America, an area that Yankees had taken for granted, the old policies no longer served very well. In 1954 the Central Intelligence Agency organized a successful rebellion against a Communist-leaning government in Guatemala. Only four years later, Vice-President Nixon's goodwill tour of Latin America demonstrated that the United States could no longer dictate to the rest of the hemisphere. The Vice-President's car was nearly overturned in Caracas, and jeering mobs in Venezuela and Peru stoned and spat at him. When Fidel Castro took over Cuba in 1959, he confiscated American property, sold his sugar to the Soviet Union, and proclaimed his island a Marxist state. Eisenhower protested and early in 1961 broke diplomatic relations, which hardly seemed a new hemispheric policy to meet a new situation. To cope with Castro, the CIA devised a scheme like the one that had succeeded in Guatemala. The debacle that followed waited for Eisenhower's successor.

In every upheaval, from Havana to Hanoi, the American public saw the devious hand of the Kremlin. Yet the Eisenhower administration had relatively little direct diplomatic difficulty with the Soviet Union. Disagreement about the future of Germany, particularly the status of Berlin, furnished grounds for made-to-order crises. Otherwise, the two great powers avoided a face-to-face confrontation.

The iron curtain not only remained in place; it took on an air of permanence. Western nations drew more closely together, both in the NATO alliance and in a "common market" that seemed a first step toward the economic unity of Western Europe. To be sure, the cooperation of France was grudging when it could be secured at all. In 1954, in spite of great pressure from Dulles, the French assembly killed an American plan for a European Defense Community to raise a multinational army to complement NATO. Although France eventually accepted the Western Europe Union that Dulles designed to replace the abortive EDC, French suspicion of Britain and of West Germany lingered. And French determination to pursue an independent course stiffened in 1958, when Charles de Gaulle became the first President of the Fifth Republic.

As France resisted Western unification, so also did part of Eastern Europe resist amalgamation into the satellite system. But while France could maintain a somewhat independent policy in the West, the satellites were kept on a much shorter leash. In 1953 East Germany erupted in futile anti-Russian riots; as the uprisings were suppressed, a steady flow of refugees poured into West Berlin. Three years later, demonstrations in Poland did secure a new government under Wladyslaw Gomulka, a Communist whom Stalin had once had imprisoned. In October, 1956, simultaneously with the Suez crisis, Hungarians overthrew their repressive regime. The Soviet Union hesitated and then dispatched an overwhelming force to crush the rising. The United States sympathized with East European rebels but gave them only moral support; indeed, after Russian tanks ended resistance in Hungary, Eisenhower said that the United States did not advocate open rebellion behind the iron curtain. With that statement the administration tacitly accepted the permanent division of Europe.

Direct negotiations between President Eisenhower and Soviet leaders failed to uncover a specific formula for German unity or a general plan for reducing international friction. In 1955 Nikolai Bulganin, the Soviet Premier, and Nikita Khrushchev, who controlled the Communist Party, met at Geneva with Eisenhower and British Prime Minister Anthony Eden. The meeting at the "summit" radiated good will but produced no diplomatic result. Eisenhower surprised the conference when he suggested that each bloc permit aerial inspection of its armaments and defenses. Although the "open skies" proposal was warmly applauded in the West, Soviet leaders displayed a chilly lack of interest. Within a year, the United States opened

Soviet skies without an agreement. In 1956 pilots employed by the CIA began regular photographic missions over Russian territory in U-2 planes, which flew above the reach of Soviet antiaircraft weapons.

In 1959 Khrushchev made his own ceremonial inspection of the United States. Now Premier as well as party chief, Khrushchev visited farms in the Midwest, expressed puritanical disapproval of what he saw on the movie sets of California, ate at the Waldorf and spoke at the United Nations in New York, and spent a pleasant weekend with Eisenhower at the presidential retreat at Camp David, Maryland. The Premier, suddenly amiable, dropped his demand that Western troops leave Berlin, thereby lifting an ultimatum he had issued late in 1958. Khrushchev invited the President to tour the Soviet Union and the two leaders made arrangements to meet again in 1960.

But the meeting was not to be. In May, 1960, as final preparations were being completed for a summit meeting in Paris, the Soviet Union shot down an American U-2 plane more than 1,300 miles inside the Soviet frontier. When American spokesmen lamely explained that the craft had strayed off course while seeking meteorological data, Khrushchev spiked

Eisenhower and Khrushchev, 1959

that story with the announcement that the pilot, Francis Gary Powers, was alive and well and had admitted that his mission was photographic espionage. After further bureaucratic fumbling in Washington, Eisenhower admitted that he had authorized the flight. Khrushchev self-righteously proclaimed his refusal to sit down with an admitted spy, and although both men went to Paris, their meeting produced only recrimination.

Democrats, warming up for the presidential campaign, claimed that the loss of the U-2, the humiliation in Paris, and the anti-American riots that forced cancellation of Eisenhower's projected good-will tour of Japan revealed the low ebb of American diplomatic prestige. Senator John F. Kennedy, the attractive Democratic nominee, built his campaign on a promise to "get this country moving again," an implicit criticism of Eisenhower's static policies. Kennedy proved that Roman Catholicism need not disqualify a national candidate and thereby did much to remove a man's religious faith from political controversy. To mollify the South, Kennedy picked Senator Lyndon Johnson of Texas as his running mate and set off to win the electorate with wit and abundant youthful energy.

The defense of the administration fell to the Vice-President almost by default. Governor Nelson Rockefeller of New York thought briefly about seeking the nomination but quickly discovered the futility of a contest. Nixon dominated the convention, wrote modern Republicanism into the party's platform, and chose Henry Cabot Lodge, the Ambassador to the United Nations, to complete the ticket. The President entered the campaign only when Nixon asked him to take the stump just before the election. The enthusiasm and the size of Eisenhower's crowds showed that he retained a political magnetism neither nominee could match. Kennedy's narrow margin of victory—about 100,000 popular votes—was no repudiation of the President and might have been reversed had Nixon invoked Eisenhower's aid earlier. Kennedy's campaign implied that Eisenhower had not led the nation, a charge the President might well have conceded. The task of a President, as Eisenhower conceived it, was to preside; he had done so with dignity, if not with imagination.

THE NATION AFTER MID-CENTURY

Through a decade of dizzying change President Eisenhower was a reassuring symbol of stability. His prestige and personal warmth, his adherence to economic and moral orthodoxy, and even his fractured syntax stayed constant while the American people uneasily sensed that things were not so placid as he seemed. The social profile at mid-century differed profoundly from that of 1900; the popular mood shifted with the speed of images on the omnipresent television screen. Yet Dwight Eisenhower's smile made it all seem less bewildering.

The changes were as superficial as rising skirts and as profound as rising population. The irritants were as trivial as zip codes and as alarming as the impersonalization of American life. Students complained that campuses were ivory towers and turned them into battlefields; pastors complained of apathetic congregations and then worried when aroused parishioners asked questions for which no seminary provided answers. Joe McCarthy went from hero to ogre to clown within a few months. The middle class attained its collective heart's desire in the suburbs and then worried about crabgrass, conformity, and potential black neighbors. What had been luxuries became necessities, and the old necessities became obsolete. Drivers abandoned the old-fashioned manual gear shift for automatic transmissions and then went back to the "sporty" stick on the floor. Bigger had always meant better in America, and everything was bigger by mid-century: take-home pay and taxes were bigger; church membership was bigger; the national debt was bigger; and the crowds in the waiting rooms of the nation's psychiatrists were growing bigger every year.

There were, of course, more Americans every year. Between 1900 and 1940, the total population climbed from 80 million to 130 million; three decades later the total passed 200 million. Increased life expectancy and a marked jump in the birth rate created a completely different kind of population: more than half of the population was under thirty years of age; since, in addition, one in ten Americans was over sixty-five, the most economically productive part of the population was a shrinking percentage of the total.

Population 1950

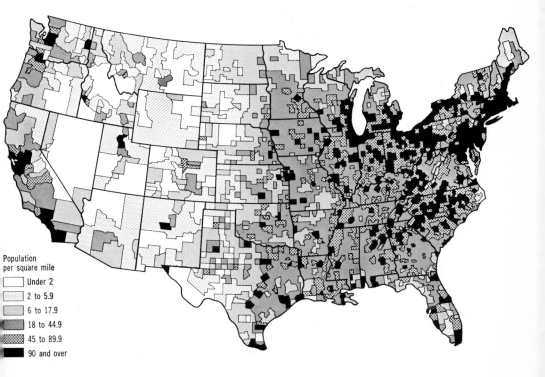

Population
per square mile

☐ Under 2
▨ 2 to 5.9
▧ 6 to 17.9
▰ 18 to 44.9
▨ 45 to 89.9
■ 90 and over

The proportion of blacks remained at about one-tenth of the nation between 1900 and 1960, but a rising birth rate promised that black Americans would soon become a larger minority.

Black and white alike, Americans lived more closer together. Crowding extended well beyond the confines of the notorious ghettoes. About 70 percent of the American people occupied 1 percent of the American landscape, a statistic that gives meaning to the term Megalopolis. Suburbs sprouted shopping centers and office buildings, while businesses and stores abandoned the congestion of the central city. The result was an increasingly urban suburb and a deteriorating city inhabited by the poor and the black, to whom suburban living was not available.

Suburban growth meant that depleted urban tax revenue could not keep pace with mounting demands for public service. When public transportation proved inconvenient, traffic clogged the streets, so that private transportation became equally inconvenient and parking became impossi-

CITIES WITH HIGH PERCENTAGE OF BLACKS

	Census 1960	Estimate 1965	Projection 1970
Washington, D.C.	54%	63%	68%
Richmond, Va.	42	47	51
Compton, Calif.	39	45	51
Gary, Ind.	39	44	50
Jacksonville, Fla.	41	44	47
Baltimore, Md.	35	41	47
Detroit, Mich.	29	39	47
Newark, N.J.	34	40	46
St. Louis, Mo.	29	37	46
New Orleans, La.	37	41	45
Nashville, Tenn.	38	41	43
Trenton, N.J.	23	34	42
Birmingham, Ala.	40	40	40
Shreveport, La.	35	37	40
Atlanta, Ga.	38	38	39
Memphis, Tenn.	37	38	39
Oakland, Calif.	23	31	39
Chattanooga, Tenn.	33	36	38
Cleveland, Ohio	29	34	38
Winston-Salem, N.C.	37	36	34
Jackson, Miss.	36	35	34
Newport News, Va.	34	34	34
Savannah, Ga.	36	34	33
Mobile, Ala.	33	33	33
Montgomery, Ala.	35	33	32

Source: *Congressional Quarterly, Guide to Current American Government* (Fall, 1970), p. 139.

ble. Entrenched educational bureaucracies and idealistic young teachers bickered about the schools, which were often as segregated as those in rural Georgia. Public employees left the garbage uncollected, the streets unswept, the subways unmanned, and the pupils untaught in an attempt to pressure the community into paying higher wages it could ill afford. The police department needed more men to combat a rising crime rate; the public-health department needed more trained people to cope with drug addiction; the department of public welfare needed more social workers and ever so much more money. Meanwhile, the air became progressively more foul, so that the wrong weather conditions brought an epidemic of respiratory infections and required stringent restrictions on furnaces, automobiles, and incinerators. And the water became so polluted that Lake Erie, for instance, was transformed from a recreational asset to a noisome nuisance. The city budget, which could barely provide substandard education, could hardly purify the entire environment.

	Census 1960	Estimate 1965	Projection 1970
Portsmouth, Va.	34%	33%	32%
Baton Rouge, La.	30	31	32
Philadelphia, Penna.	26	29	32
Camden, N.J.	23	28	32
Chicago, Ill.	23	27	32
Columbus, Ohio	16	23	32
Cincinnati, Ohio	22	28	31
Berkeley, Calif.	20	27	31
Beaumont, Texas	29	29	30
Greensboro, N.C.	26	28	30
Dayton, Ohio	22	26	30
Saginaw, Mich.	17	24	30
Youngstown, Ohio	19	25	29
Indianapolis, Ind.	21	24	29
Miami, Fla.	22	26	28
Kansas City, Kan.	23	25	28
Columbia, S.C.	30	29	27
Charlotte, N.C.	28	27	27
Ft. Lauderdale, Fla.	23	25	27
Houston, Texas	23	25	27
Flint, Mich.	18	22	26
Columbus, Ga.	26	26	25
Dallas, Texas	19	22	25
Paterson, N.J.	15	20	25
Elizabeth, N.J.	11	18	25

Let alone solve the race problem. Fifty years earlier, blacks had been out of sight and out of mind. By mid-century they were highly visible in deteriorating urban neighborhoods. Victimized by discriminatory employment practices, badly trained in inadequate schools, barred from many unions, the black became accustomed to poverty; in 1960 government statisticians reported that more than half the black population fell below minimum income levels. Northern urban blacks developed a more articulate racial consciousness, expressed in a more militant, more secular idiom, than that of southern rural blacks.

The black was not alone in his economic distress. He had company not only from Mexican-Americans, Puerto Ricans, Indians, and other members of minority groups but also from indigent whites, for about one in five white families was poor. Appalachia attracted more public attention, but the poverty was just as grinding in the barracks of migrant agricultural workers, in the flop houses along skid row, and in the small towns that progress had passed by. The "other side of the tracks" had become what Michael Harrington called "The Other America."

The rest of the nation, the amorphous middle class, grew and prospered. Every year the number of workers engaged in manufacturing and farming dropped; every year more white-collar workers took the clerical, technical, professional, and managerial jobs that indicate a mature industrial economy. As more people became more comfortable, the term "middle class" itself provoked an almost automatic apology. Middleclass man was the "organization man." He amused himself in the same way his neighbors did, with barbeques, golf, skis, and motor boats. He went to an innocuous church and worshipped whatever bland God was fashionable in the neighborhood. Social critics decried middleclass taste, middleclass complacency, middleclass values, middleclass conformity. The middle class, these critics suggested, was incapable of significant social relationships; people related to one another only through things—telephones, memoranda, martinis, and punch cards. Men rapidly changed jobs, communities, and wives, thus tearing up social roots their parents would have spent decades nurturing. Modern man for all his social contact, was lonely; the crowd was "the lonely crowd."

The picture of the critics, while recognizable, was overdrawn. Although the growing middle class was imitative, not all its models were bad. Never had so many people read so many books, listened to so many records, looked at so much art. Although many of the books were trash, the publishing revolution, especially the wide distribution of paperbacks, also put great literature in the rack at the corner drug store. Although most of the recordings were banal, even some of the popular music had social content and employed complex instrumentation and rhythms; the flood of classical recordings made the entire Western musical heritage available to the farmer in rural Nebraska. The national concern for visual beauty showed not only in the torrent of artistic work in wildly changing modes but also in the desire to eliminate billboards from the highways and junkyards from the landscape.

The middle class spent a great deal of its growing income on education. Middleclass citizens voted to allot a large slice of their taxes to schools. College tuition became an almost universal expense, although tax support materially reduced the burden. Publicly supported colleges and junior colleges, once the second-class citizens of higher education, overflowed their first-class facilities before the paint dried and attracted first-class faculties and first-class students. A diploma became the union card of the middle class.

While the middle class grew, the growth of labor unions tapered off. The merger in 1955 of the AFL with the CIO was not an entirely happy match and did nothing to provide fresh leadership; some of the older leadership, particularly in the Teamsters' Union, proved distressingly dishonest. As pension funds mounted, unions lost their militance. When automation threatened established jobs, labor organizations proved as anxious to preserve past gains as to post new ones. White-collar workers and professionals resisted the old organizing technique and no new ones replaced it. Many unions, particularly in the construction trades, kept out black applicants, which indicated that organized labor's once great interest in social reform had about run out. Even the unions had become middle class.

For many Americans who did not "understand" their "kids" the "generation gap" was the clearest sign of mid-century change. Part of the difference was in taste and style—hair, clothing, music, and speech. But the generation gap also came from a fundamental disagreement about values. Where their elders believed in absolutes, youth favored adaptability, and where their elders were adaptable, youth demanded moral commitment. Parents denounced atheism, marijuana, socialism, and premarital sex, about all of which young people kept an open mind. But they found shocking their parents' failure to oppose racial discrimination, censorship, or the direction of the nation's foreign policy.

The generation gap was a sign of change, and as change accelerated, the gap grew wider and each generation shorter. If the mark of a generation is the shared experience that provides an instinctive definition of what is "normal," a generation in contemporary America is a very short span of time. Professors discovered that each student generation passed in about half the time its predecessor had required. The "beat generation" of the 1950s differed profoundly from the "hippy" movement of the 1960s. The civil-rights movement progressed through several stages in the 1960s. Before 1970 there were already two or three generations of space explorers, an adventure that was only a decade old.

Space exploration was the most glamorous manifestation of technological change, but dozens of other innovations had a more immediate social impact. The computer was at once the marvel of the age and the scapegoat when the retailer incorrectly filled an order. For a time, computers and other electronic equipment seemed to menace the livelihood of clerks and those who performed routine industrial tasks. Technological advance did reduce the jobs available to unskilled workers, but it simultaneously demanded more skilled technicians than could immediately be provided; the shortage of qualified computer programmers, for example, meant that not all computers were efficiently used and that technological progress had temporarily outstripped those who tried to master it.

Even more influential than the computer was the ubiquitous television set. By mid-century, more families had television than had indoor plumbing, and the cultural influence and economic importance of the glaring tube could hardly be overestimated. Television unmade Senator McCarthy by revealing the low tactics with which he simplistically pursued his single theme. By common consent, television also made John Kennedy President; his appearance in a debate with Richard Nixon was apparently the decisive moment in the campaign. Television sold quantities of soap and automobiles, gave much of the population what little information it wanted about the events of the day, baby-sat for the kids, and provoked one member of the Federal Communications Commission to declare all programming "a vast wasteland." Psychologists discovered that children developed a physical dependence on television similar to addiction. Educators revised their classes because television had exposed children to several thousand hours of high-intensity instruction before they ever went to school. Marshall McLuhan, a Canadian professor, became an overnight sage by proclaiming that television had made print obsolete. Clergymen and civic leaders were concerned that a whole generation was seeing too much violence. Everyone agreed that television presented great cultural opportunities when it was best used, which ironically seemed to be the coverage of events surrounding assassinations. Yet thoughtful Americans agreed that television too rarely lived up to its promise, a conclusion that revealed a new, pessimistic dimension in the American mind, a nagging apprehension that perhaps everything was not going to turn out all right after all.

For centuries Americans had optimistically worked for progress and bet on the future. At mid-century some stopped working, and others hedged their bets. A few challenged the work ethic by their conduct: some young people preferred present gratification to investing time and energy for the greater future return that adults promised; some adults, in turn, casually used unemployment compensation as vacation pay. Americans of all ages became convinced that the nation's new international prominence was no advance over the days when Europeans tried to keep the peace of the world; nor was there any longer the cocky assurance that America would do the job more competently. Atomic energy and other technological changes seemed ambiguous progress at best. Even having more of the world's goods failed to produce instant happiness. It was this ambiguity, this lack of simple answers, this questioning of what had been taken for granted, that made the richest and strongest generation of Americans among the least assured.

Not all of these changes were clear when Dwight Eisenhower retired from public life, although the realization that something was amiss was spreading. Rather than examine the sources of national uneasiness, the electorate for eight years had put its faith in the smiling soldier, whose career symbolized the America that was slipping away.

Suggested Reading

There is no wholly satisfying study of the Eisenhower years. Alfred D. Chandler and his associates are editing the Eisenhower papers, which promise to create a base for scholarship. Eisenhower's own White House memoirs, *Mandate for Change* (1963) and *Waging Peace* (1965), are bland. Sherman Adams reveals something of the inside of the Eisenhower administration in *Firsthand Report** (1961). Anthony Lewis' *Portrait of a Decade** (1964) treats the struggle for desegregation. Samuel Lubell's *The Revolt of the Moderates** (1956) helps explain the politics of the decade, as does Theodore H. White's *The Making of the President, 1960** (1961). (See also the works on the Cold War cited in the *Suggested Reading* for Chapter 22.)

George E. Mowry, *The Urban Nation** (1968), gives a brief survey of the Eisenhower years and helps set the social scene at midcentury. Other sociological insights are contained in William H. Whyte's *The Organization Man** (1956), *The Lonely Crowd** (1950) by David Riesman, et al., and Marshall McLuhan's *Understanding Media** (1964). David M. Potter suggests in *People of Plenty** (1954) that abundance has shaped the national character.

*Available in paperback edition

CHRONOLOGY

1960   Presidential election: John F. Kennedy (Democrat) defeats Richard M. Nixon (Republican)

1961   Cuban exiles defeated at Bay of Pigs
Berlin Wall divides city

1961–?   The war in Vietnam:
- 1961-64: Gradual increase of American troops in Vietnam
- 1964: Tonkin Gulf Resolution
- 1964–68: United States planes bomb North Vietnam
- 1968: North Vietnam launches Tet offensive
  Paris peace talks begin
- 1970: Vietnamization furnishes first application of Nixon Doctrine
- 1971: Mansfield amendment indicates majority of Senate dissatisfied with pace of American withdrawal

1962   Cuban missile crisis

1963   Demonstrations in Birmingham lead to Civil Rights Act (1964) and Voting Rights Act (1965)
President Kennedy assassinated in Dallas; Lyndon B. Johnson succeeds Kennedy

1964   President Johnson declares war on poverty; promises Great Society
Presidential election: Lyndon B. Johnson (Democrat) defeats Barry M. Goldwater (Republican)

1965   American Marines intervene in Dominican Republic

1967   Arab-Israeli War
Urban riots

1968   Assassinations of Martin Luther King, Jr., and Robert F. Kennedy
Presidential election: Richard M. Nixon (Republican) defeats Hubert H. Humphrey (Democrat) and George C. Wallace (American)

1969   Warren E. Burger replaces Earl Warren as Chief Justice
Apollo missions land men on the moon

XXIV

"... A NEW GENERATION

OF AMERICANS"

Dwight D. Eisenhower's personal warmth radiated from television sets all over the nation as the President mused about change and closed his half-century of public service. Eisenhower was dignified and reassuringly familiar; he had not, as he might put it, rocked the boat. The nostalgic President proposed for his countrymen a proven test of public policy—the test of moderation, or what he called "balance."

> ... each proposal must be weighed in the light of a broader consideration; the need to maintain balance in and among national programs— balance between the private and public economy, balance between the cost and hoped for advantages—balance between the clearly necessary and the comfortingly desirable; balance between our essential requirements as a nation and the duties imposed by the nation upon the individual; balance between actions of the moment and the national welfare of the future. Good judgment seeks balance and progress. . . .

The President knew that balance would not be easily attained in the unsteady world of the 1960s. He warned against the combination of military and industrial establishments, whose influence threatened the America he knew. The military-industrial complex, the old soldier said, turned the tinkering inventor into a subsidized researcher, substituted the federal contract for intellectual curiosity in the nation's universities, mortgaged the country's future, and endangered its democracy. Dwight Eisenhower, born in a different world in 1890, did not seem convinced that every change since had constituted progress.

John Kennedy, however, welcomed change. He had built his campaign on a pledge to "get this country moving again," and his inaugural address began with reference to "an end as well as a beginning . . . renewal as well as change." "Let the word go forth," Kennedy said, ". . . that the torch has been passed to a new generation of Americans, born in this century, tempered by war, disciplined by a hard and bitter peace, proud of our ancient heritage, and unwilling to witness or permit the slow undoing of those human rights to which this nation has always been committed. . . ." Impatient, vigorous, and young, Kennedy was the acknowledged leader of that "new generation of Americans." His program—and theirs—would "not be finished in the first one hundred days."

> Nor will it be finished in the first one thousand days, nor in the life of this administration, nor even perhaps in our lifetime on this planet. But let us begin. . . . The energy, the faith, the devotion which we bring to this endeavor will light our country and all who serve it, and the glow from that fire can truly light the world.

These themes characterized the brief Kennedy presidency: change, challenge, youth, faith, energy, and style. Kennedy once pointed to the burden of an inherited past:

> . . . the great enemy of truth is very often not the lie—deliberate, contrived and dishonest—but the myth, persistent, persuasive and unreal-

Kennedy-Nixon television debate, 1960

istic. We subject facts to a prefabricated set of interpretations. We enjoy the comfort of opinion without the discomfort of thought.

Another time, Kennedy spoke of the strange, new world where old guideposts offered no direction:

We find ourselves entangled with apparently unanswerable problems in unpronounceable places. We discover that our enemy in one decade is our ally in the next. We find ourselves committed to governments whose actions we cannot often approve, assisting societies with principles very different from our own.

And there was no going back. The President once remarked that his political problems each week were as complex as those some of his predecessors had faced in a lifetime of public service. And, Kennedy went on, all his problems were "entirely different from those that . . . faced the Eisenhower Administration, or that of Harry Truman, or Franklin Roosevelt, or Woodrow Wilson . . . new programs, requiring new people, new solutions, new ideas."

The President exaggerated. Not all the problems were new. Poverty, disease, injustice, tyranny, war—these were as old as humanity. But the men of Kennedy's New Frontier refused to concede that perpetual problems need endure one moment longer. To find the answers, Kennedy summoned talent and ideas, as past Presidents had, from businesses and law firms. But he also turned to unusual sources like artists' studios, laboratories, foundations, and university campuses, especially his own at Harvard. Once assembled, the brilliant new administration set about shaking the American people out of their complacency.

Without, it must be said, an immediate legislative response. As a presidential candidate, Kennedy had stood for dynamic executive leadership, but the administration's performance fell short of his promises. Partly because Kennedy had won the election by an unimpressive 100,000-vote margin, message after ringing message went to Congress without an echo. The church-state controversy snarled aid to education; the American Medical Association thwarted medical care for the aged; fiscal conservatives turned back a tax cut the President wanted to stimulate economic growth. The air remained foul, the water contaminated, the cities unrenewed. Congress did expand the public housing program, broaden social security benefits, and appropriate more money to put a man on the moon—by 1970, the President pledged. Kennedy had to use executive authority to create the Peace Corps. Except for support of the glamorous space program, Congress acted as if the New Frontier had barely reached Pittsburgh. And the frustrated President remembered Hotspur's deflating response to the boast "I can call spirits from the vasty deep." "Why, so can I, or so can any man," came the reply. "But will they come when you do call for them?"

The wry quotation from Shakespeare typified Kennedy's style. If Congress did not know a fresh breeze was blowing in the country, everyone else felt it. And if Kennedy could not lift Congress, he unquestionably did

lift American civilization. Wit came back to Washington, and poetry, paint-
ing, dancing and drama, French cooking and chamber music, lively conversation, and so much more. And the glow spread from the capital to
the country.

The 1960s was a self-consciously new decade. Political candidates tied
themselves to the New Frontier by proclaiming the "new politics"; certain
movie critics wrote of a "new wave"; the old algebra became the "new
math"; the New Left plagued government and university administrators;
some referred to bureaucrats in business, education, and philanthropy, as
well as in government, as the "new class"; opponents of the nation's policy
in southeast Asia were dubbed "neo-isolationists." John Kennedy was partly
responsible for making exciting what was new. And in the end, the idea
that life in the late twentieth century can be vibrant and significant in spite
of frustration and complexity may be Kennedy's most important legacy.
But it was not the only one. While peace did not break out, neither did war.
And he nurtured an important legislative harvest that Lyndon B. Johnson
reaped in the three years after Kennedy's assassination in Dallas.

But Lyndon Johnson, for all his legislative skill, did not sparkle, nor
did he touch the nation's spirit and imagination as had John Kennedy.
Respected, feared, admired—these Johnson was, but not loved. Having
tasted Harvard, the nation did not relish Texas. Johnson's big cars and
cowboy hats, his surgical scars, barbecues, beagles, and his homely Texas
tales seemed terribly corny. Kennedy was vigor and vision; Johnson was a

President Johnson and Vice-
President-elect Hubert Humphrey on the ranch, 1964

wheeler and dealer. If the Kennedy administration was Camelot, Johnson's was the OK corral.

For a while, Lyndon Johnson seemed to make no errors. He assumed the presidential duties with dignity and humility, and he successfully courted popular and congressional support. He preempted the middle of the political spectrum and left very little to Barry Goldwater, the engagingly candid Senator from Arizona who convinced his fanatical partisans that there was an immense, hidden, conservative vote that would inundate the Democratic spenders if given "a choice, not an echo." In the 1964 campaign Johnson shrewdly emphasized Goldwater's avowed conservatism, successfully tagged him as too impetuous to be entrusted with the nation's foreign policy, and conveyed an impression of his own prudent restraint that his subsequent policy in Vietnam belied. Goldwater promised to decrease federal spending and welfare programs, opposed the civil-rights legislation of the decade, and lost the election by the largest margin in American history. He also carried a good many Republican legislators to defeat with him. The new Congress seemed almost anxious to do Johnson's bidding and produced the most impressive spate of legislation since the early days of the New Deal.

GOVERNMENT AND ECONOMIC GROWTH

John Kennedy had once labeled economic growth "the number one domestic problem" a President must meet. The Eisenhower presidency ended in recession; unemployment rates went up and population growth poured new workers into the labor market at the rate of about 25,000 per week. Technology increased the productivity of some workers and eliminated the jobs of others. In the fifteen years after the Second World War the output of the average automobile worker had nearly doubled, and farm production per man-hour increased twice as fast as the rate for the manufacturing sector of the economy. The task of fiscal policy was to provide jobs to soak up unemployment and consume the goods that flooded the market without inducing intolerable inflation.

Under the Kennedy-Johnson stimulus, the economy certainly grew. In almost any year, gross national product jumped about $40 billion, an amount nearly equal to the total GNP of Canada. The gross sales of General Motors alone exceeded the GNP of the Netherlands. The federal budget climbed from roughly $80 billion at the end of the Eisenhower administration to about $130 billion at the end of Johnson's. The GNP increased from about $500 billion to $800 billion, and unemployment fell below 4 percent of the labor force. "We are," President Johnson boasted in 1965, "in the midst of the greatest upward surge of economic well-being in the history of any nation."

Governmental encouragement of growth took two forms: increased federal spending and a simultaneous reduction in taxes to stimulate private spending. Kennedy tried to link the tax cut with tax reform, but Congress refused to enact either until 1964, when Johnson signed an act that reduced taxes by $11.5 billion without making changes in the basic revenue code. Then, vainly in 1967, and finally with success in 1968, Johnson had to ask Congress to take half of the reduction back as the war in Vietnam and a nagging deficit in the nation's balance of payments threatened serious inflation.

Federal spending programs began as conventional public construction projects, broadened briefly into a war on poverty that was to create what Johnson grandly called the "Great Society," and then became more planes, more bombs, and more troops for the war in Asia. The Area Redevelopment Act of 1961 authorized public grants to stimulate employment in areas of chronic unemployment, and public housing and urban reconstruction programs also put people to work. Administration of several of these programs was centered in 1965 in a new Department of Housing and Urban Development run by Robert C. Weaver, the first black member of a presidential cabinet.

The Economic Opportunity Act was the main weapon in the war on poverty, which Johnson declared in 1964. Passed just before the presidential election, the act established "Head Start" sessions to give poor children a better chance at academic success. The Job Corps furnished an opportunity for teen-age dropouts through work on conservation projects and through training in such trades as the operation and repair of business machines. VISTA, a domestic counterpart of the Peace Corps, sent young volunteers to teach in store-front schools and to organize community activities in less prosperous areas. The new Congress that convened in 1965 climaxed two decades of debate by passing the Medicare Bill, which financed the medical costs of aged Americans from the Social Security program. Congress also appropriated $1 billion to begin the redevelopment of Appalachia, the perpetually depressed area of the Southeast where the hills no longer produced enough coal or crops.

A former school teacher himself, Lyndon Johnson constantly stressed the importance of education in the Great Society. By any measure, education was one of the nation's largest industries, and statistics about the rise in university graduates, the comparative numbers of engineers in the United States and the Soviet Union, and the rate of increase in human knowledge were all commonplaces of the period. Both Kennedy and Johnson saw the nation's salvation in trained minds that might be able to cope with the unimagined future, and both urged federal support for the nation's schools. In 1965 Congress responded with the Elementary and Secondary Education Act, which authorized grants for curricular development, teaching materials, teacher training, and educational research.

The fiscal policy of the 1960s signaled the arrival of what one economist called "The Age of Keynes." In general terms, the "New Economics," whose patron saint was the British economist John Maynard Keynes, swept out many of the concepts that had for years been axiomatic—and still were for fiscal conservatives, who momentarily expected disaster. The balanced budget, long ignored in practice, was no longer given polite lip service; it was, new economists thought, less important than a 5 percent growth rate or full employment. Federal manipulation of the business cycle, which business deplored in good times and demanded in depression, had become second nature for bureaucratic economists and was widely accepted in the business community. Perhaps one reason for this agreement was that economic liberals realized that business was the source, not the foe, of national prosperity, while business discovered that government rarely challenged the control of those with economic power.

Economic theorists also questioned some of the simplistic concepts that had become the folklore of American capitalism. John Kenneth Galbraith, a Harvard economist whom Kennedy appointed Ambassador to India, challenged the traditional model of the capitalistic market. Well before affluence became part of the everyday national vocabulary, Galbraith argued that theoretical assumptions of scarcity were not relevant in *The Affluent Society*. Nor did competition, which assumed large numbers of small economic units, describe *The New Industrial State*. In economic practice, Americans had long since accepted the power of consolidated enterprise, and Galbraith thought economic theory ought to reflect this reality. No industry, for instance, could afford to develop new technology and then risk expensive, new products in an unplanned market. Aided by advertising, industry planned both the product and the demand for it. Only relatively unimportant parts of the market remained competitive. Three giant corporations in 1965 had more gross income than all the farms in the nation; the income of General Motors alone exceeded the total income of 90 percent of the country's farms and was eight times that of the state of New York and about 20 percent of the revenue of the federal government. When such illustrations could be multiplied, belief in equal access to a competitive market was clearly an act of faith. Indeed, Galbraith said, labeling the American economy "capitalistic" was hardly accurate:

> The services of Federal, state, and local governments now account for between a fifth and a quarter of all economic activity. In 1929 it was about eight per cent. This far exceeds the government share in such an avowedly socialist state as India, considerably exceeds that in the anciently social democratic kingdoms of Sweden and Norway, and is not wholly incommensurate with the share in Poland. . . .

THE REST OF THE WORLD

Economic growth was as vital to national defense as to domestic abundance. Both Kennedy and Johnson were intent on increasing and diversifying America's military force, and neither seemed to their critics sufficiently scrupulous about the application of this new power. In his campaign, John Kennedy had criticized Republican policy-makers for relying too heavily on the nuclear deterrent with consequent inflexibility in meeting situations that rated less than a nuclear response. Under the energetic direction of Robert S. McNamara, a former president of Ford Motor Company and by common consent the most effective Secretary of Defense in the nation's history, the Kennedy administration built up conventional forces that permitted a greater range of military policy.

One policy, already well developed when Kennedy took office, was designed to eliminate the "Communist enclave ninety miles from our shores," as Cuba had been described during the presidential campaign. Cuban exiles, supplied and trained by the United States and supported by American air and sea forces, were to invade the island and rally the dissident population to overthrow Fidel Castro's despotic regime. But Kennedy called off American air support, the Cuban civilians ignored their self-proclaimed liberators, and Castro's forces wiped out the invaders at the Bay of Pigs. Premier Castro was still in business in Havana after Kennedy's successor had retired to Texas. Castro's persistence provided a superb example of the ironic limits of power in the twentieth century. Cuba had virtually no military capacity, yet Castro had thumbed his nose at the greatest power in the world. Americans had long known that might was not right, but they were puzzled when it was not even power.

Even before the Bay of Pigs, President Kennedy had proposed an "Alliance for Progress," a transfusion of capital for Latin America that would eliminate the hunger and illiteracy that spawned communism. But Latin American oligarchs were not anxious for land reform or for educational or welfare schemes that their taxes would have to support, and the American Congress also proved niggardly with funds. Nor did Latin Americans share the Yankee obsession with Castro, who, after all, was the spectre that diverted a few of Uncle Sam's dollars to the southern half of the hemisphere.

One Castro was frustrating; two, President Johnson believed, would be intolerable. And so, when a rebellion broke out in the Dominican Republic in 1965, the President reacted quickly. Presidential advisers believed Dominican Communists were preparing to seize power. The prompt arrival of several hundred American Marines, whose number quickly swelled to several thousand, stopped both the potential communist coup and the revolution. A year later the last of the American garrison withdrew after Dominican voters had selected a new, "acceptable" President. However serious the Communist threat—some observers feared Johnson had overestimated it—American intervention seemed a return to the gunboat diplomacy that had preceded Franklin Roosevelt's effort to turn the United States into a good neighbor. To Latin Americans, the Alliance for Progress was less visible than the marines.

Cuba and the Dominican Republic were familiar areas of concern. But the nation also needed policies for places that most Americans could not even locate: Laos, the Congo, Goa, Cyprus, Angola, New Guinea, Rhodesia, the Sinai Peninsula, and over and over again, Vietnam. An increasing number of Americans wondered whether cold-war policies were valid in dealing with the developing "third world," which refused to commit itself permanently to either cold-war antagonist. Even France, under the firm leadership of Charles de Gaulle, followed an independent policy and developed an independent nuclear force. In spite of these new conditions, however, the administration often chose to pacify the public with anti-Communist phrases, rather than to create fresh post-cold-war policies.

In the absence of official leadership from Washington, ordinary citizens, with the increasing encouragement and eventual help of the administration's critics in government, sought new diplomatic precepts. Scholars suggested that decisions had been based on misinformation or on faulty assessments of the history, social structure, or ideology of new countries with which the State Department had had little experience. Clergymen of all faiths applied moral absolutes to America's contact with the rest of the world. Publishers turned out tracts, advertisements, and an unending stream of books by professors, diplomats, several able and profoundly disillusioned soldiers, and such unlikely polemicists as a longshoreman and the nation's foremost pediatrician. If at the end of the decade the cold-war mentality persisted in large segments of America, at least the new heresies were not restricted to the nation's intellectuals.

For the facts seemed to require a reassessment. Following some tense confrontations in the Kennedy administration, Soviet-American contacts were characterized, if not by cooperation, at least by restraint. The failure of the invasion of Cuba at the Bay of Pigs in April, 1961, may have led Soviet Premier Nikita Khrushchev to think Kennedy irresolute, a judgment that their meeting in June at Vienna apparently confirmed. But Kennedy's resolution did not falter in July, when Khrushchev threatened to cut Berlin off from West Germany. The President mobilized reserves and demonstrated the American commitment to Berlin with constant convoys that maintained access to the city. The Berlin Wall, constructed in August, 1961, was a tacit East German confession of permanent division, an acknowledgment that the iron curtain would not soon surround West Berlin. In 1968, East Germany again stirred momentary concern about Berlin by harassment of civilian traffic to the city. But the confrontation lacked the drama of previous Soviet-American deadlocks.

Khrushchev's most ambitious test of Kennedy's determination came in 1962, when the Soviets established missile bases in Cuba. When American reconnaissance revealed these facilities in October, the President ordered a naval blockade of the island. Russian ships carrying additional missiles, already at sea when Kennedy proclaimed the blockade, turned aside at the last moment. "We were eyeball to eyeball," Secretary of State Dean Rusk was reported to have said, "and I think the other fellow just blinked." Khrushchev offered to remove the Soviet equipment in return for an American guarantee not to invade Cuba, which Kennedy promptly gave. A month later, when Kennedy was convinced the missiles had been completely withdrawn, he lifted the blockade.

The Cuban crisis may have had a healthy effect on Soviet-American relations, for the two nations had reflected seriously on nuclear war and decided against it. In 1961 both countries had announced the resumption of nuclear testing; in 1963 a Nuclear Test Ban Treaty ended atmospheric testing with the attendant danger of radioactive fallout, a step Kennedy thought might be historically his most important presidential act. A "hot line" provided direct communication from the White House to the Kremlin. Americans seemed to feel an almost personal rapport with Premier Khrushchev that did not entirely vanish when the Communist party decided in 1964 to replace him as Premier with Aleksei Kosygin and as Secretary of the party with Leonid Brezhnev. A Soviet-American consular treaty, negotiated in 1964, was finally ratified in 1967, after the Johnson administration had turned aside several attempts to weaken the accord. The two countries reopened consulates that had been closed in 1948 and guaranteed one another access to nationals detained on criminal charges, a protection the United States had particularly sought. A few months after ratification, President Johnson and Premier Kosygin met in Glassboro, New Jersey, in the wake of the Arab-Israeli War. Although the two superpowers had exchanged public recrimination in the United Nations while Israeli troops routed Syria, Jordan, and the United Arab Republic, in private both acted to limit the conflict. And although the war in Vietnam required the continuation of a minimum of cold-war rhetoric, nevertheless in 1968 the Soviet Union quietly returned an airplane full of troops that had strayed over Soviet territory, signed a treaty to prohibit the spread of nuclear weapons, inaugurated direct air service from New York to Moscow, and opened discussions to curb the missile race. To be sure, Russian tanks also rumbled into Prague in the summer of 1968 and smothered incipient Czech independence. But the measure of the thaw in the cold war was that cooperation was no longer unthinkable and had already begun in some instances.

Cracks in the Communist monolith made modification of American policy possible. American diplomacy after 1945 had assumed an integrated, centrally-directed Communist conspiracy, an assumption that became increasingly untenable as the rift between China and the Soviet Union grew. Since China and the Soviet Union shared a long frontier, Chinese expansion worried Russians, as it did Indians and other residents of East Asia. The Chinese nuclear force, demonstrated in tests beginning in 1964, was not necessarily trained exclusively on the "capitalist aggressors"; perhaps part of it was designated for those "revisionist Communists" in Moscow who had "sold out" to the "warmongers." Evidence from China in 1967 indicated a significant internal struggle between militant "Red Guards," who espoused the tough doctrines of Chairman Mao Tse-tung, and more cautious Chinese, who advocated a more restrained foreign policy. Neither faction welcomed direction from Moscow.

Nor was it clear that direction came either from Moscow or Peking to the several Communist movements in Southeast Asia. The Department of State often acted as if Communists in Laos, Cambodia, Indonesia, and Vietnam were agents of Chinese imperialism. But while these groups clearly believed in some variant of Marxism, it seemed fused with nationalism and not part of one great wave of international communism. In 1962 President Kennedy accepted a neutralist government in Laos, in which Communists participated. In the summer of 1965 Indonesians set back their own Communist movement in a bloody purge of immense dimensions. And as the decade went on, the American people made clear their willingness to tolerate a compromise in Vietnam, however rigidly the Department of State opposed such a policy.

VIETNAM

No one can yet write dispassionately about the war in Vietnam, and no one in the decade did so. Accusations tumbled from pulpits and presses; academics published advertisements and sponsored teach-ins; senators shot barbed questions at administration spokesmen and barbed statements at the press; demonstration and counterdemonstration clogged the streets. It was, one heard, a civil war or, on the other hand, external Communist aggression; the government of South Vietnam, one read, was dictatorial or represented the legitimate aspirations of the people; American troops were there, one was told, as a result of the imperialistic ambitions of the military-industrial complex or because of sacred obligations under the SEATO treaty; the war, it was said, was part of a white man's plot to eliminate American blacks, who composed a disproportionate percentage of front-line troops, and dark-skinned Asiatics as well, or, alternately, it was a manifestation of the traditional American willingness to help others achieve peace, freedom, and democracy. The war enraged and perplexed ordinary Americans as had no other question of foreign policy in the century.

Political and military leaders never inspired the nation with a sense of unified purpose. Indeed, the "Pentagon papers" released in 1971 implied that

San Francisco demonstrators, 1969

the government's major motive was often its desire to avoid political embarrassment: intervention merely shielded the administration from partisan charges that it had passively watched the Communists take over Southeast Asia. However inaccurate the analogy between Hitler and Ho Chi Minh, the Munich agreements of 1938 haunted official Washington. Thus, President Kennedy, already burned by the Cuban fiasco, announced in 1961 that he had ordered more military advisers to Vietnam, in spite of warning from members of the administration that the step had only a remote chance of success and might well lead to a wider war. Thus, President Johnson ignored a caution that air power alone would not keep the Viet Cong at bay and authorized the use of American bombers to stiffen the resolve of the South Vietnamese. Thus, President Nixon justified an American invasion of Cambodia as a tactical maneuver to keep Communist infiltrators from the use of "privileged sanctuaries." Yet the war dragged on, and the American public grew less worried about Communist expansion in Asia and more anxious to evacuate American forces. Each reassuring pronouncement was subject to widespread public cynicism, and a credibility gap yawned between public and administration.

The mistrust existed well before 1971, when the press began publishing top-secret materials that disclosed apparent governmental duplicity. After the 1964 campaign, much of what Lyndon Johnson said was immediately discounted. When American aircraft began to bomb North Vietnam in 1965, the administration implied that this action would avoid the use of American troops and force the North Vietnamese to negotiate. The bombers dropped more explosive tonnage in Vietnam than had fallen on all of Germany in the Second World War, but the North Vietnamese did not flinch, and the participation of American troops increased nearly tenfold during that year. The commander in the field, General William Westmoreland, and Secretary McNamara made optimistic predictions that seemed absurd as months became years and casualties mounted. Professions of high humanitarian purpose did not square with press accounts of the massacre of civilians at My Lai or with pictures of American marines torching Vietnamese villages in order to save them from the enemy. No sooner did the administration praise the democratic leadership of South Vietnam, than Buddhist monks set themselves on fire to protest that leadership, or a coup overthew it, or officials in Saigon arrested a half-dozen of their most prominent critics.

Briefly, in 1964, American policy seemed to have broad popular support. Since few American soldiers were actually in combat then, and since the bombing of North Vietnam had not begun, the United States still appeared to be helping a small beleaguered state defend itself. In August, when the North Vietnamese torpedo boats attacked American vessels in the Gulf of Tonkin, the administration claimed that the enemy was seeking a wider war. At Johnson's request, by an enormous margin, Congress adopted the Tonkin Gulf resolution, which virtually gave the executive a military blank check in Asia. The Pentagon, it became evident later, had already designed the strategy that converted the war to an American, rather than a Vietnamese, responsibility.

The Tonkin Gulf consensus did not endure. As the war escalated in

CHINA

French defeat
1954
•Dienbienphu

Lang Son•
•Thai Nguyen

Hanoi•

Haiphong•

GULF OF
TONKIN

HAINAN

•Luang Prabang
Xieng Khouang•

Nam Dinh•
Thanh Hoa•

U.S. bombing halt
called
March 1968

•Vinh

NORTH
VIETNAM

•Vientiane

Nakhon Phanom•
Sakon Nakhon•

•Dong Hoi Demilitarized zone
U.S. bombing halt called
October 1968

Khon Kaen•   •Kalasin

Khe
Sanh• •Quang Tri
•Hue•

Incursion into Laos
February 1971

THAILAND
Ubon•

LAOS

•Danang

•Pakse

•Quang Ngai

•Bangkok

Tet offensive
January 1968

•Kontum

Battambang•

CAMBODIA

Pleiku• Qui Nhon•

Kompong
Cham

Tuy Hoa•

• Ban Me Thuot

Kompong Chhnang•

SOUTH
VIETNAM

Phnom Penh•

Phan Rang•

•Tay Ninh Cambodian invasion
April–May 1970

GULF
OF
SIAM

•Saigon

SOUTH CHINA SEA

1965 and 1966, so did the protests. The silent vigils of pacifists became mass marches and noisy demonstrations. Once the province of Quakers, a few academics, and political mavericks like Senator Wayne Morse of Oregon, the peace movement became fashionable. Senator J. William Fulbright allowed the Committee on Foreign Relations to become a forum for senators and citizens who opposed the war. Senator Eugene McCarthy of Minnesota gave the antiwar movement enigmatic political leadership when he entered Democratic presidential primaries in 1968; belatedly, Senator Robert F.

Kennedy of New York also declared his disillusionment with the war and announced his presidential candidacy. Neither President Johnson's retirement nor the prospect of losing the White House could hold the fragmenting Democratic party together. The fissures in the party mirrored divisions in the nation.

The American people saw their divisions in prime time and living color when the Democrats nominated a presidential candidate in Chicago. Although Senator McCarthy seemed to have given up, his rabid partisans carried the crusade through the platform committee to the floor of the convention itself, where they were outmaneuvered and outvoted by those supporting a ticket of Vice-President Hubert Humphrey and Senator Edmund S. Muskie. Then, early in the morning, after the convention had finished, Chicago police swarmed through McCarthy's convention headquarters in an apparently unprovoked mission of frustrated vengeance.

The Chicago police had cause for frustration, if not for their senseless rampage through McCarthy's command post. For days, while delegates were jostling one another inside the convention, another confrontation was taking place outside. Young demonstrators, some determined to influence the political process and others determined to reveal its futility, flooded Chicago, disobeyed the city's regulations, and taunted the police and national guardsmen who tried to enforce the laws. Marches and provocation and disobedience led to tear gas, nightsticks, and brutality as confrontation escalated to riot. The tense, gas-laden atmosphere hardly seemed conducive to deliberate decision-making.

Republicans successfully masked their divisions. Richard Nixon swept triumphantly through the primaries, brushing aside the inept challenge of Michigan's Governor George Romney, the hesitant effort of New York's Governor Nelson Rockefeller, and the last-minute blitz of California's Governor Ronald Reagan. Nixon successfully appealed to the center of his party and, in the campaign, to the center of the electorate with his pledge to extricate the United States from Vietnam without impairing national pride or national honor.

Governor George Wallace of Alabama, running on a third-party ticket, threatened briefly to win enough conservative support to throw the election into the House. At the ballot box, however, the blue-collar voter, on whom Wallace had relied, voted from Democratic habit rather than from apprehensive racism. Wallace carried five states and won about 13 percent of the popular vote. Nixon finished with 43 percent of the electorate. In the final weeks of the contest Humphrey almost shook off the burden of his association with the Johnson administration, but he finished about 500,000 votes behind Nixon.

In the last frantic days of the campaign, President Johnson announced that American aircraft would stop bombing North Vietnam and that diplomatic representatives of all combatants would soon meet in Paris to devise a formula for peace. After months of wrangling in Paris, only procedural details had been settled. As each side consumed meeting after weekly meeting with dreary recitations of grievances, disappointment within the

United States turned to embittered boredom. President Nixon sought new ways to achieve the honorable peace he had promised.

The President called his guiding policy the Nixon Doctrine, which announced something of a retreat from the global mission Kennedy and Johnson had undertaken. No longer, Nixon declared in 1970, would the United States "conceive all the plans, design all the programs, execute all the decisions and undertake all the defense of the free nations of the world." There remained, of course, the embarrassment of Vietnam. Secretary of Defense Melvin Laird, an able administrator and an astute politician, suggested that "Vietnamization" might offer a way out.

Vietnamization called for reversing the escalation of the previous five years and returning control of the war to South Vietnam. With American logistical help, and perhaps with American air power, the South Vietnamese could sustain their own independence and cover the withdrawal of American forces before the presidential election of 1972. Convinced "doves," who favored immediate, unconditional American withdrawal, scoffed that Vietnamization masked continued American participation; it was, sneered Senator McCarthy from retirement, merely Nixon's device to change the color of the corpses. "Hawks," on the other hand, worried that the policy might achieve only a face-saving delay before the Southeast Asian "dominoes" began falling to the Chinese Communists. But Nixon had a sure instinct for the political center, and his policy stilled many of his critics for a time.

The President also showed his willingness to let a big victory salvage his and the nation's honor. In the spring of 1970, American and South Vietnamese forces invaded Cambodia in order, Nixon said, to wipe out large concentrations of enemy troops and equipment. Neither troops nor equipment proved so plentiful as the Pentagon had predicted. But outrage at home ended the truce between the government and the young. Protest ended in tragedy at Kent State University in Ohio that May, when frightened national guardsmen opened fire on demonstrating students; the four victims became martyrs in the students' cause. A week later, in an unrelated incident, Mississippi police killed two young blacks on the campus of Jackson State College and the nation's colleges seethed.

Most of the campus ferment dissipated during the summer. The tense calm that replaced upheaval even survived the President's decision, less than a year later, to support a South Vietnamese invasion of Laos. The President packaged the battle in Laos as an "incursion," not an invasion. He assured the public that Americans were not involved, although television film showed conclusively that they were, and he claimed tactical success for an expedition that seemed to have been a disaster.

Although the campuses generally remained calm, Congress did not. Individual senators declared their dissatisfaction with the pace of Vietnamization, with the course of American policy, with conscription, and with the military budget. Congress had repealed the Tonkin Gulf Resolution in the summer of 1970, without producing a visible change in American policy. Almost routinely in 1971 legislation became the occasion for unsuccessful amendments setting a ceiling on military appropriation and establishing a date for the complete withdrawal of American forces from Vietnam. Congressman exhorted one another to recall their constitutional duty to check the President's military authority. In the summer of 1971, at the urging of Majority Leader Mike Mansfield, the Senate succeeded in attaching an amendment to an extension of the Selective Service Act. The Mansfield amendment called on the President to end American involvement in Vietnam within nine months of release of American prisoners of war by the North Vietnamese. Under pressure from the administration, the House refused to concur with the Senate, and the nation's authority to conscript draftees temporarily lapsed. It was only a token victory for those who wished to change the nation's foreign policy, but the open support of a majority of the Senate heartened the growing ranks of those who opposed the nation's longest war.

CIVIL RIGHTS—AND BEYOND

Patriotic folklore used to hold that the Supreme Court of the United States made no policy but only reminded the legal profession of the content of the Constitution. Like so many other certainties, that one too was challenged in the middle of the twentieth century. For the Court over which Earl Warren presided from 1954 to 1969 became an active partner with the other policy-making branches of government. Chief Justice Warren had been an extraordinarily popular governor of California, and he brought a politician's energy to the bench. Although the Court had often trailed popular opinion, the Warren Court frequently led it, and became as a result the center of controversy. Congress debated constitutional amendments to modify several decisions, and billboards demanded the impeachment of the Chief Justice. At least part of the dispute came because the Court apparently weighed justice as heavily as law.

In a series of decisions beginning in 1962 the Court demanded that political institutions live up to the democratic ideal of "one man, one vote." Previous courts had avoided such questions as legislative apportionment, the boundaries of congressional districts, and the disproportionate representation of rural voters. But the Court's evasion ended in 1962 with *Baker* v. *Carr*. This decision held that population, not any other criterion, such as land, was the only acceptable basis for representation. In effect, the ruling gave urban residents more influence in state and local governments, which had tended to overrepresent rural interests.

The Warren Court also discovered new dimensions in the Bill of Rights. In *Engel* v. *Vitale* (1962) and in two cases the following year (*Abington School District* v. *Schempp* and *Murray* v. *Curlett*), the Court held that any religious observance designated by the school infringed the rights of those who had no religion and was illegal under the First Amendment's prohibition of a religious establishment. As the 1960s wore on, the Court applied to the states the provisions of the Bill of Rights, particularly the provisions protecting the rights of accused criminals. In *Gideon* v. *Wainright* (1963), states were ordered to provide legal counsel for indigents accused of felonies. In 1964, in *Escobedo* v. *Illinois,* and in 1966, in *Miranda* v. *Arizona,* the Court restricted the interrogation of suspects by police unless the prisoner's rights were fully protected, by an attorney if the prisoner demanded one. The Court also limited police searches and ruled against electronic eavesdropping. Critics of these rulings alleged that the Court's defense of the rights of criminals had subverted the defense of society, and crime and violence became topics of increasing political importance late in the decade.

But the loudest criticism of the Warren Court resulted from its unfaltering support of the rights of blacks. However divided it was on other questions, the Warren Court brooked no challenge to the principles stated in *Brown* v. *Board of Education* (1954). White America, the Court said, must grant black America full, unequivocal equality. And the Court grew impatient with delay and subterfuge in the North as well as in the South. The Court struck down long-standing state statues prohibiting interracial marriages, upheld new federal statutes that outlawed discrimination in public accommodations, and permitted federal registrars to enroll black voters when states refused. When a referendum in California repealed an open-housing law, the Court required resumption of open-housing practices. The entire federal court system, as a matter of routine, demanded that "neighborhood schools" and "token integration" and various other euphemisms for segregated education end without further delay.

The pressure for change came predominantly from young people of both races. Northern students joined southern blacks on "freedom rides" to integrate public transportation in the South; these freedom rides precipitated an order from the ICC forbidding segregation in interstate facilities. Black students in North Carolina inaugurated a decade of sit-ins, stand-ins, pray-ins, and other nonviolent demonstrations against unequal treatment in restaurants, rest rooms, theaters, and white churches. In some instances blacks made their point with a boycott; when that failed, Martin Luther King's Southern Christian Leadership Conference often directed protests in the streets to touch the nation's conscience.

The demonstrations climaxed in 1963 in Birmingham, Alabama, which King believed the stronghold of segregation. March after protest march in the city built tension until the authorities snapped it with electric cattle prods, high-pressure hoses, and police dogs. The jails filled with waves of hymn-singing blacks. Hoses and dogs ended any self-serving assumption outside Birmingham that conditions were gradually improving and stimulated President Kennedy to a belated effort to catch up with the civil-rights cause.

Earlier, in 1962, the President and his brother, Attorney General Robert F. Kennedy, had sent several hundred marshals and a contingent of national guardsmen to uphold a federal court order admitting James Meredith to the University of Mississippi. But it was Birmingham that took the President to Congress with a bill to speed suits to secure voting rights, to ban discrimination in any program using federal funds, and most significantly, to outlaw discrimination in public accommodations, such as hotels and restaurants. Neither presidential eloquence nor the political pressure of a

High-pressure fire hoses in Birmingham, 1963

quarter-million orderly demonstrators at a massive "march on Washington" in the summer of 1963 hurried the Congress. But President Johnson kept up the pressure after Kennedy's death, and the bill eventually passed in 1964, in spite of the warning of Barry Goldwater, the Republican presidential candidate, that it was unconstitutional. When asked later in the year, the Supreme Court disagreed with Senator Goldwater.

In 1965 the Voting Rights Act opened the ballot box to many more black voters. A constitutional amendment, ratified in 1964, had removed the poll tax as a barrier to participation in federal elections. The 1965 legislation authorized the Attorney General to bring suits to end the use of poll taxes that kept blacks from voting in state elections, a power the Court promptly upheld. The act also suspended literacy tests and authorized federal officials to register voters in areas where less than half the population voted. In a sense, the movement for civil rights was over, for although Congress passed a limited open-housing law in 1968, at about the same time the Court enforced a broader Reconstruction statute that made the new act super-fluous. After 1965 black leaders changed their emphasis from rights to equality, or in the case of some black militants, to separatism.

The civil-rights movement had depended on the legal department of the NAACP, on the integrationists of the Urban League, and on the Christian nonviolence and eloquence of Martin Luther King. The demand for change was insistent, but respected due process, relied on white liberals, and believed in persuasive demonstrations. By the mid-1960s the weight of evidence crushed any conscience-numbing belief that equality was just around the corner. A decade after the *Brown* decision, schools were not fully integrated in Alabama, Illinois, Massachusetts, or California. Economic growth pushed white Americans to new levels of prosperity; family income of black Americans in several urban centers declined. Urban renewal squeezed more blacks into less space. Lack of stable employment and decent housing contributed to unstable family structure; the illegitimacy rate in Watts and Harlem approached 50 percent by the end of the decade. The war on poverty hardly affected the distribution of national income; the most prosperous fifth of the population had an income more than twenty-six times that of the lowest fifth. The promised good life was not delivered, and everybody knew it. In 1965 President Johnson laid out the facts:

> Thirty-five years ago the rate of unemployment for Negroes and whites was about the same. Tonight the Negro rate is twice as high.

> In 1948, the 8 per cent unemployment rate for Negro teenage boys was actually less than that of whites. By last year that rate had grown to 23 per cent, as against 13 per cent for whites unemployed.

> Between 1949 and 1959, the income of Negro men relative to white men declined in every section of this country. From 1952 to 1963 the median income of Negro families compared to white actually dropped from 57 per cent to 53 per cent.

> In the years 1955 through 1957, 22 per cent of experienced Negro workers were out of work at some time during the year. In 1961 through 1963 that proportion had soared to 29 per cent.

> Since 1947 the number of white families living in poverty has decreased 27 per cent, while the number of poorer non-white families decreased only 3 per cent.

> The infant mortality of non-whites in 1940 was 70 per cent greater than whites. Twenty-two years later it was 90 per cent greater.

"The harsh fact of the matter," Johnson declared, "is that in the battle for true equality too many [blacks] . . . are losing ground every day."

Urban blacks, penned in deteriorating portions of northern cities, badly educated in patronizing school systems, barely supported on surplus commodities or county funds, exploited by landlords, storekeepers, and loan sharks, knew what the President was talking about. Some blacks decided that sharing white America was a share in decadence anyway, and increasing numbers of self-conscious young blacks subscribed to one of several forms of a doctrine called "Black Power," first formally enunciated by Stokely Carmichael and the Student Non-Violent Coordinating Committee (SNCC) in 1966.

Black Power meant an end to reliance on the white man; it meant economic self-sufficiency, racial pride, and cultural autonomy. For years Malcolm X and the Black Muslims had opposed integration as the white man's trap; the organization made an important convert when Cassius Clay, the heavyweight boxing champion, changed his name to Muhammed Ali and took up the cause, even though he lost his title and risked jail as an indirect consequence. When the campaign for civil rights stalled short of full equality, the Congress of Racial Equality (CORE) and SNCC shifted to black solidarity.

The Black Panthers flouted their solidarity and their hostility toward the white world as openly as the guns they carried. Organized in mid-decade by Huey Newton and Bobby Seale, the organization imposed military discipline, adapted the ideology of Che Guevara and Mao Tse-tung to conditions in California's ghettoes, and assumed that the police, for whom Panthers popularized the epithet "pigs," were the enemy of all blacks. The Panthers appealed to the pride and the rage of young blacks and caught the imagination of white radicals who needed a following in the black community and admired the Panthers' revolutionary style. In 1968 the radical coalition formed the Peace and Freedom party and nominated Eldridge Cleaver, a prominent Panther, for President of the United States. Shortly after the election Cleaver left the country to avoid a prison term for violation of parole.

Cleaver's departure was symptomatic of the Panthers' constant friction with police. So regular did the shoot-outs become in 1969 that the Panthers' overblown accusations of conspiracy and genocide gained respectability. Bobby Seale seemed constantly involved in one trial or another—in California, in Chicago, and in New Haven, Connecticut, where Kingman Brewster, the President of Yale and a lawyer, wondered aloud whether any black man could receive a fair trial in any court in the land. Brewster's concern seemed exaggerated in 1971, when the New Haven jury failed to agree and the judge dismissed the case.

Whites tended to blame black leaders like Seale, Carmichael, and H. Rap Brown, a fiery orator whose presence always seemed to precede a riot, and black writers like James Baldwin and LeRoi Jones, for explosions in the ghettoes that began to seem as much a part of summer as baseball. In Los Angeles, Newark, Omaha, Cleveland, Louisville, Detroit, Washington, New York, and elsewhere blacks sporadically discarded peaceful protest for bricks, bottles, and fire-bombs. While violence unquestionably roused white resentment, the election of 1964 suggested that the "backlash" was less severe than some politicians had feared. And disorder unquestionably drove government agencies to stop-gap action to quiet local disturbances. In some cities blacks suddenly appeared on the police force, and all police became more sensitive to racial pride, if not unprejudiced. Recreation and summer-employment programs received belated (and temporary) injections of funds. Department stores added black clerks. And the nation sought ways of coping with the basic problem, rather than with symptoms.

But solutions proved elusive. Carmichael and more radical black separatists, for instance, rejected integration as a subtle method of maintaining white supremacy. For integration meant that some blacks moved into white America—schools, suburbs, occupations—and left other blacks mired in the ghetto. The paradoxical alliance of black separatists and white segregationists made any compromise vulnerable to virulent attack from both sides. Politicians spoke glibly of a Marshall Plan for the cities, of a massive assault on black unemployment, of rebuilding the black family, of education and training programs. But at the end of the decade, although the number of elected black officials had increased significantly even in the South, many of the promises remained unkept; some doubted that new legislation was essential until the statutes already enacted were enforced.

Prodded by the riots of 1967, President Johnson appointed a commission to investigate civil disorder. Under the chairmanship of Governor Otto Kerner of Illinois, the commission produced a long report that squarely blamed white America for the racism that lay at the root of the riots. "White institutions," the commission charged, created the ghetto, "white institutions maintain it, and white society condones it." The commission was so moderate that many discounted its conclusions before they were published. Nevertheless, the report boldly recommended an expenditure of billions of dollars in an immediate attempt to eradicate racial inequality. Some Americans quarreled with the accusation of white guilt; a few scholars pointed out that a similar commission on the Chicago riots had reached almost the same conclusions fifty years before; and the President sulked because the Commission had not written a chapter praising the efforts of his administration.

The Kerner Commission tried to impart the need for immediate action to a baffled nation. But mounting concern only resulted in mounting fear as the decade ended. Returning black veterans served notice that second-class citizenship was no longer acceptable. "When I get back," warned a black noncommissioned officer at a rest camp in the Mekong Delta, "I am as good as any son of a bitch in the states." At the end of the 1960s, the relationship of black and white showed every indication of remaining "an American dilemma," as the Swedish sociologist Gunnar Myrdal had called it in 1944.

THE NIXON ADMINISTRATION BEGINS

Richard Nixon correctly identified his first task when he took office in January, 1969. He would, he promised, bring the nation together; he would bridge the social chasms between black and white, rich and poor, young and old, city and suburb. The rhetoric was trite, the task probably impossible, and evidence mounted that the President meant to remove social divisions by choosing one side and deprecating the other. He enjoyed a televised football game while thousands of demonstrators gathered near the White House to oppose the nation's continued involvement in Vietnam. In the wake of the Cambodian invasion, when campuses became centers of political tumult, the President remarked that young "bums" were responsible. For more than a year several black Congressmen unsuccessfully sought an appointment at the White House to indicate the dissatisfaction of the black community with Nixon's failure to press for racial justice; the conference was finally held in 1971 and was predictably unproductive. The administration's political strategy was popularly known as "the southern strategy," and the chief political spokesman, Vice-President Spiro T. Agnew, seemed intent on widening every rift in American society with his alliterative phrases.

One of those rifts was that between Congress and the President. Richard Nixon was the first President since Zachary Taylor to take office when the opposition controlled both houses of Congress. Although the administration ordinarily secured cooperation from the House, the Senate became increasingly critical of Nixon's policies and appointments. The President's nomination of Warren E. Burger to succeed Earl Warren as Chief Justice won the Senate's prompt endorsement. But the Senate balked at Nixon's successive nominations of Clement F. Haynesworth and G. Harrold Carswell, both southern judges, to a vacancy on the Court. Haynsworth had not withdrawn from cases involving companies in which he owned stock, an indiscretion that seemed minor when Carswell's record disclosed consistent insensitivity on racial questions. Both nominations bespoke the "southern strategy" advocated by Attorney General John Mitchell, and both indicated sloppy investigation by the Department of Justice. The Senate's consent to the appointment of Harry A. Blackmun, Nixon's third choice for the vacancy, did not end the tension between Senate and President.

The military-industrial complex in caricature, 1969

For the Senate was also the forum for opponents of the war and of the military-industrial complex. An expensive antiballistic missile system survived two tests in the Senate by narrow majorities. The supersonic transport plane did not. After extended debate in 1971 both houses of Congress refused to appropriate funds to continue the development of commercial aircraft capable of exceeding the speed of sound. Much of the controversy surrounding the SST reflected a growing national concern about the environmental consequences of technology.

Preservation of the environment promised to become one of the major political issues of the 1970s. The public understood the perils of pollution, and politicians respected the political muscle of a lobby that could defeat the aerospace industry in Congress. Yet the vote on the SST only prevented further environmental decay and did nothing to purify air and water, which were steadily deteriorating. Various levels of government built new sewage systems, set new standards to control automobile exhaust, passed new regulations to curtail industrial effluents, and fined oil companies for fouling the oceans. But the programs hardly seemed to keep pace with the ubiquitous pollution.

Some Americans assigned a higher priority to cleaning up the planet than to exploring its major satellite. While Apollo missions were in progress, space exploration captured the nation's imagination, especially when American astronauts first walked on the moon in 1969. But when the flights were routine, and when the astronauts had safely landed, taxpayers wondered whether all those dollars might not have done people more good on earth. Somehow, if Americans could wander around the moon, they ought to be able to stroll unafraid in clean parks, drive on the highways without causing respiratory distress, and dispose of their garbage without ruining the rivers.

The nation did not lack critics to call attention to these and other shortcomings and, more rarely, to suggest solutions. Almost any grievance triggered a march on Washington, and Nixon's foreign policy precipitated several; each march brought strident oratory, sympathetic folk singers, and ineffective lobbying against poverty, racism, or war. Ralph Nader, a young lawyer who cultivated personal anonymity and publicized the grievances of anonymous consumers, became a model for other idealistic lawyers. "Nader's Raiders" tackled unsafe cars, dishonest advertising, polluting industries, and the indolent antitrust division of the Department of Justice. Another young Washington attorney forced cigarette advertising off the air and other examples of the energy of peoples' attorneys began to multiply.

But some young Americans chose to cultivate a different style of life, to tune out the problems of technological society rather than fight them. Communes sprang up in the hills of California, Colorado, and Vermont, in the urban canyons of Manhattan island, and on the plains in Manhattan, Kansas. Many of these groups shared a spiritual outlook, often derived from contemplative oriental philosophy such as Zen; others were simply an extended family; in a few, the use of drugs provided the shared experience.

Drugs emerged from the ghettoes during the 1960s and showed up in suburbs, college dormitories, high school corridors, military barracks, and high society. By the end of the decade, no issue except the war generated so much national anxiety as did drug abuse. Doctors disagreed on the long-term effects of marijuana and the genetic consequences of LSD. But few disagreed that increased mental illness among adolescents and increased petty crimes were linked with increased drug use. And when heroin addiction admittedly reached epidemic proportions among American troops in Vietnam, President Nixon used diplomacy and dollars to reduce the flow of illegal drugs into the United States and ordered the Pentagon and the Veterans' Administration to develop programs for prevention and rehabilitation.

Drug use was one indication of the sensuous culture that seemed in 1970 to be in conflict with a traditional American ethic. If drug use was often clandestine, sexuality emphatically was not. Movies became sexually explicit, while regulatory codes disappeared and censors dithered. As the decade ended, nonfiction "how-to" manuals rivaled fictional accounts of sexual activity on the best-seller charts. Local prosecutors made political capital by suppressing smut, but the suppression was usually temporary and sometimes illegal. What had seemed pornographic a few years before soon became commonplace. And no local authority could screen out the advertising that used explicitly sexual symbolism to sell automobiles, deodorants, cigarettes, and a host of other products.

The cultural conflict that seemed well begun in 1970 was usually called a generation gap. But the phenomenon was more complex than ordinary disagreement between father and son and more fundamental than the long hair and blue denim that style rebels adopted. Radical young people discarded more than razors and tweeds; they also gave up much of the value system that they held had perverted the "promise of American life." Ambition and perseverance seemed to give way to passivity; thrift and self-denial to self-gratification. But, advocates of the counterculture claimed, greed and economic individualism also gave way to social responsibility, racism to tolerance, and the closed mind to an open one.

Richard Nixon recognized the cultural flux in the troubled nation. Although he appeared to disapprove much of what he saw, two of his own objectives deserved a better hearing than they generally received among young people. Nixon backed the vote for eighteen-year-olds, a reform achieved in 1971 with the ratification of the Twenty-Sixth Amendment. And the President's basic political outlook, which he called the New Federalism, ought to have appealed to those alienated by the size and impersonality of big government. The New Federalism, Nixon said, required returning government to the local level. In practice, the federal government would share revenue with states and municipal governments and make them responsible for services, including part of the welfare program, that previously had come from Washington. That government was best, the New Federalism held, which was closest to the governed. The President's program, however, bogged down in a skeptical Democratic Congress.

Indeed, the output of the entire American political system was unimpressive as the new decade began. There was some danger that disillusionment and disappointment might develop into total alienation among young people who had attempted to secure political change. Yet when the radical

Weathermen moved beyond ballots and boycotts to bombs, they lost influence; alienated radicals simply disdained government instead. And if the number of radicals was growing, it still remained a small minority of Americans. The ritual of American politics went on: the promises, the debate (called "educating the public"), the delay (until public opinion hardened), the ceremony (to give little changes the appearance of big ones). And although the problems were momentarily indigestible and the legislative system seemed choked, most Americans still believed that answers would eventually emerge.

WHAT'S HAPPENING TO AMERICA?

Introspection has not historically been an American preoccupation. Americans have been too busy pursuing happiness to define it, too busy moving to reflect. But, recently, taking the nation's pulse has become a popular obsession. Presidential commissions outlined national goals and examined the tendency to employ easy violence as a solution to tough problems. Clergymen berated the "sick society" that condoned injustice; social psychologists offered contradictory diagnoses and conflicting prescriptions; sociologists charted the behavior of students almost to the exclusion of teaching them. Journalists summarized the conclusions of academics in pithy articles that proved that gun control, appropriations for the arts, and a more enlightened attitude toward marijuana would ease the nation's current anxieties. Even television undertook a prime-time probe of the nation's malaise, with the customary interruptions for commercials.

The psyche the country contemplated was not especially attractive. The concurrence of an interminable, dismal war and unfathomable domestic problems created a divided population with no clear sense of national purpose. The new left and the old right agreed on the sterility of the liberal consensus in the center. Critics wanted to restore initiative to the people, to remove impersonal bureaucrats, to change welfare programs, and to dismantle the leviathan state. The right nostalgically longed for an imagined past. But the left meant to destroy liberalism as the necessary prelude to new institutions—new government, new education for the new student who would live in the twenty-first century, new creeds to replace those associated with the dead God, new methods of supporting creative individuals to liberate them from artistic conventions of the past. Almost all American institutions, ran the charge, had sold their independence for the security of tax exemptions or philanthropic grants or matching federal funds. The whole structure was rotten and had to go.

Which implied violence. Violence had long been a part of American folklore. The duel, the brawl, the shoot-out, and the rope for the cattle rustler or the uppity black were not peaceful means of settling past disputes. Barring an occasional critic who wondered whether sadism was essential to the acculturation of American youth, nobody was unduly disturbed about violence so long as the victims were poor, eccentric, or black. When civil-rights workers were killed in Mississippi, or hippies in cellars in

Denver slums, or mobsters in Boston, or Black Panthers in Oakland, the news caused a shrug of the national shoulders: what, it was asked, could you expect?

But violence spread beyond those society could comfortably call misfits. Urban residents learned to avoid strange neighborhoods, dark doorways, and finally the streets themselves. The combination of idleness, discrimination, mistrust, heat, and a brooding sense of futility awaited only a spark and the chant "Burn, Baby, Burn!" News reports of looting sometimes made the summer madness seem purposeful, but it was more often impulsive than calculated, more an unreasoned blow at oppression than a system for stocking the clothes closet or the pantry.

Fire trucks, policemen, and, if necessary, the National Guard could impose sullen order in an urban ghetto, even if they could not entirely restore peace of mind to the middle-class residents who had seen the abyss of anarchy. But there seemed no way of shielding ordinary citizens from the bullets of madmen. Snipers holed up in a tower at the University of Texas, a public lavatory in New York's Central Park, a tenement in the Watts district of Los Angeles and shot random students, strollers, and firemen. Assassins stalked public men, especially those associated with the explosive issue of racial equality, for many of whom the threat of death became routine. A dissident member of the American Nazi party shot George Lincoln Rockwell, the tinhorn American führer, in a Virginia shopping center in 1967. Medgar Evers, a Mississippi official of the NAACP, was shot on his doorstep in 1963. President Kennedy died in Dallas in November of the same year. The FBI found the bodies of three young civil-rights workers under a dam near Philadelphia, Mississippi, in 1964. Black gunmen, probably associated with a rival faction, killed Malcolm X, who in 1965 had led a split among Black Muslims. A hidden sniper ended the 1966 "march against fear" of James Meredith, who was lucky and recovered from his shotgun wounds. In April, 1968, a drifting ex-convict killed Martin Luther King in Memphis, where he had gone to help the city's garbage men secure higher wages. Early in June, 1968, an embittered Jordanian immigrant killed Robert Kennedy just after he had claimed victory in the California presidential primary.

The national mourning for Martin Luther King rivaled the outpouring of grief for two martyred Kennedys. But it was the death of the President that affected Americans most profoundly. It was almost as if the nation would not admit his passing. For a time, the national appetite for books about John Kennedy was insatiable and second-guessing the Warren Commission that had posthumously convicted his assassin became a morbid obsession. The center for the performing arts in Washington, the nation's space center in Florida, an airport in New York, and schools and scholarships all over the land memorialized John F. Kennedy, and his grave in Arlington National Cemetery became the goal of countless pilgrimages.

And although he lived for only a fraction of the decade, the 1960s were the Kennedy years. His was the urging that made the nation look to the future, his the imagination that saw the possibilities and problems that lay beyond the New Frontier, his the compassion that set a generation seeking outlets for service, and his the decisions that brought the decade's war. Memorializing his brother in 1964, Robert Kennedy used a passage from *Romeo and Juliet*:

> . . . when he shall die
> Take him and cut him out in little stars,
> And he will make the face of heav'n so fine
> That all the world shall be in love with Night
> And pay no worship to the garish Sun.

After 1963 America groped by starlight, lacking the beacon of agreed political purpose, and the vision of statesmen who knew the night.

Suggested Reading

Much of the literature on the recent past is self-serving; almost all the published literature on Vietnam, for instance, should be used with great care. The same caution ought to apply even to documentary collections such as *The Pentagon Papers** (1971), which the staff of the *New York Times* has edited, or *The Great Society Reader** (1967), edited by Marvin E. Gettleman and David Mermelstein. The numerous accounts by Kennedy's aides reveal something of his Presidency: see especially Arthur M. Schlesinger, Jr., *A Thousand Days** (1965), and Theodore C. Sorenson, *Kennedy* (1965). John Kenneth Galbraith's *Ambassador's Journal** (1969) is informative about politics in Washington as well as about diplomacy in India.

Any study of the political history of the decade begins with Theodore H. White's absorbing accounts of the presidential elections, *The Making of the President** (1961, 1965, 1969). Tom Wicker has examined the contrasting presidential styles of Kennedy and Johnson in *JFK and LBJ** (1968). Barry M. Goldwater enters a conservative's dissent in *The Conscience of a Conservative** (1960).

Michael Harrington, *The Other America** (1963), helped arouse the country to the pervasiveness of poverty. John Kenneth Galbraith's *The Affluent Society** (1958) and *The New Industrial State** (1968) are other influential works on economics. Anthony Lewis' *Gideon's Trumpet** (1964) is a remarkably informative account of one case decided by the Warren Court, *Gideon* v. *Wainwright*. The struggle for racial justice can be followed in several books by Martin Luther King, such as *Why We Can't Wait** (1964) and *Stride Toward Freedom** (1958), in Charles E. Silberman's *Crisis in Black and White** (1964), and in *The Autobiography of Malcolm X** (1966). William I. Thompson suggests stimulating lines of inquiry about contemporary America in *At The Edge of History* (1971).

*Available in paperback edition

APPENDIX

THE DECLARATION OF INDEPENDENCE*

The unanimous Declaration of the thirteen United States of America.

When, in the Course of human events, it becomes necessary for one people to dissolve the political bands which have connected them with another, and to assume, among the Powers of the earth, the separate and equal station to which the Laws of Nature and of Nature's God entitle them, a decent respect to the opinions of mankind requires that they should declare the causes which impel them to the separation.

We hold these truths to be self-evident, that all men are created equal, that they are endowed by their Creator with certain unalien-able Rights, that among these, are Life, Liberty, and the pursuit of Happiness. That, to secure these rights, Governments are instituted among Men, deriving their just Powers from the consent of the governed. That, whenever any form of Government becomes destructive of these ends, it is the Right of the People to alter or to abolish it, and to institute new Government, laying its foundation on such Principles, and organizing its Powers in such form, as to them shall seem most likely to effect their Safety and Happiness. Prudence, indeed, will dictate that Governments long established should not be changed for light and transient causes; and,

* The original spelling, capitalization, and punctuation have been retained.

accordingly, all experience hath shewn, that mankind are more disposed to suffer, while evils are sufferable, than to right themselves by abolishing the forms to which they are accustomed. But, when a long train of abuses and usurpations, pursuing invariably the same Object, evinces a design to reduce them under absolute Despotism, it is their right, it is their duty, to throw off such Government, and to provide new Guards for their future Security. Such has been the patient sufferance of these Colonies; and such is now the necessity which constrains them to alter their former Systems of Government. The history of the present King of Great Britain is a history of repeated injuries and usurpations, all having in direct object the establishment of an absolute Tyranny over these States. To prove this, let Facts be submitted to a candid world.

He has refused his Assent to Laws the most wholesome and necessary for the public good.

He has forbidden his Governors to pass Laws of immediate and pressing importance, unless suspended in their operation till his Assent should be obtained; and when so suspended, he has utterly neglected to attend to them.

He has refused to pass other Laws for the accommodation of large districts of People, unless those People would relinquish the right of Representation in the legislature; a right inestimable to them and formidable to tyrants only.

He has called together legislative bodies at places unusual, uncomfortable, and distant from the depository of their Public Records, for the sole Purpose of fatiguing them into compliance with his measures.

He has dissolved Representative Houses repeatedly, for opposing, with manly firmness, his invasions on the rights of the People.

He has refused for a long time, after such dissolutions, to cause others to be elected; whereby the Legislative Powers, incapable of Annihilation, have returned to the People at large for their exercise; the State remaining in the mean time exposed to all the dangers of invasion from without, and convulsions within.

He has endeavoured to prevent the Population of these States; for that purpose obstructing the Laws for Naturalization of Foreigners; refusing to pass others to encourage their migrations hither, and raising the conditions of new Appropriations of Lands.

He has obstructed the Administration of Justice, by refusing his Assent to Laws for establishing Judiciary Powers.

He has made Judges dependent on his Will alone, for the tenure of their offices, and the amount and payment of their salaries.

He has erected a multitude of New Offices, and sent hither swarms of Officers to harrass our People, and eat out their substance.

He has kept among us, in times of Peace, Standing Armies, without the Consent of our legislatures.

He has affected to render the Military independent of and superior to the Civil Power.

He has combined with others to subject us to a jurisdiction foreign to our constitution, and unacknowledged by our laws; giving his Assent to their Acts of pretended Legislation:

For quartering large bodies of armed troops among us:

For protecting them, by a mock Trial, from Punishment for any Murders which they should commit on the Inhabitants of these States:

For cutting off our Trade with all parts of the world:

For imposing Taxes on us without our Consent:

For depriving us, in many cases, of the benefits of Trial by Jury:

For transporting us beyond Seas to be tried for pretended offences:

For abolishing the free System of English Laws in a neighbouring province, establishing therein an Arbitrary government, and enlarging its Boundaries, so as to render it at once an example and fit instrument for introducing the same absolute rule into these Colonies:

For taking away our Charters, abolishing our most valuable Laws, and altering fundamentally the Forms of our Governments:

For suspending our own Legislatures, and declaring themselves invested with Power to legislate for us in all cases whatsoever.

He has abdicated Government here, by declaring us out of his protection, and waging War against us.

He has plundered our seas, ravaged our Coasts, burnt our towns, and destroyed the Lives of our People.

He is at this time transporting large Armies of foreign Mercenaries to compleat the works of death, desolation and tyranny, already begun with circumstances of Cruelty and perfidy scarcely paralleled in the most barbarous ages, and totally unworthy the Head of a civilized nation.

He has constrained our fellow Citizens, taken Captive on the high Seas, to bear Arms against their Country, to become the executioners of their friends and Brethren, or to fall themselves by their Hands.

He has excited domestic insurrections amongst us, and has endeavoured to bring on the inhabitants of our frontiers, the merciless Indian Savages, whose known rule of warfare, is an undistinguished destruction of all ages, sexes and conditions.

In every stage of these Oppressions, We have Petitioned for Redress, in the most humble terms: Our repeated Petitions, have been answered only by repeated injury. A Prince, whose character is thus marked by every act which may define a Tyrant, is unfit to be the ruler of a free People.

Nor have We been wanting in attentions to our British brethren. We have warned them from time to time of attempts by their legislature to extend an unwarrantable jurisdiction over us. We have reminded them of the circumstances of our emigration and settlement here. We have appealed to their native justice and magnanimity, and we have conjured them by the ties of our common kindred, to disavow these usurpations, which, would inevitably interrupt our connexions and correspondence. They too have been deaf to the voice of justice and consanguinity. We must, therefore, acquiesce in the necessity, which denounces our Separation, and hold them, as we hold the rest of mankind, Enemies in war, in Peace Friends.

WE, THEREFORE, the Representatives of the UNITED STATES OF AMERICA, in GENERAL CONGRESS assembled, appealing to the Supreme Judge of the World for the rectitude of our intentions, DO, in the Name, and by Authority of the good People of these Colonies, solemnly PUBLISH and DECLARE, That these United Colonies are, and of Right, ought to be FREE AND INDEPENDENT STATES; that they are Absolved from all Allegiance to the British Crown, and that all political connexion between them and the State of Great Britain, is and ought to be totally dissolved; and that, as FREE and INDEPENDENT STATES, they have full Power to levy War, conclude Peace, contract Alliances, establish Commerce, and to do all other Acts and Things which INDEPENDENT STATES may of right do. AND for the support of this Declaration, with a firm reliance on the protection of divine Providence, we mutually pledge to each other our Lives, our Fortunes, and our sacred Honour.

THE CONSTITUTION

OF THE UNITED STATES OF AMERICA*

We the people of the United States, in Order to form a more perfect Union, establish Justice, insure domestic Tranquility, provide for the common defence, promote the general Welfare, and secure the Blessings of Liberty to ourselves and our Posterity, do ordain and establish this Constitution for the United States of America.

ARTICLE I

Section 1. All legislative Powers herein granted shall be vested in a Congress of the United States, which shall consist of a Senate and House of Representatives.

Section 2. The House of Representatives shall be composed of Members chosen every second Year by the People of the several States, and the Electors in each State shall have the Qualifications requisite for Electors of the most numerous Branch of the State Legislature.

No Person shall be a Representative who shall not have attained to the Age of twenty-five Years, and been seven Years a Citizen of the United States, and who shall not, when elected, be an Inhabitant of that state in which he shall be chosen.

[Representatives and direct Taxes shall be apportioned among the several States which may be included within this Union, according to their respective Numbers, which shall be determined by adding to the whole Number of free Persons, including those bound to Service for a Term of Years, and excluding Indians not taxed, three fifths of all

---

* The Constitution and all amendments are shown in their original form. Parts that have been amended or superseded are bracketed and explained in the footnotes.

other Persons.][1] The actual Enumeration shall be made within three Years after the first Meeting of the Congress of the United States, and within every subsequent Term of ten Years, in such Manner as they shall by Law direct. The Number of Representatives shall not exceed one for every thirty Thousand, but each State shall have at Least one Representative; and until such enumeration shall be made, the State of New Hampshire shall be entitled to chuse three, Massachusetts eight, Rhode-Island and Providence Plantations one, Connecticut five, New-York six, New Jersey four, Pennsylvania eight, Delaware one, Maryland six, Virginia ten, North Carolina five, South Carolina five, and Georgia three.

When vacancies happen in the Representation from any State, the Executive Authority thereof shall issue Writs of Election to fill such Vacancies.

The House of Representatives shall chuse their Speaker and other Officers; and shall have the sole Power of Impeachment.

Section 3. The Senate of the United States shall be composed of two Senators from each State, [chosen by the Legislature thereof,][2] for six Years; and each Senator shall have one Vote.

Immediately after they shall be assembled in Consequence of the first Election, they shall be divided as equally as may be into three Classes. The Seats of the Senators of the first Class shall be vacated at the Expiration of the second Year, of the Second Class at the Expiration of the fourth Year, and of the third Class at the Expiration of the sixth Year, so that one-third may be chosen every second Year; [and if Vacancies happen by Resignation, or otherwise, during the Recess of the Legislature of any State, the Executive thereof may make temporary Appointments until the next Meeting of the Legislature, which shall then fill such Vacancies].[3]

No Person shall be a Senator who shall not have attained to the Age of thirty Years, and been nine Years a Citizen of the United States, and who shall not, when elected, be an Inhabitant of that State in which he shall be chosen.

The Vice-President of the United States shall be President of the Senate, but shall have no vote, unless they be equally divided.

The Senate shall chuse their other Officers, and also a President pro tempore, in the absence of the Vice-President, or when he shall exercise the Office of the President of the United States.

The Senate shall have the sole Power to try all Impeachments. When sitting for that purpose, they shall be on Oath or Affirmation. When the President of the United States is tried, the Chief Justice shall preside. And no person shall be convicted without the Concurrence of two thirds of the Members present.

Judgment in Cases of Impeachment shall not extend further than to removal from Office, and disqualification to hold and enjoy any Office of honor, Trust, or Profit under the United States: but the Party con-

[1] Modified by the Fourteenth and Sixteenth amendments.

[2] Superseded by the Seventeenth Amendment.

[3] Modified by the Seventeenth Amendment.

victed shall nevertheless be liable and subject to Indictment, Trial, Judgment, and Punishment, according to Law.

Section 4. The Times, Places and Manner of holding Elections for Senators and Representatives, shall be prescribed in each state by the Legislature thereof; but the Congress may at any time by Law make or alter such Regulations, except as to the Places of Chusing Senators.

The Congress shall assemble at least once in every Year, and such Meeting shall [be on the first Monday in December,]⁴ unless they shall by Law appoint a different Day.

Section 5. Each House shall be the Judge of the Elections, Returns and Qualifications of its own Members, and a Majority of each shall constitute a Quorum to do Business; but a smaller number may adjourn from day to day, and may be authorized to compel the Attendance of absent Members, in such Manner, and under such Penalties, as each House may provide.

Each House may determine the Rules of its Proceedings, punish its Members for disorderly Behavior, and, with the Concurrence of two thirds, expel a Member.

Each House shall keep a Journal of its Proceedings, and from time to time publish the same, excepting such Parts as may in their Judgment require Secrecy; and the Yeas and Nays of the Members of either House on any question shall, at the Desire of one fifth of those Present, be entered on the Journal.

Neither House, during the Session of Congress, shall, without the Con-

⁴ Superseded by the Twentieth Amendment.

sent of the other, adjourn for more than three days, nor to any other Place than that in which the two Houses shall be sitting.

Section 6. The Senators and Representatives shall receive a Compensation for their Services, to be ascertained by Law, and paid out of the Treasury of the United States. They shall in all Cases, except Treason, Felony, and Breach of the Peace, be privileged from Arrest during their Attendance at the Session of their respective Houses, and in going to and returning from the same; and for any Speech or Debate in either House, they shall not be questioned in any other Place.

No Senator or Representative shall, during the Time for which he was elected, be appointed to any civil Office under the Authority of the United States, which shall have been created, or the Emoluments whereof shall have been increased, during such time; and no Person holding any Office under the United States shall be a Member of either House during his continuance in Office.

Section 7. All Bills for raising Revenue shall originate in the House of Representatives; but the Senate may propose or concur with Amendments as on other bills.

Every Bill which shall have passed the House of Representatives and the Senate, shall, before it become a Law, be presented to the President of the United States; If he approve he shall sign it, but if not he shall return it, with his Objections, to that House in which it shall have originated, who shall enter the Objections at large on their Journal, and proceed to reconsider it. If after such Reconsideration two thirds of that House shall agree to pass the bill, it shall be sent, together with the objections, to the other House, by which it shall likewise be reconsidered, and if approved by two thirds of that House, it shall become a Law. But in all such Cases the Votes of both Houses shall be determined by Yeas and Nays, and the Names of the Persons voting for and against the Bill shall be entered on the Journal of each House respectively. If any Bill shall not be returned by the President within ten Days (Sundays excepted) after it shall have been presented to him, the Same shall be a Law, in like Manner as if he had signed it, unless the Congress by their Adjournment prevent its Return, in which Case it shall not be a Law.

Every Order, Resolution, or Vote to which the Concurrence of the Senate and House of Representatives may be necessary (except on a question of Adjournment) shall be presented to the President of the United States; and before the Same shall take Effect, shall be approved by him, or being disapproved by him, shall be repassed by two thirds of the Senate and House of Representatives, according to the Rules and Limitations prescribed in the Case of a Bill.

Section 8. The Congress shall have Power To lay and collect Taxes, Duties, Imposts and Excises, to pay the Debts and provide for the common Defence and general Welfare of the United States; but all Duties, Imposts and Excises shall be uniform throughout the United States;

To borrow money on the credit of the United States;

To regulate Commerce with foreign Nations, and among the several States, and with the Indian Tribes;

To establish an uniform Rule of Naturalization, and uniform Laws on the subject of Bankruptcies throughout the United States;

To coin Money, regulate the Value thereof, and of foreign Coin, and fix the Standard of Weights and Measures;

To provide for the Punishment of counterfeiting the Securities and current Coin of the United States;

To establish Post Offices and post Roads;

To promote the Progress of Science and useful Arts, by securing for limited Times to Authors and Inventors the exclusive Right to their respective Writings and Discoveries;

To constitute Tribunals inferior to the Supreme Court;

To define and punish Piracies and Felonies committed on the high Seas, and Offenses against the Law of Nations;

To declare War, grant Letters of Marque and Reprisal, and make Rules concerning Captures on Land and Water;

To raise and support Armies, but no Appropriation of Money to that Use shall be for a longer Term than two Years;

To provide and maintain a Navy;

To make Rules for the Government and Regulation of the land and naval forces;

To provide for calling forth the Militia to execute the Laws of the Union, suppress Insurrections and repel Invasions;

To provide for organizing, arming, and disciplining the Militia, and for governing such Part of them as may be employed in the Service of the

United States, reserving to the States respectively, the Appointment of the Officers, and the Authority of training the Militia according to the discipline prescribed by Congress;

To exercise exclusive Legislation in all Cases whatsoever, over such District (not exceeding ten Miles square) as may, by Cession of particular States, and the acceptance of Congress, become the Seat of the Government of the United States, and to exercise like Authority over all Places purchased by the Consent of the Legislature of the State in which the Same shall be, for the Erection of Forts, Magazines, Arsenals, dock-Yards, and other needful Buildings;—And

To make all Laws which shall be necessary and proper for carrying into Execution the foregoing Powers, and all other Powers vested by this Constitution in the Government of the United States, or in any Department or Officer thereof.

Section 9. The Migration or Importation of such Persons as any of the States now existing shall think proper to admit shall not be prohibited by the Congress prior to the Year one thousand eight hundred and eight, but a tax or duty may be imposed on such Importation, not exeeding ten dollars for each Person.

The privilege of the Writ of Habeas Corpus shall not be suspended, unless when in Cases of Rebellion or Invasion the public Safety may require it.

No Bill of Attainder or ex post facto Law shall be passed.

[No capitation, or other direct, Tax shall be laid unless in Proportion to the Census or Enumeration herein before directed to be taken.][5]

No Tax or Duty shall be laid on Articles exported from any State.

No Preference shall be given by any Regulation of Revenue to the Ports of one State over those of another: nor shall Vessels bound to, or from, one State, be obliged to enter, clear, or pay Duties in another.

No Money shall be drawn from the Treasury, but in Consequence of Appropriations made by Law; and a regular Statement and Account of the Receipts and Expenditures of all public Money shall be published from time to time.

No Title of Nobility shall be granted by the United States: And no Person holding any Office of Profit or Trust under them, shall, without the Consent of the Congress, accept of any present, Emolument, Office, or Title, of any kind whatever, from any King, Prince, or foreign State.

Section 10. No State shall enter into any Treaty, Alliance, or Confederation; grant Letters of Marque and Reprisal; coin Money; emit Bills of Credit; make any Thing but gold and silver Coin a Tender in Payment of Debts; pass any Bill of Attainder, ex post facto Law, or Law impairing the Obligation of Contracts, or grant any Title of Nobility.

No State shall, without the Consent of the Congress, lay any Imposts or Duties on Imports or Exports, except what may be absolutely necessary for executing its inspection Laws: and the net Produce of all Duties and Imposts, laid by any State on Imports or Exports, shall be for the Use of the Treasury

[5] Modified by the Sixteenth Amendment.

of the United States; and all such Laws shall be subject to the Revision and Control of the Congress.

No State shall, without the Consent of Congress, lay any duty of Tonnage, keep Troops, or Ships of War in time of Peace, enter into any Agreement or Compact with another State, or with a foreign Power, or engage in War, unless actually invaded, or in such imminent Danger as will not admit of delay.

ARTICLE II

Section 1. The executive Power shall be vested in a President of the United States of America. He shall hold his Office during the Term of four years, and, together with the Vice-President, chosen for the same Term, be elected, as follows:

Each State shall appoint, in such Manner as the Legislature thereof may direct, a Number of Electors, equal to the whole Number of Senators and Representatives to which the State may be entitled in the Congress: but no Senator or Representative, or Person holding an Office of Trust or Profit under the United States, shall be appointed an Elector.

[The Electors shall meet in their respective States, and vote by Ballot for two persons, of whom one at least shall not be an Inhabitant of the same State with themselves. And they shall make a List of all the Persons voted for, and of the Number of Votes for each; which List they shall sign and certify, and transmit sealed to the Seat of the Government of the United States, directed to the President of the Senate. The President of the Senate shall, in the Presence of the Senate

and House of Representatives, open all the Certificates, and the Votes shall then be counted. The Person having the greatest Number of Votes shall be the President, if such Number be a Majority of the whole Number of Electors appointed; and if there be more than one who have such Majority, and have an equal Number of Votes, then the House of Representatives shall immediately chuse by Ballot one of them for President; and if no Person have a Majority, then from the five highest on the List the said House shall in like Manner chuse the President. But in chusing the President, the Votes shall be taken by States, the Representation from each State having one Vote; a quorum for this Purpose shall consist of a Member or Members from two-thirds of the States, and a Majority of all the States shall be necessary to a Choice. In every Case, after the Choice of the President, the Person having the greatest Number of Votes of the Electors shall be the Vice-President. But if there should remain two or more who have equal votes, the Senate shall chuse from them by Ballot the Vice-President.][6]

The Congress may determine the Time of chusing the Electors, and the Day on which they shall give their Votes; which Day shall be the same throughout the United States.

No person except a natural-born Citizen, or a Citizen of the United States, at the time of the Adoption of this Constitution, shall be eligible to the Office of President; neither shall any Person be eligible to that Office who shall not have attained to the Age of thirty-five years, and

[6] Superseded by the Twelfth Amendment.

been fourteen Years a Resident within the United States.

[In Case of the Removal of the President from Office, or of his Death, Resignation, or Inability to discharge the Powers and Duties of the said Office, the same shall devolve on the Vice-President, and the Congress may by Law provide for the Case of Removal, Death, Resignation, or Inability, both of the President and Vice-President, declaring what Officer shall then act as President, and such Officer shall act accordingly, until the disability be removed, or a President shall be elected.][7]

The President shall, at stated Times, receive for his Services a Compensation, which shall neither be increased nor diminished during the Period for which he shall have been elected, and he shall not receive within that Period any other Emolument from the United States, or any of them.

Before he enter on the execution of his Office, he shall take the following Oath or Affirmation:—"I do solemnly swear (or affirm) that I will faithfully execute the Office of President of the United States, and will, to the best of my Ability, preserve, protect, and defend the Constitution of the United States."

Section 2. The President shall be Commander in Chief of the Army and Navy of the United States, and of the Militia of the several States, when called into the actual Service of the United States; he may require the Opinion, in writing, of the principal Officer in each of the executive Departments, upon any subject relating to the Duties of their respec-

[7] Modified by the Twenty-fifth Amendment.

tive Offices, and he shall have Power to Grant Reprieves and Pardons for Offenses against the United States, except in Cases of Impeachment.

He shall have Power, by and with the Advice and Consent of the Senate, to make Treaties, provided two thirds of the Senators present concur; and he shall nominate, and by and with the Advice and Consent of the Senate, shall appoint Ambassadors, other public Ministers and Consuls, Judges of the supreme Court, and all other Officers of the United States, whose Appointments are not herein otherwise provided for, and which shall be established by Law: but the Congress may by Law vest the Appointment of such inferior Officers, as they think proper, in the President alone, in the Courts of Law, or in the Heads of Departments.

The President shall have Power to fill up all Vacancies that may happen during the Recess of the Senate, by granting Commissions which shall expire at the End of their next Session.

Section 3. He shall from time to time give to the Congress Information of the State of the Union, and recommend to their Consideration such Measures as he shall judge necessary and expedient; he may, on extraordinary occasions, convene both Houses, or either of them, and in Case of Disagreement between them, with respect to the Time of Adjournment, he may adjourn them to such Time as he shall think proper; he shall receive Ambassadors and other public Ministers; he shall take Care that the Laws be faithfully executed, and shall Commission all the Officers of the United States.

Section 4. The President, Vice-President and all civil Officers of the United States, shall be removed from Office on Impeachment for, and Conviction of, Treason, Bribery, or other high Crimes and Misdemeanors.

ARTICLE III

Section 1. The judicial Power of the United States, shall be vested in one supreme Court, and in such inferior Courts as the Congress may from time to time ordain and establish. The Judges, both of the supreme and inferior Courts, shall hold their Offices during good Behaviour, and shall, at stated Times, receive for their Services, a Compensation, which shall not be diminished during their Continuance in Office.

Secion 2. The judicial Power shall extend to all Cases, in Law and Equity, arising under this Constitution, the Laws of the United States, and treaties made, or which shall be made, under their Authority;—to all Cases affecting ambassadors, other public ministers and consuls;—to all cases of admiralty and maritime Jurisdiction;—to Controversies to which the United States shall be a Party;—to Controversies between two or more States;—[between a State and Citizens of another State;]⁸—between Citizens of different States,—between Citizens of the same State claiming Lands under Grants of different States, and between a State, or the Citizens thereof, and foreign States, Citizens or Subjects.

In all Cases affecting Ambassa-

⁸ Modified by the Eleventh Amendment.

dors, other public Ministers and Consuls, and those in which a State shall be Party, the supreme Court shall have original Jurisdiction. In all the other Cases before mentioned, the supreme Court shall have appellate Jurisdiction, both as to Law and Fact, with such Exceptions, and under such Regulations as the Congress shall make.

The trial of all Crimes, except in Cases of Impeachment, shall be by Jury; and such Trial shall be held in the State where the said Crimes shall have been committed; but when not committed within any State, the Trial shall be at such Place or Places as the Congress may by Law have directed.

Section 3. Treason against the United States, shall consist only in levying War against them, or in adhering to their Enemies, giving them Aid and Comfort. No Person shall be convicted of Treason unless on the Testimony of two Witnesses to the same overt Act, or on Confession in open Court.

The Congress shall have power to declare the Punishment of Treason, but no Attainder of Treason shall work Corruption of Blood, or Forfeiture except during the Life of the Person attainted.

ARTICLE IV

Section 1. Full Faith and Credit shall be given in each State to the public Acts, Records, and judicial Proceedings of every other State. And the Congress may by general Laws prescribe the Manner in which such Acts, Records and Proceedings shall be proved, and the Effect thereof.

Section 2. The Citizens of each State shall be entitled to all Privileges and Immunities of Citizens in the several States.

A Person charged in any State with Treason, Felony, or other Crime, who shall flee from Justice, and be found in another State, shall on demand of the executive Authority of the State from which he fled, be delivered up, to be removed to the State having Jurisdiction of the crime.

[No Person held to Service or Labour in one State, under the Laws thereof, escaping into another, shall, in Consequence of any Law or Regulation therein, be discharged from such Service or Labour, but shall be delivered up on Claim of the Party to whom such Service or Labour may be due.][9]

Section 3. New States may be admitted by the Congress into this Union; but no new State shall be formed or erected within the Jurisdiction of any other State; nor any State be formed by the Junction of two or more States, or parts of States, without the Consent of the Legislatures of the States concerned as well as of the Congress.

The Congress shall have Power to dispose of and make all needful Rules and Regulations respecting the Territory or other Property belonging to the United States; and nothing in this Constitution shall be so construed as to Prejudice any Claims of the United States, or of any particular State.

Section 4. The United States shall guarantee to every State in this Union a Republican Form of Government, and shall protect each of them against Invasion; and on Application of the Legislature, or of

[9] Superseded by the Thirteenth Amendment.

the Executive (when the Legislature cannot be convened) against domestic Violence.

ARTICLE V

The Congress, whenever two-thirds of both Houses shall deem it necessary, shall propose Amendments to this Constitution, or, on the Application of the Legislatures of two-thirds of the several States, shall call a Convention for proposing Amendments, which, in either Case, shall be valid to all Intents and Purposes, as part of this Constitution, when ratified by the Legislatures of three-fourths of the several States, or by Conventions in three-fourths thereof, as the one or the other Mode of Ratification may be proposed by the Congress; Provided that no Amendment which may be made prior to the Year One thousand eight hundred and eight shall in any Manner affect the first and fourth Clauses in the Ninth Section of the first Article; and that no State, without its Consent, shall be deprived of its equal Suffrage in the Senate.

ARTICLE VI

All Debts contracted and Engagements entered into, before the Adoption of this Constitution, shall be as valid against the United States under this Constitution, as under the Confederation.

This Constitution, and the Laws of the United States which shall be made in Pursuance thereof; and all Treaties made, or which shall be made, under the Authority of the United States, shall be the supreme Law of the Land; and the Judges in every State shall be bound thereby, any Thing in the Constitution or

Laws of any State to the Contrary notwithstanding.

The Senators and Representatives before mentioned, and the Members of the several State Legislatures, and all executive and judicial Officers, both of the United States and of the several States, shall be bound by Oath or Affirmation to support this Constitution; but no religious Test shall ever be required as a qualification to any Office or public Trust under the United States.

ARTICLE VII

The Ratification of the Conventions of nine States shall be sufficient for the Establishment of this Constitution between the States so ratifying the same.

Done in Convention by the Unanimous Consent of the States present the Seventeenth Day of September in the Year of our Lord one thousand seven hundred and Eighty seven, and of the Independence of the United States of America the Twelfth. In Witness whereof We have hereunto subscribed our Names.

Articles in Addition to, and Amendment of, the Constitution of the United States of America, Proposed by Congress, and Ratified by the Legislatures of the Several States, Pursuant to the Fifth Article of the Original Constitution.

AMENDMENT I[10]

Congress shall make no law respecting an establishment of religion, or prohibiting the free exercise thereof; or abridging the freedom

[10] The first ten amendments were passed by Congress September 25, 1789. They were ratified by three-fourths of the states December 15, 1791.

of speech, or of the press; or the right of the people peaceably to assemble, and to petition the Government for a redress of grievances.

AMENDMENT II

A well regulated Militia, being necessary to the security of a free State, the right of the people to keep and bear Arms shall not be infringed.

AMENDMENT III

No Soldier shall, in time of peace, be quartered in any house, without the consent of the Owner, nor in time of war, but in a manner to be prescribed by law.

AMENDMENT IV

The right of the people to be secure in their persons, houses, papers, and effects, against unreasonable searches and seizures, shall not be violated, and no Warrants shall issue, but upon probable cause, supported by Oath or affirmation, and particularly describing the place to be searched, and the persons or things to be seized.

AMENDMENT V

No person shall be held to answer for a capital or otherwise infamous crime, unless on a presentment or indictment of a Grand Jury, except in cases arising in the land or naval forces, or in the Militia, when in actual service in time of War or public danger; nor shall any person be subject for the same offence to be twice put in jeopardy of life or limb; nor shall be compelled in any criminal case to be a witness against himself, nor be deprived of life, liberty, or property, without due process of law; nor shall private property be taken for public use, without just compensation.

AMENDMENT VI

In all criminal prosecutions, the accused shall enjoy the right to a speedy and public trial, by an impartial jury of the State and district wherein the crime shall have been committed, which district shall have been previously ascertained by law, and to be informed of the nature and cause of the accusation; to be confronted with the witnesses against him; to have compulsory process for obtaining witnesses in his favor, and to have the Assistance of Counsel for his defence.

AMENDMENT VII

In suits at common law, where the value in controversy shall exceed twenty dollars, the right of trial by jury shall be preserved, and no fact tried by a jury, shall be otherwise reexamined in any Court of the United States, than according to the rules of the common law.

AMENDMENT VIII

Excessive bail shall not be required, nor excessive fines imposed, nor cruel and unusual punishments inflicted.

AMENDMENT IX

The enumeration in the Constitution, of certain rights, shall not be construed to deny or disparage others retained by the people.

AMENDMENT X

The powers not delegated to the United States by the Constitution, nor prohibited by it to the States, are reserved to the States respectively, or to the people.

AMENDMENT XI (1798)[11]

The Judicial power of the United States shall not be construed to extend to any suit in law or equity, commenced or prosecuted against one of the United States by Citizens of another State, or by Citizens or Subjects of any Foreign State.

AMENDMENT XII (1804)

The Electors shall meet in their respective States and vote by ballot for President and Vice-President, one of whom, at least, shall not be an inhabitant of the same State with themselves; they shall name in their ballots the person voted for as President, and in distinct ballots the person voted for as Vice-President, and they shall make distinct lists of all persons voted for as President, and of all persons voted for as Vice-President, and of the number of votes for each, which lists they shall sign and certify, and transmit sealed to the seat of the government of the United States, directed to the President of the Senate;—The President of the Senate shall, in the presence of the Senate and House of Representatives, open all the certificates and the votes shall then be counted; —The person having the greatest number of votes for President, shall be the President, if such number be a majority of the whole number of Electors appointed; and if no person have such majority, then from the persons having the highest numbers not exceeding three on the list of those voted for as President, the House of Representatives shall choose immediately, by ballot, the President. But in choosing the President, the votes shall be taken by

[11] Date of ratification.

states, the representation from each state having one vote; a quorum for this purpose shall consist of a member or members from two-thirds of the states, and a majority of all the states shall be necessary to a choice. [And if the House of Representatives shall not choose a President whenever the right of choice shall devolve upon them, before the fourth day of March next following, then the Vice-President shall act as President, as in the case of the death or other constitutional disability of the President.]¹²—The person having the greatest number of votes as Vice-President, shall be the Vice-President, if such number be a majority of the whole number of Electors appointed, and if no person have a majority, then from the two highest numbers on the list, the Senate shall choose the Vice-President; a quorum for the purpose shall consist of two-thirds of the whole number of Senators, and a majority of the whole number shall be necessary to a choice. But no person constitutionally ineligible to the office of President shall be eligible to that of Vice-President of the United States.

AMENDMENT XIII (1865)

Section 1. Neither slavery nor involuntary servitude, except as a punishment for crime whereof the party shall have been duly convicted, shall exist within the United States, or any place subject to their jurisdiction.

Section 2. Congress shall have power to enforce this article by appropriate legislation.

¹² Superseded by the Twentieth Amendment.

AMENDMENT XIV (1868)

Section 1. All persons born or naturalized in the United States, and subject to the jurisdiction thereof, are citizens of the United States and of the State wherein they reside. No State shall make or enforce any law which shall abridge the privileges or immunities of citizens of the United States; nor shall any State deprive any person of life, liberty, or property, without due process of law; nor deny to any person within its jurisdiction the equal protection of the laws.

Section 2. Representatives shall be apportioned among the several States according to their respective numbers, counting the whole number of persons in each State, excluding Indians not taxed. But when the right to vote at any election for the choice of electors for President and Vice-President of the United States, Representatives in Congress, the Executive and Judicial officers of a State, or the members of the Legislature thereof, is denied to any of the male inhabitants of such State, being twenty-one years of age, and citizens of the United States, or in any way abridged, except for participation in rebellion, or other crime, the basis of representation therein shall be reduced in the proportion which the number of such male citizens shall bear to the whole number of male citizens twenty-one years of age in such State.

Section 3. No person shall be a Senator or Representative in Congress, or elector of President and Vice-President, or hold any office, civil or military, under the United States, or under any State, who, having previously taken an oath, as a member of Congress, or as an officer of the United States, or as a member of any State legislature, or as an executive or judicial officer of any State, to support the Constitution of the United States, shall have engaged in insurrection or rebellion against the same, or given aid or comfort to the enemies thereof. But Congress may by a vote of two-thirds of each House, remove such disability.

Section 4. The validity of the public debt of the United States, authorized by law, including debts incurred for payment of pensions and bounties for services in suppressing insurrection or rebellion, shall not be questioned. But neither the United States nor any State shall assume or pay any debt or obligation incurred in aid of insurrection or rebellion against the United States, or any claim for the loss or emancipation of any slave; but all such debts, obligations, and claims shall be held illegal and void.

Section 5. The Congress shall have the power to enforce, by appropriate legislation, the provisions of this article.

AMENDMENT XV (1870)

Section 1. The right of citizens of the United States to vote shall not be denied or abridged by the United States or by any State on account of race, color, or previous condition of servitude—

Section 2. The Congress shall have power to enforce this article by appropriate legislation.

AMENDMENT XVI (1913)

The Congress shall have power to lay and collect taxes on incomes, from whatever source derived, without apportionment among the several States, and without regard to any census or enumeration.

AMENDMENT XVII (1913)

The Senate of the United States shall be composed of two Senators from each State, elected by the people thereof, for six years; and each Senator shall have one vote. The electors in each State shall have the qualifications requisite for electors of the most numerous branch of the State legislatures.

When vacancies happen in the representation of any State in the Senate, the executive authority of such State shall issue writs of election to fill such vacancies: *Provided,* That the legislature of any State may empower the executive thereof to make temporary appointments until the people fill the vacancies by election as the legislature may direct.

This amendment shall not be so construed as to affect the election or term of any Senator chosen before it becomes valid as part of the Constitution.

AMENDMENT XVIII (1919)[13]

Section 1. After one year from the ratification of this article the manufacture, sale, or transportation of intoxicating liquors within, the importation thereof into, or the exportation thereof from the United States and all territory subject to the jurisdiction thereof for beverage purposes is hereby prohibited.

Section 2. The Congress and the several States shall have concurrent power to enforce this article by appropriate legislation.

Section 3. This article shall be inoperative unless it shall have been

[13] Repealed by the Twenty-first Amendment.

ratified as an amendment to the Constitution by the legislatures of the several States, as provided in the Constitution, within seven years from the date of the submission hereof to the States by the Congress.

AMENDMENT XIX (1920)

The right of citizens of the United States to vote shall not be denied or abridged by the United States or by any State on account of sex.

Congress shall have power to enforce this article by appropriate legislation.

AMENDMENT XX (1933)

Section 1. The terms of the President and Vice-President shall end at noon on the 20th day of January, and the terms of Senators and Representatives at noon on the 3d day of January, of the years in which such terms would have ended if this article had not been ratified; and the terms of their successors shall then begin.

Section 2. The Congress shall assemble at least once in every year, and such meeting shall begin at noon on the 3d day of January, unless they shall by law appoint a different day.

Section 3. If, at the time fixed for the beginning of the term of the President, the President elect shall have died, the Vice-President elect shall become President. If a President shall not have been chosen before the time fixed for the beginning of his term, or if the President elect shall have failed to qualify, then the Vice-President elect shall act as President until a President shall have qualified; and the Congress may by law provide for the case wherein neither a President elect nor a Vice-President elect shall have qualified, declaring who shall then act as President, or the manner in which one who is to act shall be selected, and such person shall act accordingly until a President or Vice-President shall have qualified.

Section 4. The Congress may by law provide for the case of the death of any of the persons from whom the House of Representatives may choose a President whenever the right of choice shall have devolved upon them, and for the case of the death of any of the persons from whom the Senate may choose a Vice-President whenever the right of choice shall have devolved upon them.

Section 5. Sections 1 and 2 shall take effect on the 15th day of October following the ratification of this article.

Section 6. This article shall be inoperative unless it shall have been ratified as an amendment to the Constitution by the legislatures of three-fourths of the several States within seven years from the date of its submission.

AMENDMENT XXI (1933)

Section 1. The eighteenth article of amendment to the Constitution of the United States is hereby repealed.

Section 2. The transportation or importation into any State, Territory, or possession of the United States for delivery or use therein of intoxicating liquors, in violation of the laws thereof, is hereby prohibited.

Section 3. This article shall be inoperative unless it shall have been ratified as an amendment to the

Constitution by conventions in the several States, as provided in the Constitution, within seven years from the date of the submission hereof to the States by the Congress.

AMENDMENT XXII (1951)

No person shall be elected to the office of the President more than twice, and no person who has held the office of President, or acted as President, for more than two years of a term to which some other person was elected President shall be elected to the office of the President more than once.

But this Article shall not apply to any person holding the office of President when this Article was proposed by the Congress, and shall not prevent any person who may be holding the office of President, or acting as President, during the term within which this Article becomes operative from holding the office of President or acting as President during the remainder of such term.

AMENDMENT XXIII (1961)

Section 1. The District constituting the seat of Government of the United States shall appoint in such manner as the Congress may direct:

A number of electors of President and Vice-President equal to the whole number of Senators and Representatives in Congress to which the District would be entitled if it were a State, but in no event more than the least populous State; they shall be in addition to those appointed by the States, but they shall be considered, for the purposes of the election of President and Vice-President, to be electors appointed by the State; and they shall meet in the District and perform such du-

ties as provided by the twelfth article of amendment.

Section 2. The Congress shall have power to enforce this article by appropriate legislation.

AMENDMENT XXIV (1964)

Section 1. The right of citizens of the United States to vote in any primary or other election for President or Vice-President, for electors for President or Vice-President, or for Senator or Representative in Congress, shall not be denied or abridged by the United States or any State by reason of failure to pay any poll tax or other tax.

Section 2. The Congress shall have power to enforce this article by appropriate legislation.

AMENDMENT XXV (1967)

Section 1. In case of the removal of the President from office or of his death or resignation, the Vice-President shall become President.

Section 2. Whenever there is a vacancy in the office of the Vice-President, the President shall nominate a Vice-President who shall take office upon confirmation by a majority vote of both Houses of Congress.

Section 3. Whenever the President transmits to the President pro tempore of the Senate and the Speaker of the House of Representatives his written declaration that he is unable to discharge the powers and duties of his office, and until he transmits to them a written declaration to the contrary, such powers and duties shall be discharged by the Vice-President as Acting President.

Section 4. Whether the Vice-President and a majority of either the principal officers of the executive department or of such other body as Congress may by law provide, transmit to the President pro tempore of the Senate and the Speaker of the House of Representatives their written declaration that the President is unable to discharge the powers and duties of his office, the Vice-President shall immediately assume the powers and duties of the office as Acting President.

Thereafter, when the President transmits to the President pro tempore of the Senate and the Speaker of the House of Representatives his written declaration that no inability exists, he shall resume the powers and duties of his office unless the Vice-President and a majority of either the principal officers of the executive department or of such other body as Congress may by law provide, transmit within four days to the President pro tempore of the Senate and the Speaker of the House of Representatives their written declaration that the President is unable to discharge the powers and duties of his office. Thereupon Congress shall decide the issue, assembling within forty-eight hours for that purpose if not in session. If the Congress, within twenty-one days after receipt of the latter written declaration, or, if Congress is not in session, within twenty-one days after Congress is required to assemble, determines by two-thirds vote of both Houses that the President is unable to discharge the powers and duties of his office, the Vice-President shall continue to discharge the same as Acting President; otherwise, the President shall resume the powers and duties of his office.

AMENDMENT XXVI (1971)

Section 1. The right of citizens of the United States, who are eighteen years of age or older, to vote shall not be denied or abridged by the United States or by any State on account of age.

Section 2. The Congress shall have power to enforce this article by appropriate legislation.

Presidential Elections (1789–1968)*

Year and number of states	Candidates	Parties	Popular vote	Electoral vote	Percentage of popular vote[1]
1789 (11)	George Washington	No party designations		69	
	John Adams			34	
	Minor Candidates			35	
1792 (15)	George Washington	No party designations		132	
	John Adams			77	
	George Clinton			50	
	Minor Candidates			5	
1796 (16)	John Adams	Federalist		71	
	Thomas Jefferson	Democratic-Republican		68	
	Thomas Pinckney	Federalist		59	
	Aaron Burr	Democratic-Republican		30	
	Minor Candidates			48	
1800 (16)	Thomas Jefferson	Democratic-Republican		73	
	Aaron Burr	Democratic-Republican		73	
	John Adams	Federalist		65	
	Charles C. Pinckney	Federalist		64	
	John Jay	Federalist		1	
1804 (17)	Thomas Jefferson	Democratic-Republican		162	
	Charles C. Pinckney	Federalist		14	
1808 (17)	James Madison	Democratic-Republican		122	
	Charles C. Pinckney	Federalist		47	
	George Clinton	Democratic-Republican		6	
1812 (18)	James Madison	Democratic-Republican		128	
	DeWitt Clinton	Federalist		89	
1816 (19)	James Monroe	Democratic-Republican		183	
	Rufus King	Federalist		34	
1820 (24)	James Monroe	Democratic-Republican		231	
	John Quincy Adams	Independent Republican		1	
1824 (24)	John Quincy Adams	Democratic-Republican	108,740	84	30.5
	Andrew Jackson	Democratic-Republican	153,544	99	43.1
	William H. Crawford	Democratic-Republican	46,618	41	13.1
	Henry Clay	Democratic-Republican	47,136	37	13.2
1828 (24)	Andrew Jackson	Democratic	647,286	178	56.0
	John Quincy Adams	National Republican	508,064	83	44.0

* Before the passage of the Twelfth Amendment in 1804, the Electoral College voted for two presidential candidates; the runner-up became Vice-President. Figures are from *Historical Statistics of the United States, Colonial Times to 1957* (1961), pp. 682–83; the U.S. Department of Justice; and *New York Times Encyclopedic Almanac, 1972*, p. 101.

[1] Candidates receiving less than 1 per cent of the popular vote have been omitted. For that reason the percentage of popular vote given for any election year may not total 100 per cent.

Presidential Elections (1789–1968) (cont.)

Year and number of states	Candidates	Parties	Popular vote	Electoral vote	Percentage of popular vote
1832	Andrew Jackson	Democratic	687,502	219	55.0
(24)	Henry Clay	National Republican	530,189	49	42.4
	William Wirt	Anti-Masonic	33,108	7	2.6
	John Floyd	National Republican		11	
1836	Martin Van Buren	Democratic	765,483	170	50.9
(26)	William H. Harrison	Whig		73	
	Hugh L. White	Whig		26	
	Daniel Webster	Whig	739,795	14	49.1
	W. P. Mangum	Whig		11	
1840	William H. Harrison	Whig	1,274,624	234	53.1
(26)	Martin Van Buren	Democratic	1,127,781	60	46.9
1844	James K. Polk	Democratic	1,338,464	170	49.6
(26)	Henry Clay	Whig	1,300,097	105	48.1
	James G. Birney	Liberty	62,300		2.3
1848	Zachary Taylor	Whig	1,360,967	163	47.4
(30)	Lewis Cass	Democratic	1,222,342	127	42.5
	Martin Van Buren	Free Soil	291,263		10.1
1852	Franklin Pierce	Democratic	1,601,117	254	50.9
(31)	Winfield Scott	Whig	1,385,453	42	44.1
	John P. Hale	Free Soil	155,825		5.0
1856	James Buchanan	Democratic	1,832,955	174	45.3
(31)	John C. Frémont	Republican	1,339,932	114	33.1
	Millard Fillmore	American	871,731	8	21.6
1860	Abraham Lincoln	Republican	1,865,593	180	39.8
(33)	Stephen A. Douglas	Democratic	1,382,713	12	29.5
	John C. Breckinridge	Democratic	848,356	72	18.1
	John Bell	Constitutional Union	592,906	39	12.6
1864	Abraham Lincoln	Republican	2,206,938	212	55.0
(36)	George B. McClellan	Democratic	1,803,787	21	45.0
1868	Ulysses S. Grant	Republican	3,013,421	214	52.7
(37)	Horatio Seymour	Democratic	2,706,829	80	47.3
1872	Ulysses S. Grant	Republican	3,596,745	286	55.6
(37)	Horace Greeley	Democratic	2,843,446	[2]	43.9
1876	Rutherford B. Hayes	Republican	4,036,572	185	48.0
(38)	Samuel J. Tilden	Democratic	4,284,020	184	51.0
1880	James A. Garfield	Republican	4,453,295	214	48.5
(38)	Winfield S. Hancock	Democratic	4,414,082	155	48.1
	James B. Weaver	Greenback-Labor	308,578		3.4

[2] Greeley died shortly after the election; the electors supporting him then divided their votes among minor candidates.

Presidential Elections (1789–1968) (cont.)

Year and number of states	Candidates	Parties	Popular vote	Electoral vote	Percentage of popular vote
1884 (38)	Grover Cleveland	Democratic	4,879,507	219	48.5
	James G. Blaine	Republican	4,850,293	182	48.2
	Benjamin F. Butler	Greenback-Labor	175,370		1.8
	John P. St. John	Prohibition	150,369		1.5
1888 (38)	Benjamin Harrison	Republican	5,447,129	233	47.9
	Grover Cleveland	Democratic	5,537,857	168	48.6
	Clinton B. Fisk	Prohibition	249,506		2.2
	Anson J. Streeter	Union Labor	146,935		1.3
1892 (44)	Grover Cleveland	Democratic	5,555,426	277	46.1
	Benjamin Harrison	Republican	5,182,690	145	43.0
	James B. Weaver	People's	1,029,846	22	8.5
	John Bidwell	Prohibition	264,133		2.2
1896 (45)	William McKinley	Republican	7,102,246	271	51.1
	William J. Bryan	Democratic	6,492,559	176	47.7
1900 (45)	William McKinley	Republican	7,218,491	292	51.7
	William J. Bryan	Democratic; Populist	6,356,734	155	45.5
	John C. Wooley	Prohibition	208,914		1.5
1904 (45)	Theodore Roosevelt	Republican	7,628,461	336	57.4
	Alton B. Parker	Democratic	5,084,223	140	37.6
	Eugene V. Debs	Socialist	402,283		3.0
	Silas C. Swallow	Prohibition	258,536		1.9
1908 (46)	William H. Taft	Republican	7,675,320	321	51.6
	William J. Bryan	Democratic	6,412,294	162	43.1
	Eugene V. Debs	Socialist	420,793		2.8
	Eugene W. Chafin	Prohibition	253,840		1.7
1912 (48)	Woodrow Wilson	Democratic	6,296,547	435	41.9
	Theodore Roosevelt	Progressive	4,118,571	88	27.4
	William H. Taft	Republican	3,486,720	8	23.2
	Eugene V. Debs	Socialist	900,672		6.0
	Eugene W. Chafin	Prohibition	206,275		1.4
1916 (48)	Woodrow Wilson	Democratic	9,127,695	277	49.4
	Charles E. Hughes	Republican	8,533,507	254	46.2
	A. L. Benson	Socialist	585,113		3.2
	J. Frank Hanly	Prohibition	220,506		1.2
1920 (48)	Warren G. Harding	Republican	16,143,407	404	60.4
	James N. Cox	Democratic	9,130,328	127	34.2
	Eugene V. Debs	Socialist	919,799		3.4
	P. P. Christensen	Farmer-Labor	265,411		1.0
1924 (48)	Calvin Coolidge	Republican	15,718,211	382	54.0
	John W. Davis	Democratic	8,385,283	136	28.8
	Robert M. La Follette	Progressive	4,831,289	13	16.6

Presidential Elections (1789–1968) (cont.)

Year and number of states	Candidates	Parties	Popular vote	Electoral vote	Percentage of popular vote
1928 (48)	Herbert C. Hoover	Republican	21,391,993	444	58.2
	Alfred E. Smith	Democratic	15,016,169	87	40.9
1932 (48)	Franklin D. Roosevelt	Democratic	22,809,638	472	57.4
	Herbert C. Hoover	Republican	15,758,901	59	39.7
	Norman Thomas	Socialist	881,951		2.2
1936 (48)	Franklin D. Roosevelt	Democratic	27,752,869	523	60.8
	Alfred M. Landon	Republican	16,674,665	8	36.5
	William Lemke	Union	882,479		1.9
1940 (48)	Franklin D. Roosevelt	Democratic	27,307,819	449	54.8
	Wendell L. Willkie	Republican	22,321,018	82	44.8
1944 (48)	Franklin D. Roosevelt	Democratic	25,606,585	432	53.5
	Thomas E. Dewey	Republican	22,014,745	99	46.0
1948 (48)	Harry S Truman	Democratic	24,105,812	303	49.5
	Thomas E. Dewey	Republican	21,970,065	189	45.1
	J. Strom Thurmond	States' Rights	1,169,063	39	2.4
	Henry A. Wallace	Progressive	1,157,172		2.4
1952 (48)	Dwight D. Eisenhower	Republican	33,936,234	442	55.1
	Adlai E. Stevenson	Democratic	27,314,992	89	44.4
1956 (48)	Dwight D. Eisenhower	Republican	35,590,472	457	57.6
	Adlai E. Stevenson	Democratic	26,022,752	73	42.1
1960 (50)	John F. Kennedy	Democratic	34,227,096	303	49.9
	Richard M. Nixon	Republican	34,108,546	219	49.6
1964 (50)	Lyndon B. Johnson	Democratic	43,126,506	486	61.1
	Barry M. Goldwater	Republican	27,176,799	52	38.5
1968 (50)	Richard M. Nixon	Republican	31,785,480	301	43.4
	Hubert H. Humphrey	Democratic	31,275,165	191	42.7
	George C. Wallace	American Independent	9,906,473	46	13.5

Population of the United States (1790–1970)*

Year	Total population (in thousands)	Number per square mile of land area (continental United States)	Year	Total population (in thousands)	Number per square mile of land area (continental United States)
1790	3,929	4.5	1930	123,077	41.2
1800	5,308	6.1	1931	124,040	
1810	7,239	4.3	1932	124,840	
1820	9,638	5.5	1933	125,579	
1830	12,866	7.4	1934	126,374	
1840	17,069	9.8	1935	127,250	
1850	23,191	7.9	1936	128,053	
1860	31,443	10.6	1937	128,825	
1870	39,818	13.4	1938	129,825	
1880	50,155	16.9	1939	130,880	
1890	62,947	21.2	1940	131,669	44.2
1900	76,094	25.6	1941	133,669	
1901	77,585		1942	134,617	
1902	79,160		1943	136,107	
1903	80,632		1944	133,915	
1904	82,165		1945	133,434	
1905	83,820		1946	140,686	
1906	85,437		1947	144,083	
1907	87,000		1948	146,730	
1908	88,709		1949	149,304	
1909	90,492		1950	151,868	42.6
1910	92,407	31.0	1951	153,982	
1911	93,868		1952	156,393	
1912	95,331		1953	158,956	
1913	97,227		1954	161,884	
1914	99,118		1955	165,069	
1915	100,549		1956	168,088	
1916	101,966		1957	171,187	
1917	103,266		1958	174,149	
1918	103,203		1959	177,135	
1919	104,512		1960	179,992	50.5
1920	106,466	35.6	1961	183,057	
1921	108,541		1962	185,890	
1922	110,055		1963	188,658	
1923	111,950		1964	191,372	
1924	114,113		1965	193,815	
1925	115,832		1966	197,859	
1926	117,399		1967	197,859	
1927	119,038		1968	199,846	
1928	120,501		1969	201,921	
1929	121,770		1970	203,185	57.4

* Figures are from *Statistical Abstract of the United States: 1969*, p. 5; and *New York Times Encyclopedic Almanac, 1972*, p. 146. Figures exclude Armed Forces abroad and after 1940 include Alaska and Hawaii.

Admission of States

Order of admission	State	Date of admission
1	Delaware	December 7, 1787
2	Pennsylvania	December 12, 1787
3	New Jersey	December 18, 1787
4	Georgia	January 2, 1788
5	Connecticut	January 9, 1788
6	Massachusetts	February 6, 1788
7	Maryland	April 28, 1788
8	South Carolina	May 23, 1788
9	New Hampshire	June 21, 1788
10	Virginia	June 25, 1788
11	New York	July 26, 1788
12	North Carolina	November 21, 1789
13	Rhode Island	May 29, 1790
14	Vermont	March 4, 1791
15	Kentucky	June 1, 1792
16	Tennessee	June 1, 1796
17	Ohio	March 1, 1803
18	Louisiana	April 30, 1812
19	Indiana	December 11, 1816
20	Mississippi	December 10, 1817
21	Illinois	December 3, 1818
22	Alabama	December 14, 1819
23	Maine	March 15, 1820
24	Missouri	August 10, 1821
25	Arkansas	June 15, 1836
26	Michigan	January 26, 1837
27	Florida	March 3, 1845
28	Texas	December 29, 1845
29	Iowa	December 28, 1846
30	Wisconsin	May 29, 1848
31	California	September 9, 1850
32	Minnesota	May 11, 1858
33	Oregon	February 14, 1859
34	Kansas	January 29, 1861
35	West Virginia	June 30, 1863
36	Nevada	October 31, 1864
37	Nebraska	March 1, 1867
38	Colorado	August 1, 1876
39	North Dakota	November 2, 1889
40	South Dakota	November 2, 1889
41	Montana	November 8, 1889
42	Washington	November 11, 1889
43	Idaho	July 3, 1890
44	Wyoming	July 10, 1890
45	Utah	January 4, 1896
46	Oklahoma	November 16, 1907
47	New Mexico	January 6, 1912
48	Arizona	February 14, 1912
49	Alaska	January 3, 1959
50	Hawaii	August 21, 1959

INDEX

Gerry, Elbridge, 108, 109, 110
Gettysburg, Battle of, 219
GI Bill of Rights, 428
Gideon v. *Wainwright*, 486
Gilbert, Humphrey, 19
Glass, Carter, 376
Glass-Steagall Act, 392
Glassboro, New Jersey, 480
Glorious Revolution (*1688*), 48
Godspeed, 21
Gold rush, 269
Gold standard, 291–92, 296, 297–300
Goldwater, Barry, 475, 488
Gompers, Samuel, 274, 275, 295, 328, 336, 351, 400
Gomulka, Wladyslaw, 460
Good Neighbor policy, 377, 409–10
GOP. *See* Republican party
Gospel of Wealth, 294
Gould, Jay, 251, 288
Government, colonial, 46–47
Government, federal: and Adams (John) administration, 108, 110, 112; and Adams (J. Q.) administration, 143–44; and antitrust actions, 258–59; and Articles of Confederation, 82–83; and Buchanan administration, 207–09; and Constitutional Convention, 90–92; contributions of Federalists to, 112; corruption in, 288–89; in critical period of *1783–87*, 86–90; and disfranchisement of blacks, 241–42; and Eisenhower administration, 456; English influence on, 3–4, 6; and first state constitutions, 83–84; and First World War, 343; fiscal policy of, *see* Fiscal policy; future outlook for, 495–97; and Harding administration, 367–68; and internal improvements, 161; and Jacksonian foreign policy, 180–81; and Jackson administration, 145–50, 152–53; and Jefferson administration, 115–22; and Kennedy and Johnson administrations, 475; and laissez faire approach, 289–92; and Lincoln administration, 213–23; lending policies of, 249–50, 387; McCarthyism and, 445, 447; and Madison administration, 122–28; and Monroe administration, 131–36; and New Deal, 401–05; and patronage, 189; and Pierce administration, 197–98; and political parties at end of 19th century, 285–88; and Polk administration, 184–90; and railroad interests, *249*, 250–51; and regulation of industry, 328–30, 350–51; and regulation of railroads, 251–53; and Second World War controls, 421; and slavery issue, 202; and taxes, 99; and Tyler administration, 156, 191–93; and Van Buren administration, 153–55; and Washington administration, 97–108. *See also* Elections; Politicians; *specific branches*
Government, municipal, 279–80; in de-

pression, 387; and Progressive movement, 323–24; and urbanization, 280
Government, state. *See* State governments
Governors: in colonial America, 46; in early states, 83
Grady, Henry, 240
Grafton, Duke of, 60, 63, 65
"Grandfather clause," 242
Grangers, 252, 394
Grant, Ulysses S., 219, 221, 286, 287; in Civil War, 216; corruption in administration of, 288–89; and currency issue, 291; and expansion, 307
Grasse, Comte de, 79
Great Awakening, 42, 44
Great Britain: and American Civil War, 218–19; and American Revolution, 76–77, 79, 82; and attitude toward Loyalists, 76; colonial policies of, 19–28, 37, 40; early explorations by, 19; and Embargo of *1807*, 122; and First World War, 342–43; and Five Power Pact, 376; and France, 49–53; and French Revolution, 104–05; and Hitler, 412; and Japanese alliance (*1902*), 314; and Jay Treaty, 105–08; and Jefferson, 119; and Latin American independence, 133–34; and League of Nations, 360; and Oregon dispute, 187–88; and Second World War, 419, 422–25; and Suez Canal dispute, 459; taxpayers' revolt in, 61; and U.S. shipping, 121–22; and War of *1812*, 123–28; and westward expansion, 57, 183. *See also* Anglo-American relations; Parliament
Great Lakes, 125, 128
Great Migration, 26
Great Plains, map of, *270*
"Great Society," 476
Great War for Empire. *See* French and Indian War
Greater East Asia Co-prosperity Sphere, 412
Greece, and cold war, 436–37
Greeley, Horace, 206, 217, 266, 286
"Greenbacks" 222, 291, 392
Greensboro, North Carolina, 456
Greenville, George, 59, 60, 106
Gresham, Walter Q., 304
Grew, Joseph C., 417
Griffin, Cyrus, 94
Grundy, Felix, 123
Guadalcanal, 418
Guadeloupe, 52
Guam, 311–12
Guatemala, 459
Guevara, "Che," 490
Guffey Coal Act (*1935*), 394
Gun control, 495

Hague, The, 344
Haiti, 17, 307; U.S. intervention in, 318, 377

Quincy, Josiah, Jr., 62
Quitrents, 35, 48, 84

Race riots, 353, 372, 490, 491
Racial discrimination. *See* Civil rights;
  Racial equality
Racial equality, 490; and Black Codes,
  230; and Black Power movement,
  489–90; and civil-rights legislation, 488–
  89; and colonialism, 304; and congressional Reconstruction, 233–35;
  and Eisenhower administration, 453–
  56; and emancipation, 225; and First
  World War, 353; and Ku Klux Klan,
  237–38; in New South, 241–43; after
  1950, 466; and Progressive party platform, 326; and Second World War,
  426–27; and southern view of Radical
  Reconstruction, 236; and Truman administration, 431, 440–41; and Versailles Treaty, 356. *See also* Black
  Americans
Radford, Arthur, 457, 458
Radical Reconstruction, 227–29, 233–40;
  and Ku Klux Klan, 237. *See also* Radicalism
Radicalism: in American colonies, 64;
  and American Federation of Labor,
  275; in election of *1866*, 234; in First
  World War, 351; and impeachment
  proceedings against Johnson (A.), 235;
  of Populists, 294; in Reconstruction,
  see Radical Reconstruction; and Red
  scare, 365–67; in Republican party,
  222, 226; and social stability, 327
Radio, effects of, 374
Radio Corporation of America, 382, 383
Railroad Control Act (*1918*), 351
Railroads: and black passengers, 230;
  building of, *250*; in China, 313–14; and
  farm prices, 252–53; financiers of,
  250–51; freight car purchases of, 254;
  freight rates, 161, 162, 251–53, 293; and
  Gadsden Purchase, 197; growth in
  mileage of, 162–63, 253; and immigra-
  tion, 280; and industrialization, 249–
  51; map of federal grants to, *249*; in
  Reconstruction period, 237; regulation
  of, 251–53, 329–30; and settlement of
  West, 14, 266; and southern indus-
  trialization, 240; and Taft, 331–32;
  transcontinental, 204, 222, 229
Raleigh, Sir Walter, 6, 19
Ramsey, David, 75
Randolph, Edmund, 92, 99, *100*
Randolph, Edward, 48
Randolph, John, 117, 136
Rationing, in Second World War, 421
Rayburn, Sam, 455
Reagan, Ronald, 484
Reconstruction: and colonialism, 304;
  and Congress, 233–35; and Johnson
  (A.) administration, 229–30; Lincoln's
  plan for, 225–26; and postwar eco-

nomic conditions in South, 231–33;
  radical view of, 227–29; southern view
  of, 236–37. *See also* Radical Recon-
  struction
Reconstruction Act (*1867*), 234–35, 242
Reconstruction Finance Corporation
  (RFC), 387, 391
Red Army, 421
"Red Guards," 480
Red scare: and Truman administration,
  445–49; and Wilson administration,
  364–67
Regulator movements, 47
Religion: in colonial America, 19–20,
  41–43; and growth of public educa-
  tion, 43; in *1920*s, 371; of Puritans,
  8–9. *See also* *individual religions*;
  Religious toleration
Religious toleration, 22–24, 85; and col-
  leges in colonial America, 43–44; and
  First World War, 353; in Louisiana,
  120; in southern colonies, 22–24; and
  Quakers, 29–30
Reno, Milo, 394
Report on Manufactures, 103
Republican party: convention of *1940*,
  415; and depression, 382; and "dynamic conservatism," 452–56; and
  Eisenhower's foreign policy, 456–62;
  in election of *1856*, 206; in election of
  1860, 211–13; in election of *1876*, 238–
  40; in election of *1894*, 296; in election of *1896*, 297–300; in election of
  1912, 333–34; in election of *1916*, 338;
  in election of *1918*, 357; in election of
  1920, 367; in election of *1930*, 386–87;
  in election of *1932*, 389; in election of
  1936, 403; in election of *1946*, 436; in
  election of *1948*, 439–40, 447–48; in
  election of *1960*, 462; at end of 19th
  century, 286–88; and Kansas-Nebraska
  Act, 205–06; and Korean War, 444;
  and Lincoln-Douglas contest, 210;
  and New Deal, 402; *1908* platform of,
  332; and Reconstruction, 233–35; and
  stock market crash, 384; and Teapot
  Dome scandal, 368; and Thirteenth
  Amendment, 228; and Versailles
  Treaty, 357–59
Republicans, Jeffersonian: and Adams
  (John), 107–08; and Alien and Sedition Acts, 110; and Bank of the
  United States, 129; after election of
  1800, 115–22; in election of *1816*, 131;
  in election of *1824*, 141; and Federalists, 112; and Jay Treaty, 106; and
  nationalism, 129; political creed of,
  115–16; and slavery issue in *1819*, 135;
  view of Hartford Convention, *127*;
  after War of *1812*, 128; and Washington's farewell address, 107
Revenue Act (*1954*), 453
Revere, Paul, view of Boston Massacre
  of, *63*
Revolutionary War, American, 55–73;